The Melody of Fire

A true story of spirituality, sexuality, and surrender.

Jen Fields

The Melody of Fire is a work of nonfiction. Some names and identifying details have been changed.

Copyright © 2023 by Jen Fields. All rights reserved.

Published by Anamchara, LLC

No portion of this book may be reproduced in any form without permission from the publisher, except as permitted by U.S. copyright law.

Every effort has been made by the author and publishing house to ensure that the information contained in this book was correct as of press time. The author and publishing house hereby disclaim and do not assume liability for any injury, loss, damage, or disruption caused by errors or omissions, regardless of whether any errors or omissions result from negligence, accident, or any other cause. Readers are encouraged to verify any information contained in this book prior to taking any action on the information.

For rights and permissions, please contact:

Jen Fields
jen@themelodyofmissjen.com

Hardback ISBN: 979-8-9886581-0-8
Paperback ISBN: 979-8-9886581-2-2
E-Book ISBN: 979-8-9886581-1-5

Dedicated to the Divine Masculine and all the beautiful ways
it has shown up for me in unconditional love.

To my Daddy, who embodies the love of the divine father in
all its human duality and splendor.

To Jesus, who went the long way around the barn to bring me home.

And to my beloved J – these 185,000 words don't even touch the wonder
and the depth of all that we are. In your own words:
"It spans across time and crosses all lines – it's you and me."

iv

"I would recognize you in total darkness, were you mute and I deaf. I would recognize you in another lifetime entirely, in different bodies, different times. And I would love in all of this, until the very last star in the sky burnt out into oblivion." - Achilles

from "Song of Achilles", by Madeline Miller

vi

Contents

Prologue 1

Part One 9
    Chapter One 11
    Chapter Two 27

Part Two 33
    Chapter Three 35
    Chapter Four 53
    Chapter Five 73
    Chapter Six 79

Part Three 91
    Chapter Seven 93
    Chapter Eight 99

Part Four 113
    Chapter Nine 115
    Chapter Ten 125
    Chapter Eleven 137
    Chapter Twelve 147
    Chapter Thirteen 151
    Chapter Fourteen 173
    Chapter Fifteen 193
    Chapter Sixteen 203

Part Five 215
    Chapter Seventeen 217
    Chapter Eighteen 229

Part Six 239
    Chapter Nineteen 241
    Chapter Twenty 247
    Chapter Twenty-One 251
    Chapter Twenty-Two 263
    Chapter Twenty-Three 269

Part Seven 283

    Chapter Twenty-Four 285

    Chapter Twenty-Five 291

    Chapter Twenty-Six 299

    Chapter Twenty-Seven 305

    Chapter Twenty-Eight 313

    Chapter Twenty-Nine 335

    Chapter Thirty 349

Part Eight 363

    Chapter Thirty-One 365

    Chapter Thirty-Two 387

    Chapter Thirty-Three 409

Prologue

I WAS BORN INTO a Fundamentalist Evangelical Southern Baptist family. Not only is that a mouthful to say it's a beast to overcome, and I highly recommend you avoid that misfortune if you get the choice.

My formative years were spent at the church every single time the doors were open, and I mean that with no irony or exaggeration. I was there every Wednesday night, twice on Sundays, the entire week if there was a revival or Vacation Bible School going on, as well as every wedding, funeral, and baby shower that occurred for any of the church members. My experience with religion was a constant and persistent presence that flavored my entire childhood. I do want to be clear, however, in letting it be known that no one dragged me to church against my will. Ever. Not only was it just so ingrained into my life for as long as I could remember, it was also my community. My sense of connectivity and purpose stemmed from our little church and the goings on therein, and it was an enormous part of my identity in my youth.

My church, a little backwoods Southern Baptist church, claimed the distinction of being the oldest church in Tennessee; a fact that went uncontested until about ten years ago when some other little church nearby had the audacity to claim that *they* were the oldest church in Tennessee. This little blip on the radar of history sparked an argument of (forgive me) biblical proportions, and only served to bolster my belief that Southern Baptists aren't happy unless they are arguing about something.

When I look back on faith and what that meant to me at the time, I have to keep it in the context of the teachings I had been immersed in since birth. You see, the Southern Baptist tradition is less about an actual connection to the Divine, and more about navigating around a minefield of booby traps (sin disguised as a perfectly good time) and sinkholes that are certain to piss off God, should one misstep.

The biggest one of these holes one can fall down is being Pro-Choice (because that's basically just a sneaky way of saying Pro-Abortion in the eyes of the Lord), with condoning homosexuality coming in hot for second place. They basically just can't even wrap their minds around the actual physical union of same-sex couples, so that part is never discussed in any detail. Instead, they set up vague ideas of what it means to be a homosexual without actually discussing the sex part, which honestly makes it extremely confusing as a young person growing up in church to determine what exactly it is that is occurring that is so despised by God. It's also never discussed as if this "lifestyle" may be taking place in *gasp* *their own congregation with actual humans*. It's going on "out there in the world somewhere" with degenerates who will look like freaks to the naked eye and will be easy to spot as "the others." Southern Baptists spend a great deal of their time making sure the message gets across that should one come across a homosexual in the wild, that one is to "love the sinner and hate the sin." The line tends to get a little blurry on that for most people though, so they just go ahead and hate the sinner too. It's best to make absolutely certain that you and God are on the same page about the hate part.

As a young teen struggling with her sexual identity, you might imagine that I found all of this poorly explained hatred terrifying, to say the least.

The doctrine that was taught to me represented a very fear-based kind of faith, so it's no wonder that during that time of my life, I felt so…afraid of God. Afraid of everything, really. That fear of the Creator instilled in a person at such a young age, soaks in like ink on fabric and spreads wide through the connecting threads. It stains all connections with a sense of apprehension and fear of failing or disappointing any of the people in your life, but especially authority figures. You become well-versed in avoiding wrath.

Southern Baptist tradition isn't such that they will try to keep you within the faith against your will, they will simply tell you things that will scare the shit out of you so that you are too afraid to leave it of your own accord. "Hellfire and brimstone" isn't just a quaint catchphrase used to describe the flair of Southern Baptist preacher stylings. That, my friends, is a direct threat of what will rain down upon your head should you step out of alignment with God.

Ah, "alignment." As I type that word now, I have such a different connotation of what that means. When I was a teen, I pictured a military-style alignment. Everyone in their place, spaced evenly behind God, and following His marching orders. Stepping out of formation was glaring to everyone and was certain to bring the wrath of the Almighty (not to mention your fellow soldier's judgment on why you can't just get your shit together like the rest of the battalion).

Now alignment looks like surrender to me. It looks like trusting God enough to know that He will move you to where you need to be, regardless of what the rest of the soldiers are doing. He's moving them too, and you are all likely going to different destinations.

"Alignment" looks a lot more like faith than it used to, in my eyes. I'm not even sure I knew what actual faith was during my youth.

Believing something just because someone tells you it's true, is faith… in a way.

It's just not a very substantial kind of faith. They always used to use the example of a chair when talking about faith in Sunday school. They would say, "Faith is having trust in things you can't see. It's like how you trust that a chair will hold your weight when you sit in it."

To which I say, those people have clearly never had a weight problem and sat down in a chair that dumped your fat ass on the ground leaving you with furniture trust issues, but I digress.

Yes, I (mostly) trust that the chair will hold my weight without having sat in it. But wouldn't that faith be so much stronger if I just tried it out? I can actually have that experience without just postulating on the outcome. What's so wrong with just sitting in the chair and finding out that it will, in fact, (probably) hold my weight?

What's so wrong with having faith in God because I have a direct connection that I have come to rely on? I think I prefer the kind of faith that is tried and true, versus the faith that requires me to trust in a chair that I've never actually sat in. Also, God never dumped me on the floor because I ate too much pasta. Which sort of goes against the "cause and effect God" or "punishment and reward God" view that Southern Baptists hold in regard to how they believe God works.

The Baptists will tell you that God is an angry God. A vengeful God. A very "Old Testament" God. I find it intriguing (or maybe just frustrating) that the teachings state that Jesus is the Son of God, and that the only path to heaven is to accept that as absolute fact and ask Him to live in your heart and be your Lord and Savior -this alone will save you from an eternity in a fiery hell. Then those exact same teachers basically disregard the teachings of Jesus and use the Old Testament as a means of assessing one another's worthiness in walking the Christian path. (A Christian path that in its very essence and name should be defined by the teachings of Christ, who makes a spectacular first appearance in the New Testament, correct? Otherwise, it's Judaism…correct? Just making sure I'm not the only one seeing a tiny little discrepancy here.)

I have lots to say about the Southern Baptist teachings, primarily because I have had a lifetime to unpack the baggage that got tossed upon me at an early age, and introspection is kind of my main gig these days. However, rather than bombard you with the levels of beef that I have with Baptist teachings, I will just say that in those early years of my life, I merely accepted what was taught to me, without question.

Fear tactics paired with strict orders to not question God (i.e., the teachings of the church) left my very young lesbian self feeling more than a little hopeless and condemned.

I started to put together that I was gay around the time I was 13 or 14 years old. During the first few years, I bounced back and forth between crushing on girls at school and hating myself for doing so. I had zero interest in boys, and for a long time didn't have the language to put into words what it was I was feeling. I was in a freshman advanced English class when somehow the word *lesbian* surfaced and I finally learned what that word meant, in the way that can only be vulgarized properly by high school boys. Suddenly I began to have intensely vivid sexual dreams about women that plagued me almost nightly. My first discovery of orgasm was through those dreams, which left me with far more questions than answers and I didn't know who to ask. The internet was just starting to become a thing, and I didn't even have it at home yet because my stone tablet and chisel took up most of my bedroom. (If you are under thirty, you were thinking that anyway, so I'll just say it before you can.) I didn't trust anyone enough to ask those kinds of questions. It was a complete solo education with major gaps that I didn't know how to fill. This is something I hear frequently from my fellow gays that are in my age group, or older. Being gay was not something that was talked about, and we had no role models or positivity surrounding that topic that we could look toward to try and figure out this whole sexuality thing in a way that wasn't completely damaging to our sense of self.

What a burden to put on a child: to discover something so intimate about yourself, only to find that the way that you are will likely cause rejection from those you love, and from the God you serve.

It is scarring on the deepest levels.

In the present environment, positive LGBTQIA+ role models abound. Young people are surrounded with open dialog and discussion about sexuality. Which is not to say that they are all accepted unconditionally at home, or that coming out is no longer scary; I know that some young people are battling the same things that I battled at that age. However, there is a strong community present and visible now, where answers and peer acceptance can be easily found. That is a blessing that wasn't available even 15 years ago. Ellen DeGeneres was the first public figure that I remember hearing about being gay and the reason that I heard about it was because our church hosted a youth lock-in on the night that her coming out episode aired.

You read that correctly.

My church literally locked its youth in the church building for a night of Bible study to keep them away from the television, lest they see a positive gay role model announce their sexuality publicly.

I went to that lock-in, despite the fact that I was already dating a girl. I was absolutely terrified of anyone finding out that I was a lesbian, and I knew that whispers had already been going on throughout the church about myself and my "bestie." I knew that I had to show up in solidarity with the church that night, or I would have been questioned to no end, but it broke my heart to do so. I was so longing for a place where I could be myself. I wanted to see someone else bravely do what I couldn't do. Most of all, I wanted to feel a little less alone. I knew no other gay people at the time (except my girlfriend, obviously), and I desperately just wanted to feel a little more understood.

Understanding was something that I would never find in the circle that I was surrounded by.

By the time I was in high school, I was very active in the church, which made my position considerably more precarious. I've always been a performer and love theater with all of my heart; in high school, I was in competition theater and improv, and it was my favorite part of school. I began to do skits on Sunday mornings as part of the church service with a few other members of the youth group. At first, we bought the skits from companies that sell short scripts for worship, but over time I began to write them. Then one year, my youth pastor visited a bigger church in Nashville that had begun to do these walk-through plays called a "Judgment House" and asked if I would help him write a script for our church to host this phenomenon as well.

I agreed to help him and went back to Nashville with him and a few others to see what this was all about.

If you have never heard of a Judgment House (it's a fairly common thing now), allow me to fill you in. Basically, it's a haunted house for Jesus. The storyline is always some variance of the same premise – two people dying simultaneously and one going to heaven, while the other burns in hell. It's a terrifying, but effective way to get people to "accept Christ" by threatening them with an eternity of torment if they don't. (Like…right now. Also, you should probably sign up for church membership while you are here…)

I'm embarrassed to say that I was a part of that fear-mongering, but here we are.

One of my friends refers to those plays as a "Judgmental House," which cracks me up but also makes me want to cry a little over the accuracy. If I had known then what I know now, I would never have been able to help write those scripts in good conscience.

Fear. That fear that had been so deeply instilled in me I passed right along to other young people, believing that I was helping them find God.

Fear. Fear of the wrath of God that was so strong it could shove you into salvation. Manhandle you into the arms of the Lord.

Scare you to Jesus.

It would take me a long time, and a lot of heartache, to realize that I had it all completely backwards. I had been taught the exact opposite of what I truly needed to know in order to connect with the Divine.

What I've learned with age, and through trial and tribulation is this:

The opposite of Love is not "hate."

It's fear.

Fear and Love are polar opposites in the way that dark and light are.

If God is Love (and that may be the truest definition of God that has ever been articulated), then I feel very confident in stating that it is impossible to successfully scare someone into a relationship with the Divine. The path of fear does not lead to love any more than the path of love would lead you to fear. The path of love leads to……more love. Deeper love. Bigger love. Agape Love.

The path of fear leads to therapy and anxiety medication.

You can't access light in the darkness without, well… light. Until someone lights a candle so that you can find the dang light switch, you just keep fumbling around in the darkness.

Just like you can't keep scrambling around in fear looking for God's love. It's too far removed. There has to be a spark, an experience with that kind of love to light the path. It takes a candle to illuminate the journey. You have to know what you are seeking intimately. Hold it in your hands. You can use that smaller flame to find the all-encompassing fire that is the Love of God.

And yes, I did just use fire, which we normally associate with hell, as a metaphor for Love.

Funny that Christianity uses that imagery for what we consider to be the worst thing that could ever happen, isn't it? "The fires of eternal damnation."

As far as I can tell, if you ask anyone who has ever loved anything, they will tell you that love in its most potent form…sets you aflame.

This story is the story of the journey that brought me into the arms of Love. It is how Spirit moved me through the dark forest of fear that I had spent the majority of my life wandering through, and into the Light of all that is holy. This story is the true recounting of how I fell "In Love."

It all began with an ember.

Spirit blew on that ember until it became a spark.

I carried that spark in my hands, until one day I met a twin flame that combined with my little flickering light to start a wildfire that couldn't be extinguished.

That wildfire illuminated the skies and burned the path that I followed all the way home to the hearth of Love.

The journey was a strange and difficult one.

I've been brought to my knees many a time, though not in the ways that my childhood church leaders had hoped, I'm sure. I was never taken to the woodshed by God Almighty to be beaten for my evil ways.

My ego, however, is mighty handy with a switch.

I inflicted onto myself most of the lessons and the pain that I encountered on this path.

My sense of direction was terrible, and out of clumsiness, I fell quite a bit.

I walked most of the way with a limp.

I still do.

It feels important for me to tell you here, at the very beginning, that everything that you are about to read is true. This is not a book of metaphors, however unbelievable parts of it may appear. Most names have been changed, and a few things have been shuffled (timeline-wise as well as characters present/not present during a few scenes) for the sake of story flow, but all of these things actually happened, and I am retelling them (to the very best of my recollection) as closely as possible to the manner that they unfolded.

This is my true story, though it isn't an easy one to tell.

It is my love story with Spirit, and with the flame that brought me to It.

We will get to the wildfire in time.

For now, let us go back to the ashes....

Part One

kindling - *noun*

: easily combustible material for starting a fire

Chapter One

It was my daddy's favorite story. He loved to tell it, and I loved to watch him tell it. His features would come alive with delight. I loved the sparkle in his eye, the inflection in his southern drawl, and best of all his booming laughter.

"She was just a tiny little thing," he would start. He always put his hands in the air around an invisible small object as if to say, "No bigger than this."

"Not even three years old, I don't think. She shouldn't even have been talking like she was, but that girl started to speak just about the minute after she was born. She loved to play outside, but we had a dangerously steep bank that led down to the driveway that I was always worried she would get hurt on. I had told that child, and told that child, and told that child not to run down that section of the yard because I didn't want her to fall. I even went out there one spring and built a retaining wall around part of it to keep it from being so steep. Didn't make any difference of course, she just ran around to the side that wasn't walled up and ran down that part instead."

He would always stop and look at me with complete exasperation at this point. As though I were still toddling down steep banks against his wishes. As if it were yesterday that this story happened instead of so many years ago.

I would roll my eyes of course, but it was all part of the tale.

"Anyway, it had come a pretty good snow that day while I was at work. As anyone around here will tell you, snow and mountains aren't a good mix. I had just pulled in the driveway, and I saw her up the hill playing in the snow. Her momma was out there with her, and they were making snow angels. I guess Jen saw me before her momma did, because the next thing I know she is running full speed down that icy bank yelling 'Daddy! Daddy!' all excited because I was home."

He would grin at me proudly. "She always was a daddy's girl!" he would add.

It was true. For as long as I could remember, my daddy had two shadows.

"I tried to holler at her to stop, but she didn't hear me and before I could do anything she began to slip. I thought for a minute she was going to catch herself with those tiny little arms, but all she did was straighten back up and start to slide again. By the time she had gotten down to the asphalt, she had built up a pretty good momentum, just in time to completely lose it and fall backwards."

He would always pause right here, and I knew from his expression that he was replaying every instant of that fall in his head.

He would look perfectly horrified as he said, "I saw her little head bounce off of the concrete and heard her start to cry out in pain. I don't even remember how I got from my truck over to her, but the next thing I recall is scooping her up off of the ground and shaking her. She scared me so badly, that out of panic I just started fussing at her. 'How many times have I told you not to run down that hill?! How MANY?' I thought she was probably all right, but it could have been so much *worse*."

Daddy would pause and sigh before continuing, the fear in his eyes still visible.

"It was then that she did the funniest thing. She took her little hands and put them on either side of my face like this." He would put his large, workman hands on both of his cheeks as he told it.

"She looked up at me through those big crocodile tears, and said very seriously, 'Daddy, when little girls are hurt, you shouldn't yell at them. You should kiss them and hold them and tell them everything is going to be just fine.' "

He would then throw his head back and roar with laughter.

"She sounded just like a little grown-up! Anybody else's kid would have just been wailing their head off - mine gives me a parenting lecture!" He would double over with laughter and slap his leg with delight.

"She was right of course - I just panicked and lost it when I saw her fall. Made me feel terrible when she said it, even though I couldn't help but laugh."

Usually, the recipient of this story would still be laughing as well. Dad would always lean over and hug me at this point, almost as if to double-check and make sure that I was still safe from that fall.

"Parenting Jen has always been interesting, for sure. Sometimes I'm not sure who is teaching who," he would finish with a bemused grin.

He would look at me and we would laugh together as he shook his head.

I met my first girlfriend, Molly, at the little backwoods Baptist church that I grew up in. Oh, the irony.

It was about a month before our annual Judgement House play (written and directed by yours truly) was to be performed when suddenly the youth director brought a new member of the youth group to me to see if there was a spot in the production that I could squeeze her into. He told me that her family had just joined the church, and that he wanted her to feel included. It was short notice, and I was a little annoyed to be asked to reshuffle cast members at this point. I looked carefully at the girl standing in front of me. She was quite a bit shorter than me, which even at sixteen years old was par for the course. At nearly six feet tall, I was used to towering over my peers. My height, paired with extra-long curly flaming red hair assured that no matter where I went, I was pretty hard to miss – a fact that made my early teen years a little more unbearable than I thought they should have been. Like most blossoming young women, all I had wanted was to fly under the radar unnoticed, and instead, I found that no matter where I went, people stared. This moment was no exception. The girl in front of me was looking up at me slightly wide-eyed as she said, "Wow. You're really tall." I merely shrugged in response. I could tell she was a few years older than me (18 I was guessing?) and she had long wavy blond hair, and beautiful big blue eyes. I was kind of taken aback at how pretty she was. She told me her name was Molly in a very soft voice and was quick to add that she didn't want a speaking role in the production. I was relieved that I wasn't going to have to rewrite anything, and quickly decided to plug her into the heaven scene as an angel because everyone knows that Jesus and all the angels are sexy white people with blond hair and blue eyes. (Plus, all the angels basically had to do in the show was stand there and look pretty and I thought she was already doing awesome at that.)

Molly had caught my attention in a big way, and I began to make the cast rehearse the hell out of the heaven scene (see what I did there?) so that I would have multiple chances a week to be around her. I don't know how I knew that she was gay, because my experience with such things was exactly ZERO at that point, but I definitely picked up on something that made me strongly suspect she was like me.

Gaydar is a thing, y'all. I don't know why. Maybe it's just survival equipment that gets installed with the base model. Perhaps the universe puts it there to help us out in the coupling department, in the same way, foxes know to mate with other foxes and not jaguars. I don't know what exactly it was that made me think that Molly also liked girls. She certainly never said anything that would indicate that was the case. She mostly just stood quietly in the corner of the heaven scene in her angel robe and men's Crocs (Wait…) looking like a dream and sending out some kind of invisible rainbow vibe that drew me to her like a magnet.

There was an undeniable attraction and intrigue, and just when I thought she couldn't get any cooler I stepped out the back door of the recreation building to get some prop materials and busted her smoking around the corner.

We stared at each other wide-eyed for a minute before I finally blurted out, "You smoke?!"

She shrugged. "Not in front of anyone, usually."

"You'd better put that out before anyone else sees. I'm pretty sure you'll get in trouble.", I said, though I was super impressed. Sneaking a smoke behind the church was definitely the ballsiest thing I'd ever seen anyone do.

"What are they gonna do, kick me out of church? That doesn't seem very Christian-like. Shouldn't everyone be welcome here?" she said.

"Yeah, I guess in theory. It doesn't really seem to work out that way, though."

She raised an eyebrow.

"So I've noticed. Your little play in there has people going to hell for all eternity for drinking a beer," she said.

I bristled slightly. I didn't know if she knew that I was not only the director of the show but had also written the script.

"That's not why. They go to hell because they live a lifestyle that isn't in God's will. The beer is just an example," I said timidly.

"Seems like bullshit to me," she replied. My mouth fell open in shock.

"Aren't you afraid to say that?"

"Afraid of what? It's just an opinion. I'm allowed to have one too," she said. She took another drag off of her cigarette.

I pondered this. I was terrified to say a word against the church teachings, and it had never occurred to me that I might have been *allowed* to think something in opposition.

"Afraid to speak against God's Word like that. Aren't you afraid you'll be punished for it?"

She paused and seemed to consider it for a moment.

"Not really. It seems to me like it's the people doing the judging in there, not God," she said with a nod toward the church building. She stamped out the butt of the cigarette on the pavement and walked past me to go back inside.

"Wait!" I said. She stopped and looked at me.

"Do… you want to hang out sometime? Like… not here?" I asked. "I won't say anything else about you smoking, I promise. I really don't mind."

At this, she laughed. "Yeah, ok. As long as you don't go writing scripts about me for next year's Judgement House hell scene."

I blushed. So she *had* known. Oddly, the fact that she had openly challenged me in that way made me like her even more.

"Deal," I said.

And so, it began. It wasn't long before we were inseparable friends.

We discovered that we only lived about a half mile away from each other.

Suddenly, my new "friend" was picking me up on a Tuesday evening to get gas in her car that we would run out by the end of the night, just driving around and listening to music like high school kids do.

We started showing up at each other's schools and workplaces. We would leave church together and go get lunch, and then come up with some asinine reason to spend every single minute between services together before we had to come back to church that evening.

We didn't really have much in common, other than a love of music that we would use as an excuse to be in each other's presence as often as possible. We would take turns buying new CDs so that we could share them with each other. It really probably wasn't enough to base a whole relationship on, but we were young and dumb, and I was fairly certain she was the only other person like me on the whole planet. I was afraid if I lost her, I would be entirely alone in this scary place of being attracted to girls. I decided that I needed to somehow let her know how I felt.

One evening, despite every single part of my very afraid sixteen-year-old self screaming at me not to, I dared to cross the line a little.

She had driven my little ancient Nissan Sentra up to a mountain lookout not far from home. We were sitting in the car, and listening to music, and I remember every single heartbeat pounding in my ears as I reached across the center console and grabbed her hand.

Her eyebrows shot up so fast and hard that I thought I was going to have to pick them off of the car roof.

What now, dumbass? I thought. I hadn't thought about what I'd do after that, or even what I would say.… I had just been working up the courage over there in the passenger seat to make a move of some kind. Suddenly, I was worrying about how I would get home, and what exactly I would tell my parents if she kicked me out of my own car and left me there.

The *audacity*.

I still, at 42 years old, look back at that moment and can't believe I did that. I essentially threw everything that I was afraid of out the window because I wanted so badly to touch that girl. I didn't even know for sure at that moment whether or not she also liked women.

I just… went for it.

Reaching across that console was a defining moment in my life. I've never been a particularly brave person. In fact, I am more akin to a bunny that bravely hops into your yard like a badass until he sees your dog and then heads for the hills. But I was brave in that moment.

That was a moment when I chose the voice that was screaming inside of me over everything else. For the first time in my life, I hung up the expectations of what others wanted for my life and did what felt right in my heart.

I felt fairly certain that she felt the same way about me that I felt about her. She looked at me the same way I looked at her. I thought. Right?

I backtracked in my head as I sat there with her hand in mine and panicked that maybe I had misread everything. Perhaps I had built a whole story in my head because I so desperately wanted to be with her?

She squeezed my hand tight.

My heart fluttered. I had to let her know that I knew…this was more than friends, wasn't it?

"Don't change, ok?" is what came out of my mouth.

It was enough.

She nodded and smirked slightly. "Don't you change either," she said knowingly. She paused for a moment, and I could tell she was trying to work out something in her head.

"I need to ask you something. Did…did someone say something to you about me? Is that why you are doing this?" she asked as she squeezed my hand tighter.

I didn't have a clue what she was talking about.

"What do you mean? Said something about you like what? I've been working up the courage to say something for weeks."

She went on to tell me that the reason that she and her family had suddenly appeared in the congregation out of nowhere one day was that she had been caught in the act, in bed with another girl. She had been given an ultimatum at that point. No more sex with girls (obviously), and she could choose between either being checked into the local asylum or she could go to church with her family in hopes that religion would save her from continuing down the path that she was on.

I wish I was making that up.

They didn't fuck around when it came to homosexuality down here in southern Appalachia 20 years ago. They would either try to shock it out of you or pray it out of you, and Molly was lucky that they'd given her the option.

She told me her plan had been to just tough out the whole church situation until she could save up enough to move out of her parent's house, and then she could just do whatever she wanted. I'm sure when she was carefully crafting that plan, she didn't think for a second that she would end up holding hands with the church drama leader.

I was honestly *beyond shocked* to find out that information when she disclosed it.

"What? Why didn't you say something? I've been over here scared shitless that you might punch me in the face if I told you what I was feeling, and the whole time you had already been with a woman? If you would have just told me that… this would have been so much easier," I said.

"Are you kidding? You are such a sheltered little church girl, Jen. You are the

LAST person I thought I could tell that to. There is no one more surprised by this conversation than me," she said.

I wanted to be offended, but I knew she was right. I could hardly believe I was going through with any of this myself. I knew that no one else would ever have thought it was in the realm of possibility that I was attracted to women (let alone would act on it), given my position in the church. I couldn't think of any way to respond so I just kissed her... which definitely sealed the deal on her being the more surprised of the two of us for the evening.

The conversation that evening pushed us into a full-fledged relationship with the speed that can only be attained by a lesbian couple. There is an old joke that some of you will be familiar with:

"What does a lesbian bring on the second date?"

The answer is, "A U-Haul."

That, my dear ones, is one of those jokes that is funny because it is true.

Two lesbians will leave from their first coffee date together and swing by the animal shelter on the way home and adopt 3 cats and start a family before dinner at whichever house they have decided they will cohabitate from that point on. (Usually for the next 25 years.) Lesbians excel at nesting.

Due to our age, we didn't exactly U-Haul (yes, I did just use that word as a verb), but we did the best we could under the circumstances. We already spent nearly every free moment together, so nothing changed there, but suddenly there was kissing and touching and virtually trying to be on top of each other every waking second.

One thing led to another until I (finally!) had my first sexual experience.

It's funny, because I was of the age that I was getting a lot of feedback from my friends about their first sexual experiences (all with men, of course) and it was honestly such a mixed bag that I didn't even know what to expect. If I had been reading Yelp reviews on high school fucking, I'm not sure that I would have patronized that establishment.

Luckily, she was wonderful. She obviously had a little more knowledge and experience under her belt than I did, and she made me feel comfortable and beautiful.

She also "showed me the ropes," as any information I had gotten up to that point had been from straight women and was not helpful. I was an eager student. I loved sex with her, and it felt a bit like a beast had been unleashed that I hadn't known had been sleeping inside me. If we had been able to have sex every day that would have been great with me. My sexuality became something I wanted to explore in every way possible. I learned so much during those months and my attraction to women, and women alone, became solidified in my mind. I couldn't even imagine sharing that intimacy with a boy, and the thought of it honestly made me a little nauseated. I reveled in the curves and softness of my girl.

I began to notice other women constantly and would find myself daydreaming about touching them. Sex with a woman took what had just been a whisper in the back of my mind and moved it to the forefront of my thoughts and gave it a microphone. It was distracting, showy, and…. hot.

I was open to anything Molly wanted to try in bed, but my language and knowledge were so limited at that time that it didn't take much to shock me. I was definitely still a sheltered church girl at heart. This amused her tremendously, but she was patient and kind.

We once took a day trip to Knoxville, which was fairly close and a much bigger city (where we were certain not to run into anyone we knew), where Molly took me to my first sex shop. I walked around that place with my jaw dragging the floor in what must have been a clear flag that they should check my ID/age, because I got kicked out about 5 minutes after we walked in. Just the fact that such objects even existed was a whole new world that I hadn't ever been aware of, and by the time Molly had purchased a few things and gotten back in the car I was bubbling with a thousand questions.

She had purchased our first strap-on and a vibrator that trip, which I won't lie, blew my mind before we even used them. I could not even wrap my little Bible school mind around how those things were going to work. I spent the whole way home looking at them and asking her so many detailed questions that she finally told me with a laugh that she would show me later and asked me to shut up.

We began sneaking off at any opportunity to fuck somewhere. It was exciting and scary and exhilarating. I was happy, but terrified.

Tongues were wagging at church. Eyebrows were being raised at school. Both of our parents were definitely starting to notice that something wasn't normal about this connection.

Molly was kind of lucky in that way though - her parents thought it was wonderful that she had such a close church friend. They (well, anyone who knew me at all during those years) would have never ever guessed in a million years that we were sleeping together.

My parents, on the other hand, who had barely let me breathe without a permission slip in 16 years, found this new friendship exceedingly strange. They began to fish a bit. They would ask questions about why neither Molly nor I had boyfriends, or why we had to spend every waking minute together, etc. They never came straight out and asked if anything romantic was going on, but they danced all around it.

Things were escalating and I felt it.

Molly and I were in love. It made my last year of high school nearly impossible.

I felt like I was living a double life. Home/school Jen and church Jen were not the same as lesbian Jen. I felt like a one-person boy band where one of the members kept derailing on pills and booze and couldn't keep up with the choreography. It felt impossible to contain or direct, and I couldn't see a way to get us all together in a happy whole unit that could stand together onstage in front of the world. I couldn't reconcile the group. It began to feel like my sexuality was going to have to start a solo career if it wanted any sense of validity, but we were all afraid of the negative press.

My senior year is tinged with memories that are still painful to recall. I somehow got nominated for homecoming queen, and I remember riding into our football stadium on the back of a convertible, only to look over and see Molly in front of the bleachers looking like she had been crying. She hadn't been able to be with me while I got ready, did our group photos, or rode in the homecoming parade. She wouldn't be able to attend the dance after the game with me. It broke my heart to see her standing there while a guy friend of mine escorted me onto the field in front of the entire school when we both knew it should have been her.

I remember feeling so helpless. And like a fraud.

My senior prom I snuck out of the dance a few times to call her from the payphone outside the ballroom, only to have her pick up the phone sobbing. She should have been there with me, but we both knew there was no way that I could have taken her. People were talking enough at that point that we could never have passed it off as going together as friends. Who brings their older college-age buddy to their senior prom? No one. Unless they go to Rydell High where there is a nationally televised dance competition, and they need some help from ChaCha.

It was excruciating.

I broke her heart multiple times that year. I still carry guilt about that.

Towards the end of the school year, my dad came home from work early one day and damn near caught us having sex. I heard him come through the downstairs door of our split foyer house and take off up the stairs as fast as he could. I jumped up, grabbed my dress and ran to the bathroom, and told Molly to act like she was getting dressed to leave. I heard him knock on my bedroom door just as I shut the bathroom door behind me. I called to him that we were getting dressed to go to a movie. I could tell he didn't quite buy the lie, but it did manage to keep him from opening the door.

It scared me so badly that I decided something had to give. It was one thing to have to tell them about my sexuality, it was a whole other thing to be physically caught in the act with a girl. Not to mention the trauma response/reaction that the incident brought to the surface in Molly. I didn't think anyone could be more afraid of getting caught than I was, but I watched her crumble in fear. She already had been down that exact path before and still hadn't recovered from the aftermath. For days afterward she was still shaken, even more so than I was.

I knew I had to get out of that house before we got caught.

At the time, I was working at a quirky little retail store in the mall that was a kind of hipster hub long before the word "hipster" was used. The day I got hired I formed an instant connection with a beautiful brunette named Lila, who was a few years older than me. She was stunningly beautiful, with large doe-like brown eyes, and I initially talked to her because that seemed like a better option than just open-mouthed staring at her. I found her to be incredibly down to earth which helped me let go of my little crush (well, that and the fact that she was VERY straight, by her own admission), and we quickly became close friends. Lila's boyfriend, Jason, worked across the hall from us at the music store in the mall. He was a tall broad-shouldered boy who always wore a newsboy cap. Though his size seemed intimidating, he had a gentle kindness about him that made me take an instant liking to him as well. Around the time that my dad nearly caught Molly and me in bed together, I overheard Lila and Jason talking about moving in together. They had apparently found a cheap apartment that wasn't very far from where I lived, and I asked them about it.

"I think the apartment below us is open, Jen. You and Molly should move in! That would be so fun for us all to be neighbors! We could hang out more… plus, it would be nice to have people we know living beside us, rather than strangers or someone we may not like," Lila said.

I jumped on the opportunity.

Molly and I moved in together into that apartment as soon as we possibly could. Soon the four of us were all spending a great deal of time hanging out together. Lila was an amazing cook and would often make dinner for all of us. I tried to reciprocate the favor, but there are only so many times you can ask a group of people to politely choke down your horrible "first attempt" at meals before you have mercy on all involved and just leave the cooking to someone who knows how. We all shared a big love of music and we spent most of our time together taking turns introducing the group to our favorite artists. Molly and I quickly found out that Jason was an incredible musician- not only was he an amazing bass guitar player he actually had a beautiful singing voice as well. I heard him practicing upstairs (it was a pretty shitty apartment, and the walls were thin) quite frequently, and he even played a few songs for us sometimes when we were all together for dinner.

The sweetness in the overall connection among the four of us somehow made the place feel like home despite the fact that the apartment was a dump, and we were sleeping on a mattress in the floor and eating off paper plates. We were all poor, but the relationships were rich, and we all became very good friends over the three years that we were neighbors.

My parents basically just stayed away. They initially did everything they could think of to stop Molly and me from moving in together (including using my young age as a reasonable protest for why I wasn't ready to move out), but once it actually happened, they just pretended like I lived alone and somewhere really far away from them. I only saw them at church and when I came by their house. Looking back, I think they knew what was going on but none of us had the balls to have that conversation. I wasn't ready to come out of the closet, and they weren't ready to face the music either.

Luckily for all of us, no one in the family had to initiate that conversation because our local church gossip ringleader saw Molly and me having a picnic in a park one day (holding hands, no less) and decided that this was the most amazing opportunity that she had ever had; she could destroy the lives of TWO families for the price of one with that little nugget of knowledge.

I'm sure it was the proudest moment she had ever had, calling first Molly's family, and then mine, and then the rest of the entire goddamn prayer chain to make sure everyone at our little backwoods Baptist church was aware of the lesbianism she had witnessed with her very own two eyes.

What a saint! What a deliverer of justice! She was truly out in our community doing the work of the Lord. After all, it may have completely devastated all of the lives of both families involved, but it's without a doubt what Jesus would have done. He would have sniffed out that sin, judged it harshly, and basked in the glory of the spotlight shining on him for bringing this to light for everyone else to judge as well. The deliverer of the news. The stirrer of the proverbial pot.

I'm sure she secured herself a bigger mansion in heaven that day.

I showed up at my parent's house for a visit one day right after that phone call had taken place, and my mom happened to be there alone. I had no idea whatsoever what I was walking into. Apparently, when Betty "Bigmouth" Bible called she had spoken with my mother, and Mom hadn't yet passed this newfound knowledge on to my father because she had decided to confront me about it first. We were sitting on the porch together and I could tell something was wrong. Really, *really* wrong.

She started out tentatively. "I need to ask you something….and I need for you to tell me the truth."

I stared at her with big eyes. Where was this going? "Ok," was all I could muster up to respond with.

She took a deep breath.

"Is Molly gay?" she asked.

Oh fuuuuuuuuuuuuuck.

My mind somehow bypassed answering that question because I knew with certainty what the next question would inevitably be.

This was actually happening. My greatest fear had just been made tangible - newly born into reality on this porch between these rocking chairs. I could physically feel the fear between us both, naked and screaming for attention while we both tried not to look at it.

My mind whirled. We were about to start down a path here that we couldn't backtrack from. I thought I would give her the option to halt it before it started.

"Mom. I will answer that question, if you want, but we both know that there may be information disclosed in this conversation that you don't actually want to hear. Are you sure you want to have this talk right now?" I said, trembling.

My body had gone cold and numb. I had never truly experienced fear until this moment. I prayed that she would say she'd changed her mind.

I wasn't ready. I couldn't do this. Not now. Not here.

I had always thought I would eventually tell them the truth when I was more stable. When I had my life a bit more together. When I wasn't in college and working retail and everything wasn't precariously hanging on paycheck to paycheck. When I had made a better life for myself, so that I could say, "See? Being gay isn't the worst thing. I've built a beautiful life, and I just so happen to share it with a woman."

Not in this moment. Not sitting there as a broke-ass college kid dating another broke-ass college kid with not a single thing to our names. I had no good points to bring up in this argument that I had rehearsed in my head a thousand times, because it wasn't when I thought it would unfold.

Stupidly, I had believed that I would have been in control of the when and how the coming out would occur. Instead, there I sat with it crammed in my face against my will. I could barely breathe.

When Mom replied, she did so slowly and intentionally. I could tell the words were painful for her to say.

"I think I have a right to know the truth about my daughter," she said.

We sat in silence for a moment.

When I could muster up the guts, I finally said, "Yes, Mom. Molly is gay."

I braced myself for what I knew would follow.

"Are you?" she asked.

It occurred to me that I could still lie. I could still not tell her.

My mind briefly went down the rabbit hole of what that would look like, but then all I could see was a future scenario where we inevitably would have to have this same conversation again and I would have to confess the truth.

Then they would be mad that not only was I gay, but that I had once lied about it when directly asked.

No, this truth would always be true. Better to just rip off the Band-Aid.

When I met her gaze, my lower lip began to quiver uncontrollably. I felt the hot tears forming behind my eyes.

"Yes," I whispered.

There it was. A single word released from my lips and hung heavy in the air between us. No way to put it back in my mouth now.

"Yes???!" she half-shouted. Then she tightened her lip into a firm straight line. I knew that look. She was beyond angry. She raised her voice and began a series of questions/statements that were fired so rapidly at me that I had no time to respond to any of them.

"How did you get here, Jennifer? All of that time at church……we raised you better than this. You know very well what the Bible says about that lifestyle. Who else knows? You two have apparently been flaunting this all over town. Did you really think it wouldn't get back to us? I thought you had been saved!? You know better. This is a direct sin against God. You need to ask for forgiveness and turn from your ways NOW. It's the only hope you have…" She stood up and stormed inside still shouting. It was as if I could have been there or not been there. She was in her own personal dramatic monologue, and I was just another actor present on the stage.

She slammed the door hard behind her and I sat there in a stunned silence for a moment before I heard a loud crash of what sounded like something being thrown against a wall and shattering.

I ran inside to find her, arm raised above her head, with another dish that she was about to send flying.

You have to understand that while my mother did have a temper, I had never known her to be loud or throw anything when she was angry. She is more the "slice a major artery with class by saying the most hurtful thing you can think of without raising your voice and walk away with a smirk while they bleed to death" kind of arguer.

Seriously. Example: "Oh look, you've made me angry. Probably stems from your weight problem or the fact that your father loves your sister more than you. Byeeeeeeeee."

That was her style.

Not this dish-slinging ninja standing before me.

I stood there in disbelief for a moment just watching her lose her shit.

She finally collapsed in a heap with her back against the kitchen cabinets, sobbing audibly about how all that she had ever wanted in life was to be a mother and that she had failed miserably at it.

Of course, that cut me to the core. But my way of dealing with uncomfortable situations has always been humor, and unfortunately, I can't turn that off.

Sometimes it's my favorite thing about myself, and sometimes I loathe it. This was one of the latter because after watching that impressive display what came out of my mouth and pierced the now quiet room was…

"And the award, for unnecessary dramatic performance in a not very supporting role goes to…….." I said, complete with slow clapping.

If Mom could have set me on fire with her eyeballs, it would have happened in that instant.

"The fact that you have destroyed your own mother is funny to you?" she seethed.

I sighed.

"Of course it isn't, Mom, but I don't really get why you are making it about you…like it's something you did or didn't do that made me this way. It's not. I can't help who I'm attracted to," I said, as gently as I could. I didn't want to send her back into an outburst again.

She sat, still in the floor, absolutely shaking with rage.

"Don't you DARE tell your father."

"Umm…I have no intention of it. I didn't want to tell YOU. You asked, remember?" I replied.

"What if I hadn't? Were you never going to tell us? Were you just going to let everyone in town and at church know except for us? Did you just want us to look foolish?" she said.

"I would never want you to look or feel foolish. I just wasn't ready to tell you yet," I said dejectedly.

She kept rapid fire questioning me from the floor, and my answers became more and more shaky. I don't know how exactly I thought this conversation would go when it eventually happened, but it certainly wasn't like this. My arguments were weak. I didn't have my Bible verses that I had thought I would use in retaliation memorized.

I finally left with my tail between my legs.

The next day was Sunday, and I always, *always* came to visit Mom and Dad after church. I knew that if I wasn't going to tell Dad that I would have to come by like everything was normal, or he would know something was up. I had to stick to the usual script.

I walked in the door, said hello, and sat down on the couch across from where Dad was sitting in his recliner watching tv.

He picked up the remote, cut the tv off and looked me dead in the eye.

"Do you have something you need to tell me?" he asked firmly.

What the hell? Seriously?

"Actually, I was told NOT to tell you," I replied, as I turned to glare at my mother who stood in the adjoining kitchen.

She burst into tears.

"I had to tell him, Jen. He knew something was wrong with me. I couldn't hide that. I had to…." she let the sentence trail off into tears.

My dad's voice boomed across the house as he lit into me about all of the ways that I had let him and Jesus down with my "lifestyle choice".

I'd tell you all of the details, but I honestly can't remember most of them. Self-preservation allowed me to tune out a great bit of that speech, or maybe I didn't and it's a trauma response that blocks the memory of every single exact word.

The sentiment remains unmistakable in my memory, however.

The "not enough-ness."

The disappointment that I had become.

The disgust.

The condemnation.

The…. dare I say it…. hatred?

The anger.

The belittling.

The exact phrases might be fuzzy, but all of those elements are still swimming around in my memory, ready to be fished out and examined any time I choose.

I do remember with clarity how it finally ended, though.

"I cannot condone this perverted sex that you are engaging in. I refuse to believe that you are not CHOOSING to do this, to yourself and to others. It's not natural. And it's not simply 'who you are.' Other people might...but I will NEVER, EVER accept this. EVER," he said.

He stood up and stormed toward the door. Right before he walked through it, I called out to him.

"DADDY!"

He stopped to listen but did not turn around.

Tears had been streaming down my face the whole conversation. I knew that arguing would solve nothing. I searched quickly for something that would bring back some compassion from him. I tried desperately to think of something that would remind him that this was his child he was screaming at. His own daughter that he had once thought hung the moon.

How could I make him see that his words were destroying me?

"Daddy…. when little girls are hurt, you shouldn't yell at them. You should kiss them and hold them and tell them everything is going to be just fine," I said through my tears.

I watched his head drop for a brief moment. His hands were still on the door frame.

I thought for a second that he might turn around to look at me. He seemed to consider it, but then he stood up a little straighter and walked out the door without looking back.

It would be nearly ten years before my dad would look me in the eye again.

Chapter Two

THINGS WENT so terribly at home with my coming out, I have no idea why I thought they would go any better at church. There is optimism, and then there is just stupidity. The way I scurried off to church with my girlfriend that next Sunday as if nothing had happened was definitely the latter.

I suppose I thought that my parents wouldn't want their child (or themselves) to be discussed in a harsh and negative way, so they wouldn't engage the congregation in any gossip about it.

That turned out to be wishful thinking, and I quickly began to understand that I did not know my parents nearly as well as I thought I did. (I'm aware that they felt the same way about me.) The prayer chain (gossip hotline for Jesus) had been activated without my knowledge, and apparently had been buzzing with excitement all week.

We were walking into a fired-up bees' nest that Sunday like two dumb little kids with lollipops who had no idea they were about to be stung to death.

We had no sooner walked into the church building that day when the pastor met us at the door and asked if he could have a word with the two of us in his office. I think I actually said "shit" out loud in the foyer in response.

Nothing like immediately making a bad reputation even worse.

As we followed him down to his office, we lagged a few steps behind.

"Did you know this was going to happen?" Molly dug her elbow into my ribs.

"Do you honestly think I would have insisted we come today if I had?", I whispered back.

When we rounded the corner, I could see that the pastor's office was full of people. I saw several of the deacons, the youth pastor, the choir director, and my and Molly's parents.

Nausea washed over me as we stepped through the door and the pastor closed it behind him.

There was no place to sit so we just stood there like two giant rainbow-colored elephants in the center of the room.

I've never felt more unnerved. I usually loved being the center of attention but not this time. I looked over at Molly and thought she looked like she might pass out.

The pastor stepped behind his desk but didn't sit down.

He had the attention of everyone in the room.

"It has been brought to our attention that there has been some…inappropriate… sexual behavior occurring between the two of you. Jen, your parents say that you are claiming that this is the lifestyle choice that you have made, and you intend to continue to make. Is that true?" he asked.

"I don't know about a 'lifestyle choice' but I am a lesbian. That's not something that is ever going to change. I'm attracted to women, and I am in love with Molly. If that answers your question," I replied. I even shocked myself with how confident I sounded with my response, considering there was a small stream of urine running down the inside of my leg. I didn't care. I was mad enough that pissing on the carpet seemed like a good revenge in the moment. I hadn't planned on my bladder betraying me, but now that it was happening it kind of felt like the right thing to do.

The pastor furrowed his brow.

"We didn't bring you down here to discuss the terminology of the sin that the two of you are engaging in. We brought you here to inform you that we cannot have an unrepentant homosexual standing before the church and delivering messages each week. It is not representative of the Christian path, nor what this church stands for. We are going to have to ask you to step down as the drama leader," he said.

I felt hot, angry tears spring to my eyes.

Theater was the thing I loved the most. I loved writing and directing our skits and plays every week. It was honestly the only thing that had kept me coming back to church after Molly and I had gotten together.

"What? The Easter cantata is a month away. I wrote the drama part. You can't get that together from scratch in four weeks," I said.

"You can just give what you wrote to the choir director. We will find someone to fill in."

I was seething.

"*I will not*. I wrote that, and I'm not just going to hand it over for someone else to direct. I can't believe you are doing this. Who I love is nobody in this room or out there in the congregation's business," I said between clenched teeth.

I turned to Mom and Daddy.

"I can't believe you all would pick loyalty to a church over your own daughter.

I know this came from you. There is no way they would have known if you hadn't told them," I half shouted.

"Don't you dare disrespect me more than you already have. The pastor is right. You can't be standing up in front of the church as a leader when you are disregarding the teachings of the Lord," Dad replied. "Turn in your scripts," he commanded.

My face was blood red. Molly had gone completely pale and still looked like she might keel over at any second.

I took the notebook that I was holding, along with my Bible that was sitting on top of it and flung them both on the pastor's desk. Papers went everywhere.

I looked up to see that everyone in the room was staring at me, aghast.

The pastor's jaw tightened as he glared at me.

"Anything else?" I asked. I straightened my shoulders in defiance.

"Actually, yes. We are going to have to ask your father to step down from the deacon position as well. The Bible says that in order to serve in that position a man and his entire family have to walk in the will of the Lord. Since your father is unable to control your behavior, he can no longer serve as a leader in this church," he said.

I turned to face my dad, expecting to see the same look of shock that was on my face present on his. I was surprised to find that he apparently had already known this was coming. He nodded his head in resignation.

"What?! This is ridiculous. I'm a grown woman! Whatever I do has nothing to do with him. I don't even live under his roof anymore. This whole thing is just…… CRAZY. You all are CRAZY!" I yelled.

I searched for other things to say- a better argument, a plea to make them see how insane this was…but nothing came to me. I had been caught too off guard to even defend myself properly.

I grabbed Molly's hand and dragged her behind me as I stormed out the door.

I was crying hysterically as we marched back up the stairs and out of the front door of the church. I hurled every single insult I could think of about the pastor, the church, and even Jesus, out of my mouth on our way to the car. It was the most un-Christian-like verbalization and display of anger that I could muster, and I must say, I even shocked myself.

Molly stared at me with saucer-sized eyeballs.

But hey…if you are going to denounce your faith…go big or go home, right?

I did both. I went big, and then we went home.

I had never been more humiliated in my entire life. My parents and my entire church family had turned their backs on me. Not only that; they all thought I was a terrible human being, and that I was going to hell.

I was devastated.

Hell, even my girlfriend was giving me the side eye after that display in the church parking lot. She had made a comment about not wanting to get struck down by proximity.

I had known that a lot of that rejection was coming, of course. It's not like I had been ignorant to the ways of the Baptist church in regard to how they felt about homosexuality.

The enormity of it though, and the way that it hurt still shocked me. It was one thing to know how they felt about my sexuality in theory. It was a whole other bag when the exclusion and the rejection was personal.

I decided that if Christianity, and especially Southern Baptists, wouldn't accept me for who I was then I didn't want to be a part of that faith anyway. If they could literally shun a person because of who they loved, then I didn't want to be associated with them at all.

I spent the next several years trying to get past what happened that week between my parents and the church and myself.

I pushed the anger down deep inside of myself.

I buried it until I could no longer see its head poking out from the soil.

I disassociated myself from any and all things "religious" or "spiritual."

I was no longer part of that flock that was willing to follow along blindly wherever they were led. I adopted the term "agnostic" to describe my beliefs to anyone that asked in the following years. "Atheist" didn't sit quite right with me. I did still believe there was a God. I just believed that he hated me, so I didn't want anything to do with him.

I was terrified of him, to be honest.

There was something charming to me about the word "agnostic." A word meaning literally, "without knowing". That seemed to define exactly where I sat on the fence of belief.

I didn't know.

I didn't know how anyone could claim to.

The only thing that I knew with certainty was that if the followers of Christ could spew such hatred, anger, and judgment about a love they knew nothing about, I wanted no part of that. If that behavior and belief system was meant to be representative of the God they served - that was a God that I didn't care to follow.

His playbook and instruction manual that had been preached at me from all sides my first 19 years felt impersonal and impossible to follow.

I felt like I had been set up for failure from the get-go.

I did the only thing that felt right to me to do.

I laid it down.

I walked away from it.

I was "without knowing."

I chose to be.

The mysteries and the structure of God and the universe were not mine to try and figure out.

I would simply "exit stage right" and leave the fighting to the church that seemed to love it so.

Spirituality clearly would have nothing to do with me, nor I with it.

I would be perfectly content in my "not knowing."

Or so I thought.

32

Part Two

spark: *noun*

A.: a hot glowing particle struck from a larger mass

B.: a latent particle capable of growth or developing

34

Chapter Three

2005 - Four years later

I STARED AT HER with disbelief.

"No way. There's no way he knew all of that," I said. Half of me was intrigued. The other half thought she was full of shit.

"Jen, I swear. I'm not the only person that has experienced it. The CIA actually uses his services to find bodies that haven't been recovered," she replied earnestly.

We were sitting at the table having breakfast. The man we were talking about was a well-known psychic in our area named Bobby Drinnon. Well-known that is, to everyone but me apparently. Julia, my wife, had just spent an hour telling me the story of her visit to him several years prior, and how all of the things that he told her that had come to pass. I had mixed feelings about the idea of psychics in general, though she told me that he preferred the term "intuitive counselor."

I didn't really know what to believe about it. I trusted Julia and honestly didn't think she was lying about her experience, but I also wondered if perhaps Mr. Drinnon had researched her background and been prepared to captivate her with his "knowledge" of her history when she walked in. I also quizzed her hard on details of his future "predictions" to find out if he had given her vague, one-size-fits-all, future storylines that anyone could make fit into their own life and future events seamlessly. Julia was eighteen years older than me and had retired early from her teaching job in order to open her own business, at the prompting of Bobby Drinnon who had "seen" her owning and running a retail store that offered her tremendous freedom and financial abundance. His prediction had come to fruition shortly after her meeting with him. I couldn't find any holes in the story, though I wondered if her memory of the meeting was accurate this long after it occurred. She could possibly have just retroactively adjusted the story to "fit" her life because she wanted so badly for it to have been real. It also crossed my mind that it could all have just been coincidence.

Still…she seemed so convinced.

I watched her run a hand through her dark pixie-cut hair and her brows furrowed over her bright green eyes. She was frustrated that I didn't seem to believe her, and I found myself appreciating how cute she looked when she was being earnest. I knew she wasn't lying. I believed that the experience was real *for her* if only in her mind. I just wasn't sure about the validity of the psychic and thought there had to be a catch. Julia was practical, and not one to be easily fooled. Her pragmatic approach to life was one of the reasons why we worked so well as a couple. She balanced out my tendency to be a dreamer without a plan. If someone who had known us as a couple had overheard this conversation, they likely would have been surprised that it was Julia and not me who was singing the praises of a psychic.

That is, they would have been surprised unless they knew my distaste and disregard for all things that claimed to deal in the spiritual realm.

That was, in fact, one of my main issues about this whole topic - to my mind anyone who professed to have knowledge of the spiritual realm also had an agenda. This time it was apparently an East Tennessee "Miss Cleo" who I'm sure had no problem accepting large amounts of money for his "counseling" services.

I asked Julia what she had paid this man for an hour of his time, hoping to call her out on that end about it. To my surprise, the rate was very reasonable. I should have known that she wouldn't have paid an astronomical amount to meet with him. She was great with money. (Yet another area where she brought balance to our partnership.) There was really only one way I was going to be able to tell what was true about this psychic guy. I was going to have to meet him myself.

I bit into the muffin that I had hardly touched during this whole conversation, and my teeth hit something small and hard. My eyes widened, and I instantly spit out the bite I had taken into my napkin to investigate. Julia, knowing that look well by now, was already on her feet.

"Do you need your Epipen?", she asked, as she headed toward my purse by the door where she knew for sure I always kept one.

"I think I'm ok…. I don't think it's a nut…just a small cluster of poppy seeds. Maybe just pitch me my allergy meds just in case?" I said.

I have a list of food allergies a mile long, with tree nuts being at the very top of the "things that will make me keel over and die if ingested" index. Julia tossed me the small medicine bottle from my purse that had my allergy medicine in it, and I quickly took one.

"I read the ingredient list twice before I bought them," she said.

There was no doubt in my mind that she had done just that. She knew all of my food allergies and was typically even more careful than I was at navigating around them. She was very attuned to my needs in general, and attentive nurturing was her favorite way to express love. When I met Julia, she served on our local Humane Society board and had about 20 foster animals, most of which had special dietary or medicinal needs that she managed to stay on top of impeccably. I often joked that she had been unknowingly practicing for our relationship long before we met, and that I had married her because she was the only person properly mentally equipped to keep me alive.

She was staring at me with concern, as I swallowed carefully and took slow breaths. This had happened enough times in my life that I knew how to assess when to be really concerned, and when I was going to be ok.

"I want to see him," I finally said.

She looked at me perplexed. "Who? Jesus?"

I laughed loudly. "No, not this time. I'm fine. Besides, I'm not sure he would be the one waiting for me if I wasn't," I said as I waved it off. "I was talking about Bobby Drinnon."

She breathed a sigh of relief as she pushed a glass of water toward me to drink.

"Ok good," she said with a laugh. "And also, good luck. Bobby normally stays booked up about three years in advance."

"That's fine. I'm pretty sure my schedule is wide open three years from now. I'll just call and get my name on the list," I replied.

I could wait. I wasn't in any hurry to find out that this man was a fraud.

"As long as you don't inadvertently off yourself with a walnut before then," she said as she dug in her wallet to retrieve his business card.

"Amen to that."

I looked at the card she handed me.

The words, "Bobby Drinnon, Intuitive Counselor" were surrounded by pastel rainbows. I smirked. This would be interesting, at least. I decided to go ahead and call while we were sitting there. His secretary answered.

"Thank you for calling the office of Bobby Drinnon, how may I help you?"

It sounded like I was calling a doctor's office, and I found that amusing.

"Yes…hello? I'm calling to see about making an appointment with Mr. Drinnon for his, um, intuitive counseling services?" I said, feeling more than a little ridiculous.

"Yes, ma'am. The first appointment we have available is in 2008 is that ok?" she asked.

I snorted. "Yes, I believe that I can work that out with this much notice, thank you."

She gave me a date and time, which I wrote down on a small scrap piece of paper as if I would be able to keep up with the corner of the phone bill that I had torn it from for three years. She also promised to call for a reminder a week prior. I laughed again at what felt like a ridiculous situation all the way around and thanked her for her time.

I looked at the paper and held it up to show Julia. "Done! I have an appointment for October of 2008."

She grinned. "I told you it would be a while." She picked up my plate to take it to the sink and kissed my forehead sweetly. "You ok?"

I nodded that I was.

"Good. I'd like to keep you around. Plus, now you have an appointment in three years that I promise you, you won't want to miss."

A FEW DAYS passed and I had all but forgotten making that appointment when my phone rang one morning as I was leaving for work. I didn't recognize the number, and I don't usually answer the phone if I don't, but for some reason this time I picked up.

"Hello, Ms. Fields? This is Kelly from the office of Bobby Drinnon. Bobby said that this morning you kept coming up in meditation for him, and he felt like he needed to speak to you sooner. He was wondering if you might be able to make it here for an appointment tomorrow at 11:00 am?" she said.

My heart stopped. What could possibly be so important that this man needed to speak to me that soon? Even though I mostly thought he was a phony, there was still part of me that worried that perhaps something terrible was about to happen. Maybe I was dying? Maybe some tragedy was on the verge of occurring to my family? I could think of no positive reason why he would need me to drop everything and come to his office so quickly. I made a split-second decision to call into work the following day to make it to the appointment. I had to find out what this was all about. I told her that I would be there.

"Wonderful. I always like to tell everyone that is coming in to take a little time and prepare what you might like to ask Bobby about. If you have specific questions about life events, or even pictures of family members you want to bring in that would be good. He is wonderful with photographs and can read energy and future events from them if you want to bring some in with you," she said.

She went on to give me directions to his house and we agreed that I would be there at 11:00.

I hung up the phone and my hands were shaking. I didn't know what all of this meant, and what had felt like a kind of joke a few days before suddenly felt very real and more than a little frightening. I went in to work that day but was distracted and nervous all day. I kept mulling over in my mind various reasons for the urgency and could think of none that put my mind at ease.

When I told Julia about it, she was no help. She also thought that it was reason for concern. She said she was excited for me that I would get to go, but she also was a little afraid of what message he might be calling me there to receive.

When I got home that evening, I tried to get my thoughts together for what I wanted to ask Mr. Drinnon about. I found a picture of Julia and me that I had printed off a few months prior and decided to take that. I wanted to ask him about our relationship. We hadn't been together very long, and I was curious to hear his take on the future.

I tried to think about other things I wanted to know about, particularly things that had been burdening my mind. I got out a notebook and pen and set to work. I came up with three questions that I wanted to ask him if he knew the answer to.

The first one was concerning my dad. He had just gone to the doctor a day or so prior for a biopsy to check for skin cancer. I was so afraid for his health. In a family of fair skinned redheads, skin cancer was prominent in our health history. We all typically made it a point to get annual checks, but Dad had let this go on for too long this time. I was worried. It had been weighing on my mind so heavily…I just wanted to know if he was going to be all right.

The second question was about my own health. I had been having excruciating menstrual cycles. They were lasting 8-10 days, and the cramping was so painful that it would often have me doubling over in agony, and sometimes would make me vomit. I hadn't been to the doctor about it yet, but I was very concerned. I was afraid that I had cancer or something that was going to cause me to have to have a hysterectomy at a young age and was terrified of getting bad news. I kept intending to make an appointment but felt fine in between my periods which made me forget to do so until the pain rolled back around again the next cycle. I hoped that maybe Mr. Drinnon could give me some insight.

The last question that I wrote down was about Julia. I wanted to know if she was my "one." I felt like she was. I loved her dearly and things were just easy between us. We had fun together, shared a love of animals and rescue work, and got along very well for the most part. I just wasn't *sure,* sure. I had always heard that you would know when you met your "person". I thought I knew…didn't I? There was just enough doubt that I wanted to ask.

I carefully looked over what I had written down. I wasn't sure if any of my questions were things that were even possible for Mr. Drinnon to see or tell me, but I thought I would give them a shot.

You took that awfully seriously for someone who doesn't believe in psychics, I thought to myself with amusement. I set my notebook beside my bed that night, and I drifted off to sleep thinking about the impending meeting.

I dreamed that I met Mr. Drinnon. When I saw him, I guessed he was older than me maybe by about 25 years. He was definitely closer to my parents' age than mine. He had long, silvery blonde hair that came to his shoulders. He embraced me in a friendly hug when he appeared, and I felt a familiarity with him that I didn't understand.

He told me there was nothing to be afraid of.

I believed him.

I told him my questions that I had come with, and he told me that he wanted to think about them and ask for guidance about the answers. He said that he would tell me tomorrow what was told to him.

I watched him as he diagrammed out a great number of things about my life on a chalkboard. I listened attentively but there was so much that I didn't understand.

I couldn't make it make sense how it all worked.

He was showing me levels of existence and talking to me about things of which I had no knowledge.

This was more than just earth, heaven, and hell- the three places I had been taught that we could exist.

I kept trying to wrap my mind around the things he told me, but I had no context, and I found them extremely confusing.

He finally seemed to realize that I wasn't following and stopped. He said he would try to explain better tomorrow when he saw me face to face, in a way that might be easier for me to comprehend.

He told me that he was looking forward to our meeting in the morning, and that he loved me.

I woke up. I thought the dream was intriguing but was convinced that it had happened because I had lain down with the meeting on my mind. My notebook by the bed reminded me that it had, in fact, been the very last thing I had been thinking about as I drifted off.

I decided the dream was probably insignificant and went back to sleep.

The next morning as Julia left for work, I left to make the hour and half drive to Mr. Drinnon's place. I typed the address in the GPS and noticed that my hands were shaking.

I was excited to go but was afraid as well. I hadn't even been able to eat breakfast that morning. I knew the drive would feel like forever.

It did.

I tried singing, talking on the phone, and stopping for snacks. and anything else I could think of to keep my mind off of the impending meeting, but nothing worked. The closer I got, the more afraid I became. By the time I pulled into the driveway, I was a mess.

The estate that Mr. Drinnon lived in was beautiful and surrounded by rolling farmland with dark picket fencing. It was breathtaking. As if I wasn't having enough trouble breathing.

I walked in the door that was marked as the business entrance to what was clearly his home. There was no one in the office area, and I was a few minutes early, so I sat down on the couch to wait. I looked around the waiting room. Articles were on the wall from both local and national newspapers, all featuring photos of the man I had seen in my dream the previous night.

I stared at them in complete disbelief.

Julia had not shown me a photo of him, I knew that for sure. I hadn't looked him up online, I had simply called the number from the card that she gave me.

How had I somehow known what he looked like in my dream?

I wasn't the psychic, HE was.

As I sat, mouth gaping open, trying to figure out what the hell was going on, suddenly the man himself appeared through a door opposite of the one I had walked in from.

His presence filled up the entire room when he entered.

He gently said, "Hello, Jen. Welcome!" as I stood up to greet him in return.

"May I give you a hug?" he asked.

I replied that he of course could give me a hug (I'm a hugger!), and as he embraced me, I felt the most peaceful feeling wash over me. I had never experienced another person's energy affecting me in that way. There was a sweet tenderness emanating from him that put my entire being at ease.

"Won't you come into my office and have a seat?" He gestured to the door that he had walked in through.

I nodded and followed him to his desk. I sat opposite him in a comfy oversized chair. I watched him put a tape in a tape recorder (I hadn't seen one of those since middle school) and press record.

I was grateful that he was going to record this session, but I honestly had no idea how I was going to listen to the playback. I was pretty sure I had sold my old boombox years ago in a yard sale along with my collection of cassettes from artists like Tiffany and Marky Mark and the Funky Bunch.

"Thank you so much for arranging to be here today on such short notice. I just wanted to tell you that there is nothing to be afraid of. I sense fear from you surrounding the sudden call for you to come so quickly. I didn't call you here to scare you or tell you any bad news. I simply felt a strong connection with you during my meditation. The guides were giving me lots of information about you, and I wanted to meet with you sooner rather than years from now. That's all. I was excited to meet you. So, I truly hope that you can relax and enjoy our session now. I also want you to know that I would never give anyone any information that Spirit tells me they cannot handle. I will say though, that they tell me you can handle a lot," he said with a laugh.

They? Who were They? I thought.

"Your guide team. We all have our own personal guide team made up of our ancestors, guardian angels, higher beings, and Spirit Itself. They watch over you at all times, and they are the ones that brought you here for guidance," he said.

I processed some of that, but I was mostly hung up on the fact that I HADN'T ASKED THAT OUT LOUD. I don't know what I had been expecting, but so far this visit had already been surprising me right and left. He had just heard what I said in my head as if I had spoken it to him. It crossed my mind that I should watch my thoughts since this man could clearly hear them, but I didn't really know how I should go about that. I had never tried to censor the things that popped in my head before and as I tried briefly to control them while he was speaking, I realized that it was much more difficult than I would have imagined. It took me no time to give up on it because I became aware that I could not focus on shutting my mind up while I was trying to listen to him.

I was extremely relieved to hear that I hadn't come all of this way to hear bad news. I took a few deep breaths and tried to release the rest of the fear that was coursing through me. I allowed myself to relax a little. This was going to be ok, I thought. If nothing else, it seemed like it was going to be intriguing.

I nodded at Mr. Drinnon to continue.

"We can just jump right into the session, if you feel comfortable."

I was a little surprised to find that I *did* feel comfortable now. Actually, the sense of peace that had washed over me when he had hugged me earlier was getting stronger, the longer I sat in his presence. His gentle voice and loving tone were helping me ease into a place where I found him engaging. I realized that I was beginning to feel genuinely excited to hear what he had to say, instead of being afraid of him.

I made eye contact, finally. I saw a mischievous glint in his eye that made me like him even more. He wasn't this somber bearer of bad news that I had built him up to be on my way to meet him. What I saw in his eyes made him very human to me suddenly. He seemed to take all of this much more light-heartedly than I had realized. I had been expecting heavy, stoic, and dark "movie-psychic" energy from him, and what I found was the opposite. He appeared to be joyful and sweet. There was a playfulness in him that I found charming. There was nothing dark here, that I sensed anyway. Nothing "supernatural" or scary in nature. No calling in of dark things from the abyss to seek counsel. As best I could tell, in the language that made sense to me at the time, this man was telling me that he spoke with my guardian angels.

I was on board. At ease. Ready for more.

I asked him to proceed.

"Last night in my dream, you asked me three questions that you wanted me to try and answer for you. I think that might be the best place to start today.", he said.

"Wait. What? Your dream? I dreamed about coming here last night…do you mean *my* dream? I'm confused," I admitted. Boy was I ever.

He laughed softly.

"Yes. Your dream…but also mine. We met last night in the dream realm. There are many different planes of existence, Jen. That's part of what I was trying to explain to you last night with the diagram. We exist in and can travel to or reach much more than this physical reality that we perceive with our five senses. Our conversation was a perfect example of that. You and I met on the dream plane last night. You asked me questions. I brought them back with me to consider, and I asked your guide team about them this morning before you came. Would you like to hear what they had to say?", he asked.

I nodded wordlessly. I tried to remember the questions that I was going to ask, and suddenly remembered that I had carried in my notebook. As I went to open it, he went on…

"Last night the first question you asked me was about your father's biopsy. They want me to let you know that all will come back well. This was just a small health issue that will be easily treated and that it is not cancerous at this time," he said.

I froze with the notebook half open in my hands and stared at him. I had to ask him to stop for a moment so that I could collect the pieces of my mind that had just been blown all over the universe.

So that was how this was going to go down.

He was not only going to tell me the answers…he was going to tell me the questions as well. I closed my useless notebook back up and continued to gape at him in disbelief for a moment or two with my mouth hanging wide open.

I tried to regain some composure but found it difficult to wrap my mind around what he had just said because I simply could not get past what was happening.

"OK. You can continue. I'm sorry. I'm just having a little trouble believing this right now," I said.

He looked at me with amusement. The mischievousness in his eyes sparkled even more. It was obvious that he was loving this, but that it was something that he was used to navigating. I'm sure all of the clients that he had sat with over the years must have had a particular "come to Jesus" moment. We were five minutes into this reading, and I was already walking down the aisle to profess my belief.

There was no way he could have known my questions ahead of time. That wasn't something he could have researched and found out. Well…maybe my dad's doctor visit could have been found through documentation somehow, but

I suddenly remembered my next two questions and I knew there was no way he could have researched them. Even if he had somehow known that Dad had gone to the doctor, it still didn't explain how he knew that was one of the questions I would ask. I waited, wide-eyed, for him to continue.

"The second question you asked me was about your own health. Your guides want me to tell you that there is nothing to worry about. You have mild endometriosis. It will come and go as far as the pain that you are experiencing during your menstrual cycle but that it is nothing serious. They told me you were afraid that you might be told you must have a hysterectomy, and they want me to reassure you that you will not," he said.

I know I must have been looking at him like I would have stared at an alien spacecraft that landed on my lawn. I couldn't even formulate words. I hadn't even been to the doctor about this. It was just something that I had been wordlessly worrying about in my mind. I had barely even mentioned it to Julia. If he hadn't already won me over, this sealed the deal.

It must have been clear to him that I couldn't speak, so he continued.

"The third thing that you asked me about was your relationship. You told me that you were in a marriage-type relationship with another woman. You also said that you would bring me a picture of the two of you with you today. May I see it?" he asked.

The question nudged me out of my stupor, and I opened my notebook once more to the place where I had the photo tucked between two pages to protect it.

It was my favorite photo of us. We looked so happy in it that it made me smile each time I looked at it. This time was no exception, and I smiled as I handed it to Mr. Drinnon.

He sat quietly with it for a brief moment.

"I know her. We have met before, correct?" he asked.

"Yes, some time ago," I replied. I was a little surprised that he would remember her. He must meet with hundreds of people a year.

"I remember her aura. She is a really beautiful soul," he said.

I agreed. She was. She was a bright light, and that was part of what attracted me to her to begin with. Her kindness was almost tangible.

"Did you know that we have many soulmates in our lifetime? A few of us have one soul that is the "other half" of our soul, in a way…and people usually use the term "soulmate" to exclusively mean that romantic connection. "The ONE." That's usually what they mean when they say "soulmate", but we have many soulmates in our lives. A soul connection is simply that. One that we connect with on a deeper level. When I look at a photo or meet two people in person that have a soul connection, I can see a golden or sometimes a red thread that connects their hearts.

When I look at this picture of the two of you, I see a golden thread connecting you which means that you are most definitely soulmates," he said.

"And it's always really sad…", he paused here and took a breath. He assessed my face before continuing.

"…when soulmates don't end up together for life," he finished.

I felt my eyebrows raise. I realized he was telling me, in the most gentle of ways, that we wouldn't make it.

I wasn't so much surprised by this disclosure as I was deeply saddened. We had only been together a few years, and we were newly married. As I sat there and allowed this information to sink in, I found myself wondering how long we would last? We were happy now, but what would be the turning point? I briefly wondered if this knowledge would affect my desire to stay. Should I even be putting time into a relationship that wouldn't ultimately go the distance? Would that even be fair to either of us or would I just be wasting both of our time? Should I even put that much stock into what this man was telling me? He could be wrong…but what if he wasn't?

My heart ached as I digested what he had said.

"Are you ok?" he asked. "They told me you could handle it."

"I'm ok. I can handle it. I'm just processing," I said.

"Ok…then I also want to tell you that I got something else from that photo. You are going to lose the biggest masculine influence in your life. Probably your father. Definitely the most prominent male, so I'm assuming it would be your father. It will be sudden… out of the blue…and very painful to you. But not soon…I don't think," he said.

"Ouch. That one is a little harder to swallow," I said shakily.

The most prominent male in my life would definitely be my father, and though things were still tough in many ways between us, I was still a daddy's girl at heart. I talked to both of my parents fairly regularly these days, but they were far from accepting of my sexuality or relationship with Julia. The strain had been intensely painful, and any conversation surrounding anything outside of work and the weather were avoided by both parents, but especially by my dad. I could only hope that this prediction was very far down the road, and that Dad and I would have come to some kind of peaceful place between us by then. I told myself that I would make extra efforts to soothe the cracks in our relationship from now on. I wanted to look back and treasure the time and memories we shared and not feel like it was tinged with this simmering anger and uncertainty that had been below the surface the past few years.

This reading had taken an unexpected turn.

While there wasn't an "emergency" situation here where something was told to me with urgency, it was still definitely bad news. I wanted so desperately to lift the mood.

"Do you have better news about the future that you can give me? Those two messages are awfully heavy," I said.

He nodded.

"Yes. Only good news for the rest of the reading. First of all, I see you singing… everywhere. I think it's your career. You are traveling and singing in all different places. You are a little older…your hair is longer. You look extremely happy," he said.

I had always wanted to sing, but literally had no control over my voice. I wouldn't even sing in the shower in case Julia should happen to overhear. I wanted this prediction to be true, but I knew it couldn't be. Theater had always been my heart, and I had secretly longed to do musicals for as long as I could remember. I never auditioned though, because I knew my voice was pretty terrible and I didn't want to embarrass myself. I had resigned myself to dialog-only performances. If you had asked me to pick any career on the planet, and there were no limitations as far as talent or education, I would have absolutely picked singing.

That was in a fantasy situation though, and I knew reality was much harsher. I simply didn't have the chops for it.

"Hmmm. I doubt that will happen. I can't sing. Like…at all," I said.

"You will be able to," he said with great certainty.

I raised an eyebrow. I wasn't sure exactly how someone could go from not singing a note to having a music career. I definitely wasn't sold on this particular vision of my future.

"I see you through many lifetimes, most recently in Charleston or Savannah, making a living as an artist. I see you painting and singing on the streets for money in this one particular past life. They are telling me that you already know how to do it, you just have to remember. It can be easily uncovered. It's already part of who you are," he said.

Past lives?

C'mon.

Seriously?

My Southern Baptist upbringing bristled inside me at this suggestion. I was open to a lot…or so I thought…. but this was just too much for me to swallow.

"So, you are telling me that we reincarnate? I don't buy that. I don't believe in reincarnation," I said to him.

What about heaven? What about hell? He was suggesting that we didn't spend eternity in either of those places, but instead came back to earth again and again to live various lifetimes. No way. Also, no thank you.

He looked at me, his eyes full of compassion.

"Dear one, I ask you to consider the idea that you don't have to believe in something for it to be true. Take the Law of Gravity for example. It's an abstract concept. I can prove to you, within reason, that it exists…but you still can't see it. You could tell me that you don't believe it exists, and I would understand why. But that doesn't make it not true. It is simply a law of the universe - one of the ways that it works. It doesn't need your belief in it to continue operating as it always has," he said.

I pondered this. Was I really just being obstinate? Was reincarnation really as reasonably proven as the Law of Gravity? I suddenly remembered fragments of my dream from the night before and recalled that this was also part of what Mr. Drinnon had been trying to tell me then. I hadn't been able to follow, because it was so foreign to me.

I definitely was going to have to research this and give it more thought. After all, I had spent the last several years claiming that I didn't believe in the religious teachings that I had been raised in. So what did I believe?

Clearly, there was much more to our spiritual presence than I had ever given thought to before. These "planes of existence" that he was giving me a crash course in during this reading had to have some credibility or he wouldn't have had the knowledge about my questions from my dream that he inexplicably had.

I knew nothing about any of this kind of "spirituality," but I was quickly realizing that I wanted to. I made a note in my notebook to research reincarnation when I got home and make up my own mind about it.

Also: "dream meetings." My notebook was becoming less of a recording of this session and more of a homework list.

"We will save other past lives for another time when you have had some time to decide how you feel about that. I'd like to talk about your aura. Your aura is a clear dark blue. People with your aura color are good leaders. Good teachers and communicators, typically. However, the darkness of your aura indicates that you might be struggling with speaking your truth in some regard….", he said.

As he said it, I felt my heart skip a beat. It was something that happened frequently. So frequently in fact, that I barely even paid attention to it when it occurred anymore.

I had been checked for a thyroid disorder several times over the last few years and my levels were always just slightly off-kilter, but not enough to go on medication. The heart palpitations were one of the symptoms that I had just gotten used to.

Mr. Drinnon stopped talking right when my heart skipped and tilted his head slightly.

"Your heart just skipped, didn't it?"

How the hell had he known that? It's not like anyone could hear your heartbeat, and I knew I hadn't reacted because I was so used to it happening.

"Yes, it did. How did you know that?" I asked.

"Your entire aura vibrated differently when it happened. You also have a discoloration around your throat chakra, which is where your thyroid is. You may have some issue going on there, if you don't already know about it. However, it could also be related to what I was just talking about… your aura color suggests you have difficulty speaking your truth. A throat chakra block would mean the same thing. Is there something you are struggling with in your life that you aren't talking about, Jen?" he asked sincerely.

Ugh. Auras and chakras. More words that made no sense to me.

I scribbled them down in my notebook as well, so that later maybe I could go back and figure out what the hell he was talking about.

As much as I didn't know about chakra blocks and floating colors, I did know with certainty that he was correct about my struggle to tell my truth.

"Yes. I came out…well…was dragged out… of the closet to my family a few years ago. It caused a lot of damage to our relationship, as well as to my relationship with people in my church. A lot has changed, and it's directly related to my sexuality and identity surrounding it. I still have a really difficult time navigating all of that," I told him.

He nodded.

"That could definitely cause chakra issues. When you are open to it, I could recommend ways to clear that block. Just if you would like. Reach out to me when that feels right to you, I'd be happy to help," he said.

I'm going to have to figure out what you are even talking about first.

He laughed as if I had said it out loud.

"I know. That's why I said, 'when you are open to it.' The positive aspects of your aura color are that you are an intellect, and probably an excellent writer, as blue is a communication aura. You have a very calming presence, and typically children and animals are drawn to your aura type the most. You are probably great with both kids and critters. They feel safe with you, because they are," he said.

I thought about my job as a dog groomer which I had been doing for a few years now. It was true, animals did gravitate towards me. Even wild animals seemed to not be afraid. Communicating and spending time with animals was one of my favorite things in life. I always felt like it was almost like they recognized me in a way. As if when they looked at me they thought, "Oh hey…there's that lady that loves us. We are safe with her." It was something that had happened ever since I was a child, and I delighted in those interactions.

Who knew it had to do with my aura color?

I was learning so much here.

"We are going to change direction a little here because your guides just showed me a major karmic lesson in your life that they want to talk about and they are giving me details about it," he said.

"You know I have no idea what you are talking about. What is a karmic lesson?"

"A karmic lesson is a lesson that keeps repeating in our lives until we learn how to navigate or heal it. This can be a stumbling block that repeats in one single lifetime until we learn the lesson, or it can be a lesson that you haven't learned from a previous lifetime. In this particular case, they are telling me that it is from previous lifetimes. They are telling me that it is a big one, and that you specifically reincarnated this time to heal it. They say that it is your only karmic lesson this lifetime, but that is because it will be so difficult. It is concerning love," he said.

Great. More difficult news. I was starting to not be very excited about my future.

I stared at him, waiting on the other shoe to drop about this "love" prediction.

"You will fall deeply in love with a man named….it starts with a J…no wait… they are telling me that it is "Jay." Yes, you will fall in love with a man named Jay, and it will change everything. It is why you came here this lifetime. He holds the lesson that needs to be learned," he said.

"Ha! Well, you are going to miss that prediction, sir. I'm not attracted to men…not even a little. I do know a girl named "Jai" though. We aren't really each other's type, but at least she's female. Are you sure they said "man"?" I asked. I was laughing. I couldn't help it. It was literally the most ridiculous prediction that I'd ever heard.

I would have sooner believed him if he had told me that I was going to sprout wings and turn into a fairy than this future singing straight girl that he was telling me I was going to become.

"They said it's definitely a man," he replied knowingly.

Ok, buddy. Either you aren't hearing them correctly or my guardian angels have been day-drinking.

I'm sure he heard that, but he apparently chose to ignore it because he didn't respond.

"One other thing that they are telling me…they are saying that you have similar gifts to mine. You are a powerful psychic, and also a medium, but your gifts haven't opened up yet. They are dormant, for now. Later in life, when the time is right, they will be activated. They will show you how to use those gifts when that happens," he said.

Well, now I had heard it all. I wasn't even sure if I believed in these "gifts" that I was witnessing at the current moment. Sure, there was obviously something to the "dream plane" thing since he had known the questions I was going to ask; but this whole "future" or fortune-telling part of this bit seemed questionable at best.

It also seemed oddly specific and more than a little bold of him to just throw out details that could easily be discounted down the road.

For example, had he told me that I was going to have a career change, and left it at that I could have easily believed him. Instead, he picked the most outlandish thing that I could have conceived to claim that I was going to do. A singing career? Yeah. Ok.

Not to mention the specific name of a man that he claimed I was going to fall deeply in love with. Wouldn't he have been smarter to just say that I had a new love interest on the horizon? That would have covered all of the bases, including my sexual preferences, and when it had happened, I would have definitely told everyone that he had "foreseen" it.

And now he was telling me that I was a psychic medium (was that the same thing or were they two different things, a psychic and a medium? I wasn't even sure of that) and I could do what he did?

Why didn't I know all of this myself then, if I had such gifts?

I liked this man. I actually liked him a lot, I couldn't help it, but I was calling "bullshit" at this point. The first part was impressive, I would give him that. The rest I would just take with a grain of salt and probably laugh about over a beer with my friends later.

We wound up the session pretty quickly after all of that because I know he could tell that he had lost me.

I felt kind of bad for not believing in him. He was sweet, and I liked his energy. I had wanted so badly for this to go well, but I felt like he just missed the mark all the way around with this reading. Maybe he was only good at the dream part.

He handed me the cassette that he had recorded the session on, and I couldn't help but smirk as I put it in my purse. He walked me to the door and thanked me for coming. I thanked him for calling me to him sooner than three years from now (although I was admittedly disappointed, at least I hadn't had to wait a very long time only to be let down), and we hugged.

As I walked to my truck, he called to ask me, "Do you want me to tell you how to get out of here?"

"No... I'm good. I have a GPS," I yelled back.

"Ok…but I'll just give you quick directions…just in case…" he started.

I shook my head.

"No, really. I'm ok, thanks. The GPS will get me home," I said.

He paused, seemed as if he were going to insist further, but then simply shrugged his shoulders and waved goodbye. I waved back and then put my home address in the GPS.

I began recapping the session in my mind as I drove down the driveway and turned onto the main road.

What a strange meeting. It was perhaps the strangest encounter I had ever had. I was still working through not only all of the personal information that he had told me, but also the larger concepts that he had been trying to enlighten me about.

It all was so different than the concepts around the spirituality, or rather, the religion that I had been raised up around. Were they even the same thing? Spirituality and religion?

They felt different in a big way to me for the first time in my life.

I tried to articulate what it was about the things Mr. Drinnon had been trying to tell me that felt so different than what I had heard at church. The main thing that I had noticed was the conviction. Preachers and teachers at church would yell and scream and try to scare you into believing what they said was the "Truth."

Mr. Drinnon just seemed to know what the truth was and furthermore, seemed to expect that I knew as well. Like his "Law of Gravity" example, he just seemed to have a confidence in his knowledge of how God and the universe worked. It was just "how it was" in his eyes.

I'd certainly never seen a Southern Baptist with that kind of deep-rooted air of assurance about themselves. They all just seemed frantic and afraid to piss off God all of the time. The only thing they seemed certain of was that God was easily angered, and that they needed to try and dodge that at all costs.

Mr. Drinnon had a peace that I had never experienced around a human being before. It was as if he had a map of the universe and God, and he was certain that it was exactly representative and to scale with how it was laid out. He was confident in it.

I wanted that peace. I wanted that knowledge.

I vowed that I would read and research and educate myself the very best I could in the ways of this spirituality; I would do whatever it took to know what he knew.

I would find that map.

I needed that map.

As it turned out, I got my very first lesson in the ways of Spirit that day, because I actually really did need a map.

My GPS had lost signal at some point while I was deep in thought, and I came to my senses only to realize that I was completely lost. It took me forty-five minutes to find my way back to a main highway where I finally got satellite signal again.

I learned many things that day. Not the least of which being this: if someone who claims to have knowledge of future events tries to offer you directions...shut up and take them.

52

Chapter Four

2010

As I RETURNED from the bathroom of the brewery, I heard our large table of friends roaring with laughter. I couldn't help but smile as I walked closer and saw them all absolutely collapsing in fits over something Julia had said. Though petite in size (she was a good half a foot shorter than me) her energy was huge. She didn't particularly like being the center of attention, so she rarely told stories or addressed the whole group, but when she did everyone listened. She always chalked it up to the way she learned to carry herself in her first career (she was a retired teacher and knew how to hold the attention of a large group), but I knew it was more than that. She was *so* likable. She had such a mischievous playfulness about her that it made everyone curious about what she was thinking. When she spoke, all eyes naturally went to her.

As I slid into my seat beside her, I felt my usual sense of appreciation as I noticed how her intellect and sense of humor once again had everyone around us enthralled. I was always so proud to be her wife.

It was a particularly sweet time in our relationship. We had built a beautiful life together that included a large group of rowdy friends who were always up for a good time and knew how to create one. Every Friday night, Saturday night, and Sunday we were wrapped up in a flurry of friends and doing something new and exciting. We hopped from brewery to concert to camping to festivals to boating and back again with a small entourage of other lesbians who over time began to feel more like extended family than friends.

I realized as I caught the tail end of what Julia was saying that she had been telling them our now slightly infamous electric fence story and that is what had sparked the hysterics.

About six months prior to this particular evening, Julia and I had rescued three half-starved horses from a terrible situation. The horses had been standing in six inches of mud all winter long on about an acre of land with no shelter. We decided something had to be done, and we had the room to take them in, so we did. There was a large empty barn on the land that came with our house when we had purchased it, so we moved the horses into it and had electric fencing installed all around our property to keep them contained. The horses transitioned beautifully and were now thriving in their new home with us.

About a month after we rescued them, we began to notice that the horses had suddenly started hanging their heads over the fence to eat the grass from the neighbor's yard. Upon investigation, we found that there were a few small breaks in the electric fencing wire, so we went out early one morning together to repair them. Julia went into the barn and flipped the switch to make sure the electricity running to the fence was off and then went to the break that was farthest away from the barn. I followed her and watched her reconnect the wire by making each end of the pieces a hook and linking them back together. It seemed simple enough, so I went down the line a bit and did the same for what I thought was the only other break in the fence. Assuming we were finished, I went into the barn to feed the horses, but when I came back out, I noticed another break in the wire that we hadn't seen. It was very near the gate, and easy to miss. Thinking that the fence was still turned off, I put my feed bucket down and went to fix it.

What I didn't know was that Julia had cut the power to the fence back on when I had gone back into the barn. When I grabbed the live side of the wire (which was very near the source) I got the biggest jolt of my life. It was as if every single cell of my body came alive on high alert. I could feel my entire system surge with an unfamiliar high-energy crackle. I could feel it in my heart, in all of my limbs, even my teeth. I screamed at the top of my lungs, and uncontrollably peed my pants.

So did Julia, from laughing so hard.

I remembered jumping back and began investigating my hands for what I was sure would be burn marks. There were none. I found it so strange that it affected me internally so strongly yet didn't leave any evidence behind physically. Every hair follicle bristling, your entire circulatory system in total freak-out mode, and all fight or flight responses screaming simultaneously isn't something you experience often in your day to day. I was no worse for the wear, really...but it was a sensation unlike any other that I had ever felt. It made a lasting impression on me.

It stuck with Julia as well. She couldn't stop laughing all day about it, and never missed an opportunity to retell the story to a captive audience like the present group. They were still howling with laughter as she now recounted how my scream that day had even scared the horses to death and sent them running across the field.

My dear friend Carson, who sat on the side of me opposite Julia, wiped away tears from her sparkling green eyes from laughing so hard. She was by far my closest friend in our large group. I had known her for ages and couldn't believe that she somehow hadn't heard this story before now. She was normally quite stoic and serene, and it was unusual to see her come undone. I found myself laughing at her laughing and soon we were leaning into each other giggling helplessly like two children.

When we both regained our composure, she pushed her glasses up on top of her short blond hair and wiped the tears from her face again.

"What did feel like? I've never touched an electric fence before. Is it a sharp shock like you get from static electricity?" she asked.

"No…it's WAY stronger than that. It goes all throughout your body. I don't know how to put it into words really…I think it's just one of those things that you have to experience yourself to understand. I will say that I now understand why the term 'wired' is an expression people use when they are wide awake or extra alert. Getting zapped with an electrical current will certainly wake you up!" I said.

"And make you pee your pants," Julia added, which sent the table back into another round of laughter.

"That too," I conceded.

As the giggles slowly died down, the conversation broke off into smaller groups around the table and Carson turned to me and asked how school was going.

I sighed heavily.

I had been taking a few master's level classes that were part of a prerequisite for a counseling and family therapy program that I had thought I might want to join. It was the latest venture in a long line of graduate classes, certifications, and degrees that I had bounced from over the last several years and I was frustrated.

"Meh," I said with a shrug. "I don't like it. I thought it would be a good direction for me to head, but now that I am in the classes I feel like it's definitely not for me. We've just been sharing between ourselves as students about our lives in a counseling-type practice setting, and I already can't separate myself from other people's emotions. I've been coming home and worrying about my fellow students and their problems so much it's giving me anxiety. There's no way I could do this as a career. I'll finish out this semester, but I won't be going back." I was embarrassed to admit yet another career path failure out loud, even to Carson who I knew with certainty wouldn't judge me for it.

"Hey, that's ok. There's no shame in recognizing that something isn't for you. You'll find your "thing" eventually, Jen, don't worry," she said.

I rolled my eyes.

"I'm starting to think my 'thing' is being a perpetual student," I replied.

Julia, who had been listening to the conversation, leaned forward and said, "So what if it is? You have the time and space right now to explore whatever you want.

You are working for me, so you know I'll be flexible with your hours for you to take whatever classes you want until you figure out for sure what career you want to pursue. I'd rather support you while you figure it out now than watch you do what I did and be stuck somewhere you aren't happy for a long time."

I thought back to how Julia had left her teaching job at the prompting of Bobby Drinnon's vision. I had met Julia shortly after she had made that jump, so I wasn't with her when she was struggling financially in the teaching job she had grown to dislike, but she talked about it frequently as a very difficult time period in her life. She knew the value of being in a career that brought you joy and often encouraged me not to settle until I found the thing that absolutely felt right in my heart. She had offered me a job at her store early on in our relationship, as a secure place to work while I explored other options, and I had gratefully accepted it.

I had initially worried that maybe working with my wife would be too much time together since it would basically put us in close proximity 24/7 with very little time apart, but it had ended up only strengthening our partnership all the way around. We almost never fought, and I never really found myself wishing that we worked in separate places. She was so supportive of me while bounced around all over the place chasing my damn "purpose" like a kid chasing a unicorn (it actually was beginning to feel that elusive) that I felt safe and loved enough to continue doing so until one actually came along. In fact, I was far harder on myself about it than she ever was.

I pointed at Julia as I said to Carson, "Did you hear that? She actually believes that I'll figure out this whole 'purpose' thing one day. Her unfounded belief in me is astounding. It's pretty cute how blind love can make you, isn't it?" I reached over and ruffled her short pixie-cut hair affectionately.

Julia laughed and then leaned over to kiss my cheek.

"You will figure it out, I know you will. You're too smart not to. And I'll support you every step of the way."

FIVE YEARS HAD passed since my own meeting with Bobby Drinnon, and I had long since pushed that meeting to the back of my mind with the exception of the journey it sparked to deconstruct the miseducation of my youth surrounding spirituality. The homework notes that I had taken that day had led me down rabbit hole after rabbit hole in search of what the "truth" was. My thirst for spiritual knowledge had increased exponentially over the years that followed that meeting.

Shortly after my meeting with Mr. Drinnon, Elizabeth Gilbert's book *Eat, Pray,*

Love was published, and I devoured it. It changed my life almost as drastically as that meeting did.

It resonated so deeply with me that I must have read it ten times in a row.

Gilbert made spirituality feel less…woo-woo. It gave me a stepping-stone after that meeting with Mr. Drinnon to explore the concepts that he talked about in a way that was much more palatable to me than some of the ancient texts I had been struggling to wade through in my research. That book talked about meditation and enlightenment in a way that a beginner could connect with. For someone who was coming from an entirely different direction to join this path, it was exactly the starting place I needed. The author's rawness and humility, as well as the ability to laugh at herself, drew me to her instantly. She was a real human navigating real-life pain through a spiritual journey.

This was a brand of spirituality that I could connect with.

I even tried to mimic her experience in hopes that walking down the same path would give me the same results. I went to Italy for 6 weeks to teach an art history class. It was a wonderful experience, and I loved every second of my time there. However, I'm not sure how enlightening it actually was because I *only* made it to Italy, which means that I only got to the "Eat" part of the journey.

Honestly, that was so typically me and pretty representative of the headway I was making all the way around on my spiritual path.

Fuck all of this hard work, can't I just eat?

I ate all of the foods. Devoured all of the books I could stomach. Consumed whatever I could find that told me how to connect spiritually.

I didn't do any of the practices, mind you. I just scarfed down the words and moved on to the next instruction manual. I have always excelled at living in my head. If I have one strong God-given gift, it is that I am a quick learner. The problem is that, while I understand concepts very well in my head, putting them into practice is a whole other issue. It is very like me to watch a YouTube video on changing the oil in my car or read an article on growing strawberries, only to walk away and do neither. I mean, I learned how to do it, right? Wasn't that the point?

It's definitely been a lifelong issue. Learning is intriguing and fun for me. Practice feels an awful lot like work.

My approach to spirituality was no different. I learned a whole hell of a lot about what other people said a connection to the divine feels like without actually experiencing one iota of it.

In the spirit of this "all play and no work" mentality that I live by, I agreed to go to a yoga class with my sister, Whitney, one day just to check it out. She'd been going on and on about yoga this and yoga that for quite a while, and though she knew I had been resistant to group exercise ever since a particularly scarring gym class in middle school in which I accidentally ripped what was subsequently known as the "fart heard round the world" into the face of a fellow student who was holding my feet down to the floor while I was trying to do as many sit-ups as possible in sixty seconds… she still somehow talked me into going. Whit pointed out that maybe we could heal my gym class trauma AND strengthen my core in one fell swoop. She was still quick to add that she would not sit beside me during this yoga class nor hold my ankles down for any reason, just in case.

My sister is my best friend, and not just because she knows about things like gym class farts and spectacular falls down flights of stairs at formal events (I will not be sharing that story here, sorry) and other blackmail-worthy stories, but because she is smart and hilarious, and I would choose to hang with her even if we weren't sisters. She is six years younger, which ended up being the perfect amount of age gap to make for peaceful coexistence between siblings. We had nothing to fight over. We couldn't share clothes, we had totally different friend groups, and she was only ten when I started driving so when she got too annoying, I would just leave. We've only had one fight that we both remember, but it was a doozy. It started when I ate a hot pocket (the last one in the freezer, and according to her, the ABSOLUTE LAST EDIBLE THING IN THE HOUSE) and ended when she hit me in the face with her shoe.

Basically, I didn't fuck with my little sister anymore after that because I learned what everyone else would soon come to find out: *She is not the one*. She will not put up with shenanigans, bullshit, unfairness, or discrimination from anyone including me or even more impressively, our parents.

Whit had still been living at home and was about to start high school when all of the shit had hit the fan with Mom and Dad and the church over my sexuality. I had been really afraid that our parents' reaction would somehow filter over into a rift between my sister and me, since they basically had her ear all of the time and I felt like I had a pretty good idea of what they were saying about me to her. I thought they would convince her that I was a terrible person, and that she would just stop talking to me altogether to keep them happy. To my complete shock, the exact opposite happened. Not only did she not stop talking to me, my fourteen-year-old little sis completely went to bat for me in every conversation that I wasn't present to defend myself for. She dug her heels in and stood up for me against any and everyone who dared to insinuate that I was "less than" because of who I loved.

I couldn't believe it. I would never have expected her to stand up against her own parents (who I knew from experience could be terrifying) at such a young age. I was so touched by this, and so impressed by the bravery that I made every effort to repay her over the next few years with highly desirable high school contraband like alcohol and marijuana any time I could sneak it to her. This only served to make me an even cooler big sister than she already thought I was, and it put us in a never-ending closed circle bond of protecting each other and keeping each other's secrets from our parents that lasted into adulthood.

It wasn't lost on me though, what those last few years of high school must have been like for her because of me. I knew speaking up on my behalf had lasting repercussions on her own relationship with our parents, and that it had provided her with her own trauma surrounding the fracture in our family that looked very different than mine.

I had once asked her years later why she continually spoke up for me the way she had, when she could have made the rest of her time in the house so much more peaceful if she had just kept her mouth shut and her head down.

"I adored you. Always. I wanted to be just like you when I grew up. You were almost larger than life to me in so many ways. I told all of my friends that you were the smartest, kindest, most loving person alive. I knew that if Mom and Dad couldn't see who you were – regardless of who you loved…that the problem was them and not you. I couldn't bear to hear them talk about you the way they did… and I was the only one there to stop it," she replied.

I looked over at her now from the passenger seat as she drove us to the yoga class. She had her strawberry blond hair up in a messy bun, and her big sunglasses covering half of her face. Our physical appearances were so similar- people always instantly knew we were sisters. I found myself wondering with amusement how two people who looked so much alike on the outside, and were raised by the same two parents, could turn out so very differently. I still, at nearly thirty years old, was terrified of Mom and Dad.

As far as I could tell, Whit wasn't afraid of much of anything.

"Did Mom and Dad ask you about the beach trip?", she suddenly asked.

"No. What beach trip?"

She hesitated. I searched her face to try and figure out why but couldn't tell much through the sunglasses.

"Wait. Did they ask you to go to the beach with them? I mean… that's fine. I wouldn't really expect them to ask me to go," I said.

"Not exactly. What they said was that they wanted to do a family beach trip… and they invited Nathan and me. And they were just going to invite you. I told them that if they didn't invite you AND Julia, then Nathan and I wouldn't come either," she said.

I turned fully in my seat to look at her.

"Well, they didn't mention it so I guess they decided they would rather cancel the family beach trip than invite my wife."

"I'm sorry. I shouldn't have brought it up. I really hoped that maybe they had invited you two. I just thought that maybe after all this time they would have loosened up a little…" she said softly.

I sighed.

"Yeah, me too. Thank you for sticking up for me, by the way. Again. You don't have to keep doing that, you know?"

"I feel like I do. I feel like the only time they ever stop to think about the ways they treat you differently is when I point it out. I don't mind doing that for you. I love you." She reached over and squeezed my hand.

"Still not sitting beside you in this yoga class, though," she added with a laugh.

Whit tried to get me to buy a package at the door instead of a single yoga class to save me some money and I laughingly declined. I had no intention of doing this on a regular basis. I had mostly agreed to tag along just because I had been reading an awful lot about yoga and spirituality and wanted to see what the fuss was all about. I had heard it reiterated repeatedly in my studies that yoga could teach you to strengthen the mind-body-spirit connection.

I mean… surely I could learn that in one class, right?

We came into the yoga studio and began setting up our space. I had just taken the plastic packaging off of my brand-new mat right before we walked in, and when I tried to unroll it was stuck together tightly and made a sound similar to that of duct tape being pulled off of flooring as I tried to unstick it from itself.

My sister rolled her eyes at me from her own mat that she had already unfurled and was sitting cross-legged upon several feet away.

"Sorry," I whispered.

I finally got the thing spread out and plopped myself down on it just in time for the instructor to walk in. She was a little bit older than me but much more fit, which I found intimidating. She had shoulder-length curly dark hair that she was pulling back into a ponytail as she greeted everyone. She obviously knew the other women in the room, so I gathered that they were all regulars. I was the only one she didn't greet by name.

Whit introduced the two of us, and I told her that I was excited to be there.

That wasn't exactly true. I wasn't really excited…. mostly just curious and ready to be done with the workout part so that I could go get sushi with my sis afterward and talk about how awesome it felt to have my body and spirit so connected.

"I'm excited that you are here too, Jen. Just a heads up, I'm probably not the most orthodox yoga instructor that there is. Our music for this class is a playlist of pop and hip-hop, and I kind of just like to let the class unfold however it feels right. I don't follow a sequence of poses every single time, and I'm more concerned with teaching you to be present in your body than I am with getting you into pretzel poses that are uncomfortable. Just so you know what you signed up for," she said with a smile.

"That sounds great, actually," I said. I liked her laid-back manner already.

She walked over to the stereo at the front of the room and started the music.

"We are just going to start with some simple stretches to get everyone warmed up." she said.

As she walked us through the stretches, she sang a few lines of the song that was playing, and then burst out laughing suddenly.

"Girls, that just reminded me…I need y'all to pray for me. A good friend of mine SWEARS that she can teach anyone to sing, so I've agreed to take voice lessons from her in exchange for yoga classes. As you just heard, she's definitely going to have her work cut out for her!" she dissolved into laughter at the thought. Some of the other women giggled along with her, but I had completely stopped mid-stretch and was staring at her.

Had I heard her correctly? Someone had said that they could teach anyone to sing? Was that even something that was possible to learn? I had always been under the impression that singing was just something you were either born able to do or not. I had a very visceral reaction to this new possibility. My heart had quickened and was pounding in my ears. I even got a little clammy. There was an intense longing suddenly pulsing through me. Every single part of my being seemed to cry out,

"I WANT TO LEARN TO SING!"

I realized, with some astonishment, that *I wanted it more than anything.* Could this woman that she was talking about teach me to sing? Was that even possible? I was pretty terrible…but still…she said *anyone.*

I got not a single solitary benefit out of that entire yoga class because I spent the whole hour going through the possibilities that might exist to me if I could only sing.

I could do musical theatre! Maybe I could even write songs…I loved to write!

Maybe I could sing with my theatre friends, or even finally have the guts to sing at karaoke. How amazing would it be to just know that you could sing at the drop of a hat…or at the very least know that you didn't sound like a dying cow when you opened your mouth to try?

The class couldn't end fast enough for me. Literally the minute that we sat up after savasana I jumped to my feet and ran up to the instructor to ask if I could get the name and phone number of her friend that taught voice lessons. She wrote the information down for me on the back of one of her yoga cards, and I realized as I took it from there that my hands were trembling.

This felt big for some reason.

Every cell in my body seemed to know it.

I talked Whit's ear off the whole way home about it, and only realized when she asked me what I thought about the yoga class that I hadn't really even paid attention to it. I couldn't remember much about it at all and realized that I had been completely not present during an hour-long practice that was designed to make you "more present."

It was par for the course for me. Always in my head, once again.

The minute that I got home, I dialed the number that was on the card and spoke with the woman who would become my very first vocal coach.

The lessons were expensive, and I wavered a bit when she told me how much it would be monthly. Could I justify paying that much money a month for something that might not even work?

I suddenly remembered that my 30th birthday was coming up in a few weeks. I would have some birthday money coming in soon. I decided that for once, instead of using my birthday money on bills or necessities, I would give myself something that I truly wanted. I had always wanted to sing…this was worth a shot if I meant that I could have that. I pulled out my credit card and paid her over the phone for what would end up being the best gift that I had ever given myself.

The entire trajectory of my life changed with that phone call.

Two weeks before my thirtieth birthday the stars aligned with a yoga class and a phone number that would lead to far more than I could have ever comprehended as I hung up the phone that day.

If you had asked me about the phrase "written in the stars" at that particular juncture, I would have told you that I didn't believe in such things. I felt pretty certain that we made our own choices and picked our own paths, and that none of it was predestined.

While that may be true in some regards, I have learned over time that there are still stopping points (or starting points, depending how you look at it) that are meant for us along the way. You can think of them as cities along the highway of our journey. If you are traveling from point A to point B, you can choose any number of ways to get there but you are going to have to stop for gas every now and then.

I look at those pitstops as the predestined part of our journey. You can drive whatever road you want to drive, but you are going to have to stop around a certain mile marker if you are going to proceed forward. Sooner or later a city will pop up in the middle of nowhere and you will have to pull over because you won't know when you will get another chance.

"Saturn return" is one of those cities, and it affects every single human around the same mile marker.

Around our thirtieth birthday, each and every one of us experiences a major event in our astrological charts. Around that time period, Saturn returns to the exact longitude position in our birth charts as it did the moment that we were born. Saturn return (as it is referred to) signifies a crossing over into the next phase of life. It occurs around thirty years old for everyone and marks the beginning of adulthood and maturity. In other words, it's when you technically "grow up," astrologically speaking.

Usually, there are major changes and shifts that accompany a Saturn return that will move you onto the new portion of the path that you are supposed to travel. If you are over thirty, I encourage you to think back on your life around that time. You will find that you weren't exempt. Maybe it was the end of a big relationship or a marriage. Maybe you went back to school or had a career change. Perhaps you had a child. Whatever it was, I guarantee you that it affected you in a big way. The universe brought you into maturity with a bang.

Up until my thirtieth year, I had been searching and wandering around fairly aimlessly looking for my path and my purpose in life. It was something that I often talked about with Julia, and with my friends. I just felt like I couldn't seem to get my shit together, and that every direction I had tried to go had just ended up leaving me feeling empty. I hadn't really known where I was supposed to be, I just felt pretty damn certain that it wasn't where I was currently.

I didn't find out about Saturn return until I was nearly ten years on the other side of it, but if I had known then what I know now, I might have relaxed a little. I may have been able to let go and trust that the universe would pick me up and move me when it was time.

We like to think we have so much control over our lives.

We do….and we don't. As far as I can tell, it's a cooperative effort. The shifting of the cosmos offers us a timeline of transitions that we can ready ourselves for if we have knowledge of them.

Saturn swooped back in on a mission at the appointed time, gobbled me up, and then spat me out onto the path that I was meant to walk. I wish I had known at the time that the stars give us a map of sorts to alert us to times of major change ahead. Then again, I still probably wouldn't have seen it coming. After all, I literally had someone who could see future events tell me that I would become a singer and I not only had disregarded the information as ridiculous…I had forgotten about it entirely.

My voice lessons worked like a magic wand.

The very first lesson that I had, my instructor had me sing scales (which I, of course, had never done before) and I was a nervous wreck. I would give anything to have a recording of that first lesson to go back and listen to, and especially to play for people who don't believe me when I tell them that there was a time when I couldn't sing.

Those scales that I sang reminded me of music class in elementary school when they gave us all a recorder to play and tried to teach us "Twinkle, Twinkle, Little Star."

We didn't know how hard to blow or where we put our fingers, so we just gave it our best effort and squeaked out a series of unrelated half-muted/half-car horn notes that sounded like we were strangling a flock of ducks.

I bet our music teacher wanted to kill herself on "recorder day" every year.

I bet my voice teacher wanted to kill herself on my "lesson one" day.

I knew it was bad. I honestly have to give her kudos for not just giving my money back and sending me home never to return that day. Instead, she just backed waaaayyyyyy up in the vocal lesson playbook and came out from behind her keyboard. Apparently, I wasn't ready for even beginner singing lessons because she abandoned that whole approach instantly and instead made me lie down on the floor.

She sat beside me, put my hands on my abdomen over my diaphragm, and gave me a class in remedial breathing.

The entire hour of that first class she literally spent teaching me how to breathe.

It surprised me to find out that I hadn't known how, considering I had been doing it my whole life but honestly, I found it quite difficult.

I followed her through exercise after exercise. She showed me how to control my breath. How to place it in different areas in the body -chest, head, mask (which is your sinus cavity area), etc. She gave me exercises to learn how to hold my exhale steady for lengthy amounts of time.

I left the class light-headed and pissed off.

So much for learning to sing. I couldn't even breathe correctly.

This was literally the very first time in my life that I had ever paid attention to the very action that kept me alive. I had just been taking it for granted this whole time.

It occurred to me that maybe if I had paid more attention in that yoga class that led me here that I might have been a little better at this. There was clearly an awareness of my body that I had been missing this entire time There was a presence in the "now" that I hadn't been tapping into. There was, within my body, something that happened moment to moment that I had the ability to control and direct and yet I hadn't even given it a thought. Ever.

I had been ignoring my breath…my life force, my entire life.

I found the exercises she had given me to practice at home extremely difficult.

We spent a month just working on breath.

A month.

For someone who desperately wanted to sing, that felt like cruel and unusual punishment. I kept asking her when she thought I would be ready to try actually singing again, and all I got from her was "not yet."

On the day that she finally decided to let me try scales again, I was excited but the memory of how it went the first time was still present in my mind. I didn't want to embarrass myself again and honestly, I couldn't really see how all of this breath work I had been doing was supposed to help when it came to actual musical notes. However, as we began to sing the first few notes, something happened this time that felt like magic to me. As I worked my way step by step up the scale, my instructor reminded me each and every note of all that we had been working on with my breath.

"Breathe from your chest this note."

"Place this one more in your nose."

"Make sure you support the note with your breath all the way through."

I was doing it!! I could do it!

What had felt like completely uncontrolled and almost random noises before were now sounds that had intention. I could direct them with my breath to match the notes that I was hearing. It was the light bulb moment that changed everything.

It was like playing an instrument. I was learning to "play" my breath. Move it this way and get this sound. Push it into my nasal passage, and get a higher tone. Every single facet of the sound stemmed completely from how I controlled my breath.

One of the notes I was singing collapsed into uncontrollable laughter.

I had been making this so hard this whole time, and it had been so easy!

My instructor grinned up at me from the piano bench and nodded.

"You just figured it out, didn't you?" she said. She had seen it click into place in my mind.

I nodded, still laughing.

Why had no one told me this? My whole life singing had been such a mystery to me. I was in awe of anyone that could do it, thinking they had some kind of gift that only got handed out to a select few. Instead, I had just discovered that it was one of the most physiological exercises that existed. It felt scientific now…just recreate the method that's been proven to work, and you can sing the note. It felt obtainable. Learnable.

Honestly, it almost felt like cheating a little…like someone gave me the code for the back door that no one was supposed to know about.

I was over the moon.

The mystery was gone now. I *knew* I could do this.

So, I did.

I became a singer.

I did it with both commitment and gleeful abandon. I practiced my exercises and songs every free moment that I had. I hammered out my technical skills until they became second nature, and then I used them to play with sound in new ways that I hadn't tried.

I learned my voice inside and out.

We had just met, my voice and I, but she was my new best friend.

We sang jazz. We sang Broadway. We even sang a little opera.

Like driving a new car wide open on curvy backroads, I just wanted to see what she could do. What were we capable of now that we knew the secret? What magic could we create now that we knew the spells?

My voice teacher ended up moving away a few months after we started working together, and I immediately sought out another vocal coach. I was learning with a voracity in leaps and bounds that surprised even me.

My next teacher was a well-known piano and vocal instructor in the area. He was also often the musical director of shows for a renowned professional theatre company in our area. I knew that working with this new instructor would be taking my education to another level entirely. He was known in the area for being a perfectionist and a tough critic, but also for pushing his students to their full potential.

I wanted to be pushed. I longed for it.

He intimidated the hell out of me in the beginning, but it wasn't long before we learned to speak each other's language and in no time at all I was singing complex pieces of music that he normally reserved for his most advanced students.

Make no mistake though, he definitely kept me humble about all of it. There were days when he made me sing the exact same line of music 75 times in a row, only to end the lesson by telling me that it still sucked but we were out of time for the day.

There were days that even the simplest melodies that I sang were "off."

There were lots of days that I left crying.

There were a few days I wanted to punch him in the face.

Even through all of that, an absolutely beautiful working relationship bloomed between us. He learned the ins and outs of my voice in ways that I wouldn't have known to look for. He knew more of what I was capable of than I ever could have seen with a beginner's mind, and he knew exactly how to coax it out of me.

Over time, I became as easily fine-tuned in his hands as an old baby grand piano.

My instructor would just move a weight slightly here, adjust the tuning a tad there, and the sound he was looking for came out of my mouth in perfect clarity. The way he directed and extracted sound from me felt like sorcery in a way, and I was enchanted with it all.

I lived for lesson day. It became the highlight of my week. In between classes, I practiced every single second that I was able to.

I had blossomed into a songbird.

My wife, Julia, didn't exactly know what to think of this new creature that she was living with. She had married a person whom she had never heard sing a note before, and it must have felt as though she suddenly had walked into a flash mob in her own home.

SURPRISE! You live in a musical now!

I never really asked her how she felt about it in the beginning because I just assumed that she would be as happy about my magical new transformation as I was. In hindsight, maybe thinking that she would feel about it the way that I felt it about was too much to expect, because I thought it was pretty fucking rad. That was probably too high of a bar of expectation.

As it turned out, she did not think it was rad at all.

She was confused about it, and...annoyed? That was the only word I could find to describe what I thought I was detecting. *I felt like I was annoying her.*

I didn't let it stop me though, or even slow me down for that matter. I just charged on ahead, singing all the while. There was going to be no "Raining on My Parade" except on Streisand day in vocal lessons.

I didn't really realize at the time that what I had been picking up on was much, much deeper than what I thought was just slight annoyance. I just continued plodding along in my own little personal concert and didn't worry about those moments when I felt like I was being a bother to her with my singing. In fact, I didn't give it much of a second thought until one day that "annoyance" reared its head in my face in a new way and waved a tiny little red flag.

Around the year mark of my vocal lessons, I had decided that the time had come for me to put all of this hard work to use. I was going to audition for a musical! I had been in so many shows throughout my whole life, but I had never once been in a musical.

I didn't know what to expect, but I knew I was a very strong dancer, and thought surely my vocal skills had reached the point that I could be cast as a backing ensemble member.

I selected my sheet music carefully and went down to the local theater to audition for their upcoming show, which was a classic country music revue of sorts. I chose to sing a Patsy Cline song; one which my vocal coach had recommended because he thought it suited my voice and showed off my tone.

It wasn't a particularly difficult song for me to sing, and I breezed through it in the audition with no bumps or wobbles. The dance portion of the audition was easy steps and went extremely well. I walked out of the theatre feeling great about how it went, and confident that I would be a good fit for the background ensemble.

I was so excited and proud of myself. I had just auditioned for a musical!

A year ago, I had sounded like a wounded animal when I tried to sing, and now I had come far enough to stand on a stage in front of a director and not feel like I humiliated myself entirely.

The next day I was on my way home from work when my phone rang. I looked down and saw the theater's number on the display and felt my stomach tighten a little.

Here goes! My first offer to be in a musical!

"Hi, this is Brett, the director at the theater from yesterday. Is this Jen?" the voice on the other end of the line said.

"Yes! Hi, Brett. How are you?" I asked.

"I'm well, thanks for asking. I'm just calling you back about your audition yesterday. You did a really fantastic job, and after discussing it with the assistant director and music director, I wanted to call on behalf of all of us and offer you the lead role. Would you accept it?" he asked.

"What?!" I shrieked into the phone.

"You blew us away yesterday. We all want you as the lead in the show. Will you accept the role?" he repeated.

I pulled over to the side of the road because I had begun crying so hard, I couldn't see.

"YES! Oh my GOD…YES! Thank you!!!" I squealed excitedly.

He laughed at my reaction.

"Good! I'm so happy to hear that. Glad to have you on board. Rehearsals begin Monday at seven- so we'll see you then, ok?" he said.

I agreed and hung up the phone. I was bursting with joy! The lead??!! How did that even happen? I was crying and laughing at the same time. I actually got out of the car and did a joyful dance right there on the side of the highway, and then got back in panting and giggling. I had to call Julia! She would be so excited for me!

My hands were shaking as I dialed the phone.

She had barely picked up when I let the news come spilling out of my mouth excitedly.

"BABE! You aren't going to believe this….the director from the play that I auditioned for at the theater yesterday just called and told me that I blew them away and they offered me the LEAD ROLE and of course I accepted it but I honestly can't even believe it because I thought they would just put me in the ensemble because I really haven't been singing that long you know and I hope I don't let them down because I haven't been doing this as long as a lot of other people there so I'm probably behind when it comes to being in a play but I'm so EXCITED and HAPPY and IN SHOCK because this is just CRAZY isn't it???" I said without taking a breath.

The line was silent.

"Hello?" I said.

"I'm here. I just don't really get why you're flipping out. Is that a big deal? The lead for a show at the community theater?" she asked.

"Um. YES. It's a huge deal. Well…to me anyway. A lot of those people who auditioned have been doing musical theater for years. They picked me over them for this show. I feel like that's a major accomplishment for someone who hasn't been singing very long," I replied.

Seriously? She couldn't see how that might be something to be excited about?

"Oh. Ok. Well…congratulations then. Where are you? Could you pick up dinner on the way home? I didn't have time to stop," she said.

"Uh…. yeah…I could do that, I guess," I replied.

"Cool. See you in a little while then," she said and hung up the phone.

I stared at the phone in shock.

Talk about bursting my bubble.

What the hell had just happened? I probably had been expecting too much for her to be as excited as I was, I could understand that. But just… nothing?

My face was still wet from my happy tears that I had been crying only seconds ago, and now here I sat feeling completely deflated. I took a napkin out of the glove box and cleaned up my mascara before I put the car back in drive and headed home. As I drove, I thought about the conversation we had just had. Was I the one out of line here? Had I overreacted? After all, she was right…it was just a community theatre role. It didn't feel like just that to me though. It felt so much bigger than just getting a singing part in a tiny volunteer show. It felt like the start of something huge.

I tried to sort it out in my mind. Why *did* this feel so important to me?

Ever since I had started singing lessons, I had begun to feel like I had a sense of purpose – an identity. I finally had something to look forward to when I woke up. It felt like more than singing to me. It felt like my true self was finally coming out. It was as if for thirty years, there had been a part of me that had been bound and gagged somewhere in a back closet and I had finally let her free.

Music made me feel alive.

Living was finally happening.

Purpose was finally happening.

As I pulled back into the driveway, I thought about how important those things were to me, and how long I had waited for them to happen. There was movement in my life, finally. How could Julia not see this? The entire time that we had been together I had bemoaned to her my feeling of purposelessness. I had gone through degree program after degree program, career after career, and new hobby after new hobby searching for something that lit me up. Each time I had started down a new path I just ended up feeling a sense of restlessness and an uneasy *knowing* somehow that it wasn't the right thing.

Singing had been the only thing that stuck. It was the only thing that felt right. The only thing that had brought me a deep sense of joy and satisfaction. Singing had allowed me to step into the fullness of my being. For the first time in my life…I saw my own potential. The human that I wanted so desperately to be had just been waiting this whole time for permission to sing the song of her soul.

I couldn't silence that now.

I couldn't un-know it, or un-feel it, or unsee it.

I didn't even want to. I had waited my entire life to find something that would mean to me what music now did. I wasn't sure exactly what Julia's issue was with all of this, but I knew that I couldn't let her bring me down enough to stop what had finally begun.

I needed this.

I needed this far more than either one of us had realized, I think.

I knew that singing had changed me dramatically- I felt like a whole new person and I could understand why that might be scary to my wife. Even I didn't know this woman that I was becoming, but I liked her. I wanted Julia to like her as well. I wanted her to see that this strange new songbird was a much better version of me. It was certainly a much happier one. I didn't know how to convey to her that if she would just stick with me through these shifts and let me bloom into the person that I felt like I was starting to become that it didn't have to be frightening; it could be a journey we took together.

The way that she was responding to even this new small step (a step that as she had noted, wasn't a big deal in the scheme of things) worried me though. If a small role in a small show was causing a reaction like the one I had just witnessed, how would things be between us if I took bigger (or more) steps? She had said she would always support me in following my heart, but the way she had been reacting to music hadn't felt very supportive at all.

Here I sat, feeling like I finally had discovered a way that I might be able to have it all - a happy marriage and a purpose that was fulfilling to me…but something deep down inside told me that it wasn't going to be that easy. There was a nagging at the back of my mind reminding me of my conversation with Bobby Drinnon years ago.

He had predicted that I would become a singer, and though I had thought the idea ludicrous at the time…he had ended up being correct about that. I felt an uneasiness in my stomach as I recalled how he had also told me that Julia and I wouldn't make it.

I took a moment right there in the driveway to bow my head and whisper the first prayer that I remembered saying since I had left the church so many years ago.

"God… if you actually hear prayers or grant wishes or whatever… I would just like to ask you…please, *please* don't let Mr. Drinnon be right about everything."

Chapter Five

THE FIRST READ-THROUGH of the play was a clusterfuck.

This was my first musical that I had ever been a part of, so I had no way of knowing that all first read-throughs for a musical are a disaster, and I nearly walked out that day never to return. It was extremely unsettling to me because it appeared as though not a single person in the entire theater had the slightest clue of what they were doing. I found absolutely no reassurance that an actual show might develop from what I was witnessing around me.

I hadn't realized that a "read-through" for a musical is always awkward by nature because the majority of the story is told through song. Songs, I might add, that most of the cast haven't heard.

I'm sure you can imagine what that looks like.

While it was apparent that the cast was very talented, it still felt like I was sitting in a room full of bumper cars. There so were so many starts, stops, and changes of direction that my head was reeling.

This particular show was also set to feature a live band, which presents a whole other set of issues that would have to be worked out. This was the first time that any of the musicians had played together or even seen the music for the show… and it sounded like it.

The directors were still trying to work out casting details; they were still filling in some holes in the cast. Parts that they hadn't found a great fit for were still on the table and they spent a good deal of time at the end of rehearsal asking all of us if we knew anyone who might be a good fit for various roles. They also needed a bass player for the band. I knew quite a few actors, but not many singers or musical performers since music was so new to me.

However, it did occur to me that I knew a bass player.

My friend Jason, who had lived above me when I was seventeen and was still dating Molly. Even after Molly and I split, I had remained fairly close with both

Jason and Lila throughout the years and had even been a bridesmaid in their wedding. Jason had played in a number of bands in the area for as long as I could remember, and I had been to several of his shows in the past and was always impressed with him. I felt pretty certain that I remembered him doing some musical theater himself at times. I knew he was extremely talented and would be a great addition to this show if he was interested.

I told the music director about him, and he encouraged me to reach out and see if he was available. To my delight, Jason was not only interested in playing for the show- but he was also very excited about it. He told me that he hadn't had the chance to do any theatre in a very long time, and that he had actually been thinking about trying to get back into it even before I had called.

He agreed to come to the next rehearsal.

I hung up the phone feeling excited that I was going to have a good friend beside me in rehearsals and for the show. It made me feel a little less like I was out on a limb in new territory all alone.

The next rehearsal was a music rehearsal in the theater itself (the read-through had been in a conference room), and they had pushed a small piano out to the middle of the stage to accompany us.

I was nervous. There was something about being on an actual stage and singing that intimidated me far more than simply singing alone in a voice lesson at my instructor's house.

Even the audition had been in a small room with just a few people present. I looked around nervously at the other cast members. This would also be my first time singing in front of a group. I was beyond intimidated.

As we warmed up with easy scales, our voices filled up the entire theater in a magical chorus. It made hairs on my arms stand up as my entire body responded to the sound.

It was my first time experiencing something that I would grow to love dearly.

This was a side of theatre that I had never been a part of before. The unbelievable sensory experience of so many talented voices blending together to echo off of the house walls was a delight to my ears. I had to stop singing for a moment because I got a little choked up with the emotion that it brought to the surface in me.

I hadn't known what I had been missing. I closed my eyes and let myself be carried away by the music surrounding me.

I was in love.

When we finished the scales, the director flipped through some pages on the piano, and then suddenly turned and looked at me.

"Jen, you are up first since you are the lead. Let's start with the Patsy song that you auditioned with just to get you good and warm. Ok?" the musical director said.

I immediately tried to swallow down the lump that had suddenly formed in my throat. I was going to sing *first*? At the piano alone? In front of all of these very talented people?

Ugh.

I handed him my sheet music that I had tucked inside my script. I hoped he didn't notice the paper shaking as I handed it to him. I knew that I was going to have to get used to this sooner or later. I had just expected it to be…well…later.

I took a few deep breaths as he played the intro.

My first few notes betrayed me a little. In my nervousness, I had forgotten to support them with my breath, and they came out a little wobbly.

I focused harder, dropping down into my body. I began to command my breath the way that I had been taught.

Support fuller from your chest, Jen.

Even out the tone with your breath.

Remember, there is a slight flip here, let it go into your head a bit.

Raise your soft palate.

That's it. You've got this.

I coached myself silently in my head and the notes falling from my mouth began to cooperate. I had talked myself back into the place where muscle memory and instinct took over. I could hear my own voice echoing through the theater. It surprised me how strongly it reverberated.

I looked back out over the house to see exactly how big of a space it was that I was filling up with sound, and I saw a single figure standing in one of the aisles.

I recognized the tall silhouette instantly from the newsboy cap that he always wore.

It was Jason.

He must have come in late, from the back of the theater, and had been walking down to the front but now he wasn't moving at all.

He was frozen in place, watching my every move. His eyes were wide, and his mouth was open slightly. He seemed mesmerized and slightly shocked.

We made eye contact.

I was happy to see him. It made me feel a little less afraid to see a friendly face in this moment, and I began to direct my singing to him out of gratitude.

I smiled as we held each other's gaze, and he slid quickly into one of the aisle seats as he smiled and nodded back to me.

I relaxed fully into the song and let the buildup of the bridge be as full and as resonant as it seemed to want to be. Seeing the approval on his face had been the reassurance I needed. I was on a roll now, and this felt like a performance. I wanted to impress him.

I wanted him to be proud to call me his friend on that stage.

I wanted him to believe that I deserved to be here.

I sang my heart out.

When I finished the song the entire cast, including the music director, applauded for me. The showering of appreciation made me blush. I had barely looked up from gathering my sheet music when I found myself being pulled by my arm to the side of the stage. Jason had to have run from the seats to the stage to get to me that fast.

As soon as we were out of direct earshot of anyone, he turned me around to face him. He was a little taller than me and he looked down at me slightly, his blue eyes wide. He looked around once again to make sure no one could hear and put a hand up to the side of his thick beard before whispering fiercely, "Oh my GOD, Jen! I had no idea you could do that. You never told me you could sing!"

I laughed.

"Well…I couldn't sing. I started taking lessons last year and this is the first project that I've done musically. So I guess you found out the same time as everyone else did," I said.

"I'm so impressed! Your voice is beautiful. We should work together…outside of this show. Let's start a band! Would you want to do that? I know you are a writer - I bet you could write songs. I could teach you. I think we would be awesome together. We already know we would get along well since we've been friends for so long. What do you say?" he asked.

The suggestion caught me completely off guard. He wanted to start a band… with me? With someone who literally just sang in front of a crowd for the first time only seconds ago?

I didn't know what to say.

"Are you sure, Jason? I don't really know anything about any of that. What if I suck?", I said.

He grinned widely at me, his blue eyes sparkling with delight.

"Not possible. Plus, you know I won't judge you for anything that you don't know. I'll help you. I could play guitar and sing with you. I have some friends who would probably love to be a part of it. A drummer. Another guitar player. Say yes. Just say yes, Jen, and we will figure out all of the details later."

His excitement was rubbing off. How much fun would it be to sing in an actual band? I briefly let myself imagine what it would be like. All of this was happening so fast… first this musical and now an opportunity to start a band? I could hardly believe it.

But I wanted it.

"Yes. Ok. Yes. I'm in… but you will have to be the one to organize everything because I don't even know where to begin," I replied. The butterflies in my stomach went nuts.

He beamed at me.

"I'm on it! This is going to be something really special, Jen. I promise," he said.

I felt those words enter my heart and then echo back to me from the depths. There was a stirring in me that I couldn't interpret. I'd never felt anything quite like it before. It was different than excitement…there was a knowing that came attached to it that was unfamiliar. Almost like an anticipation of something that I had already experienced before.

Yet… that wasn't possible because this was all new ground.

Wasn't it?

The feeling confused and unsettled me.

There was no way for me to know what the future held, yet I somehow got the distinct feeling that part of me did. It was similar to deja vu, but that wasn't quite the way to describe it either.

There was a flicker of recognition there somewhere in my soul, and I felt a shift in my entire being. The excitement was radiating throughout me, and as hard as I was trying, I literally couldn't pinpoint the reason why. Sure, the possibility of starting a band was exciting, but the reaction happening in me felt hugely disproportionate.

I walked out of the theater after rehearsal that night still mulling it all over in my mind.

Jason passed me in the parking lot in his car and waved at me and gave me a thumbs-up sign.

What was happening here? I had no idea, but the flurry of energy coming from deep within my bones seemed to indicate that whatever it was that was coming was monumental. I seemed to be teetering on the edge of something very significant, and the only way that I was going to find out what lay ahead was to close my eyes and leap.

78

Chapter Six

"ABSOLUTELY NOT. I don't want you to do it," Julia said sharply.

"Why? That makes absolutely no sense, Julia. Why does it matter if I sing in a band or not? You have your hobbies and animal rescue work that you like to spend your free time doing. This is how I want to spend mine," I replied.

I was exasperated. We had been arguing on and off about this for days. I hadn't even let Jason set up an official first practice yet because even the *theoretical* band had been such a source of contention at home.

"I don't think you realize how much time a band will take, Jen. Not to mention, it will affect my time as well. You will probably have shows every Friday and Saturday night, and that's just not how I want to spend my weekends…going to see you sing the same songs over and over all of the time. I'm not going to be your groupie," she said. Her cheeks were flushed with anger.

It was like she had tossed a match on kerosene. I exploded.

"So, you don't want me to do it because your time is more important than mine, really is what you are saying? I never said you had to come to shows. I don't care if you come or not, actually. Plus, you are acting like we are some big-name band that will be booked all of the time. WE DON'T EVEN KNOW ANY SONGS YET. Hell, we might suck. I don't know what any of this is going to look like right now, so I don't know why you think that you do. I'm doing this. It's happening. I don't have to have your permission to sing. You are my partner and not my parent," I said.

"Fine. You are right, you don't have to have my permission. But I don't have to like it, and I don't. So don't expect me to support it." She was seething.

I walked out of the house, slamming the door behind me, and called Jason to tell him to let me know when and where he wanted to practice, and I would be there.

I had been correct in thinking that other steps with music would lead to bigger contention at home. The initial red flag that I had seen with being cast in the play had turned into a giant red quilt that seemed to wrap around our entire relationship.

My journey with the band had started off on the wrong foot with Julia, and that misstep was without question indicative of how it would continue to play out the entire time I was a part of it.

The week after we finally played our first show (a tiny little 5-song set opening for another band); the residual fighting landed us in couples' therapy.

She kept saying it was about the time the band would take up, but that never sat right with me. I felt like it couldn't be the real reason that she was so vehemently against it. We lived together and worked together. Outside of work, we spent quite a bit of time with our friends that we had dinner with a few times a week and went on vacations and camping trips with. She and I were always doing something together, even in our free time. Apart from school, this music venture of mine was the very first time that I had stepped away from our constant time together to do something that I wanted to do that didn't involve her.

She couldn't handle it, and I could not for the life of me grasp why.

Even our therapist seemed to have difficulty understanding what the actual issue was.

"Why can't you just let her do this, Julia?" she asked her one session.

Of course, that just led to us walking out of the office that day with Julia wanting to look for a new therapist because she thought the current one was on "my side."

I thought she seemed so as well, but I refrained from pointing out that if she WAS taking my side that perhaps Julia might actually take into consideration that she could be in the wrong here.

Investigating that possibility was an idea that she was never open to.

Meanwhile, the band itself was quickly becoming the "something special" that Jason had promised. We had started off our work together by staying after theater rehearsals to write songs and learn cover songs for an hour or so each night.

I, of course, hadn't told Julia that we were doing this in order to avoid a fight every single night. I just told her rehearsal ran until 11:00 and stayed accordingly. I wanted to make sure that this whole band thing was even going to be something worth fighting for and over before I fully committed.

It only took a few sessions for me to see that it was.

I had always liked Jason. His laid-back and easy-going manner had long ago made him one of my favorite friends. Throughout the years, whenever a good amount of time had passed since we had seen each other last, we effortlessly seemed to pick back up where we left off in an easy camaraderie that never changed with time.

We had never worked together on any kind of project though, so I had been curious to see how that would go both with the musical and the band that we were working on simultaneously.

He won over everyone involved, on all accounts.

The director was so charmed by him and impressed with all of the talents that he brought to the musical, that he ended up giving him a speaking/singing role in the production in addition to his house band position. He also promptly asked him to be in the next musical production that was scheduled on the lineup.

Jason and one of the other band members hit it off so well that they asked him to play on an album recording that they were working on. He made friends and connections right and left throughout that show.

When it came to working one on one with me, Jason was kind, gently encouraging, and very forgiving when it came to how little I knew about creating music. He would play guitar to accompany me while I learned to sing new cover songs, never complaining even once when it took me twenty (or more) tries to get it right.

He gave me a crash course in songwriting over the span of that production's rehearsal that rivaled any paid course that I've seen to this day. He broke it down for me step by step and showed me how to turn poetry into song.

I was amazed at how knowledgeable he was about songwriting, and even more impressed with the way that he was able to convey it to me so easily.

By the time the musical ended, I knew without a doubt that the band was something that we had to continue to do. Jason told me that he rented a shared practice space downtown already. He had been practicing there for years, and a few other bands used it on different nights. The rent was cheap, and there were all kinds of amps, mics, and sound equipment that stayed in the room that we could use if we wanted.

We set our practice nights for Thursday nights, and I could hardly wait to go to the first one.

At least... I was excited about it until the actual day arrived.

I fought for a solid hour with Julia before I left for practice that night.

Jason opened up the door of the practice room to find me in tears with my makeup running down my face. I was unsure if I should even stay. I thought about just turning around and going back home. Was this even going to be any fun for me if each time I came to practice it was going to start with a screaming argument at home?

"Well...you are already here now. The fight is over for tonight, so you might as well stay and make it worth it. I'm sorry that she's being like that though - I really am. I want you to want to do this, and I certainly don't want to make your life difficult because of it. Lila is like that too sometimes about music, so I get it," he said. He gave me a big hug and handed me his bandanna from his pocket to wipe my tears as I sat down on a futon. "It'll be ok, Miss Jen."

Miss Jen. It was the first time he ever called me that, though it would go on to be not only how he addressed me most of the time, but also how he introduced me to everyone in his life. I remember it sounding so charmingly southern and old-fashioned to my ear at first – almost humorous. Over time it took on a feeling of sweet comradery – like a nickname that had been bestowed on me that I wore proudly as a symbol of the kinship between us.

He gave me a warm smile.

"So… if you are ready to get started…I hooked up the mics before you got here and I thought we might try singing a few of the cover songs that you learned at the theater, just to get the feel for how that sounds coming through a P.A. system. Are you open to that?", he asked.

"Um… yes…but I've never sung into a mic before. I'm sure it's different…what do I need to know?" I asked.

"I figured that you hadn't, that's why I wanted to try it tonight. It *is* very different, but I'm not sure it's something I can explain - you'll just have to see for yourself. The main difference is the way that you hear yourself. You won't be able to actually hear your voice as it comes out of your mouth because the guitar will be too loud. You'll have to hear it through the monitor," he said.

I stared at him blankly. I had no idea what he was talking about.

He laughed at my expression and motioned for me to come over and stand in front of one of the mics. He adjusted the height for me.

"Talk into it," he instructed.

I did so, and my voice came blasting back at me through a small speaker on the floor in front of me.

"That's your monitor," he explained. "Everything that we are doing comes through there in the same way that the audience is hearing it. So, if you can't hear yourself, or me…or the guitar…. tell me what needs to be adjusted and I'll fix it, ok?"

I nodded. He picked up his guitar and stepped behind the other mic he had set up beside me.

"Let's start with 'Jolene' since we've been working on that one." He began to play the intro.

As I began to sing, I realized exactly what he had been talking about. The guitar was so loud that as I sang the words, I couldn't hear my vocals in the normal way. I had to adjust things on a slight delay as they made their way back to me through the monitor. This was going to take some getting used to. It was also going to require that I learn my vocal instrument on a whole different level. I was going to have to be absolutely certain of where I was placing a note before I sang it because there was no way for me to hear it instantly as it came out to make an adjustment.

I must have been doing something right though, because as I got to the chorus something shifted.

My voice suddenly sounded richer. There was a new depth of sound coming back at me from the monitor that I had never heard before. It was so incredible that it made the hairs on my arm stand up.

I looked over quizzically at Jason to see if he heard the difference too, and suddenly realized with great shock what it was.

He was singing with me.

He had placed a harmony line just below mine, so tightly that it had only seemed to enrich my own voice.

It was so perfectly aligned that I had mistaken it as something that had come from myself.

I stopped singing and was now just staring at him wide-eyed.

He quit playing.

"Holy shit, Jason. That was incredible. I couldn't even tell us apart," I said breathlessly.

He grinned sheepishly, and looked down at the floor, refusing to make eye contact.

"Yeah…I kind of thought we would blend well. I'd been wanting to try that for a while. Sounded pretty good though, didn't it?" he said.

"Pretty good? No…it sounded amazing. I honestly don't even know what to say. I have goosebumps!" I replied, holding my arm up for him to see.

He nodded, still looking down, and ran a hand through his beard. Was he blushing?

"Can you do that on all of the songs? How did you even learn how to blend like that? I have such a hard time with harmony. I have to memorize it, and it takes nothing for me to get pulled off and sidetracked on someone else's note," I said.

"I can teach you. In the meantime, you can just take lead on the songs we do, and I'll sing the harmony," he said.

And so, it began.

What would come to be known as our signature sound was born that night in that little practice room.

Our vocals would become so tightly woven together that oftentimes we were indistinguishable.

He did try to teach me how to sing harmony, but I was never as naturally good at it as he was. Oftentimes in performance, I would get lost and screw up my line. He would always save the song somehow though, adjusting through my mistakes on the fly. Thanks to him we always came out smelling like a rose no matter how badly I messed up.

It became a sweet partnership.

So much trust was built between us during that time.

We learned every nuance of each other's voice and featured and lifted each other up every single chance we got. We chose our cover songs with great care, only bringing in those that showed off the very best of what we could do.

Writing original songs brought a tender intimacy to our friendship. Songwriting by nature involves showing the most vulnerable and raw parts of yourself. Having a songwriting partner means allowing that person to stick their fingers into those places - to help shape and mold them into art with you. It's a surrender to the other to be seen and known in the places of yourself that are the hardest to look at. When two people create together, the connection has to be strong for the art to be strong. It's absolutely crucial to be on the same wavelength as the other person, or at the very least, to be flexible enough that you can meet them where they are.

This "education" about each other that we received was a deep dive that I had never experienced with another human before.

It grew into something unlike any relationship that I had ever had.

When it came to relationships with my closest friends, my partners, and even my wife, I had gotten to know them in all the ways that I thought mattered the most. I knew their backgrounds, their family dynamics, their favorite foods and colors, their politics, and their spiritual affiliations. I knew their favorite music, their clothing preferences, the places they liked to travel to, and whether they were a dog or cat person.

When it came to Julia, I knew her sexual desires and preferences, her family members that she loved (or hated) the most, her secret fears, and the exact way she liked her coffee.

I thought I knew all there was to know about the people I was closest to.

Yet…over time I was surprised to find that I had come to know Jason in a completely different way.

I knew how his mind worked when he was piecing together a line of poetry. I knew what he looked like when inspiration was flowing through him like water. I knew the sore spots that were guaranteed to make him teary-eyed, and I knew the face he made when he was trying to cover that up.

I knew when he was holding a note out extra-long, when we were singing together for the sheer purpose of reveling in the blend of our voices.

I knew exactly how happy music made him.

I knew his strengths, and I knew the secret places where he only pretended to be strong.

I knew what motivated him. I knew what moved him. I knew how he saw himself and his place in the world, and how that was reflected in the songs he wrote.

I knew him in all of the ways that can only be known by creating with someone.

He grew to know me in all of the same ways.

It made me wonder if I had ever really "known" anyone before.

Certainly no one had known me before, at least not in these depths of creativity. I already had felt as though I had only just met my true self for the first time when I began singing. That was the version of me that Jason got to know. We got to know that "Jen" together. I became that woman with him by my side.

When the connection is that strong the music is bound to be good, and ours was no exception.

It wasn't long before we brought a few more musicians on board with us to create a five-piece band. These other players rounded out our sound and we began to attract the attention of many local venues. Soon we were booking shows right and left.

The band became my happy place. Jason's and my partnership had now blossomed into a little music family that I took my refuge in.

Julia and I would fight, and then I would flee to the safety of rehearsals or shows to get away from the growing tensions at home. The demand for the band was escalating, but so was the animosity in my marriage. Julia's worst fear about the time that the band would take up was manifesting quickly before our eyes.

We were still going to therapy.

It wasn't working.

One day our therapist tried to explain what she thought was happening with Julia to me in a way that she knew I would understand.

"All of this fighting… the things that she is saying… I wonder if you could look at that as the lyrics to a song you are hearing? There is a melody running behind that though, and if you listen harder, I think you will hear all of the things she is not saying. She's afraid she is going to lose you, Jen. Music is scary to her because she felt like she had built this whole life with you…a life she was proud of and a life that she wanted from now on. She is older than you. She thought things were settled and that you were happy in that stability the same way that she was. Now it feels like you are being pulled away from her by something out of her control. Music is stealing you away. You are putting all of your time and focus there…time and focus that you used to give to her…and it just keeps getting bigger and bigger. Can you see that?" she said.

"I can see what you're saying. In a way, I can understand why she would feel that way. But the thing is…it never had to be like this. Music didn't steal me away -she pushed me away before it ever even had a chance to. Musical pursuits and a good relationship shouldn't have to be mutually exclusive. She's the one who made it a problem. She made it clear from the get-go that she wouldn't let me have both. I wanted both. I still want both. I just can't see her backing down from making every single conversation about it miserable," I replied.

And trust me…there were a LOT of conversations about it.

Over the next four years, my life was a constant push and pull between singing and fighting about singing. I wanted to do music more than anything, so I was willing to pay the price to continue to write and perform, but that didn't make it any less exhausting.

Oftentimes, Julia would come to our shows, and I would invariably look out in the crowd while I was singing only to see her sitting at a table looking like she'd rather be sawing her nipples off with a butter knife.

I would walk down off of the stage like a scolded puppy during our set breaks and sit with her and try and raise her mood.

"Are you ok? You don't have to stay if you don't want to," I would say.

("Please, Jesus. Just go. You are killing my show buzz.", is what I wanted to say, but refrained.)

It felt an awful lot like babysitting a fussy toddler who was just tired enough that they didn't know what they wanted. She didn't want to leave, but it was beyond obvious that she didn't want to be there either. I hated the whole situation, and it sucked every bit of the joy out of my show for me every single time she came.

Jason would often check on me when I would get back onstage after these interactions ("You ok, Miss Jen?"), but he knew it was inevitable that I would come back from those set breaks just wanting to be done with the show.

It really wasn't fair to anyone involved, but I felt especially bad for Jason and the other members of the band who had nothing to do with the situation.

I mentally checked out on everyone and left them hanging. It always caused a noticeable decline in my performance, which I knew reflected badly on the band, but I didn't know how to fix it. I just couldn't seem to separate myself from her energy when I was performing.

It affected me every single time she came to a show.

Oddly enough, I was having an entirely different experience with my family when it came to my music. They were regulars at my shows. They all came to every musical performance they possibly could, be it for theater or the band. It was the one area of my adult life where my parents were unwaveringly supportive. They had been *delighted* at my move into the world of singing from the get-go and showered me with pride and approval surrounding my newfound skills. They truly were my biggest fans. Because of this, they had made a big effort to get to know Jason since he had been the reason that I joined a band to begin with. Per usual, he had charmed his way into their hearts instantaneously, and I would often find him sitting with my family instead of his own on set breaks or after shows. It bothered me on multiple levels that my parents so openly welcomed connection with Jason while Julia was often barely spoken to at the same shows, but Julia was usually in such a foul mood at my music events that I didn't push it. That wasn't exactly the side of my wife that I wanted to insist they get to know, so I just let them be cordial from a few tables over to spare everyone involved.

Whit, my sister, was the blessed peacemaker (per usual) whenever she came to the shows. She and Julia loved each other, and they would always sit in close proximity in order to talk, which kind of forced my parents to do more than just acknowledge Julia's presence with a wave. Whit also adored Jason from the minute that she met him. She found him hysterically funny and always jokingly referred to him as her "fun uncle" because she said he felt more like family than friend. She was the common bond that crossed all the unspoken boundaries between Julia, my parents, and music. I was filled with gratitude every single time I saw her out in the crowd at a show, because I knew she would easily smooth over any and all interactions that were awkward or uncomfortable. Her presence was the only time I felt totally free to just focus on performing and enjoy doing what I loved to do.

A few years in, Jason decided one day to invite two more musicians to play with us. He asked me if that would be all right, and I told him to just do whatever he thought was best. If he thought they would add to our sound, then I trusted his judgment.

The new additions were a banjo and fiddle duo that had been playing together for quite some time in various bluegrass bands. The first time they came to rehearsal, I was blown away by their talent. They were not only both tremendous musicians, they could both sing and their harmony blend was nearly as strong as mine and Jason's.

I knew that bringing them in would change our sound dramatically. We currently had a classic country sound, and the addition of banjo and fiddle would definitely swing us more into the bluegrass genre.

I thought it would be interesting to see what that would look like, but I couldn't for the life of me figure out why they wanted to play with us.

It seemed to me that they were already successful as a duo in their own right.

Why would they want to come into another band just to be backing musicians? It didn't make sense.

As it turned out, my intuition that something was off about the situation was correct.

They didn't want to be backing musicians…they wanted to front the band. Our songwriting and growing notoriety in the area had attracted them to our project, and there was an agenda that slowly began to emerge the longer they played with us.

It started out with minuscule moves. Nearly undetectable at first.

They brought in a few songs that they wanted to add to the setlist.

No biggie. We expected that things would shift a little when they joined us.

Next, they brought in a few duets that they wanted to sing lead on.

Ok. That's fine. We could use some more songs in our shows anyway. Plus, they were amazing singers, so it was hard to argue with featuring them some.

The next thing that happened was that every single song began to feature a banjo or fiddle solo when we were performing live.

Again- they were awesome, so we really couldn't complain that it was "too much."

Then one day they asked if they could be the singers on the newest duet that Jason and I had written. That particular move didn't sit so well with me. Songs felt like my babies, and I didn't really want anyone else to sing them. Jason seemed ok with it though, so I gave in.

Everything happened in such small increments that I still can't look back and pinpoint the moment that it occurred, but one day I looked up and realized that I was only singing lead on four songs in a three-hour set. I didn't play an instrument, so a good portion of the time I just stood to the side watching the action with my thumb up my ass. I might as well have popped some popcorn and sat down in the audience for all I was contributing.

There had somehow been a quiet coup.

I had been nudged off of the team inch by inch…so slowly I hadn't even noticed what was happening until I was standing on the sidelines with no playing time. Jason was still singing quite a bit, and of course, he played guitar on every single song, so it wasn't quite the same for him.

Had he even noticed that I was barely singing anymore? It didn't seem as though he did.

The final straw was the day that we walked into the practice room to find a "band manager" present to talk to us about financial matters. She had a contract written up for us all to sign, dictating how money from shows would be split fairly amongst the band (and her).

We were completely taken aback.

No one had asked Jason (or myself) about hiring a manager. He and I exchanged looks and understood that neither one of us would sign that contract. As it got passed around, we both just passed it on without adding our names. When it got back to the manager, she said that she still needed two signatures.

In response, Jason asked her to leave.

As she walked out the door, he turned to the band members and asked everyone else to leave as well. His voice was very low and controlled and I knew he was trying very hard to cover up his anger.

Everyone packed up their instruments and quietly filed out of the room.

Everyone but me.

As soon as the door closed, he wheeled around to face me.

"What the hell, Jen? What was that? Why would they just bring someone in like that without asking us first?" he said. He was furious.

"Because it's their band now," I replied.

He looked at me with a mixture of confusion and anger.

"What do you mean? This is OUR band. Mine and yours, remember? We started this whole thing together. We write the songs. It's ours," he said.

"Not anymore, Jason. In fact, I don't even feel like I'm IN this band anymore. Haven't you noticed? Look at the setlist. I barely even sing anymore. They are singing our originals, plus adding in their instrumentals. They've maneuvered the whole setup, and you are singing background vocals most of the time. They front this band now, not you and me. Can you really not see that?" I asked.

He was staring at me, speechless.

Apparently, he really had not noticed. I could see him working through it all in his head.

I watched the lightbulb click on.

"Oh my God. You're right," he said. "But what can we do? We can fix it, right? We'll just demand that the setlist be reworked. We will go back to our old set, and just let them play on a few songs," he said. I could see the wheels turning as he spoke. He was trying to figure out exactly how we could backtrack gracefully.

"That will never work. They're never going to be content to go back to that now that they are basically running the band. Why would they? I would say that I wouldn't let myself be squashed like that either, but that is exactly what I've done. I allowed this to happen because for the longest time I didn't see it," I said.

"I didn't see it either. I'm so sorry, Miss Jen. I'll make this right, just let me have some time to think about how to handle it, ok?" he said.

I agreed that I would. I left that night trying to decide what my place was with this band now. Was it salvageable? I wasn't sure. I knew needed music in my life. It was something that had grown to be such a huge part of who I was and what I believed my purpose to be. Singing in this band had given me opportunities that I never would have had otherwise. Could I be ok with just singing a few songs in a set and contributing with the songwriting? The thought of that didn't sit quite right with me, but neither did walking away entirely.

When I got home that evening, I relayed the events from the band practice to Julia.

She said that she thought that I should just quit. It obviously wasn't going to be what it was in the past ever again, and she couldn't see why I would want to put all of that time into a band that I was barely singing in.

She wasn't wrong. In fact, she had a very good point and if it had come from anyone else, I probably would have readily agreed. But because of all that we had been through over this band, it enraged me when she said it because I felt like she was just jumping on the opportunity to shit on my music from a different angle. The conversation escalated once again into the same old screaming argument about music that we had been having for four years.

We went to bed so mad at one another that neither of us was speaking any longer.

As I lay down that night, I realized that it just wasn't worth it anymore. Julia was right, as much as it pained me to admit it.

It wasn't worth fighting her tooth and nail to get to sing if I wasn't even really getting to sing.

It wasn't worth putting myself and Jason through hell to try to take our band back when there was a good possibility that nothing was going to change. Even if we somehow managed to step back to the forefront of the band, tensions would be high, and it would likely be miserable in a different way.

I just couldn't do it anymore.

Not for this kind of payoff. It wasn't a good trade.

I decided that quitting the band was the right decision after all, and I let it be known to Julia before I cut the light out on the nightstand.

I cried myself to sleep that night, knowing that on the other side of the bed Julia was breathing a giant sigh of relief. The four-year-long argument was finally over, and she had won.

Part Three

ignite - *verb*

a.: catch fire or cause to catch fire

b.: arouse or inflame (an emotion or situation)

92

Chapter Seven

JASON,
I APOLOGIZE in advance for the length of this letter, but it is one of the hardest things I have ever had to write. I also want you to know that I am writing this to you instead of talking to you face to face, not because I am afraid to talk to you in person or don't respect you enough to do so….on the contrary, I know that if I try to tell you this face to face I will get emotional and cry, and not end up saying half of what I want to say, and you deserve more than that, my dear friend.

After much thought and consideration, and many tears, I have decided that it is time for me to step down from the band. I know that you know me well, and that this probably does not come as a total shock. There are many factors that have contributed to this very difficult decision. The most pressing is Julia. As you know, she has not been on board with my musical endeavors in any shape, form, or fashion. From the minute that we started this band it has been a battle with her at home. I know you have seen some of it, but there is a lot that I have kept hidden because I didn't want you to not like my wife.

I know it affects my performance. It definitely affects my head space about it at all times. I feel as though it is unfair to everyone for me to keep trying to stick this out and make it work when I am fighting a battle that I can't win. I think I am probably holding you back as a band in a lot of ways because of this.

The second factor we discussed the other evening. I feel as though I have been nudged out of the band. Everyone there is amazingly talented. I can say in truth that everyone there deserves to let their talent shine. I just feel like I have lost my place, and it's so far gone that I can't ask to have it back. And at the end of the day……I realize that you are getting to play with one of the most talented groups of musicians in the area, and I genuinely want that for you. You deserve it, and your songs deserve to get to be heard in that way.

Through all that we have shared musically, I have come to consider you my best friend. I hope that you can understand this decision and that you are not angry with me. When I made a list of reasons to go vs reasons to stay, you were really the only valid reason for me to stay. I have enjoyed all that we have created, and I have loved spending time with you and getting to know you so well. I love performing with you, and I will so miss being onstage with you and looking over and feeling like you had my back to the end of the earth. I can't thank you enough for that. If it is ok, I would like the theater gig on Friday to be my last show. I think it is symbolic and synchronistic that the idea for this band was born in the theater, and that our time on this journey together will end in the theater. I wanted to tell you that I was leaving before the theater show, because I wanted us to both be able to know and appreciate our last time performing together in that moment. I thought we would have wished for that opportunity in hindsight had I not said anything. The theater was always a place of magic for us.

Finally, I need for you to know that what I want more than anything is for us to come through this transition with our friendship intact. I really want to thank you for believing in me all of this time. You helped me become confident in my talent, helped me grow so much musically, and showed me that I was more capable than I ever imagined. Thank you for teaching me to fly. I love you and appreciate your friendship beyond what I could ever tell you.

Love always,
Jen

Jen,
Of course, I wouldn't be mad at you, and we are still friends… but this is an epic break-up letter. You know I'm not good at these things, but I can say that my heart hurts. I love you, my friend. Indeed, as poignant as the theatre show will be, it will also be twice as bittersweet.

It's been a great time…the best time. I'm really going to miss seeing you regularly. I understand how serious the band is to you and I know you wouldn't make a decision like this hastily. I do understand where you are coming from. Thank you for being a part of this.

The second part, actually.

See you Friday at the theater.

Love,
J

The theatre show was brutal.

I couldn't keep my shit together for a solid song the whole show.

Jason wore dark sunglasses onstage the whole time (in a dark theater, nonetheless) to keep from having to look me in the eye, I presumed.

The rest of the band was almost giddy that I was leaving, and though they all made an effort to not let that show onstage, I still felt it. I was out of the way for them now. They were free to take this band in any direction they chose with me out of the loop. They had divided and conquered the partnership between Jason and me.

As we packed up our equipment when the show was over, I saw the marker board that had our setlist for practice on it amongst the pile. They had already erased my songs.

It was like I had never even existed as part of the band.

It was such a simple, yet hurtful gesture.

Feeling deeply the insult to my injury, I walked back into the theater crying as they all drove off.

The crowd had thinned out, and only a few theater staff remained to clean up.

I went into the ladies' room and tried to clean myself up a little, but every time I wiped my tears away more spilled from my eyes. I finally just gave up and had a good cry in one of the stalls for a solid five minutes. When I felt like I had finally gotten myself under control, I came back out to the mirror and attempted a half-assed makeup reapplication. I felt certain that everyone that had come for the show was gone at this point, so I decided it was probably safe to go on back to my Jeep, even if I did still look like a hot mess.

The second that I walked out the backstage door, I looked up to see Jason standing underneath the streetlight a few feet away, his cap pulled down low.

He had clearly been waiting for me.

"Miss Jen," he said with a small wave.

My heart ached when he said it.

Miss Jen.

What had started as his playful nickname for me had turned into so much more over time. I hadn't known anyone in the local music scene in the beginning, and he had always introduced me to fellow artists and venue owners like that.

"This is Miss Jen…"

Now it sort of felt like my stage name. Or at least the name that people who knew me from music called me.

"Miss Jen."

I briefly wondered if anyone would ever call me that again, now that I wouldn't be singing. I could add that to the list of things I was really going to miss.

"Can I walk you to your Jeep?", he asked. He offered his arm to me, and I slipped my own arm through it. The side parking lot was empty except for our two vehicles, and it was extremely dark. I was glad he had waited to walk me, I felt much safer with him there. He turned to face me, and I realized that he still had his sunglasses on.

"For fuck's sake, will you take those things off? I can't see your eyes and I don't even know how you can see to walk out here," I said as I reached up and grabbed them off of his face.

What I uncovered beneath those glasses broke my heart. His eyes were red and swollen. Tears were running down his cheeks just as freely as mine had been all night.

He hadn't been avoiding looking at me this whole time.

He had been hiding his tears.

He pulled me into a tight embrace and then collapsed onto my shoulder in heavy sobs.

I didn't know what to say. I had never seen a man cry. Ever.

My dad, the closest male figure in my life, had always seemed superhuman in his ability to never break down. If my guy friends ever cried, it was never in front of me and it most certainly was never *because* of me.

Yet here I stood, holding my very best friend in my arms as he shook with sobs that he could not hold back….and it was my fault.

I wept with him.

No words were said for a very long time. Just the longest, most tearful embrace that I had ever been held in.

He finally pulled away slightly, and wiped the tears from his face, though they continued to fall.

"I'm so sorry. I feel like I let you down. It should have never gotten that far gone with the band without my noticing. I should have stuck up for you better," he said.

"It's not your fault…I should've stuck up for myself. That wasn't on you. I just didn't have the fight left in me. I couldn't fight Julia at home and the band at practice. It was just… too much fighting," I said. I hung my head. It was true. I was overwhelmed and exhausted.

"It should've been me. I should have done the fighting. You are worth fighting for," he said.

I sighed heavily. He was so sweet.

"I'm really going to miss you, J. You know… a long time ago someone told me that we have many soulmates in our lives. That there are just certain people that we have a deep soul connection with. I believe that's true, and in that way…I believe that you are a soulmate of mine," I said.

He reached out and wiped tears from my cheek. Looking into his eyes unsteadied me. They were deeper than anyone's eyes I'd ever seen. Had I never looked into them before? I tried to think back over the time we had known each other…I couldn't recall ever being this close to him, let alone staring into his eyes like this.

How had I never noticed how beautiful and expressive they were?

It felt like they were pulling me in.

"I believe that too, Jen. We're definitely soulmates. I always think of you that way…but there is also something more, on my end anyway. This is something that I couldn't say to anyone else, especially my wife…she would never understand… but you are my muse. Ever since we began this journey together with music, I've been so inspired. Writing music became so simple. It just poured out of me like water. Ideas for arrangements and riffs just popped into my head so easily. Inspiration surrounded me the moment you became a part of music with me. That came from you, my dear. You're my muse and now…I don't even know if I want to continue to do music anymore without you…" he said. He disintegrated into sobs again.

Seeing him like this made me crumble inside. He was killing me.

"You *have to.* You have to keep doing this. You are so unbelievably talented, J. That doesn't come from me…it comes from you. You were doing music long before I came into the picture." I whispered back. He cupped his hand under my chin and raised my face to look him in the eye again.

"Not like this, I wasn't. I need you, Jen. This was supposed to be ours…this whole project began between the two of us. It should stay that way. It could still be that way…let me try to fix it?" he said.

He took a deep breath and whispered urgently, "I don't want you to leave."

He was still looking deeply into my eyes as he said it, and it unsettled me in a way that I didn't understand. It felt like he was searching my very soul…looking into my being for an answer…to…what?

What was the question? It felt deeper than the words he was saying.

I felt like he was reading my thoughts, and it made me uncomfortable. I looked away.

He let his hand drop from my face.

"I think it's just time, J. I think leaving is the right thing to do. It feels like I have to. I can't see a way for either of us to fix this…though I really wish we could. I'm so sorry. I'm just going to have to let it go," I said softly.

He took a step back away from me and seemed to consider this for a moment. He took his cigarettes out of his shirt pocket and busied himself with lighting one as he leaned up against my Jeep. We stood in silence for a long while, looking out over the empty parking lot. There were a thousand things I wanted to say, but I couldn't seem to find the words.

As he finished up his cigarette, he finally broke the silence.

"Have you ever had your heart broken before? Just…anytime in your life…has anyone ever broken your heart, Miss Jen?" he asked.

The question caught me off guard. I couldn't see how this related to the band, but I decided I would go along with it.

"Yes. Once. I was crazy about this girl that I dated in college. We had been friends for a while before we got together, and I thought she was just the greatest thing. She was smart, funny, and beautiful. The connection was really something special…or so I thought. She showed up at my doorstep one day out of the blue and just broke up with me. No good reason. No excuses. Just BOOM…didn't want me anymore. I wanted to die. I think I cried an ocean. It took me forever to get over that. Actually…to be honest…I don't know that I ever truly *did* get over it. It's still painful to think about," I answered.

"It's terrible, isn't it? The worst pain. It just cuts you to the core, and there is absolutely nothing you can do about it. The worst part is, like you just said…you never really get over a hurt like that," he said.

"Sounds like you have also had your heart broken before," I replied.

"Yeah. Twice, actually. I was crazy about my first girlfriend in high school. You know how it is with your first love…it's all new and feels so special and you are just inseparable. Well…that's how it was until I found out she was cheating on me with a good buddy of mine. I was just destroyed. Couldn't eat. Couldn't sleep. Like you said -wanted to die. You know how it is," he said with a shrug.

"Ouch. That's terrible. Especially since you had to experience that so young. What a horrible way for your first love to end. I'm sorry that happened to you, J. But you said there were two…what about the second one? When was your second heartbreak'" I asked.

He began to walk away from me as he said over his shoulder, "Oh, that one? That one was just now."

Chapter Eight

I COULDN'T FUNCTION.

I had been crying for weeks.

Every single time I thought about music or J it felt like someone reached inside my chest and ripped my heart out all over again.

Why had I walked away from the thing that mattered the most to me?

Why had I allowed myself to be manipulated into giving up the thing I lived for?

Every weekend that passed I would see the band post their shows on social media and I wanted to scream at the top of my lungs.

That should be me. I should be singing at that show. (Insert sailor words and name-calling. I can be super petty when I'm mad.)

I had let myself down in a way that I couldn't seem to come to terms with.

Giving up on the band felt inextricably like giving up on myself, and it was too late to do anything about it now. I felt like I would never sing again. It seemed as though I had blown the best opportunity that I was ever going to get to make music a big part of my life.

And J…I couldn't even think about J without weeping. The last conversation we had in the theater parking lot was still ringing in my ears. Why hadn't I just let him try to fix it like he asked me to?

Julia was no help at all. While she made little effort to hide the fact that she was over the moon happy that I had quit the band, she clearly hadn't anticipated the level of heartbreak that it would cause me in the aftermath.

"Now tell me again why you are so upset, exactly? No one made you quit- you made that decision all on your own. I just don't get why you are acting like you will never sing again," she said for the fiftieth time.

"Because it feels like that. I'm afraid I *won't* sing again. I don't play any instruments and I don't know anyone who I would want to start a different band with.

99

I need J. We always worked so well together, and I just don't think I'll find anyone else that I have a creative connection with like that," I replied.

It was true. That was a huge part of my sadness. He had always been so easy for me to write with because he never judged me for the things I didn't know musically. He just taught me what I needed to learn and helped me grow. He was my right hand onstage. I couldn't sing without him. It just didn't feel right.

I cried so frequently, and was so full of deep sadness about it, that I could tell it worried Julia. She began to make a genuine effort to ask about it with a little more compassion. At first, I thought this was a nice gesture on her part, and responded to her attempts to talk about it with gratitude. Then I gradually began to realize by the way she was tiptoeing around me at home constantly that her newfound compassion was stemming from fear of the way I was behaving.

I had actually scared her with this dive into despair.

She thought I was losing it. I wanted to reassure her, but I wasn't so sure that she was wrong.

About a month after that last show, I was at work one day at Julia's store and I looked up to see J's wife, Lila, coming in the door. I waved at her, and she smiled at me as she came over to the register I was working. We exchanged pleasantries, and then she asked me, "Would you have a minute to step outside to talk? I won't keep you long."

"Sure. Let me just get someone to cover my spot for a minute," I said. One of my coworkers overheard and stepped behind the register so that I could follow her outside.

As soon as we rounded the corner of the building, she turned to face me. She tucked her long dark hair behind her ear and took a deep breath.

"I need to ask you something. I need to know why... every single day for a solid month, I have walked into a room to find my husband crying over you leaving the band," she said.

This took me aback. I stared at her in shock for a moment.

'Is he doing that?" I half whispered. So, it wasn't just me that was dying over this.

"Yes. He is doing that. And in the almost twenty years that we have been together I have never seen him cry until you quit the band. He didn't even cry when his mother passed away. So, I would like to know exactly what is going on that has made him so upset about this. You need to know that if this were any other woman but you…because I know you are gay…. that I would be very…. not ok with this," she said.

It seemed to me that she was very "not ok" in the present moment anyway.

"I don't know, Lila. All I can tell you is that I've been crying every day about it too. My wife thinks I'm a fruit loop and I can't seem to keep it together or move past this either. There is nothing…inappropriate…going on between us, if that is the reassurance that you are looking for. There isn't and there never has been. We are close friends though, in a way that is hard to explain. It's just that…we were amazing at creating together. That kind of connection is very hard to let go of….at least, it has been for me," I said.

It sounded like he was having just as difficult of a time as I was.

As much as I hated to admit it, it made me happy to know that he was struggling as well.

"Well, this can't continue on. As much as it pains me to say it - I can't fix this, you are going to have to. I don't like it, but you have a piece of my husband that I don't have. I'm not musical, and he has always kept that part of his life very separate from me. Music has always felt like 'the other woman' in a lot of respects. I think that is why this is so upsetting to me… now the 'other woman' is actually *another woman*, not just a group of guys that I lose him to several nights a week. I felt pretty certain that nothing romantic was going on between you…. I am aware of your sexuality, and I also know that my husband is a very good man. I know he wouldn't do anything to hurt me or our family in that way, but I'm still jealous. I can't help it. I'm here though because I'm willing to try and get past that…for his sake. I can't bear to watch him hurt like this. For some reason, this has broken his heart in a way that I've never seen before. Will you call him? Maybe you all can figure out a way to continue music together. Maybe you could just come back to the band?" she said.

"Not possible. Unfortunately, I'm afraid I've burned that bridge for good. I don't want to have to walk back into that practice room with my tail between my legs. I do have some pride left," I said.

"Well, maybe you all could just write together or play as a duo or something. You can figure it out. Just…call him? Please? I can't stand to see him like this," she said.

I sighed heavily. Did she not think that I had been trying to figure out a way to repair this damage? I had been hurting just as deeply but couldn't seem to come up with a solution.

'Ok. I'll call him. I'm not sure that I can say anything that will help. I've been pretty devastated myself…but I'll talk to him," I said.

She gave me a hug. We talked for a few more minutes about work and the kids, and then she left.

As I walked back into work, I thought about how badly J must be hurting over this for his wife to come to me with that conversation. I also thought about how Julia had been handling the whole thing, and how she probably would have rather poked her eyeballs out with a stick rather than go ask J to play music with me again.

I was kind of jealous myself - jealous that his spouse loved him enough that she put her own issues aside because she couldn't bear to see him hurting.

I called J.

We had a very tearful, heartfelt conversation about what the last month of not playing music together had been like.

We had both been miserable.

We agreed that it was crazy to not be creating and singing together if being separated hurt this much.

"What if we just got together once a week, just to write and sing a little? Just the two of us, no band. Do you think that would be enough to make us feel better? We don't have to perform or anything, but we could still create," he offered.

"Well...it's more than we have now. I think that would be good. We could still make music, but it wouldn't be as big of a time commitment if we aren't playing shows. I think that would go better with Julia, at least. Let me think about it for a few days, and I'll run it by her and see how she feels about it, ok? I'll let you know something by Friday," I said.

We agreed that we would touch base on Friday.

I mulled it over for a few days, but I couldn't bring myself to talk to Julia because the idea of reinstating our standing argument made me sick to my stomach. The idea of just meeting once a week for music excited me tremendously though. I quit crying every five minutes, and Julia noticed. I was obviously feeling better.

When she asked me what had lifted my spirits, I blew off the question. I didn't have the guts to bring it up yet. I made up my mind I would tell her Thursday night, because I have no balls and torturing myself is one of my favorite pastimes.

It felt like the longest week EVER.

Thursday around lunchtime, I got a call from J. When I saw his name pop up I briefly worried that maybe he had changed his mind, but when I answered he sounded excited.

"Hey! Sorry...I know you are at work. I won't keep you long. I have a surprise for you though...are you sitting down?" he asked.

"No... do I need to be?" I said with a laugh.

"Maybe. I just talked to a friend, and I ended up booking us a very short gig. It's just a six-song set...we would be opening for one of my friend's bands. I told them that we were starting a new acoustic duo together and this would be our first show. It's next Saturday. Isn't that awesome?" he said. He could barely contain himself as he spoke.

"Um. Yes...that is awesome...but I haven't even talked to Julia about any of this yet. Also, I thought we decided that we wouldn't perform - just write and sing for a while. We don't even have six songs worked up that you aren't using with the band," I replied.

My heart sank. Julia was going to flip her shit. She was also now going to realize why I had suddenly perked up at home, and there was no way in a million years that she would believe that I hadn't been hiding this new show from her the whole time.

"Miss Jen… it will all be fine. We have a week to work up some songs for that set, and we can just do covers if we need to. It will be a good way to break the ice with this new project. As far as Julia goes, it's just a tiny set. Surely, she won't get too mad about that?" he said.

"She will kill me," I replied confidently.

I was right.

When I told her the news that evening, she completely and utterly lost it.

In all of our fights about music, she had never screamed at me the way she screamed at me that night.

"You couldn't even wait a MONTH to start playing music together again? What the HELL?! And you couldn't even be bothered to discuss it with me before you booked a show?!!", she yelled. I didn't even have a good argument. I knew I had handled the whole situation terribly.

I sat in silence. Our dogs had scattered when she started yelling, so I didn't even have them for backup support. She had never physically hit me before, but if she decided to in this moment, I knew I was going down. I didn't think she would ever do that, but I also had never seen her this angry before. She was shaking with rage. I stared at the floor while she railed on me.

"You have zero regard for my feelings. ZERO! Do you even love me anymore, because it sure doesn't feel like it? You just do WHAT you want to do, WHENEVER you want to do it, and you don't give a single SHIT how I feel about it," she continued.

I couldn't take it anymore. I exploded.

"I don't have to ask you how you feel about it, because I KNOW how you feel about it. You've made it perfectly clear in the LAST FOUR YEARS that you hate music. ABUNDANTLY CLEAR! I will NEVER understand why you can't just let me do what makes my heart happy. It doesn't feel like you love me either! You have literally watched me DIE over the last month since I quit the band…. and you don't care because it means I'm here. At least you 'have me,' huh? I'm devastated and depressed, but I'm home! I'm SO ANGRY WITH YOU about all of that, Julia. I have SO MUCH ANIMOSITY towards you for not just supporting me while I follow my dreams. So, to answer your question…NO. I don't love you anymore. I'm SO ANGRY with you that I don't even have room in my heart for that anymore. I care about you, I always will…. but I am not in love with you anymore," I screamed back at her.

We both stared at each other as we caught our breath.

I realized what I had said.

I also realized that I meant it.

"I'm sorry," I whispered after a long while. I wasn't taking it back, but it destroyed me to see the hurt on her face.

"Get your shit and get out. Nearly thirteen years together and you are throwing it away over some piece of shit local band? You aren't even that good, Jen. But this was. This was good once…for a very long time…until you decided that you loved singing more than you loved me. I can't even look at you right now. Get out," she said.

I packed a single bag and went to stay at my parents' house that night. I didn't know where else to go. It was a difficult conversation with them, but they were very accommodating.

Julia called me early the next morning and told me to not come back to work, and that I had until the weekend to come get the rest of my things out during work hours while she was gone.

Two weeks later, she served me with divorce papers.

I met her down at the lawyer's office with no representation, and no desire to fight with her over anything ever again.

I signed immediately and contested nothing. She kept it all, and I didn't care.

It would have been almost laughable if it weren't so tragic. She had pages and pages of things listed that she wanted, or that she was claiming as hers.

On my side of that list of "who got what" was simply my old Jeep.

My name had never been on the house or the property, so I never expected to be offered a chance at keeping those things, but I knew enough about divorce to know that I could have asked for some kind of financial support. I chose not to. There was a huge part of me that felt like not pushing the issue of splitting money or material things was the best I could do for her. I knew it wouldn't fix the hurt I had caused, but I also knew those things were very important to her. She was a practical realist. She was great with money and enjoyed the finer things in life that her business allowed her to afford. If I had insisted on taking half of everything, I knew it would have injured her far more than the already difficult truth of my falling out of love with her; it would take away her stability and lifestyle that was so important to her. Walking away from the marriage with the only thing that I walked into it with seemed the best way to offer any kind of consolation to her for the heartbreak that I had caused.

Here. Have the things, without a fight. I'm so sorry that I broke this.

As we walked out of the lawyer's office that day, she turned to me and gave me a hug.

"I really do wish you the best," she said right before she got in her car and drove away.

I remember thinking that she was acting like we were rivals on opposing basketball teams instead of longtime partners who were separating.

Good game. I know our schools hate each other and I don't want to hang out with you or anything, but I really do wish you the best.

My dusty old Jeep and I moved in with my parents until I could figure out what my next move would be.

Mom and Dad were on the porch when I broke the news to them that I was going to need a place to stay a little longer than I had anticipated. My heart was heavy, and I sat down on the porch swing across from where they were sitting with a hefty thud that made the swing chains creak.

As soon as I opened my mouth to speak, tears started streaming down my face.

"Is… is it ok if I stay here for a few months longer? Julia and I are done. I had hoped maybe we could work things out, but I just signed divorce papers… and I don't really know what my next move will be."

Mom's eyebrows raised in surprise. "You already signed papers? That seems awfully fast. Had you two already been talking about divorce before this fight?" she asked.

"No," I answered. I didn't know what else to say. I was as shocked as everyone else at the speed that this had all unfolded.

Dad chimed in, "What are you going to do about work? I assume you won't be working for her anymore either?"

"Yeah, she let me go from work too. Not that I would have wanted to continue. I can't be around her right now…but I don't really know what I'm going to do workwise at the moment," I said. I sighed heavily. I really didn't want to be answering twenty questions about all of this right now, but the plain and simple truth was that I didn't have anywhere else to go, and my parents needed to know exactly how dire things were. I felt like the fact that I was asking them to stay here should have been a huge indication to them that I was out of options.

"Well, honey, you can stay here as long as you need to until you can get back on your feet. We will have to do some rearranging in the house… it probably won't be ideal for any of us space-wise, but we will make it work," Mom said.

"Thank you," I whispered. I was deeply grateful and relieved. I searched for more words but couldn't seem to find them.

"I think you made the right choice, you know," Dad said. "It seems to me like Julia forced you to pick between her and music. You light up onstage, Jen. I've never seen anything make you that happy." Dad took a deep breath and handed me a handkerchief from his pocket before he continued. "I know you are sad and disappointed, and I'm sorry that you are hurting right now… but you know, sometimes God removes things from our lives that aren't good for us. I think maybe he just showed you some mercy. Your sexuality has always been your stumbling block. Maybe music was his way of getting you away from that," he said.

I groaned audibly. I should have known that this is how my parents would look at this loss. "A blessing." God saving their child from sexual deviance.

"Look, I know that you all think that being gay is the absolute worst thing that a person can be or do, but can we not do this right now? I'm feeling pretty brokenhearted and hopeless at the moment, and if you can't meet me here with compassion can you at least not preach at me?" I said.

Dad paused for a moment.

"I actually don't think that anymore - that homosexuality is the worst sin. I've had a lot of time to consider all of that over the years, and I don't feel the same way about it that I did when you first told us you were gay. All of us sin. We all have our shortcomings because we are human. There are people who show up at church every single Sunday who are committing adultery. I certainly don't think they are any better than someone living a homosexual lifestyle. I think sin is sin in God's eyes, and I've really been convicted over my desire to try and judge which one is worse. It's not my place. I've never thought you were a bad person, Jen. Your sexuality just makes me sad now because it's the one thing that I feel like keeps you away from God. That's why I said that. You were such a leader in the church, even at a young age… I feel like it's such a waste for you not to be serving. Maybe now that there isn't a relationship with a woman in the way, you can just try to come back to church. But even if you don't… you can stay here as long as you need. We do love you. And I'm not angry at you anymore. I haven't been for a long time," he said.

I was deeply touched.

And kind of excited that I had at least been upgraded to the same sin level as an adulterer in my dad's mind. (*Bonus level unlocked.)

It wasn't full acceptance, but it was certainly a more loving angle than I had heard him express in the past. I didn't want to pick it apart by coming back at him with all the instant points to argue that popped into my mind (like how it wasn't so much my sexuality that kept me away from the church as it was the way I had been treated over it). Besides, we had already had those arguments dozens of times, and after all that I had recently been through with Julia, I didn't really have it in me to fight with anyone else right now. I decided to just be grateful that things had shifted to a place where I didn't feel unwelcome or unloved in the presence of my parents during this very difficult transitional time. At least they were offering me a soft place to fall. I decided to simply reply with, "Thank you for letting me stay. I love you too."

I was homeless, jobless, and wife-less.

Part of me knew I deserved it. God knows I hadn't been putting my marriage first the last four years. I was deeply disappointed and sad, but once the chaotic dust began to settle another part of me began to realize that I had just been handed a magnificent opportunity for an entirely fresh new beginning.

It was the first time in my entire life that I wasn't partnered with someone. The first time every single minute decision I made didn't affect someone else in the least.

I had never even lived alone. I started to feel an excitement for the possibilities that seemed to be endless. For the first time, I was holding something in my hands that I had never touched before.

Freedom.

I wasn't even sure what it was.

What did freedom truly mean?

I hadn't consciously made this move. "Freedom" hadn't exactly felt like my choice, but had it been on some level?

I have often looked back at the strange disintegration of my marriage and marveled at the speed with which that uncoupling unfolded. On paper, it didn't make sense that a relationship that had lasted for nearly thirteen years (and had been fought for and over for a third of it) could simply evaporate in a few weeks.

In terms of alignment though, it was textbook.

My divorce was my first masterclass in the ways of the universe.

When the universe knows it's time for you to move, it simply moves you.

It doesn't move you because you did anything wrong.

It doesn't move you to punish you.

It doesn't even move you to reward you.

It moves you only (and always) at the exact moment that you change your vibration to align with something other than where you are sitting.

Vibrational alignment is a funny thing.

When you are a vibrational match to something, it's in your life.

When you are no longer a match, it leaves.

It exits as quickly as it entered to make room for the next thing that you are aligning with to come in.

"Divine timing" was a term I heard often in church growing up, and it was used almost always as a way to make someone feel better when they were seemingly stuck in a situation that they weren't happy with. Much like the conversation I had just had with my dad, where he was seemingly convinced that God had taken away my marriage because it was displeasing to him. It was an aspect of God that fit nicely with the "punishment and reward" Santa-Claus-type of God that the church had already introduced us to at a young age. If you behaved in a way that was pleasing to the Lord, then when he woke up on the good side of the bed one morning and felt like it, he would reward you by bringing something amazing into your life.

Until that day came, you were basically just out of luck and needed to sit there with your mouth shut and be grateful for the shitty situation you were living in because it could be worse. (Don't make God angry or it will be.)

The more I think through the cheap gumball machine version of faith that I was handed as a youth, the angrier it makes me. Christian fundamentalists constantly belittle the power of God far more than the atheists that they so readily condemn. If they should be afraid of anything, it should be that.

They should fear underestimating the Almighty, not because they fear the wrath, but because they should fear missing out on all of the wonders that he is capable of.

God doesn't only move with power when he is angry.

If we are going to make the grand claim that God cares about us as an individual, then shouldn't we believe that he cares about us all of the time?

Wouldn't that mean that he would be constantly working in our lives - moving just underneath the surface to orchestrate and direct us every single second?

Or does he only pop into our lives occasionally to put a lump of coal in our stocking or bring us a Christmas present based on how pleasing (or displeasing) our behavior has been to him?

Please.
God cares about us much more than that.
He knows how we feel one hundred percent of the time.
He is responding to us each and every second.

Actual divine timing, as I have come to understand and experience it works in a much more multileveled and personal way.

It all has to do with energy and vibration.

Everything in the universe is made up of energy (including you) and vibrates at a certain frequency. The highest frequency that exists is agape love. (That is, the omnipotent, unchanging, and unconditional love of God.)

The lowest vibrational frequency exists in the energy of Fear.

They are polar opposites.

Sound familiar?

(It should, unless you took a pee break and accidentally skipped part of the first few pages of this book.)

The energy that we emit out into the universe vibrates at various points on the spectrum of the love/fear scale constantly, whether or not we are aware of it. For example, anger, grief, boredom, hopefulness, and joy all emit a different frequency. God…or the Universe, or Source energy, or Spirit (whatever name makes the most sense to you and resonates with you is fine to use for the purposes of this) responds and connects with us through those vibrational energies.

It is ever-present.

Constantly listening and responding to our energy that we are sending out via our thoughts and *especially* our emotions.

In our life, we can only and always receive experiences (relationships, inspiration, even material things) that we are a vibrational match for.

The best example or way to describe this that I can think of is a radio.

If you want to hear country music, you have to tune your radio to a country station, correct?

If you change your mind and decide you are now in the mood for some soft pop, you have to adjust your radio to a different frequency. You change your tuner to a different station.

The Universe works exactly like that.

If you are tuned into the frequency of "gratitude", for example, the soundtrack of your life will be one of thankfulness. You will keep receiving more and more things to be grateful for. As long as you stay in that vibration gratitude will continue to pour out of the speakers of the universe and accompany your life.

The same goes with the frequency of "worry." If you tap into that vibration and stay there for a while, you will be inundated with all kinds of things to worry about. The universe will be sure to provide you with all kinds of new experiences that fit the programming of that channel because it appears as though you want to listen to that.

After all, you set your tuner there, didn't you?

We all have our tuners set to different channels, and we stay there for various lengths of time before we decide we want something different.

Some people never change the station. Ever.

They are just comfortable where they are and they don't know what the other stations might play so they just don't ever touch the dial.

They've listened to eighties music their whole life, and they don't know any of the new artists over on the pop station, so they just keep singing along to the songs they know.

The universe just keeps bringing them Whitesnake and Duran Duran because that's what they want to listen to. It's comfortable and familiar. Safe.

It's also pretty boring, but most of us will take boring if it comes along with "safe."

However, for most people, every now and then something will happen that makes us shift our vibration a little. Sometimes it's something we choose to do. We get tired of working the same old soul-sucking job every day, so we decide to go back to school to try a different path, or we move to a new city to be closer to our spouse's family. Whatever it is that sparks the change comes from our own willful decision.

When we do that the realm of possibilities for our lives opens up.

Our vibration shifts from the radio station of "dissatisfaction" to "hopefulness" and the universe switches up the program accordingly.

Other times something entirely beyond our control occurs and shakes up our radio and we land on a station we have never listened to before.

Maybe something like a divorce, for example.

You might have been cruising along listening to the "conflict" station for thirteen years or so when suddenly you hit a pothole and your radio skips over to the "freedom" station just long enough for you to hear a couple of songs.

The universe is riding shotgun and notices that you are loving this new sound.

You switch the station back to "conflict" quickly though because you know every word of those songs and you can sing along.

Still…you can't seem to get those new songs out of your head. The melodies were so intoxicating…

The universe saw that glimmer in your eye. It can tell that you secretly want to listen to that new station, so as you round the curve up ahead with both hands on the wheel, it reaches over, changes the station for you, and pulls the knob off of the radio.

You want to protest, but you know that your shotgun buddy was only responding to you. It saw you light up a little when you heard that new station. It heard you singing those songs in your head. It knew you were ready for a change.

Divine timing works just like that.

It's not that the new music gets delivered when God decides he is ready to change the station….it happens when you finally decide you are.

When you shift your energy, you indicate that you are ready for something different.

You align with something else…something new…something that you are not currently experiencing.

The old simply falls away because you are no longer receiving that signal.

The Universe allows the new to come rushing in with a whole different set of melodies for you to listen to.

When you move, the Universe supports you every single time.

The night that J and I talked in the parking lot of my last show, something big had happened in my vibrational field. I had begun to think about possibilities that I had never considered before. For the first time in thirteen years, I had assessed my life and asked myself if I was happy with where I was. Could I go home that night knowing that I had chosen to walk away from singing and my best friend and live with the consequences? Could I be content sitting at home in a life I had grown to resent, all the while wondering what "might have been" possible if I had chosen a different path?

I couldn't.

I had cracked just wide enough open to make space for something new.

I had turned the tuner just slightly enough that I picked up the crackle of a new station.

The Universe felt it and jumped in to help me.

The signal sharpened, the old station fell out of earshot, and as quickly as that......I was listening to a whole new set of songs.

Divine timing. The dance of the cosmos.

When you move, the Universe supports you.

Every. Single. Time.

Part Four

wildfire – *noun*

: a large, unplanned, and uncontrolled fire that
spreads quickly over combustible material

114

Chapter Nine

J AND I WERE walking together downtown after one of our first performances together as a newly formed acoustic duo. It had been a few months since we had started writing together again, and my divorce was being processed. I was filling him in on all that had transpired between Julia and me over the last few weeks and was lamenting to him the absolute overwhelm I was feeling from the sudden massive changes that I was in the middle of. My life was completely upended. I had decided to go back to dog grooming because it was a skill that I had that I knew was always needed. I had been able to find a job almost instantly, once I decided that was going to be the most beneficial move. Grooming also paid extremely well, so I was already putting aside deposit money for an apartment so that I could move as soon as possible. While I was grateful that my parents had opened their home back up to me when I needed it, they were already driving me a bit crazy, and I was chomping at the bit to find a place of my own.

J listened attentively as we walked. We came upon a brewery that had outside picnic tables. He nodded to an empty one and asked if he could buy me a beer. I agreed to it, and he handed me his guitar. I took it to the table and waited while he went inside and got our drinks. He came back out and sat down across from me, and I asked him how he thought the show went. I was tired of talking about the divorce and just wanted some relaxing conversation with a beer and my best friend.

I took a few sips as we recounted the highlights of the show to each other. We both thought it had gone extremely well. This new acoustic singer-songwriter approach that we were trying felt like a perfect fit for us. We were still building a setlist, but we both agreed that it was coming along very nicely.

As we talked, I slowly became aware that J wasn't drinking his beer.

He seemed nervous, and even though the conversation was light, and we were laughing a lot, something just seemed…off. I could tell he was thinking

115

about something else. I wondered if I had burdened him too much with all of my depressing divorce-talk earlier.

"You ok? You seem a little distant," I asked finally.

He looked at me, took a deep breath, and then looked down. He stared at the table for what felt like an eternity.

When he finally met my gaze again there was a rawness and a vulnerability present in his eyes that I'd never seen before in the 20 years that we had been friends. The depth of it almost swallowed me. It was similar to the way that he had looked at me that night outside of the theater when I quit the band, but this was more than just sadness. I watched him struggle internally with something. I physically saw it behind his eyes, and it scared me that he was unguardedly allowing me to see so much of him in this turmoil.

"I need to tell you something, and I don't know how you will react. I'm scared to death that you will never speak to me again if I say it," he whispered.

I was taken aback. What could he possibly say that would make me not talk to him? Hadn't we just proven through continuing our music together that we both valued this friendship so much that we would do anything to maintain it?

"J...you can tell me anything. I thought you knew that. There is nothing you could say to me that would ever make me stop talking to you. You stood by me when I made the stupid decision to quit the band. Do you really think I wouldn't be there for you in the same way no matter what this is about?" I said. I noticed that his hands were shaking. I had seen such a different side of him these last few months. This always confident, seemingly fearless man who I had always thought of as unshakable...was trembling.

"Please tell me. You can tell me. Whatever it is," I added. I leaned forward and nodded reassuringly, though his palpable fear was unnerving to me. Whatever he was about to say must be really bad. I tried to brace myself for whatever might come next.

He took another deep breath, holding my gaze with that searching, pleading rawness that was unraveling me.

"I know we have been friends for a very long time. The music and creating with you the last few years have been so special to me, and when you left the band, it made me realize some things. I...I thought I had lost you. I thought you were gone out of my life for good, and nothing has ever hurt me like that before. My heart was just completely broken," he said. Tears were forming in his eyes now, but he continued.

"It took me a while to come to terms with this because it's so messy... but you are gorgeous, and the most intelligent and talented person I've ever met. The connection I have with you is like nothing else. I love you, Jen. I'm *in love* with you, and I hope I never have to know what life without you feels like again."

I was speechless. Hot tears were slipping down my cheeks now too. I certainly hadn't expected him to say that. He was searching my face for a response, but I couldn't find words. I just stared at him with my mouth slightly open from shock.

"I know…I *know* that you are gay. And I am married. And that this is probably the most fucked up thing I could ever say to you, especially now, with all that you are going through. But I've had a lot of time to think about it, and I've cried a lot over it, and I just couldn't go on without telling you. I'm *so* in love with you. Please, Jen. Please say something." The tears were falling steadily from both of us now as he held my gaze

"I can't lose you again," he said earnestly as he slid his hand across the table to grab mine.

The instant that our hands entwined it was like a bolt of lightning exploded between them. We both pulled away in shock and he knocked his beer over as he jumped away from me. We both stared at our hands and then at each other in disbelief. My entire being was still vibrating from the surge of energy that had just gone through what felt like every single cell of my body.

"What the hell?! Jen! You felt that too, didn't you?" he frantically asked as he grabbed napkins to try and mop up the spilled beer.

I nodded. What the hell, indeed. What had just happened? I still had no words; I was reeling from both his confession and the sharp physical jolt that had just occurred between us. That hadn't been just a mild static shock like you would experience after pulling a sweater over your head in the wintertime. It had blown through my entire being like a tsunami of electricity.

"Just so I don't feel so crazy…what, exactly, did that feel like to you? I can still feel it, kind of.", he asked as he checked his own hand again for physical evidence.

I could only think of one thing that it compared to.

"It felt like grabbing an electric fence. I felt it all through my body…I can still feel it too, even in my teeth," I answered shakily.

We stared at each other, a little warily. He slowly inched his hand toward mine again. When he got a few inches away from my fingers I began to feel a warm buzz, almost as if it were radiating from his hand.

He hesitated. I knew he felt it too.

He slid closer and closer until finally our fingertips were touching. Everything in me felt alive. It was as though we were both crackling with a fire that we were creating simply by touching. I slid my hand fully into his and the lightning bolt of energy happened again, but this time, even though we both jumped, neither of us let go.

It was as if the energy enveloped us both. We sat there radiating, glowing together in what felt like a halo of electricity. My heart rippled and swelled and felt like it might explode, but I didn't want it to stop. The feeling was exquisite.

I was staring into his eyes for what simultaneously felt like the first time and the hundredth time. There was a truth there that I couldn't deny.

I thought back over the last few months and the searing pain that I had felt when I had been separated from him after I had quit the band. The way that it had destroyed us both hadn't made sense to anyone. Both of our spouses had thought it was odd. I had just chalked it all up to simply the agony of losing music because it was the thing that mattered most to me, but now…sitting here holding his hand in a warm electric buzz I wondered if that had been entirely true. Had it been losing music? Or had losing him been the reason that my heart had hurt so badly?

I had never even looked at a man before as a romantic possibility.

I had never been attracted to a boy, let alone loved one. It had literally never even crossed my mind. I had lived my entire life in a world where men only existed for me in platonic friendships.

I thought back to J's wife coming by my workplace after I quit the band because she thought there must have been something deeper going on between us than just music. I would have found the whole conversation laughable at the time if I hadn't been inexplicably wounded more deeply than I had anticipated as well. I hadn't been able to figure out why I felt the way I did, but it certainly wasn't funny.

Had I unwittingly lied to her? Nothing romantic had ever been talked about between us, and no lines had ever been crossed, that much was true. However, was it possible that there had been feelings buried below the surface that I simply hadn't given any credence to because I hadn't recognized them for what they were? As I sat there staring into his eyes, I felt pieces of the puzzle begin to click into place.

It made sense now why I had been so destroyed.

I knew him better than I had ever known anyone. We had created something truly beautiful together through our music, and it was much deeper than just the songs we were writing.

There was something here that was much more than friendship, and now that he had brought it to my attention I couldn't unsee it for what it was.

I was in love with him.

The realizations began to pour in. How had I been so blind? Why had I not realized that the reason why my heart had broken when I left the band was because I loved him? It made perfect sense. It was why I couldn't seem to get past the pain until we were back together again. I hadn't even looked into his eyes until that last night at the theater, and I remembered that once I did something had stirred in me that I hadn't known was there. It was so unfamiliar - I hadn't even thought I was capable of feeling anything for a man that wasn't friendship. I had written it off as just feeling bad for hurting him, but as I sat here with my eyes locked to his once more, I realized for the first time with clarity exactly what was happening.

We were in love with each other.

There was a fire here between us. The lightning jolt between the touch of our hands had just awakened me to it.

I felt like a fool for not seeing it sooner.

There was so much to consider. He had been right in stating that this was messy.

It was *sooooo* messy. I let my thoughts briefly flip through all of the reasons why this conversation alone was a terrible idea, but none of them could overpower the one thought that kept echoing loudly in my mind.

I was in love with him.

I was in love with a *boy*.

What did this even mean about me? About my sexuality? About my past? About… everything? I honestly couldn't even wrap my head around it. There was going to be so much to figure out here, but I realized that I didn't even care because all that mattered in that moment was the energy radiating between us. He had pulled me into the depths of those steel blue eyes, and my heart was fluttering like a butterfly fighting its way out of the cocoon.

I finally found the words to answer him.

"I'm in love with you too, J. You won't ever lose me again, I promise. I don't know what this will look like, but we will figure it out together, ok?" I whispered.

And then, because it was so different to my tongue and I wanted to taste it I added, "I love you…boy."

I saw a look of relief and tenderness wash over him as I spoke. I reached across the table to wipe a tear from his face, and he placed his hand gently over mine as I touched his cheek.

I suddenly heard very distinctly a voice that I instantly recognized but hadn't thought of in years. It was so loud and so clear in my ear that it startled me.

"You will fall deeply in love with a man named Jay……and it will change everything."

I jumped slightly as I heard it and J looked at me quizzically. The memory came flooding back to me of the moment that I had heard those words for the first time while sitting in Bobby Drinnon's office. I had thought it ridiculous at the time, yet here I sat holding the hand of the fruit of the prophecy.

Touché, Mr. Drinnon. Touché.

Two weeks later

We had been practicing as a duo at the same practice space we had used for the full band before I quit. It was a barn that was on J's best guy friend's property; in the country and private enough that there wasn't anyone close by for the music levels to bother. The downside was that there was no heating or air, so we (and the instruments) were at the mercy of the seasons.

Late September can be particularly balmy in East Tennessee, and it's often as hot then as it is in mid-July. This particular night was one of those nights.

We were both sweaty and hot and had removed every piece of clothing possible that didn't cross the line as indecent.

I had arrived in a spaghetti strap sundress with a denim jacket over it and cowboy boots.

I was down to just the sundress and bare feet.

J had taken off his pearl snap, newsboy cap, and shoes as well, and was now just in a white undershirt and his ripped jeans.

I had brought a bottle of whiskey to practice, but there was no cooler or ice, so it was less than refreshing, and in all truth was just adding to the flush and the heat in our cheeks.

Well, that and the fact that we couldn't take our eyes off of one another.

It was smoldering.

Since our talk that night at the brewery we had been doing an interesting dance around and in between our feelings. We were in love with each other. It had been put on the table, and we both acknowledged it sitting there like a small creature between us, yet we seemed unsure of what to do with it. There was a tenderness surrounding it…almost as if we didn't want to scare it away.

We were gentle with it.

No sudden moves. No leaps into the unknown. No loud noises or words that might run it off.

But the feelings spilled out through our eyes, and now quite frequently, through our hands.

Since that first night that we held hands, we had been surprised and delighted to find that the powerful surge of energy that had nearly knocked us over the first time now pulsed between our fingers every single time we touched. We began to take any opportunity to hold hands that we could, just to feel the rush.

Every time we were close when we were talking, our fingers would end up laced together. Walking to and from anywhere. In the car. Between songs at practice. If he wasn't reaching for my hand, I found myself reaching for his.

It was the only physical intimacy that we allowed. There was an unspoken agreement that we both honored.

However, our eyes went everywhere our hands didn't go.

We marveled at each other constantly. It was as though we had never seen each other before that night that we had confessed our love. It felt like with that disclosure, a permission slip had been granted to explore each other in ways that we hadn't considered prior.

I now often felt him watching my every move.

I would turn to find him unapologetically staring into my eyes so deeply that it caught me off guard every single time.

I found myself watching him do things that I'd seen him do a thousand times (like smoking a cigarette or playing guitar) with a new awe and appreciation.

There was a new reverence for each other that hadn't been present before.

Now when we talked to one another, it was with the gentle intent of peeling back another layer…seeing each other a little deeper. Over the years of friendship, our conversations had always been fun, but fairly light. We knew each other well in most ways, and more extensively where creating music was concerned, but now we were beginning to dig a little farther down with each interaction.

This particular night, songwriting was proving to be a challenge. We were about a verse in on a new song that wasn't working. The heat, both in the barn and between us, was distracting and we were both finding it difficult to focus.

I stood up, exasperated, and walked over to the whiskey bottle that I had sat on an amp earlier.

"Do you want another shot? Maybe it will make us feel better, or at the very least, make us care less about how hot it is in here," I said.

He put his notebook down and stood up as well.

"Yeah, I'll do another shot with you."

I poured the Gentleman Jack into two shot glasses carefully. I picked them up and when I turned, I nearly spilled them both down the front of J's shirt because he was now standing right in front of me. I hadn't realized that he had walked up behind me so close.

"Oh, shit! I'm sorry!" I said as we both laughed.

He slid his hand up my arm, steadying me. When he got to my hand, he slid his fingers between mine briefly before he took the glass from me.

"Let's take a shot of whiskey….and kiss," he said, tentatively.

My eyes widened.

My pulse quickened.

Did he just say that?

He raised his free hand and gently brushed a damp curl back from my cheek. His touch sent a shiver through my body.

"Only if you want to…." he added gently. He was looking through my eyes, into my soul, searching intently for my response.

There was no hiding the "yes" that was emanating from my entire being.

I raised my glass to his and tapped it with a soft clink. We both threw back the shots in unison and I could hear my heartbeat thundering in my ears after I swallowed.

He sat his glass back down on the amp and wrapped his arm around my waist.

His other hand he put on my cheek, and his thumb caressed my bottom lip gently. He separated my lips with it ever so slightly, and then leaned in and replaced his thumb with his mouth.

If I thought the electric current between our hands was fire, it was nothing compared to the jolt that went through me when his lips touched mine. We both inhaled sharply, and pulled away briefly from the shock of it, but then like two magnets we pulled back into each other as if we had no other choice.

He kissed me slowly at first, tasting my lips tenderly. Then he slid both of his hands to hold my head between them, entwining his fingers in my hair. I found myself melting into the deepest, most passionate kiss that I had ever had. His tongue found mine and the rhythm between us was intoxicating.

The way he drank me in made me weak. The tender way his strong hands held me was so new and wondrous to me. It was nothing like kissing a woman.

I felt his beard brushing my face and found myself surprised at its roughness in comparison to the softness of his lips.

I felt safe in his hands.

I surrendered to him completely.

It seemed to go on forever and I never wanted it to end.

When he finally pulled back, I was reeling. I couldn't speak.

He was still inches from me. We continued to stare into each other's eyes in wonder. He began to gently caress my lips and face while he whispered to me.

"I've wanted to do that for so long, Jen."

"Since that night at the brewery?" I managed to somehow croak out hoarsely. I was still unsteady and finding it hard to recover. I had never, in my 36 years, been kissed like that. I had never felt *so much*. It was like everything in me was glowing. I wanted more, but his answer caught me off guard.

"No…I've wanted to do that for much, much longer than that. I've known you for almost twenty years. That whole time it was like…you were…this book…in a glass case. I always admired it, every single time I walked by. I thought the cover was beautiful, but I couldn't touch it. Sometimes when I would pass by the case, the book would be open, and I could read a page or two. I fell in love with the words, but that's all I ever got to see - a page or two at a time.

I feel like you just opened up the case and put the book in my hands…and I can't wait to read every single word," he said.

I stared at him, touched to the core by his words. It was the most romantic thing I'd ever heard. I could barely find the breath to answer.

"Oh, J…that was the most beautiful thing anyone has ever said to me. If I wasn't already hopelessly and completely in love with you that would have done it."

I laughed, even though tears slipped from my eyes as I said it.

I had never been more moved.

I had never felt more seen.

As he pulled me in to kiss me again, I had the realization that I was already in deeper with him than I had ever been with anyone.

He already had more of my heart than anyone had ever had.

I already trusted him more than I had ever trusted another human in my life.

And we had only just begun.

Chapter Ten

Five weeks later
11/11/17

TRYING TO DESCRIBE sex with J feels a bit like trying to take a picture of the moon with your phone camera. You are trying to document the splendor of the colors of the moonlight, the subtle nuances of her surface, the way the very atmosphere explodes with her energy and ethereal glow. What you end up with is a tiny white dot in a sea of black that could easily be mistaken for an accidental snapshot of the bottom of your purse where the light is reflecting off of your keys.

But I will try.

The first word that comes to mind stems from my earliest understanding of "rebirth."

Baptism.

I willingly allowed myself to be submerged and arose a new woman with an entirely new understanding. A clean slate. A fresh start.

We talked to DEATH the actual act of physicality before it happened. I had to come to terms with my lesbian man-hater thirty-six-year-old self and her first date U-Haul full of baggage. We had to have a man-to-man outside in the parking lot about it. I told her I loved him. I told her that his gender didn't matter.

She pointed out that the only naked man I'd ever seen was in the paintings and sculptures of my 42 art history books that I'd written pages about in my bachelor's program, and that I hadn't the slightest fucking idea of what to do with any of that equipment. She said that was cute when you're 16, but not when you are 36.

She had a point.

I had expressed these concerns to J.

I told him that I hadn't the least bit of experience with a boy and that if we were to touch sexually that he would have to teach me what to do.

His response: "My God, that's so… endearing. And so hot."

We wrote what was, in my humble opinion, our best song during that time. The words have nothing to do with that sentiment, but the title is "Teach Me." We could barely introduce that song on stage together for a very long time without blushing.

The sex talks had gone on for weeks.

What would this mean, for both of us?

I had very strong emotions tied to my identity when it came to sex.

What would this sudden shift mean for my sexuality, and more importantly, for my relationship with my family? I had fought for nearly two decades with my family to find acceptance and love because of my lesbianism.

I had been so certain of my sexuality that I had gone toe to toe with the people that I loved the most for years and demanded that they accept me. I had insisted that I be included back into the fold regardless of my love for women. It had never really come to the level of acceptance that I had hoped. My wife of nearly 13 years had never even come to a Christmas with my family. In many ways, I felt like I was still fighting. Even my recent brief stint of living with them had been peppered with conversations that indicated that full acceptance was still out of reach.

And now I was so in love with a goddamn boy that I could barely breathe, and was sure enough about my attraction that I was willing to take it further physically?

I found it extremely difficult to process.

How was I to proceed here? Obviously, we couldn't tell anyone for a myriad of reasons so it's not like I planned to show up at my parents' house with balloons and announce that I had finally made all of their dreams for me come true and fucked a boy. But eventually, if my and J's relationship continued this would be a discussion that I would have to have with them.

I feared that conversation would end up making it look as though I had put our entire family through the most strenuous thing we had ever endured as a unit……for nothing.

It was a lot to take into consideration.

J was quite a bit more fluid with his sexuality than I was. He never did really grasp exactly how big of an issue his penis was to me. (Pun intended.)

We were discussing it one day (my issue, not his penis), and he took my face in his hands and said simply,

"Miss Jen. People don't fall in love with genders. They fall in love with people."

He clearly didn't understand, so I tried to put it the only way I could think of that might make him see.

"What if I were a man? Wouldn't that be an issue for you to come to terms with? Wouldn't you waffle a bit when it came to physical intimacy?"

His reply was simultaneously maddening and flattering.

"If I felt about a man the exact same way that I feel about you, I would have zero issue sleeping with him."

If anyone but J had said that to me, I would have just thought they were exceedingly desperate to get in my pants, but I knew he meant it. That's just how he was. Gender and sexuality were non-issues for him.

Of course I would end up with the one straight boy who would be fine fucking another boy as long as there were feelings involved.

As bad as I thought my side of the issue was, his side wasn't any better. In fact, it was much worse. Married to his high school sweetheart with two beautiful children, he had a stable and solid life that he had worked hard to build. He was respected and loved and had been comfortable for a very long time. Like myself, he had suddenly found himself in a situation that he didn't know what to do with.

It flipped everything he thought he knew on its head.

He didn't want to lose his children. He didn't want to hurt his lifelong partner who had been nothing but loyal to him. He didn't want his dad to think less of him.

He had no one to talk to about it but me, and that was just painful and confusing for both of us.

The tears he shed.

My heart shattered for him, but I also hurt for many of the same reasons. I adored his children and didn't want them to be hurt by our actions.

And *Lila*.

I couldn't even think about what this would do to her without crying. Prior to music, I had been closer to Lila than to J. I never in a million years would have thought that I would ever hurt my friend for any reason, let alone this one.

"This will destroy Lila," J said with his head in his hands.

"I know," I whispered. "What are we going to do? I love her too. Do you want to stop? We could just pretend like nothing ever happened…go back to just being friends and music partners."

He raised his head and his red, swollen eyes met mine. "How?? How could we ever walk away from this now? I can't turn off all that I feel for you and just be friends. Could you actually do that?" he asked.

"No," I said as I looked away. "But betraying Lila isn't a clear-cut front-runner in the options department either. I know that you don't want to hurt her, or anyone in your family… and I don't either. There is no good solution here, love." It was true. I had no helpful answer. It hurt me for all parties involved. "On the bright side, my dad just informed me that he now thinks adultery and homosexuality are equal sins, so *my* family won't hate me more than they already do. We can just focus all of our attention on your family's reaction."

My attempt at lightening the mood only extracted a halfhearted smile from J.

"Well, that's something anyway."

Not much, all things considered.

Several times over those weeks we sat together, playing with the energy between our hands…

"How close do we have to be before we feel the shockwave…there? No…farther away? Still there?"

We conducted our very own Bill Nye experiments to distract us from the hard stuff until we couldn't anymore.

We would kiss until combustion seemed the only outcome, and then we would back off and talk about all of the reasons why we couldn't go farther.

Too much explanation. Too many hearts hurt. We would end up back in the same position each time. Hands entwined, tears streaming down our faces.

One day I laughingly told him, "Well…if we ever do have sex, no one can ever accuse us of jumping blindly into bed together. We've talked this to death. If it happens, there is no excuse. We've weighed the pros and cons and we've already grieved and celebrated both sides. We've already decided to betray who we betray and to be uplifted in whatever way we are uplifted. There's nothing left to talk about. No one can accuse us of negligence. We can never claim it was an accident."

He agreed, with deep sadness in his eyes.

No matter how we looked at it, there was no easy solution.

The night it finally happened we were in my new little loft apartment, where he had made a habit of sneaking over to before or after his theatre rehearsals to see me for a bit. That theatre was our small community theatre and I had done so many shows there by now it felt like a second home. It was exactly .4 miles from my new place.

The hours surrounding rehearsal times became the best part of my day. He would come by for a kiss, a touch, a word, or just to bounce a song or idea from rehearsal off of me to see what I thought.

He had just finished a show a few days prior to this particular night, but because it was a volunteer theatre the cast was always expected to clean up and paint, etc. for the new show that would begin rehearsal soon after. This meant he could claim to be there for an extended amount of time, and it wouldn't be questioned.

He cut out of cleaning early and appeared on my doorstep, guitar in hand.

I was delighted to see him with it because it meant that he intended to stay for a while.

He came in and we started practicing almost immediately, working on a new song that we had started the week before.

We were on my new couch laughing and singing together, when suddenly he caught my gaze and we both got very quiet.

He put his guitar down and stood up and put his hand out to ask me for a dance.

I loved dancing with him. He was an amazing dancer, and it's something that we had always done, even as friends.

When we had the full band, oftentimes we had an opening act, and he would pull me out onto the floor with him while they played. I knew how to two-step and at some point, showed him how to lead, not that he needed much more than the steps. He picked up on that in one dance and before I knew it, he was leading me like a champ every time we got the opportunity.

After our confession of love for one another, we danced so often that it just became something that we did as a couple.

J and I. We sang and we danced. We created and we glowed.

It was magical.

One night, around this time period I went to dinner with J and Lila after a show. Somehow dancing came up in conversation and she said, decidedly…

"Yeah…we don't dance. Neither of us really like it."

I looked at him and raised an eyebrow. He looked at me sadly, shook his head to indicate that I shouldn't say anything, and shrugged.

My heart broke, more than a little.

My boy was a dancer. He loved it, and he was amazing at it.

I considered myself lucky to be in his arms, anytime I got the chance. I'm not a follower unless I feel safe, and I would follow him across any dance floor.

How long had he hidden that part of himself before I came along?

I didn't know. It felt like a big thing to keep secret given how often he danced with me.

How could she not know this about him?

I wondered what other things he had shared with me that he had kept silent before.

That particular night at my loft as he stood before me with his hand out, I looked in his eyes and I knew that he was asking me for more than just a slow dance. I put my hand in his as I had done so many times before, and he slid me through a turn and stopped me in front of him.

He grabbed the hem of my dress and began to raise it up, but then paused.

"Is this ok?" he asked gently.

I nodded.

He kept his eyes locked on mine as he slipped the dress up my body and over my head.

As he let it fall to the ground he stepped back slightly, and I watched him take in every inch of me with his gaze.

His warm hands touched my sides and slowly found their way to the back of my bra where he expertly unhooked it.

I let it fall to the ground without a fight.

"You're so gorgeous, Miss Jen. Even more beautiful than I could have imagined," he whispered, his breath a bit ragged.

He kneeled to the ground in front of me and slipped my panties off slowly.

"Clean shaven? I wouldn't have guessed that," he said with an amused smirk.

"Why? Do I give off '70s bush vibes?" I retorted back.

We both laughed.

"Not at all, ma'am," he answered as he kissed my stomach softly.

He looked up at me from the ground and stared deeply into my eyes as he undid the buttons on of his own shirt. I pushed it down his shoulders once it was open and he let it fall to the floor. He slowly stood back up as he undid his belt, and then slipped off his pants and underwear.

My love. Naked, and in front of me.

I looked at him, unabashedly.

He was beautiful.

His long, muscular limbs were softly chiseled and defined. He had always seemed so physically strong to me, and now I could see why. His body was solid and perfectly proportioned. His broad shoulders that I had often held onto while dancing, tapered only slightly from his chest down to his waist. His torso was thick, but not fat. I realized he could probably move me or pick me up easily if he wanted to.

This was new territory. The women I had been with had all been smaller than me.

I always had the upper hand, strength-wise. At nearly six feet tall, I realized that for the first time in my life, I felt small and feminine in my nakedness. Standing beside him made me naturally want to yield to his physical power almost subconsciously.

His strength wasn't the only new thing I was witnessing.

Though I had no other experience with naked boys to compare the size of his dick to, I had certainly been on the wearing and receiving end of many a strap-on in my lesbian escapades. I had always felt like there was probably no way that dildos were good representations of actual real-life penis size; I assumed that they were likely exaggerated in size since straight women always seemed to me to be talking about how "size matters."

I found myself proven wrong in that assumption. The cock in front of me put the size of my strap-on to shame. I remember thinking in that moment that it was huge, but that it somehow perfectly fit the rest of his naked frame. Thick and solid, like the rest of him. I was more than a little intimidated, but still found him exquisite.

It shocked me how powerfully I was attracted to him. How much I wanted to touch him. All of him. He was the first naked boy I'd ever seen in the flesh. He stood there before me not only naked but wanting me with an energy I'd never felt from another human of either gender. Desire emanated from him like warmth from a fire. It unsteadied me that I could feel it radiating from him as if it were a tangible thing.

He pulled me close and kissed me, and though we had kissed dozens of times before, the sensation of his bare skin next to mine did something to me that felt similar to an internal firework show.

I stepped back, quivering.

"Are you okay?", he asked earnestly. "Are you afraid?

I shook my head no.

"Not afraid of you…I could never be afraid of you. I am a little afraid of this, though. What is this, J? Why does it feel like it's everything? I'm scared of that. I'm afraid of the power that already exists between us. Just feeling you against me was like the energy between our hands…. times ten. The thought of more feels a little terrifying."

He spun me around to face away from him. He put both hands on my shoulders and marched me to my bed like a child being put in time-out.

He put his hand behind my head and laid me down on the side of my bed gently.

He kissed me all over- first my forehead, and then my nose, and then my mouth, hungrily. Then he made his way to my neck as he laced his fingers in my hair (my absolute weakness), and I felt myself yield to him even more. Suddenly, my nipples were in his mouth, and he sucked first one, and then the other in the most beautiful display of tenderness and desire that I'd ever felt. He looked up at me as he did this, and I remember feeling slightly shocked to see a man's face from this angle, yet simultaneously smitten by his eyes.

This wasn't just any man. This was my boy. My chosen love. It felt powerful and sensual and beyond electrifying.

He kissed a trail from my large breasts down to my navel, and then my hip bones.

I could feel my wetness dripping down from me to the bedsheets. It was soaking the spot where I was lying.

He finally took one of his thick fingers and gently slid it down the slit to my pussy, found it soaking wet and throbbing, and whispered, "Miss Jen…you're so wet…I want to taste you so badly. May I?"

I could barely speak but somehow managed to get out, "Yes, please."

The spark of that first touch of his tongue against my clit nearly sent me off of the back of the bed.

I gasped as he took more of me in his mouth, slowly licking in perfect momentum.

It struck me suddenly that I could feel his beard on the softest parts of my inner thighs, and I giggled softly. He looked up at me quizzically.

"Your beard…I'm just not used to feeling that……" I said.

"Uncomfortable?", he asked.

"Not at all. Just different. I love it actually…please… don't stop."

He responded by putting his hands on my hips and pulling my entire body closer to his face. I briefly marveled at his strength but was soon distracted entirely by the pulsating rhythm of his tongue. My back involuntarily arched as waves of pleasure rocked my body. It felt like he was devouring me in the most beautiful way. So tender, but so intense. Every vibration I put out he picked up on, and soon he fell into the perfect pressure and the perfect movement.

"There…" I whispered, but there was no need. He already knew. He continued to hold steady in perfect execution and it took no time before I cried out in climax. I writhed in pleasure, panting and throbbing, as he cupped his hand to me where his mouth had been and felt each spasm as it slowed.

He smiled up at me from between my legs.

"Jesus, J…that was *fucking incredible*………" I couldn't even formulate a thought. I had never orgasmed so quickly before.

He raised himself up in front of me at the foot of the bed, stroking his huge cock.

He had grown harder and now appeared to be even bigger than he was before, and I suddenly found myself feeling intimidated once again.

He locked eyes with me, and I felt him search my entire being with his gaze.

"Are you ok? Do you want to do this still?" he asked.

I looked at him, naked and vulnerable before me, knowing that whatever I said he would defer to. I could call it off, and he would be the most perfect gentleman that had ever existed. He would put his clothes back on and leave, and I somehow knew that it wouldn't even change anything between us.

But I couldn't do that. I wanted him too. Maybe even more than he wanted me. Definitely more than I'd ever wanted anything in my life.

"I need to feel you, J. As powerful as we are together…what will that even be like with you inside of me? I want this with you. I feel like it was always meant to be yours. I've been here. Waiting. Holding this space. For you. For this. Please," I fervently whispered.

He nodded, "You're sure?"

The Melody of Fire

"Yes. Are you?" I asked.

"My love…yes. I've never been more certain of anything in my entire life," he said almost reverently.

"Are you ready?"

I nodded.

Something inside of me that I'd never felt before was aching for him. My body felt like it was crying out in yearning.

I felt him begin to rub his cock on me. It even shocked me how wet I was.

His eyes were locked on mine as I felt him slide slowly into me.

The sensation made us both inhale sharply together. We both laughed a little at the synchronized response.

We never released eye contact.

He slid further into me, and we both moaned with delight.

And then…things began to get strange.

It felt like time stopped. It literally seemed as though the minutes halted completely and left us suspended in some kind of in-between space.

I looked up at him in wonder as he thrust into me again slowly.

I could see auras of color around and behind him, and in between us that were confusing but captivating. The deeper he plunged into me the less I felt like myself and the more I felt like an extension of him. He began to feel like a physical piece of myself (an organ or an artery) that had been missing this whole time that had finally found its way back inside of me. I felt complete for the first time in my life.

Our consciousness merged into one unit, and I honestly couldn't tell if my thoughts were my own or his. There were vibrations and reactions, and I knew not from who they originated, only that we both were responding in synchronization. The whispers and murmurs between us merged in the same way, and I had no idea who was speaking, only that each breath caused another ripple of pleasure and sound.

I looked into his eyes and found myself drowning in lifetimes of consciousness that I suddenly began to remember.

This wasn't the first time we were making love……it was the millionth.

I knew his every breath and movement, and he anticipated mine like they were his own.

He leaned forward and cupped my head in his hand with his fingers laced in my hair, his eyes centimeters from my own as we drowned in the depths of each other.

My ego dissolved.

There was only "Us."

We.

Love.

133

My first dose of universal consciousness.

My first encounter with the Divine.

Shiva and Shakti.

Hieros Gamos. The sacred marriage of the Divine.

There…suspended somewhere in time and space, my entire existence realigned.

My fears about my past history and "knowing what to do" vanished as a hundred past lives reawakened within me.

I knew how to touch him, just as he knew how to touch me.

Not just surface level…the deepest parts.

He penetrated the depths of my being, while I received the most vulnerable parts of him into my soul.

The exchange felt otherworldly and beyond my wildest imagination, yet somehow as familiar to me as breathing.

We had been right here, sharing this same exchange God knows how many times.

I *knew*.

He *knew*.

We periodically laughed at the comfort and intensity of it all together.

We went from the uncertainty of those first few moments with him on top of me, to boldly exploring every position that occurred to us one after another in an endless euphoria of lovemaking.

He flipped me around and fucked me from behind. We found ourselves in a sixty-nine pleasing each other in the most tender ways. I sat on his face, and then he fucked my mouth afterward, I found myself riding him and then reversed and rode him that way.

We delighted in each other the way that longtime lovers do.

So much rawness…so much vulnerability…and yet, so much trust. There was an inexplicable familiarity.

We made love with the ease and joy that is normally found in lovers that have been together for decades.

Or maybe lifetimes.

Centuries.

His face changed in the aura ever so slightly and our surroundings shifted over and over again. I bore witness to the two of us engaging in the same physical connectivity in other spaces. Other times. It happened so quickly and so fluidly that I simply watched it happen without trying to make sense of it. I heard languages unfamiliar to my ear come out of both J and myself, and we somehow knew what the other one had spoken. There was a deep inner knowing attached to what was happening. We were somehow connecting in that moment to past versions of ourselves that had made love in this very way. Each time I tried to consciously grab onto a moment to figure out what was occurring, the intensity of the pleasure pulled me right back into my body and the scene would shift once more. I heard over and over again a word that I had never heard or read prior: "Lemuria."

When we finally came to our senses, four hours had passed.

I looked at him wide-eyed. "*How is it midnight?!*" I said. He shook his head in shocked disbelief as well. Where had we gone, that time had ceased to exist?

"I know I'm new at straight sex, but I have to ask you….is it always like that?" I asked.

He laughed my favorite laugh of his. Deep, hearty, and knowing.

"Oh, my love. No. Not at all. I've never experienced that before. That wasn't like any sex that I've ever had. I'm not even sure that it *was* sex – that word feels too small to describe what just happened. But whatever that was… it wasn't new to the two of us. You saw that… heard that…felt all of that with me, didn't you? I was beginning to feel a little crazy there a few times," he whispered.

"The different places? Different languages? Yes. At one point you looked at me and your beard was gone, J. You said something to me in a way that I knew I shouldn't have comprehended, but I did. What do you think happened? What *was* that? I feel like if it had happened at any other time, with anyone but you, I would have been so freaked out and scared. But it just felt… right. And really beautiful," I said. I was lying on his stomach looking up at him while he twisted my long hair around his fingers. He sighed with relief.

"I feel exactly the same way. It was like every time I started to freak out a little you would do something that would make me almost come and I had to focus so hard on holding back that I let go of the panic. And then everything would shift all over again. That's crazy about my beard. I swear Jen… at one point you had flowers braided in your hair. And then I looked again, and they were gone," he said. His eyes were wide, and he shook his head. We were both dumbfounded.

"Lifetimes, Miss Jen…MY Miss Jen," he whispered so quietly that if I hadn't been watching his mouth I wouldn't have heard.

"What really feels nuts is that we are just lying here talking about what probably should have been a mind-blowing mystical experience that we shared, and it just feels…normal. Comfortable. Almost like we aren't surprised at all," I said. It was true. If someone else had told me that they had just experienced the very thing that had just happened between J and me, I would have laughed at them. I certainly wouldn't have believed them.

J shrugged in response. "You're right. I mean… I'm definitely shocked on some level. But in the same breath, I wouldn't have expected any less. It's weird," he said.

"Hey… what's 'lemuria'? Do you know? I kept hearing that word," I said.

He shook his head. "I don't know, but I heard it too. Well, I don't know if "heard" is the right word. More like… it just kept popping into my mind. There's a lot I don't know about what just happened, Jen. I'm going to have to sit with all of this for quite a while, I think," he said.

I nodded solemnly in agreement.

"The only thing I know with certainty in this moment is this: I am yours and you are mine. It has been that way since the beginning of time… and it will be that way when time no longer exists," he said.

He pulled me up onto his chest, kissed my forehead, and held me tight.

I melted into him and felt like after this single difficult lifetime of searching, I was finally home. Hearing him articulate what I felt so precisely, unraveled what was left of me. I was standing in the presence of a Truth here that felt sacred. I surrendered to it entirely.

I raised up out of the baptismal waters with eyes that were clear for the first time. Ears that could hear for the first time. No matter the strangeness of all that had just occurred, there was no going back. No un-knowing of what I had just experienced.

My old self was gone, never to return.

Unbeknownst to me in this moment, a serpent that had long been fast asleep and nestled in a neat coil at the base of my spine, had been awakened.

Her bright golden eyes had dreamily opened through the physical reconnection to the divine energy created that night.

She would begin her ascension that evening, weaving her way up my spine and touching my chakras as she slid past.

As dumbfounded and blown away as I was from this first experience of sex with J, there is no way I could have known what we had activated in me.

The awakening had just begun.

My soul exploded in song as I looked around with my new senses.

I wanted to sing the praises of my baptism by fire to the world.

I was reborn.

New eyes to see.

New ears to hear.

A new heart to understand.

"The knowledge and the secrets of the kingdom of heaven have been given to you."

Matthew 13: 10

Chapter Eleven

THE NIGHT THAT I found out that our first sexual experience had unlocked telepathy between J and me was the night that I almost died.

I was driving home from a fun night of karaoke with some friends one evening about a week or so after J and I had slept together for the first time. I had the radio blaring in my soft top Jeep and was singing at the top of my lungs as I made my way down the curvy backroads that were the long way home. To my dismay, it began to sprinkle outside and then became a full-on downpour as I got further away from the city on the country roads that I had chosen to take. I considered pulling over. I couldn't see well in normal conditions through the plastic windows of the soft top, and the large mud tires that I had put on the Jeep for four-wheeling were great in rough off-road conditions but terrible in rain.

I knew there was a church parking lot about a mile up the road and decided that if it was still coming down this hard when I reached it that I would pull over there until it slacked off. There was a sharp curve up ahead and I slowed down considerably before I turned into it, but as I came out of the other side the back end of the Jeep fishtailed a little bit.

I quickly turned the wheel the same way of the tires and managed to get it straightened back up, but then to my absolute horror, I hit a patch of standing water in the road as soon as I gained control of the vehicle.

The entire Jeep slid to the left, all four tires were facing forward but I seemingly floated across the left lane and toward a ten-foot embankment off of the shoulder. I turned the wheel both ways, but quickly realized that it made no difference what I did, nothing was stopping the trajectory. If there had been a car coming, we would have had an unavoidable head-on collision, but luckily the lane was clear. I turned my attention to the impending embankment.

I was going over. There was absolutely no way to stop it.

Panic gripped my heart. There wasn't much time to mentally react, but I remember very clearly thinking,

"This is it. This is how I'm going to die."

I braced myself for the impact. As the left side tires flew over the bank, I felt the Jeep begin to roll. It creaked and thudded as it flipped upside down…once…twice…three times. It slowed a little each time it rolled over and on the third flip, it finally stopped.

I was completely disoriented, and it took me a moment to realize that it had come to rest on its top. I was completely upside down.

The engine was still running, and I cut it off with hands that were trembling so badly that I could barely make them work.

I sat there in stunned silence for a moment.

I was alive.

Holy shit. *I was alive.*

How? That roll bar had taken three hits in a row and somehow hadn't cracked. The only other thing between my head and the ground was the fabric of the soft top. I should be dead.

I moved all of my limbs, one at a time. Nothing seemed to hurt. Was it just adrenaline that was masking a major injury somewhere? Perhaps. It was pitch black so I couldn't tell if there was blood anywhere. There was no dome light in the Jeep, and I couldn't see a thing.

I had to get out somehow. I tried my door, and it was jammed tightly. It must have been dented in when I rolled. I had taken the backseats out of my Jeep right after I bought it so it might be possible to climb out the back…

It occurred to me suddenly that I needed my phone. I was going to have to call for help.

Fuck. I was upside down. The entire contents of my seat and console had been strewn about everywhere. There was no way I was going to be able to find my phone in this darkness.

I raised my arm above my head to touch the ground (but what was actually the roof of the Jeep), and my hand landed on a slim rectangular object.

I couldn't believe it. It was my phone.

Relief washed over me as I gratefully grabbed it and tucked it in my bra. I unsnapped my seatbelt and carefully maneuvered my body to the ground above me. As I reoriented myself, I managed to find the zipper for the back window and began to work it open from the inside. I squeezed a few fingers, and then my entire hand through the hole until I could grasp the pull and unzip it enough to free myself.

I crawled on all fours out into the middle of waist-high grass in the open field where the Jeep had landed. I began to cry with gratitude as the enormity of what had just happened sunk in.

I lay down on my back panting with exhaustion and began to say out loud over and over, "Thank you thank you thank you thank you thank you…."

My phone rang suddenly. I pulled it out of my bra and saw that it was J. I was shaking so badly that it took me three tries to answer it. As I put it to my ear, I heard him yell,

"ARE YOU OKAY??"

"I…I think so. Yes. I think I'm ok…." I answered. I was so confused. I still felt disoriented from the whole wreck, and I couldn't work out why or how he knew about it.

"Jesus Christ, Jen. I almost had a heart attack. I'm so glad you answered," he said.

"Huh? I'm sorry, babe…what's going on…I'm I in a coma or something? Is this a dream? I'm so confused," I said. I was still breathing heavily, and my body was trembling. I was still trying to recover, and the physicality of my response indicated that this had to be really happening, but it didn't make sense that he knew about it.

"Where are you?" he asked.

"Lying in a field. Off of Pickens Bridge Road."

"I'm on my way. Are you hurt? Do I need to call an ambulance?" he asked.

I considered this. I had climbed out of the Jeep with no problem. Nothing seemed to be broken or sprained. In fact, as I looked myself over carefully…I was shocked to see that I didn't even seem to have a scratch. Had I hit my head though? I was beginning to think I was delusional with this phone call.

"I think I'm all right. Just come and get me. But J…how did you know something was wrong?" I asked.

"I was sitting at home, and I had a panic attack out of nowhere. It just came over me out of the blue…I couldn't catch a breath and I was terrified for no reason…. but then I started to get these visuals in my mind of your Jeep going off of a cliff. I saw it flip over a few times. It scared the shit out of me. Is that what happened?" he asked urgently.

"Yes," I said in a near whisper. I was in complete disbelief. He had seen and felt the accident happen? How was that even possible?

"*Fuck*. I'm so glad you are ok. I'll be there as soon as I can be, love. Hang tight," he said.

I lay back down in the grass and tried to make sense of everything that had just unfolded as I waited for J. The cool rain pelted my face as I lay there feeling so very grateful to be alive.

I looked up at the stars and watched the rain continue to fall down on me from the heavens. I thought about how small I was, how insignificant.

I didn't know why my life had been spared.

People died all of the time in car wrecks that didn't involve flipping multiple times in a soft-top vehicle. For some reason, God was allowing me to walk away from this accident without a single hair on my head being harmed.

There had to be a purpose for that, right?

Whatever the reason was, I felt like it had to be tied to the boy that had just seen the entire catastrophe unfold in his mind's eye.

I didn't understand any of what was going on right now. It was obvious that I was in far over my head. There was clearly a force at play here that was much stronger than anything I could comprehend.

I was just going to have to surrender to this ride. The connection between him and me felt predestined in every way.

Hadn't it already felt as though I hadn't really had a choice in the matter?

Our love was foretold to me over a decade prior.

Now we were feeling and seeing each other's thoughts somehow.

I felt like it was pointless to even try and figure out what the big picture was here.

At the moment, I was simply thankful that I was going to be alive to experience any of it at all.

I suddenly heard footsteps rustling through the high grass towards me. I slowly sat up. I could see the thin beam of a flashlight sweeping over my Jeep.

"Jen??" I heard J yell.

"Over here…" I said as I raised a hand up. The light suddenly blinded me, and I put my hand over my face.

He was kneeling beside me in an instant. He hugged me to him tightly.

"Holy shit, Jen…the Jeep is upside down! How are you ok? You *are* ok, right?", he pulled back and used the flashlight to look me over carefully.

"Yeah, I'm ok. Just shaken up," I replied. I reached out for him to hold me again. I just wanted to feel safe again for a moment.

"Woman…don't you ever scare me like that again!" he said. "Look at me."

He lifted my chin gently with his finger.

"You promised me that I wouldn't ever lose you again, and then I thought I just did. Could you stop putting me through that?" he said.

"That would have been a tragedy, wouldn't it? We only just fell in love. I would hate to think that we could lose each other so soon," I said as I pulled myself up to a standing position. "Look. I'm fine." I turned around slowly with my hands up so that he could see that all body parts were working.

"Ok. Let's get you out of the rain," he said, and he picked me up easily and began to carry me to his car.

"HEY! I can walk!" I protested.

"That may be so, but I'm not sure I'm ready to put you down. I may never let you go again since you seem so intent on leaving me," he said.

I laughed and leaned into his chest.

"I'm not going anywhere, J. I promised, remember?"

"Do you know what a twin flame is?," J asked me one night as we walked to our cars after a show.

"Twin flame? No…I've never heard that term before."

"Well, I know you love to read so check that out when you get a minute. That's what I think this connection is," he said.

"Well, I'd love to have an explanation for all that is happening between us. Wanna give me the Cliff Note version?" I said with a laugh. I was deeply intrigued. I had been researching on my own as well. Something about this love just felt deeper on a cosmic level. I had found nothing in my spiritual books that had come anywhere close to adequately describing what was occurring between us.

He pulled me close and pushed my long hair away from my face and behind my shoulders. He searched deeply into my eyes until he found my soul, the way he always did now when we spoke.

"A twin flame is more than a soul mate. At the beginning of their creation, some souls were split in two, each half inhabiting a different body. Throughout various lifetimes, usually only one soul will incarnate at a time in an earthly frame, while the other stays in the spiritual realm and supports and guides the other half through that lifetime. When both halves of the soul are ready, they incarnate during the same lifetime in order to learn important lessons together. The connection is overwhelmingly powerful because twin flames are literally two halves of the same whole. They are a perfect mirror to each other: boosting each other's best qualities, but also reflecting back flaws that need to be addressed. Hallmarks of a twin flame connection are a deep understanding of each other that can't be explained from one lifetime's experience…" he stopped because my eyes had widened.

I thought of all of the ways I knew him. All of the little things that didn't make sense for me to understand. The way he could just breathe slightly differently, and I could know volumes of his thoughts in an instant. I thought back to the night of my wreck and how he had literally seen my thoughts and felt my panic.

As if on cue, he said,

"Strong telepathy…"

I smiled. He nodded in acknowledgment and continued,

"And what feels like a massive awakening, both spiritually and sexually. There's more. A lot more. You should read about it, love. I think you'll agree that the connection that we have is definitely that."

"I already agree, but you know I'll research it," I responded.

I was staring deeply into his eyes, lost in our thoughts.

Our thoughts. That's what I began to think of them as, over the next few years. This conversation was the beginning of trying to piece together an understanding of a depth of connectivity that I never was able to define or fully convey to anyone else.

Twin flames, indeed. It's the only thing that even touches what it felt like. If we were two halves of the same soul, it would explain so many things.

Why often times our energy was indistinguishable from one another.

Why thoughts felt like they originated from both of us.

Why sex and singing were this otherworldly, shared ecstasy that felt like we were the only two beings in existence, but I couldn't tell us apart in those moments. There was no "I end, and he begins," or visa-versa. There was only the space of "we create in this moment." We were an energy - a force that together, felt whole and complete and perfect in a way that both of us found ineffable.

I have often looked back on exchanges and synchronicities between us and been awed not only that they happened, but that at the time they felt so normal to us.

I didn't trust it in the beginning. I didn't believe (or sometimes even consciously realize) that we were sharing thoughts and energy.

When we first got together if I felt something, I just assumed it was coming from me. Time and consistency changed all of that. There were times when I would wake up with a disturbing level of anxiety that felt foreign. Talking to J would always later reveal that it was coming from him. Something had happened to spark his inability to sleep, and we would compare times to find that we had been awake at the same hour with that vibrational disturbance.

It wasn't always negative. Sometimes I would find myself feeling absolutely enveloped in love. A warm glowing feeling would suddenly catch me off guard, and usually precede a phone call from J that just simply was to say he loved me, and I was on his mind.

It took a while, but once I realized what was happening, I began to be able to distinguish the feelings and energies that came from me and the ones that originated from him.

I began to trust the information I was receiving. When we were in the same

The Melody of Fire

space it was difficult for me to tell whose energy was whose, but when we were apart, I became proficient in knowing the origin.

As time progressed, I found myself coming to rely on its trustworthiness the way I trusted that the sun and moon would rise at their appointed times.

J was far ahead of me in his spiritual wisdom and was my mentor and teacher in all of the ways. When he wasn't helping me expand my consciousness through our sexual exploration, he was sending me books and articles or walking me through exercises to assist my spiritual growth. He taught me how to meditate, and how to use my breath to bring myself into the present moment and clear my mind. I took to meditation easily, and it quickly became a part of my daily routine that I looked forward to. I began to seek out moments that I could squeeze in more meditation practice, and soon I was meditating for a few hours a day. At some point, it occurred to both of us that since we could hear and feel each other's thoughts even when we weren't trying to, that we might be successful at doing so with concentrated effort.

With this new goal in mind, I began to intentionally try and access his mind when I would meditate. To my absolute delight, I found that when I tapped in, not only could I see what he was doing at any given moment, I could talk to him as clearly as if we were speaking on the phone. One particular morning, I had been talking to him in meditation and my session got cut short because my neighbor stopped by for a moment. When I got in the car to go to work later J called me and finished the conversation as if nothing was out of the ordinary.

"What I was saying this morning was…" he started out. We picked up right where we left off as though it were perfectly normal that the beginning of that conversation had only occurred telepathically.

So began a beautiful intentional practice of connecting across the barriers of physical space. It gave us a way to stay deeply entwined in each other's energy no matter what was happening in our day-to-day lives. It became the most beautiful reprieve from what was becoming an increasingly more and more difficult situation with J's marriage. We both longed to be in each other's presence constantly, but it simply was not possible at the time. Connecting in meditation offered a little bit of peaceful connection in a way that we hadn't expected but were both deeply grateful for.

The more time that passed, the stronger the magnetism and connection became. It felt more and more apparent that we truly were two halves of the same whole. I began to have dreams in which we were indistinguishable as entities. I would look in a mirror only to find his reflection staring back at me. There were dreams when I would look at him and see me instead. He told me on more than one occasion that he was experiencing the same phenomenon.

I dove in deep when it came to studying the twin flame connection. When J first suggested this, there wasn't a lot of information available about the dynamic.

At the time of writing this book, the topic of "twin flames" is so overwhelmingly popular that it virtually takes over any website or social media group that publishes information on spirituality.

They may state that their mission is to connect lightworkers or discuss ascension, but it isn't long before someone brings up questions about twin flames and suddenly the group spirals into a twin flame chat room.

I've witnessed it time and time again.

The twin flame dynamic is anything but easy - it's not meant to be. In fact, it is virtually a guarantee that meeting your twin flame will not only show you love like you have never known before, but it will also show you the depths of your own shadows that need to be healed. People don't typically come to research the twin flame journey because they are blissfully in love, the way that J and I did. They reach out because they are in torment, and they want to know what the hell is happening to them.

There is a popular belief among twin flame "experts" that one of the souls is "awakened" to the connection and the other one is not.

They claim that there is a "runner" and "chaser" dynamic that exists between the two because the connection is so powerful that it is scary to the party that is not awakened.

This leaves the awakened twin in a world of hurt, as they chase after the other twin trying desperately to make them wake up.

In my opinion, it's a brutal perspective on a relationship that is already very difficult to navigate. I'm not entirely sold on the idea that the dynamic works that way (with a runner/chaser), because it wasn't my experience, but there are thousands of people who seem to think that is one of the defining characteristics of a twin flame connection.

Wicked people are clever, and they know that people who are hurting will pay any amount or do anything to stop the pain they are going through.

There are charlatans galore, each pushing their own brand of twin flame snake oil medicine. I now watch with dismay as people charge hundreds (sometimes even thousands) of dollars for sessions and courses that they claim will help "reunite you with your twin flame."

They know that once you have had a taste of the love that exists between flames, you will do anything in your power to get it back, including filling their pockets with exorbitant amounts of money. It breaks my heart to see people preyed upon when they are hurting.

I know without a shadow of a doubt that had either J or I have been a "runner" in our situation, either of us would have fallen into that trap. Luckily, we were both wide awake to the connection. Neither of us had to try and figure out how to somehow shake the other awake to what was happening.

I am so grateful that we both knew what we had. It allowed us to truly treasure and explore all of the depths of our inexplicable connectivity in glorious ways.

We remained constantly curious about it, testing the waters of the spirit realm together.

Can you hear me in meditation?

Did you just feel what I was thinking?

What happens if we touch this way?

Where do we go during sex or singing? (It's definitely not an earthly realm.)

How are we bending the rules of time?

What happens when we apply intention to sending messages from a distance?

We reveled in every bit of it. It was amazing to have a partner that was so open and willing to explore with me. We never questioned any of it, we just allowed ourselves to be continually amazed as we discovered new ways to love each other.

I delighted in the discoveries we were making. It began to spill over into other areas of my life. I became fiercely curious about the possibilities of the spirit realm. I had read so many books on spirituality up to this point, but now I was receiving actual real-life downloads and experience. My realizations with and through J when it came to working with Spirit made me want to learn more and more.

It was like reading book after book on flying an airplane. Your research would likely tell you how to operate the aircraft, what to expect in various air conditions, how to handle issues that might arise, etc. but until you actually try to fly the plane you can't really grasp what they are telling you. Someone can tell you what air pockets or turbulence feels like, but until you actually feel that for yourself, they are just abstract concepts.

I was beginning to see that it was the same with all of the spiritual knowledge I had been trying to absorb through books. The descriptions of things like telepathy and tantric ecstasy that I had read ultimately turned out to be fairly accurate- but there was no way of knowing that until I had felt them firsthand.

J taught me that being fearless yet playful about exploring Spirit opened you up to the most amazing experiences a human could have.

What else I had I been missing out on by not trying to put what I had read about into practice? How else could I experiment and open myself to receive more? What other ways could I allow mystical experiences to show up in my life?

This twin flame love (and label…which started me down a rabbit hole of reading all I could get my hands on about the deepest spiritual connection possible between two human beings) opened me up in the most beautiful way. I allowed all of the newness in. I wanted to feel it all - to let it touch my insides and change me forever.

I began to exist solely for the magic, both between J and me, and in whatever other ways Spirit wanted to bring it to me.

New experiences began to flood my life right and left.

The twin flame experience was going to be the candle that lit the way of the path to the Source.

I could already feel it in my soul.

Chapter Twelve

IT WAS AROUND this time that I began to connect the dots between the spiritual and mystical experiences that I was having and the teachings of the Bible. I'll be honest, I kind of hated it.

I had spent a very good portion of my adult life trying desperately to poke holes in the teachings of the church. I had a deep-rooted animosity still for all things surrounding Christianity, and particularly Christians themselves. The farthest thing from what I had hoped would happen was that the things I was learning firsthand would support the beliefs of those assholes.

Don't get me wrong, I've never experienced one iota of the judgment or discrimination that seems to be all-prevailing in the Christian church in any of my encounters with the Divine.

Particularly when it comes to sexuality and gender (which is still a hot topic in the Southern Baptist community), my experiences seemed to suggest that God does not give a single solitary shit about who you love. I know that would ruin a whole lot of bullet point sermons down in the South though, so I guess they will just continue to preach about "the gays" like they are the most pressing issue on the planet until the end of time.

I had used the hatred and fear-mongering that I had experienced in my youth as an excuse to try and push away every single one of the teachings that had been hammered into me growing up.

I felt justified in that. In fact, I still do, even now. Those interpretations of the teachings of Christ feel so off base that it was and still is easy for me to write them off as delusional and not representative of what Jesus was trying to teach.

It was simple for me to put distance between myself and the church that I knew because none of it resonated with me. However, my relationship with the actual teachings of the Bible became an interesting dance. I began to discover that the further I tried to get away from the Bible, the more I got brought back to it from a new angle.

I'll give you an example.

One of the first things that I did as I began to interact with Divine energy was throw the word "God" out of my vocabulary. I hated it. Every time I said "God" I got flashbacks of hellfire and brimstone threats and lightning bolts. It brought up connotations of an Almighty being who was cold, unreachable, and angry. The name "God" also felt super masculine and that ignited a whole other distaste in me that I found hard to work around.

The interactions and experiences I was beginning to have with Source Energy felt completely opposite of all that I had been taught about "God."

For starters, I wasn't sure this presence was a dude.

Sometimes it felt masculine, but sometimes it was decidedly feminine.

It felt limiting and inaccurate to try and assign it one gender. I began to make the claim that "God" was non-binary (because I am clearly cutting-edge and this bold assertion on my part got lots of attention and at the end of the day, I am still a Libra and we live for that shit).

I referred to "God" as They/Them to anyone who would listen. The more I toyed with this concept though, the more I disliked even saying the name "God" because it still just felt so predominantly masculine to me. I decided that the title "Spirit" felt so much more appropriate. There was a genderless quality about that word, and I also loved identifying an energy that seemed omnipresent yet invisible as a ghost-like entity.

I adopted "Spirit" as my name of choice for the Almighty.

I began to contemplate how it was that we were connected to Spirit. I recognized that we each had this little spark of that divinity that lived inside of us and that it was through that connection that Spirit worked through and with us. This was why meditation was such an effective tool for listening to the guidance of the Divine. When we were able to quiet our human ego, we could hear the voice of Spirit inside of us. We had a piece of whatever it was that Spirit was made of inside of our own individual consciousness to access at any time.

As I was working through this concept in my meditation practice, it suddenly dawned on me one day that I had heard this theory before…but in a slightly different way.

The Bible teaches about the Holy Trinity. I had been told when I was a child that when a person accepts Jesus as their Lord and Savior that the Holy Spirit would enter into their heart to live. They told me that The Father, The Son, and The Holy Spirit were three parts of the same entity, but that the Holy Spirit was the part of God that resides within us.

I sat there on my yoga mat feeling like an idiot. Here I had thought I had been so clever in my discovery that "Spirit" was part of our being, and the whole damn time all I had done was worked my way backwards to a principle that was explained to me as a five-year-old. Basically with the same terminology.

This kind of thing continued to happen. The more I learned (not through reading, as I had previously thought was the way to learn spiritual truths, but through actual experience) the more I learned that I was just relearning things that I had already learned.

The farther away I tried to walk from the Bible, the more I found myself right back in front of it.

It was exasperating. I didn't want to be a Christian. I hated Christians. They hated me.

Yet I was finding that the more that I wished for a written guide to show me how to connect with the Divine, the more I was shown that I had already read it.

It had simply been taught to me in a way that I couldn't receive. I hadn't been able to hear the truths over all of the fear and ignorance that had been screamed over top of them by those who were supposed to know better.

I began to see that I was going to have to loosen up my own hatred and judgments if I was going to get any further in my spiritual growth. Spirit took me right back to pre-K Sunday school and put a little picture book of Jesus stories in my hand and said, "Let's try this again, the right way, shall we?"

It is said that spiritual growth occurs not in a line but in a spiral. We continually revisit lessons and principles that we thought we previously understood, we just see them each time from a little higher up on the staircase. That became the reality of my relationship with the teachings of Christ. No matter what new and novel way I thought of to try to work with Divine energy, I found myself walking around the same truths that I had started at.

No matter how hard I fought it, each time I surrendered I was brought back to the beginning.

Spirit began teaching an alchemy course in my heart.

I had to learn how to separate Christianity from Christians.

I had to learn how to integrate Spirituality with Christianity.

I learned how to separate Fear from Love in test tubes.

I began mixing universal consciousness with personal experience.

Spirit began to show me how the fire of unconditional Love has the power to transmute and purify all things.

It was a pretty good class. I'm hoping one day to be accepted to the sophomore level.

I began to make a little peace with Jesus – just a little.

I started to let go of the animosity - just a bit.

One baby step at a time my new faith began merging back with the faith of my childhood– in tiny ways.

Things began to shift ever so slightly. I wasn't exactly running back down to the altar of my youth, but I also wasn't hurling rotten fruit at it anymore.

The middle ground and the meeting place of the beliefs I grew up with and the new ones I was forming started to feel like a more neutral place.

After all, I did know with certainty that I could never reject or walk away from what was happening between J and me. If anything was real… it was that. And if the Bible offered any kind of clues or assistance on how to bring more of THAT into my life, then I realized I could never discount it entirely. There was going to have to be some kind of integration on my part, that much was obvious.

So, I just stopped running from it.

I decided to just be in a space of curiosity about it all.

One by one I began to loosen my fingers from the fist I had been holding up in defiance, trying to create an open palm that could freely receive the new knowledge and experiences that were arriving in my life. Without judgment. Without assumption. With surrender.

Chapter Thirteen

I WAS SOBBING.

EVERY cell heaving with jealousy.

I had just watched him kiss Lila goodbye.

Something I had witnessed 1000 times before we were together.

Something that I should have expected.

Something that I had no right to be jealous about.

Something that I knew in theory was still happening.

Something that I hadn't seen with my own eyes since before we fell in love.

Something that killed me in a way I hadn't anticipated.

I was sitting in the basement of a venue that I shouldn't really have been allowed access to, but the owner loved me and had taken one look at my tearful face and offered it as a refuge.

He had handed me the key and I fled.

I had intended to just wait out everyone leaving. I could hear the footsteps and the laughter of the crowd above. I thought that when it died down, I would sneak out and no one would be the wiser.

As I sat there alone, I mulled the whole situation over in my mind.

J's marriage was the Achilles heel of us both. He was constantly wounding himself with the betrayal that he was acting out, and it brought out the absolute worst in me.

Being the "other woman" made me feel like the lowest human being on the planet. I was constantly forced to be in the same space with his family at various band gigs, and would come off of the stage only to put on a whole other show for them in which I pretended that I wasn't in love with J.

I loved Lila. I always had. I didn't want to hurt her like this. Lying to her constantly was making me miserable. I loved his kids like they were my own children. What was this going to look like when the truth came out? A whole lot

151

of hurt, that's what. They would all no doubt hate me, and I wouldn't blame them one bit.

I felt like a piece of shit. An entitled piece of shit, no less, because here I sat absolutely seething with jealousy as if I had witnessed her kissing *my* husband instead of her own.

It's not like we hadn't known what we were getting into from the very beginning, but it sure felt different sitting on this side of that leap. We were both dying over it in completely different ways. I missed him constantly and longed to be with him the entire time we were apart. The space in between the days that I saw him were breaking me. On top of that, I felt beyond guilty for my part in the betrayal to his family. He carried the burden of our love with him day in and day out when he was at home with his wife and kids; the knowledge of what he was doing to them as a unit weighed on him constantly. Every time I looked at him, I saw the pain of that guilt just below the surface. I wondered how it was possible that Lila wasn't seeing it? Was he better at hiding what he was going through when he was at home, or was I just more aware of the suffering he was in because I felt every fluctuation of his emotions as if they were my own?

The whole situation was a constant reminder that no matter what etheric and mystical heights we were reaching as a couple, at the end of the day we were still inextricably human.

As I sat there crying, I wondered for the thousandth time if breaking it off was even a possibility anymore.

I thought back to how a single month apart *before we had even spoken a word of love to each other* had destroyed us both. How could we possibly lay it down now that we were in this deep? What would that do to both of us? Neither of us would be a whole person again without the other. Our souls were entwined like barbed wire. If we tried to extract ourselves from one another now, it would feel as painful as splitting our actual physical bodies in two.

I knew walking away now would never work. We would somehow end up back in each other's arms. There was too much beyond our control occurring here, that much was obvious.

I knew at this point that nothing could truly keep us separated.

Nothing, that is, except the thing that already did.

The door to the basement opened, and there stood a tall, broad-shouldered silhouette that I didn't even have to look up to see. I had felt him long before he had touched the door. The energy knocked me over as he stepped inside.

He closed the door gently behind him and took his long strides over to me under the light of the single dangling bulb overhead.

"You can't, Jen. You can't be jealous. You can't let that make you crumble like that," he said.

It infuriated me.

"Oh. I can't be jealous? Why? So that you can lead us both on in this fucked up game you are playing without feeling guilty? Your side chick…your mistress…your piece of ass …can't be hurt by your affection with your wife? Because that's the REAL thing, right? That's the thing that matters. I'm just for fun. I can't be stepping outside of my lane, right? I've seen this movie, J. That's not the role I want." I was teeming with anger and jealousy and hurt. I again wondered if breaking it all off would somehow make this pain stop. The thought made me want to die, but so did the visual of the two of them kissing that kept replaying in my mind.

I was sitting on an unopened keg with a board on top. He dropped to his knees in front of me. I couldn't meet his gaze. He grabbed my hand, and I tried to ignore the usual zing of fire that passed between our fingers.

"Will you look at me, please?" he asked.

I refused.

"I can't, J. If I do, I'll just give in to whatever bullshit that you are about to say, and I feel like my feelings are valid right now," I said.

He sighed.

"Ok. You don't have to. Of course your feelings are valid, that's not what I meant. I know that it hurt you to see that. I never see the dates you go on, or what you do apart from us, but it kills me to even know when you are at dinner with another person. I can't imagine if I actually saw you touch someone else how that would feel," he said.

I had done that intentionally. From the first moments that we had been together, I had gone on dates with other people, took pictures while doing it, and posted them all over social media to make sure he saw them. Ninety percent of the time my dates were with women, but occasionally I went out with a boy just to make him wonder. It was never serious. I never slept with any of them, and few got a second date or even a follow-up call. I had done it primarily for appearances (should anyone question J and me), but also to let him know that he wasn't the only one who had someone who wanted them.

Petty, I know. Some of those moments weren't my finest.

He would go on to lose his fucking mind a few times over people that I saw. Desperate times call for desperate measures, and there were moments when I was a desperate asshole. I knew that he wanted me for his own (the same way that I wanted him to myself) and there were times when I intentionally did things just to try and kick up his emotions in hopes that he would make a move to be with me. I'm not proud of that.

In fact, this conundrum was bringing out quite a few behaviors and reactions from myself that I wasn't proud of -the jealousy that I was battling at the current moment being one of them.

"Jen, please," he said.

"Ugghhhhhhhhh. FINE," I grumbled in reply.

I looked at him. It was a stupid decision, because I melted before he could even say the words that would echo off of my heart as if my own mouth had uttered them.

"THIS. This is real, right?" he asked. He touched my chest, and then his own. He touched between and above my eyebrows, where my third eye sits…and then he touched his own to indicate that he was also talking about the psychic connection. He held up our entwined hands in front of me and shook them gently.

I nodded, wordlessly.

"It's so real…that nothing else compares. Everything else… all of existence in fact, is just…background noise to *this*." He paused. Tears filled his eyes.

"You will do what you feel like you have to do, and I'll do what I feel like I have to do…but *nothing* is real, except for this. It's the most real thing that two people have ever been given. Isn't it maybe too much to ask that it be easy too? Shouldn't there be a price for this gift? This fire? This magical connection that exists between us? This love that permeates everything? THIS is real, Jen. That's what we have… *the most real thing*. We can argue and be jealous over everything else that exists outside of this, and that would be VERY easy for both of us. But we could also choose to just latch on to what we have found. Let it *be* the most real thing that we both have and don't taint that by worrying about what exists outside of it. I need you to trust that I am trying to handle this in the very best way that I can. My family didn't ask for this to happen, and I am trying to figure out how to minimize the pain that this will inevitably cause them. There is nothing easy about it, but I will do whatever I have to do because I want to be with you more than anything. I promise you that I will figure out how to make that happen…but that's not going to be today. *Please*. Please stick with me until we can make that day happen?"

His words (and tears) lowered my guard. It was always in moments like these that the dynamic of the twin flame connection was most apparent to me. If what they say is true…that your twin is literally the other half of your own soul (and that feels accurate to me), then their words and thoughts will resonate with you in the same way that your own words and thoughts do.

It was as if my own being had spoken a truth to me that I already knew and asked me to have faith that there was something greater at play.

I couldn't tell him no any more than he would have been able to if the roles had been reversed. Of course I would ride this out with him. What choice did I have?

Whatever this power was that existed between us, it had long since spiraled out of our hands. We were simply going to have to let this unfold the way the universe intended because being without each other was no longer an option.

No matter what things looked like in the earthly realm, J had been right in what he said the very first time we made love:

I was his and he was mine….and it had been that way since the beginning of time.

We were slow dancing naked in the middle of my apartment. I was wrapped in his strong arms, swaying side to side blissfully. Intermittently, we would press our foreheads together…third eye to third eye, and stare into the endless horizon of each other's eyes that were so close it was all we could see. It felt like drowning in ecstasy and periodically gave way to kisses that were so deep that we nearly forgot to breathe.

We began slowly tracing each other's bodies, each one mirroring what the other did. He ran his fingers slowly down the curve of my left side, and I found myself matching the movement as my fingertips made their way down his right side. He let his hand find its way to the back of my neck and entwined his fingers in my hair, and I followed with the mirroring and locked my fingers around the back of his head. Foreheads touching again, I worshipped at the altar of his eyes. I swooned slightly from the intensity of the love that was washing through me, and I felt him do the same. I realized with a smile that it had unsteadied him. He was drowning too.

I let my hand slowly slide down his chest and abdomen until his hard cock was in my hand. He mirrored my movement down my body, fingertips as gentle as droplets of water until he slowly pushed a finger inside of me. Still swaying to the music, we left our hands like that for what felt like infinity. Gently stroking each other, feeling so connected and so in the field of each other's thoughts that the energy pulsed around us and through us like a warm electric glow.

He finally moved his hand away first, sliding his way up my hipbone, back up the curve of my waist. He caressed the side of my breast tenderly before inching his fingers down my arm and to my wrist. I didn't follow this time with the mirroring, because I sensed an intention with this movement, and I was curious. He slid his thick thumb and finger around my wrist like a handcuff and studied the circumference intently.

"What are you doing?" I murmured, watching him mentally note where finger and thumb met.

He smiled. "Don't worry about it," he said as he then slid his entire hand into mine and led me into a spin and a dip which reminded me that we had been dancing playfully before things had escalated into the intensity that we had been reveling in for the last hour. I giggled as he pulled me back close to him. He waltzed me backwards to my bed and when we were close enough, he threw me onto it; and so began several fevered hours of lovemaking where I gave the idea of his finger and thumb wrapped around my wrist not another thought.

A week later we had a show, and as usual, we had gotten there early to set up (and also to simply have more time with each other). We stepped outside together so that he could smoke, and he held my hand while he finished his cigarette. He flicked the butt to the sidewalk and as he extinguished it with his boot, he reached into his pocket and pulled something out. He turned to face me and raised my hand that he was still holding to him, eyes sparkling mischievously.

"I made you this," he said, as he showed me a beautiful brown leather cuff bracelet. He set to work putting on my wrist, and while he fastened three tiny eye hooks, he told me that it was made from his belt and that he'd made himself one that matched. He pushed up his sleeve to reveal the wider, more masculine version of the bracelet that he had just put on my wrist. We placed them side by side and I admired his work. He had not only cut and somehow finished off the edges of the cuffs, but he also had stitched twine through them in careful decorative patterns. They were beautiful. I felt giddy at the thought of wearing them onstage together, hidden by our sleeves; just one more way that we would be connected in that moment.

"Oh, J… I love it. Thank you so much," I said as I stared again at the craftmanship. I was so happy to have something physical as a gift from him that had obviously taken so much time and attention. I spent a good deal of time during and after the show glancing at it when I could. I would smile at him in gratitude all evening and he would nod knowingly, sometimes softly adding a "yes ma'am" in acknowledgment of my silent thank yous.

When I got home that evening, I went to take off the cuff and to my surprise when I went to unhook the clasps, I found it difficult to get off. It fit so exactly…. so perfectly did it match the circumference of my wrist that moving the eye hooks inward to release them was tricky. How did he get the fit so perfectly?

The image of his thumb and finger wrapped around my wrist from the week before flashed through my mind and I began to laugh.

He had measured me without my knowledge.

Like every gift that passed between us, it was a perfect fit. As close as skin.

I HAD ONLY told three people in my life about J and me – my friend Carson, my sister, and my therapist, Alice.

Alice I had told immediately because I value her opinion and I knew she wasn't allowed to repeat the information. I also knew she would believe me because she was deeply spiritual herself, and I consistently used her as a kind of gauge to assess whether or not I might be on my way to the looney bin by the way she reacted to the stories I relayed of all that was transpiring between J and me. She never once made me feel crazy, recommended medication for a mental disorder, or brought in a team with a straitjacket. I felt like those were good signs.

The fact that J was married made me hesitate to tell Carson or Whit because I felt like the fewer people that knew, the better. However, the more time that passed and the deeper the relationship with J went, I found myself yearning for a place to talk to about the enormity of what was happening to me that wasn't someone I was paying to listen. I knew neither Carson nor Whit would judge me, so I finally entrusted them both with the knowledge.

Neither one was mean to me about it, but they also didn't fully get it, and I couldn't blame them. I knew I wasn't doing a great job at describing the connection because every time I tried, I just felt like I sounded like a fucking nutcase.

"You can hear each other's thoughts?" Carson asked with a raised eyebrow.

I sighed. "I know how that sounds, ok? I can look at it objectively and see the crazy, believe me. But I swear to you, I'm telling the truth."

"It's not that I don't believe you, Jen. I've just never heard of anything like that…even in movies or books. Is it like… you just hear what he is saying in your head, or what? Can you describe what's it like?" she asked.

"Sometimes it's like that, yes. I hear his voice as clearly as if we were speaking on the phone. Sometimes it's like I just *know*. I feel his emotions in my body, and I think a thought that I am fairly certain is my own…but then he will say it out loud. Especially during sex. It's the most confusing then. I can't really tell who is thinking or saying what. It's just this amazing union of energy that's so immersive it feels like we are one entity," I answered.

"That actually sounds really magical," she said. And then, "How in the world are you able to watch him go home to someone else after that?"

I felt the tears welling up in response. "It's *so* hard…but it's not really my decision, you know?"

Where Carson was sweetly empathetic to my position, my sister was flat-out angry and protective.

"Look, you know I love J. I really do. But if he continues jerking you around, I will cut him," she said.

"That's just it, Whit. He's not jerking me around. We walked into this eyes-wide-open, and I can't just ask him to dump his family and run away with me. He and I are in the wrong here, no matter how sure we both are that we belong together. I fully understand why he's staying where he is for the time being. He's trying to figure out the best way to support his kids and Lila before he makes a life-changing move. I know from the outside looking in on this situation that this is probably hard to see… but he really is a good man. I can't be angry at him for doing what a good man in a terrible situation *would do*. As a matter of fact, I feel like I can say with certainty that if he were the type of father that could just abandon his kids without a second thought that I would never have fallen in love with him to begin with. I think it is a testament to the man he is that he can put aside all that I know he feels for me in order to try and do this the right way. If there is even a 'right way' here. God knows, I just want him to show up on my doorstep for good one day, but I also love Lila and the kids, and I feel terrible for putting innocent people in this position," I said.

"And you love him enough that you are ok being a mistress?" Whit asked.

"It's more than that. I don't even know how to explain it, but it's so much more than that. I've told you about the connection – the telepathy. I can remember being with him in other lifetimes, sis. I know that we belong to each other and that this is all for a purpose much bigger than I understand. The intensity of what we have was enough for me to walk away from a sexual identity that I was so sure about that I was willing to let it destroy my relationship with Mom and Dad. That should speak volumes."

"It does. Speaking of Mom and Dad, how do you think they will take this when it all comes out?"

I sighed heavily. Our parents adored J. He had formed a special bond with my dad in particular and it wasn't unusual for them to go fishing together or for Dad to loan him tools or show him his latest home improvement project.

"I don't know. I think they will probably think that we are both terrible people. That will kill J more than me – I'm used to them thinking that, but he looks up to dad so much," I said.

'Yeah, not to be worst-case-scenario here, but I don't see any way of it going well either."

"Listen, I don't want you to think you have to defend me over this, ok? You've done more than enough of that since you were fourteen. If it comes out…when it comes out… I'll take the hit. I deserve it," I said.

She shrugged, "I'll always defend you. Against anyone who doesn't see what a beautiful soul you are. That includes J, by the way. If he hurts you, I'll go after him."

I couldn't help but smile at her, though I knew she wasn't joking.

"And you don't deserve to be punished over this, Jen. You've been punished enough over who you love your entire life. I don't know a human being alive that could walk away from the kind of connection that you have described to me that you two have. It's just not the best circumstances and I worry for you, you know? I just want you to be happy, and I can see how much you love him. I won't talk shit about him or try and talk you into breaking it off if this is really what you want. But…can you just reassure me that it's worth it to you, no matter what happens?"

"He has taught me about the existence of something that I thought wasn't real… unconditional love. The way Mom and Dad rejected me over my sexuality made me feel like love could easily be lost. And then the way Julia reacted over music… I've just walked away from the relationships with the people who were supposed to love me the most with this realization that there was *always something* you could do to make a person stop loving you. There was always some sort of invisible boundary that, once crossed, the love ended. I didn't think human beings were capable of loving unconditionally, myself included. I couldn't imagine willingly trusting my heart to anyone ever again after all of that. I felt like I would always hold back a little bit of myself, so that when I found the "thing" that would make the other person stop loving me that I wouldn't be utterly destroyed. J has changed all of that. I don't even know if I can fully put this into words, Whit, but I will try. When I look into his eyes, I see a love that is ancient and completely unwavering. Whenever it was that my soul was created, I know that he was right there, loving me just the way he is now. No matter what is going on externally in our lives, what is happening internally is solid, steady, and unchanging. And I trust it. I trust *him*. With every single part of me. I have the deepest knowing of his soul. I know the origin of his motives and I know why he chooses the actions that he does… and I know that that man acts out of a desire to lovingly protect everyone that he cares about. When it comes to me, I know without a shadow of a doubt that I reside in the innermost part of that beautiful heart. I see it. I feel it.

"It doesn't matter if I walk away. It doesn't matter if he does. It doesn't matter what either of us does or says. I don't think it would even matter if one of us died. The nature of this love is the deepest love in existence. It is eternal, unchanging, and wholly unconditional and it has changed me for the better. You asked me if it was worth it, no matter what happens? No matter what happens, this love will remain the same. And for that divine gift, I will be eternally grateful."

"What's something that you've not done in bed, but want to?" I asked J tentatively one evening while we were snuggling on my couch.

"You mean…in general? Or something that I've never done with you?" he asked. I felt myself blush slightly as he said it. "And are you asking me this because there is something that YOU are wanting to try but are afraid to ask?" he added with a mischievous grin.

I pondered this before I answered. We had been pushing the envelope a little here and there with our lovemaking. He had already introduced me to an entire world of sexual exploration that I had never known before. The spiritual connectivity alone had been more than I ever knew could exist, but this question from me had been more of a physicality inquiry. I just wanted to know more about his fantasies.

"Both, I think. Something you've never done at all – with or without me – but want to. And no…I really was just asking about you. Almost everything we've done has been new to ME because you're the first man I've ever been with. I was just…wanting to offer a little more to you. BE a little more for you." I put my hand on the side of his cheek and rubbed his beard with my thumb. I looked deeply into his eyes, searching his soul the way he always did mine.

"I want to fulfill every desire you've ever had, J. I want to be everything you've ever wanted. If I can even give you a small bit of what you've given me, it would make me so happy," I whispered to him.

"First of all, you are already everything I've ever wanted, Jen. I couldn't possibly want you more. Period. You drive me crazy, in case you haven't noticed," he said as he took my hand and slid it down to his crotch for me to feel his erection beneath his jeans. "I can't even be near you without fantasizing about all of the ways that I want you. It's a little embarrassing, actually. I would like to be able to keep it together more than that. Especially in public," he said with a soft laugh.

I grabbed him firmly through his jeans.

"Well… no reason to try and hide it here," I said. He leaned his head back and exhaled sharply. I bit his neck playfully as I tightened my grip with my hand.

"That's it!" he said suddenly, raising his head back up to look at me.

"What's it?" I replied with confusion.

"Something that I've never done, that I want to do. I've always been a dominant. *Always*. I've never submitted to anyone in bed…ever. I'd… like to do that with you," he said. He brushed my hair back away from my face.

"Would you do that for me… with me, Jen? Will you dominate me?" he whispered as he stared into my eyes.

I could see that he meant it.

Could I do that, I wondered? Was I capable of dominating this over-six-foot-tall force of masculinity that was looking back at me expectantly right now? Not only had he proven repeatedly that he could move me easily anytime he pleased, he also had led the direction of each of our sexual encounters. I relied on him unquestioningly to take control in all ways. Though I trusted him fully and there was complete comfort between us, I still had moments when I was self-conscious about my inexperience with men in general. I had been happily submissive to him since sex between us first began. Of all of the things that I had thought he might ask of me, dominating him had not been one of them.

"How, J? What exactly do you want me to do? Tie you up? Just…be rough with you physically? I don't think I really know how to do what you are asking."

He gently moved me off of his lap and stood up. He walked over to my nightstand and opened the drawer where I kept my sex toys. I watched him rifle through it, pull out something, and hide it behind his back as he turned to walk back to me. I raised an eyebrow at him as he stopped in front of me.

"Well?" I asked.

This felt like an unusually dramatic presentation of what I could only imagine was a bottle of heating oil or my pair of handcuffs, both of which we had already played with together previously.

Instead, I found myself in complete and utter shock as he pulled a collection of thin leather straps from behind his back and tossed them in my lap.

It was my strap-on harness, without the dildo attachment. The assembly had been in the very bottom of that drawer and had not seen use since long before I had moved into my apartment. I briefly wondered when he had seen it in there, and if he even knew what it was. Had he mistaken it for some kind of leather restraint, I wondered?

"I don't think this is what you think it is," I said with a smirk.

He knelt down in front of me.

"Oh, I know exactly what it is, Miss Jen. It's your strap-on, correct?" he asked.

I nodded in surprise. So, he *had* known. Where in the world was he going with this?

"I saw it in your drawer the last time I was looking for a condom. I have to say, love, that the thought of you wearing that and fucking another woman with it… is extremely arousing," he said in a low voice. I met his gaze as he stared into my eyes unwaveringly.

"Hmm. Yes, I expect that you probably would *love* to watch me do that. Are you hinting at a threesome?" I asked. I was teasing him only slightly. *This* was a conversation I had expected. I hadn't come across a straight man in my entire life who wasn't interested in watching two women fuck. Or even more specifically, hadn't been interested in watching ME fuck another woman -not that I had ever agreed to let anyone.

But things were different with J. I would do anything for him. If he was asking to watch me in bed with another woman, I knew I would agree to it. I watched him carefully to try and determine if this was, indeed, what he was suggesting.

"I'd be lying if I said I wouldn't want to see that. My own beautiful, gloriously feminine, red-haired goddess just completely dominating another woman – for my viewing pleasure. What an absolutely enticing thought," he whispered as he tugged a strand of my hair playfully.

I tried to hide it, but I was a little disappointed. While this conversation hadn't been unexpected exactly, I had hoped deep down that he wouldn't have wanted the same thing that every other man that I had encountered in my life had expressed a desire for. The love between J and me was so profound, I had thought it exempt from what I considered ordinary in any way. The "expected" had been consistently defied in every single way between us. Until now.

I also had begun to think of J as some sort of male anomaly – his focus and desires seemingly way outside the box and more spiritually centered than anyone I had ever met in my life. He had repeatedly shown me experiences that felt outside space, time, and expectation and because of that, he had become a kind of super-man in my eyes. This conversation that I was having with him presently felt reminiscent of requests made of me by drunk men in bars who had just found out I was a lesbian. It felt disappointingly…ordinary. And kind of low brow.

"You didn't like that. Why?" he asked. As usual, he had felt the tiniest shift in my energy as soon as it had occurred. There was no hiding anything between us.

"It's just…kind of…a typical man thing to ask of me. And I thought it beneath you, to be honest," I replied. "Plus, I'm a little disappointed that you would want to share this thing between us that feels so deeply sacred with another person."

"I want to be perfectly clear here – I didn't ask you to have a threesome. I simply stated that the thought of watching you dominate another woman was arousing. If we ever DID decide to bring someone else into the bedroom, there would be no sharing of the depth of what we have. It would be strictly for the physical pleasure and enjoyment of both of us, and I would insist that it be a mutual decision and desire that we both shared. I would never ask you to do that 'for me,' only *with me*. And in line with that – a third party would be a person of your choosing, not mine because I would want you to feel empowered and not like you were being asked to do something that you didn't want to do," he said.

At this, I perked up.

"I would get to choose the girl?" I said. That felt safe to me. It also removed the concern that he might ask someone to join simply because he wanted to sleep with them with my permission.

He nodded.

"But we don't have to do that ever, if you don't want to. Really. That wasn't what I was going to ask you when I brought you this," he said as he looped a finger through the strap-on leather and held it up.

"Oh, thank God," I said with a relieved laugh. "I mean… I would have done it if you had really wanted to, but I wasn't exactly keen on the idea. I already have to share you far more than I want to."

"Agreed," he replied solemnly. "I don't have you in my hands nearly enough as it is. If we ever decide to think about bringing in someone else to play, it will have to be when we are together fully as a couple."

At this, I smiled. We had been talking more and more about what life might look like when we could truly be together as a couple. That possibility seemed closer now than ever. It felt like we were teetering on the brink of a new life together and I could hardly wait. If things were this deep, this meaningful, this *magical* now…what would they be like when we never had to be apart? Would life just be one long continuous adventure together? As it stood, I barely existed between the moments that we spent together. I just waited for my next opportunity to be in his presence again. To breathe again. To feel alive once more. And when I did, I couldn't get enough of him. I wanted to absolutely consume him. If I could have smoked him, drank him, or eaten him…it still wouldn't be enough to satiate the desire for him that roared to life the minute that I was in his presence. I wondered…would finally being able to be together constantly detract from the urge to completely devour each other each time we touched, or would it continue to be one new revelation after another?

I looked down at the strap-on that J had placed back in my lap.

"Why *did* you bring me this? You never said," I said as I pointed to the pile of leather.

He looked down at the floor for a moment, and when he raised his eyes back up to mine, I detected a note of fear in them.

"You asked how you could dominate me. You said it like you didn't believe that you actually could, but you have dominated women in bed before with no problem, haven't you?" he asked as he pointed to the strap-on.

"Yes, I have… but that was different, J. There isn't usually a natural delineation between dominant and submissive between two women. It's typically a trade-off. I was a pretty solid switch in the bedroom with girls," I replied.

"So be a switch with me," he said earnestly.

"How, J? I could top you, but we've done that. We both know you are still in control, even then," I said.

"How do you know that you are in control when you are in bed with a woman? How do you know when you are being dominant?" he asked.

"BECAUSE I'M THE ONE DOING THE FUCKING," I said loudly with exasperation. *My God, why was he being so thick-headed about this*? What was so hard to understand?

"Then fuck *me*, Jen. I'm asking you to dominate me and to fuck me with your strap-on," he replied.

My eyes widened, and my jaw dropped open.

"What?", was all I could get out.

"You heard me," he said, looking directly into my eyes.

"You're serious, aren't you?" I asked. I could tell that he was, even before he nodded yes in reply.

"You really want me to do that, J? Aren't you afraid? What if I hurt you?" I whispered frantically.

"I'll tell you what you told me the first time we made love- I could never be afraid of you," he replied.

"While that may be true, babe – you realize that I can't feel that thing, right? It's not attached to my body and I'm going to be putting it in an extremely sensitive place. *I'm* worried that I'll hurt you, whether you are or not," I said. "You know I'll do whatever you want – anything you ask. I'm just making sure you're thinking this through."

He grabbed the strap-on from my lap, stood up slowly, and reached out his hands for mine. When I took them, he pulled me up to stand with him.

"I trust you, love. Will you trust yourself?" he asked me gently. I looked away from him. I wasn't sure that I did trust myself at all. I knew I would never hurt him intentionally, but experience with strap-on sex had taught me that it was by nature difficult to direct and often a little clumsy. If this was all new to him, I didn't want his first time to be terrible.

"You've never done this before with anyone else?" I asked tentatively.

"I've never let anyone touch my ass. Period. I told you Jen, I've always been dominant…to the extreme. You know exactly what I'm like in bed better than anyone ever has. You make it delightful to be a dom. The innocence that you hold every time we try something new together – it's beautiful and it just brings out the most primal parts of me," he said.

"So why do you want me to step into that role? I don't understand. If you love being in control so much with me, why would you ask me to take over?"

He paused and took a deep breath.

"Because there is a side of you that I haven't seen. There's a piece of you that you haven't shared with me. You have been a dom at times – with other people. Someone out there, who isn't me, knows what you look like commanding them in the bedroom. They know exactly how you fuck when you are in control. I want to know that part of you, Jen. What's it like to submit to you? Do you fuck slowly, or fast and hard? Are you demanding of what you want? Do you give orders with your words or with your body? Do you talk dirty? I want to know. I want intimate knowledge of every single facet of you. It kills me to know that there are pieces of you that someone else has experienced but I haven't seen. I want all of it. Every part. The things that you've shared with other people, and the things that are mine alone," he replied.

This touched me deeply. I realized that while my asking him about something he would like to do in bed but hadn't yet had been an off-the-cuff question on my end, this was something that he had given a great deal of thought to before I even brought it up

"Would you have asked me to do this if I hadn't started the conversation?" I asked.

"Eventually. Yes. The thought of you giving someone else something that you hadn't given me has been eating away at me for a while," he replied. "I would have asked you at some point."

"And this is what you really want? The thought of me fucking you turns you on?" I asked.

He nodded. "The thought of you dominating me is very arousing. Does it turn you on at all? I never want you to do anything that doesn't feel right. Actually, I never want you to do anything sexually with me that isn't exciting to you. It's all about deepening what is between us, love. That's the whole point. We explore together, or we don't at all," he said.

I pondered this. Did it turn me on? I had to admit that the thought of J submitting to me was a little exciting. Intimidating, but exciting.

"I'm intrigued. I have concerns, but I'm willing to do this if it's what you really want," I replied.

He laughed.

"Well, we can't start like that. That was the least dominant sentence I've ever heard," he said.

I laughed as well.

"Yeah, I guess it was, wasn't it? Sorry."

"I'll tell you what. Why don't you grab the attachment to this and go put it on. I'll meet you in the bed in a few minutes, and we will start over." He handed me the leather strap harness.

"You want to do this now?" I asked incredulously.

"Yes. We never know when we are going to get time together, do we? We have it right now, love. Let's make the most of it. Plus, I feel like more time to think would just make one or both of us chicken out. Let's just go with it," he replied.

"So, you *are* a little afraid," I said with satisfaction. He turned me around to face the nightstand and smacked my ass…hard.

"Go. Now," he said in a low growl.

"So much for being submissive…" I muttered as I walked to retrieve the dildo from my drawer.

I went to the bathroom and as I was taking off my clothes and stepping into the leather straps, I noticed that my hands were trembling slightly. This was not at all where I had expected my earlier question to lead. I would have never guessed in a million years that J would have wanted to submit to me. He was such a beautiful epitome of strength and masculinity, yet sensitive to even my tiniest shifts of thought and energy. He exuded a power that was so perfectly mixed with empathic conscientiousness that it floored me every time. I felt like he was born to be a dominant. Designed and constructed for it.

And now he was willingly relinquishing that role to me?

He was asking to see a side of me that I had shared with other lovers, but those women had never been the dom that he was. It was far less intimidating to top another person who was willing to switch roles from the get-go. It felt like a fairer playing field. There is no way I could compare to the powerhouse that was J in the role he was born to embody – and I was afraid to try.

I thought about him waiting on me in my bed and tried to tap into what he was feeling. After the first time we had made love, he had teased me a bit about the first moment that he had entered my body. The next day when we were recapping the experience he laughingly said, "When I looked in your eyes, I could tell there was still a little fear there. You were… eighty percent sure you wanted to do it."

"Eighty percent?" I was laughing with him, but I realized he was spot on. How wondrous it was to be so connected with someone that they had that good of a read on your emotions at any given time. And that was even before the telepathic connection had blossomed into what it was now. As I felt out for him in this moment, I sensed mostly excitement coming from his energetic field. The only uncertainty seemed to be radiating from myself.

I took a few deep breaths as I finished buckling the straps on the harness.

You can do this.

You've done it a hundred times before with women.

He's given you so much. You can give him this.

I kept repeating those words to myself as I walked out of the bathroom and into my bedroom.

When I stepped into the room, J was sitting naked on my bed and stroking himself. He froze when he saw me.

"Oh my God," he said breathlessly as he looked me up and down. "That is… sexy as hell." He stood up to meet me at the edge of the bed and took me in his strong arms as he whispered to me. "I've tried to imagine what you might look like wearing that dozens of times. It doesn't hold a candle to what actually seeing you in it feels like." He ran a finger underneath the waist strap and tugged on it roughly. I inhaled sharply.

"Oh, so you can feel something when I do that?" he asked with surprise.

"The bottom strap is between my legs. For stability I assume. It's sitting on top of my clit. So, to answer your question, yes… I can feel a little," I replied.

"Good to know," he said with a mischievous grin. He grabbed the cock attachment and pulled it towards him. I gasped as the strap between my legs shifted forward and my knees buckled a bit from the sensation.

"I guess there is a little bit in this for me after all," I said with a nervous giggle.

He looked at me solemnly. "This is *mostly* for you, Jen," he said.

"Well, I wouldn't take it that far. You will definitely be feeling much more than I will," I said.

"That's not what I mean. I'm not talking about physically. While it's true that I do want to experience the side of you that can be dominant, there's one more thing you need to know. One more reason that I want so badly to do this. You gave me the biggest gift I've ever been given the night that we first slept together. You gave me the surrender and the innocence that you hadn't given another man, ever. You trusted me to be the first man to make love to you. I…want to give you something equal to that. I'm gifting you something that I've never shared with another human, in the exact same way that you gave that to me. It's something that I'm a little uncertain about. Something that requires complete trust in you, and it's an experience that I've never had with anyone else. Submission is a piece of myself that no one but you has ever or will ever have - and I'm offering it to you with all of my heart. I'm giving you back what you gave me, love," he said.

He brushed my long hair back away from my face as he spoke and caught a tear with his thumb as it slipped from my eye.

This man.

This gloriously sensitive, thoughtful, astoundingly romantic man.

What had I ever done to deserve a love like this?

Why and how had this beautiful human fallen for me so deeply that he could love me so completely?

I was speechless.

He kissed me tenderly again and again, searching my eyes in between for the thoughts that I knew he could easily see.

"Say something?" he finally asked with a smile. I shook my head.

"I don't even know where to begin. Just… thank you, J. Thank you for loving me so beautifully in ways that I didn't even know I needed," I said as I met his gaze.

"Thank YOU. Thank you for sharing the incredible experience of this love with me. Thank you for waking me up. Thank you for bringing me to life. Most importantly, thank you for showing me what love with no boundaries feels like. I just want to stay in the magic with you, Jen. I want to keep finding new ways to love you – keep expanding and deepening and discovering all that is between us. Is that all right?" he said.

"Yes. I want that too," I replied with a nod. I wiped away a few more tears and when I went to embrace him, the strap attachment bumped against his leg reminding me what had sparked this entire conversation. Despite the deep emotional reaction that his words had brought to the surface in me, I knew that I was going to have to put the tears away for the moment and step fully into the role he had asked me to play in order to receive the beautiful gift he was offering to me.

The feel of the strap-on cock pressing against the inside of J's leg brought back the recollection of exactly how I had embodied the role of a dominant with the women that I had fucked while wearing it. I knew that I was going to have to turn up the volume on that persona in order to pull off the same level of control with J. I briefly considered talking to him about how to start but decided that this would likely be much more of a turn-on for him if he never saw it coming. This was a side of me that he knew nothing about, and I was holding cards he hadn't seen.

It knew it was time.

I leaned into him enough that it shifted his weight slightly off balance. As he went to take a step back to steady himself, I quickly wrapped my leg around his knee and pulled it sharply towards me, causing him to fall backward onto the bed. I was on top of him in an instant, straddling him and peering down at his very shocked expression. I pressed my knees into his arms near his shoulders effectively pinning him to the mattress with my own weight.

"MISS JEN!" he said with surprise as he tried briefly to move from beneath me but then gave up with a laugh.

"Oh, you've been holding out on me, you naughty girl," he said as he bent his arm just enough to grab my ass tightly. I slapped his hand away hard, and his eyes widened.

"You don't touch me unless I say you can," I told him flatly.

"Yes, Miss," he replied in a half-shocked, half-delighted whisper. The sound of him using the name he had always called me, "Miss Jen," as a title to indicate his submission sent a thrill through me. I knew I would never hear it quite the same again.

The dildo was hanging just inches from his face. It crossed my mind to scoot up above his head and straddle his face, move the strap to the side, and demand that he get me off with his tongue – but then something different flashed through my mind and I halted. As in most moments when were in bed together, I wasn't sure if the image I saw had come from me or from him, but it had been such an arousing thought that I quickly shifted my intention. I began to stroke the strap-on cock the way I had seen J stroke his own so many times.

"I want you to take this in your mouth. I want to watch you suck it the way I suck yours," I demanded. The thought must have come from him because it was instantly clear that he had known I was going to ask. He seemed not the least bit surprised as he nodded with a soft, "Yes, ma'am."

As I watched him wrap his mouth around the dildo, I shifted position to release the pressure from his shoulders so that he could freely move his arms once more. He brought one hand up to hold and stroke the cock while he sucked it. I felt the strap on the underside begin to move back and forth against my clit as he very intentionally pulled the attachment forward with each stroke. I moaned with pleasure. When I looked into his eyes, I saw that he was asking permission to continue – making sure that pleasing me was ok at this time with a quizzical glance.

I nodded encouragement to him, and he increased the speed slightly.

I hadn't expected this to be so tantalizing on my end, but I was on fire.

The visual pleasure of watching him willingly take orders from me to do something that I never would have dreamed he would agree to do was *overwhelmingly* intoxicating. I felt so powerful as I pushed the cock down his throat a little. I watched him gag in response.

"Good boy," I whispered as I pulled out to give him a chance to breathe.

He laughed in disbelief. "I can't believe you've just been meekly letting me dominate you this whole time, and all of THIS was underneath. I had no idea who I was fucking, Miss Jen. I've been playing with fire, it seems," he said. His eyes were sparkling with delight.

I winked at him. "Well, you struck the match," I replied.

I slid myself back down the length of his body until I sat between his legs. I leaned forward and took his thick cock into my mouth for a moment, feeling it grow harder between my lips. He moaned softly.

I sat back on my heels, and as I did so, I spread his legs wide. I reached for the bottle of lubricant that I had sat on the edge of the bed earlier when I took the attachment out of the drawer. I poured a generous amount on the dildo and looked up to make eye contact with J while I rubbed the liquid on it. He held my gaze steady, but I could tell he was a little afraid. I bent his long legs and pushed them back towards him until his knees were over his ribs.

I thought of all of the dirty, domineering things I could say to him as I positioned the cock to enter his body, but when I looked back up at his face, they all seemed to evaporate. I really didn't want to hurt him. I looked at him quizzically, looking for some reassurance that he wanted me to keep going.

"I'm sure," he said, though I could tell he was bracing himself for the worst.

"Eighty percent?" I asked with a sly smile. He laughed out loud, and I felt his body relax as he did so. He grinned back at me and nodded.

"Eighty percent."

I took a deep breath and watched him do the same.

"I love you," I whispered. He mouthed back a silent "yes ma'am."

He began to stroke himself as I slowly began to enter his body with the attachment as gently as I possibly could. I watched his eyes widen with surprise as he inhaled sharply. When I was fully inside him, I paused, searching his face for any sign that he wanted me to stop. He smiled in response.

"You look so worried. I'm ok, Jen. YOU relax. Let's go, babe," he said.

I nodded.

I began to thrust in and out of him very slowly, going a little deeper each time. He moaned softly, his head tilted back, and eyes closed. I felt his entire body relax more fully and he began to ride the waves of each inward thrust. I was watching his face carefully to make sure that it was only pleasure that he was experiencing – ready to instantly adjust or soften if needed.

Suddenly his eyes opened and met mine. They were full of wonder.

"Is this what it feels like when I fuck you?" he asked in a whisper.

My heart melted.

I knew exactly what he meant. The vulnerability. The surrender. The body being totally entrusted to another human being.

I was witnessing him experience that for the first time.

He was in my hands. At my mercy fully.

I could easily hurt him, and we both knew it but here he was, lying beneath me with his heart wide open in complete faith that I wouldn't.

"Yes. It feels just like that, J. I've got you," I replied.

"I know," he said.

He closed his eyes again and I began to increase the speed ever so slightly, watching his every move in response to make sure he was comfortable. When he began to lean into the penetration, raising his hips up slightly to meet my thrust I knew we had just blown past any remaining boundary. The fear was gone now.

"I'm going to give you all of this cock now. I know you can take it," I said.

I felt him balk slightly and his eyes flew open to look at me once more.

"You *can*. You're doing so well… I want a little more of you…a little deeper. Surrender to me completely," I whispered urgently.

He nodded in response and took a huge breath in. On his exhale I felt the remaining resistance fall away and he relaxed completely beneath me. The instant I felt the shift I took the opportunity to penetrate him fully and he moaned with pleasure.

"Miss Jen…" he said as he received me in over and over. I watched in amazement and awe as this force of masculinity allowed me to have my way with him completely. I could feel my own wetness dripping down my thighs. Seeing him like this, feeling the absolute vulnerability of all that he was giving to me was by far the most erotic moment of my life.

He began to stare into my eyes intently as I thrust into him again and again. Our energy was fully merged now, and we were back in the space of indistinguishable thoughts and emotions. I could hear everything that was coming from him, though he was saying nothing aloud.

My love…

There is nothing here that you cannot have.

Everything I have and everything I am belongs to you.

My body and soul are in your hands.
I am yours, and you are mine.

We had met somewhere in the field between masculine and feminine – someplace outside of gender and judgment and expectation. There had been a completion of the circle that was him and me – the mouth of the snake had consumed the tail until the entire whole was so connected that there was no beginning or end. There was only "us" now. Neither he nor I. No roles. No rules. No conditions. Only pure undiluted trust, and the deepest love that has ever existed

Chapter Fourteen

THE LAW OF Attraction and manifestation began to pop up quite frequently in the books I was reading around that time. They intrigued me deeply. The more I was experiencing the exchange of cosmic energy with J, the more I was getting a feel for what sending and receiving vibration felt like.

I decided to try and play with the concept a bit. Could I do it? Could I manifest something into my life with just my will? I wanted to experiment and see if I could make this "Law of Attraction" work for me.

I decided that I would start with something that I didn't care too much about, just to see if it was possible. I tried to think about something specific that I wanted but wasn't so invested in receiving that I would be upset if it didn't happen. I settled on trying to manifest a truck to drive to work. I loved my old Jeep, but it was a manual and a very rough ride. The animal hospital that I was grooming for was nearly an hour from my new place, and every single day that I drove there I wished I had an automatic. It didn't have to be new. In fact, I didn't want to spend a lot, so it was fine if it was pretty old as long as it was reliable.

I drew out the specifics of what I was wanting to call in and wrote them down on a piece of paper that I taped to my bathroom mirror.

Used truck
Automatic
Low mileage
$6000 MAX
Black
My style

"My style" meant a very specific type of look. I had an ex-girlfriend once tell me that the second gayest thing about me (the first being actually sleeping with women) was my vehicles. I like a butch-looking automobile. I have always driven tough-looking trucks or Jeeps, and the more they look like they could tear up a country field the more I love them. The Jeep I was currently driving had both body and suspension lifts, off-road lighting, and giant mud tires (which was why it hadn't handled well on a wet road the night I wrecked). I felt like Spirit knew by now what kind of look would get my attention, so I felt like simply listing "my style" was sufficient.

I began to send out my request each morning in meditation. I didn't spend much time on it, I just repeated what I wanted and imagined what it would feel like to drive to work in my new vehicle.

When I got up from my quiet time I simply went on about my day and didn't give it another thought. I repeated this action for a few weeks.

One day, as I was leaving work, I passed a used car lot that was about a block away from the animal hospital, and there on the corner sat a beautiful little black truck that I almost wrecked trying to look at as I drove by.

It was lifted. It had off-road lighting in a bar across the top and another set near the headlights. Someone had definitely spent some money fixing up this truck, it was obvious. I turned around and went back to the lot to get a closer look.

I got out of my Jeep and walked up to the truck to look inside of it. It was an automatic. It looked immaculate, and the interior had several accessories that had been added as well. I couldn't find a price or information sheet on it anywhere. I figured that it was probably far more expensive than what I had wanted to pay, given the condition.

A salesman walked up behind me as I was looking it over.

"Pretty truck, huh?", he said.

"It's beautiful. I couldn't find a price though. How much are you all asking for it?", I asked.

"Yeah, sorry about that. We just got it in a few hours ago so we haven't made a sticker for it yet. They were going to price it at $6,500, but I know they would sell it right now for $5,999 cash."

I laughed out loud.

Maybe this manifestation shit actually did work.

I bought the truck, of course.

I was so excited not only about my new ride, but about how easily I seemed to have called in exactly what I wanted. It boosted my confidence in my ability to intentionally manifest things and I decided to set my sights on something a little bigger.

There was only one thing that I could think of that I didn't have that I desperately wanted.

I wanted music to be my full-time job.

Since the moment that J and I started the duo together, I had been daydreaming about making the move to music as a career. I wanted our songs to be on the radio. I wanted to tour with him. We had fantasized with each other about what our life would look like together on the road. A new city every day, and a show every night. An entire life together filled with singing and travel and writing and lovemaking. It sounded like heaven, and it was everything I wanted.

THAT. That was what I wanted to manifest.

The problem was, I didn't really know how to go about calling that in. It felt so multilayered and complicated. When I sat down to write out exactly what it was that I wanted it was over a page long. I knew I was going to have to try and simplify this somehow. The more I thought about it, the more I realized that the entire life that I was hoping to create for myself all stemmed back to music. It was going to take something really big to shift in order for our music to get seen on the scale that I was hoping for. We needed connections in Nashville. We needed visibility that was outside of our area. If we could just get a leg up somehow, then touring to promote ourselves would naturally follow. Music was the path to all of our dreams coming true, so I decided to focus on that aspect for my manifestation work.

I replaced the paper that I had stuck to my mirror that had my truck details on it with a new paper that only had two phrases written on it:

MUSIC VISIBILITY

NASHVILLE CONNECTION

Those words still felt vague to me because I didn't know exactly what to try and call in.

I didn't know how anything worked in the music business, so I was hoping like hell that Spirit did.

I went through the same process that I had done with my truck. Every morning and night I would send out my requests for help with our music career. In meditation, I would get lost in my fantasies about what my life with music and J was going to look and feel like. It was intoxicating. I wanted it so desperately that I found myself daydreaming about it almost constantly.

This went on for a few months.

Absolutely nothing shifted.

I began to wonder why nothing was happening.

I focused even harder on trying to call it in. I meditated longer. I voiced my desires out loud.

Still, nothing.

I went back online and searched for manifesting tips. I picked up a few new ones and added them to my regimen. I wrote down what I wanted and burned the paper. I imagined what I wanted when I lay down at night until I fell asleep.

I began to get frustrated. Why the hell was nothing showing up? It seemed that the louder I got in my requests, the less I got back. The Universe had gone completely silent on me.

I thought back to the ease with which my truck had appeared in my life. I had done the exact same process that I was using now, hadn't I?

It suddenly dawned on me that there had been one very big difference between the two scenarios.

I hadn't really cared if I got the truck.

It could have shown up in my life, or not. It hadn't really been that big of a deal to me because I had been treating it like an experiment from the get-go. In contrast, I wanted this life with J and music more than I wanted anything. It felt like the single biggest and most important thing in the whole world. In my attempt to manifest a big shift with music, I had been desperately grasping for it and trying to do everything I could to sway the Universe in my favor somehow.

I went back and reread one of the books I had bought on the Law of Attraction. It confirmed what I had begun to suspect - I had been blocking the manifestation.

I had been so focused on when I was going to receive what I was asking for that I was hindering it. The Law of Attraction states that like attracts like. So basically, the energy that you put out is the energy that you receive.

I had been so hyper-focused on the LACK of movement that I was inadvertently calling in more lack. The book stated that in order to remedy this that I would have to shift my attention and energy. I needed to let go of my attachment to the outcome of what I was asking for, and act as though the Universe had already granted my wish.

This was a big mindset shift for me. I struggled with it initially. How was I supposed to let go of the outcome of the thing I wanted more than anything? I held the memory of how I had treated my wish for the truck in my mind as a guide for how to proceed.

I started telling myself that it was fine if things didn't work out with music. J and I would figure out another way to be together, and we would always make music no matter what. When I got up from meditation, I tried to leave the fantasies about our touring life on the yoga mat. I would allow myself to revel in the images of what I wanted for a while, but then at the end of my session, I would say "It is done. Thank you Spirit for making it so." I would visualize Spirit running off to put things into place for my dream to come true, and I tried very hard to trust that I didn't need to worry about it anymore.

It took me about a week to get the swing of this new approach. I found that I was thinking about it less and less during my workday and was truly starting to just trust that Spirit had it covered.

It worked like a charm.

The Melody of Fire

In just a few weeks, Spirit brought in the answer to my prayers in a way that I could have never seen coming.

I came home from work one day to find a DM on the band's Instagram page from none other than country music singer/songwriter/producer Dean Miller, son of the legendary Roger Miller.

He said that he had come across one of our songs on Spotify and that he loved our sound. He wondered if I might give him a call to discuss the possibility of him bringing us to Nashville to produce our next album. At the end of the message, he listed his personal cell phone number.

I stared at that message for a solid ten minutes in utter shock and disbelief.

I briefly investigated his profile, website, and credentials to make sure that I wasn't dealing with some Instagram scammer. It seemed legitimate.

I showed the message to J, but he wasn't sold.

"I don't know, Jen. It wouldn't hurt to talk to him, I don't suppose, but anybody could just say they are Dean Miller in a DM, you know? I would at least ask him to FaceTime you or Skype or something so that you can make sure that is actually him you are talking to. Just before we get too excited about this," he said.

I agreed. I sent a message back saying that we were flattered that he liked our song, and that I would love to connect via FaceTime if he was available to talk. He messaged me back that he would absolutely be up for that, and we set a time for the call.

I was so antsy and nervous the whole entire day leading up to that video chat. What if it wasn't him? This was going to be so disappointing if it turned out to be a hoax.

When I got home that evening, I got ready for that phone call the same way that I would have prepared for a show. I curled my hair, and carefully applied my makeup. If this really was Dean Miller, then I wanted to look the part of a potential country music star.

If it wasn't him, I was going to feel like an idiot.

I sat down on my couch and carefully dialed the number that he had sent me. I scarcely breathed as I waited for him to answer the call.

When the call clicked over to video, I was delighted to find myself staring at the same face that I had seen in photographs on the internet standing with artists like Dolly Parton and Brooks and Dunn.

It really was him.

"Hey, Jen! I'm Dean. It's nice to finally get to talk to you," he said.

I could hardly believe it. It was nice to talk to *me*? I wasn't the one whose reputation proceeded me. I had to continually rein in my nervousness throughout our entire phone call, even though Dean was so personable and laid-back that I found him easy to converse with.

177

Together, we laid out a plan to come to Nashville and record with him. He seemed genuinely excited to produce our album. He wanted me to send him audios of our original songs that we wanted to record, along with notes to indicate what sound we were going for in order for him to select the musicians that would be the best fit for the project. He gave me a list of dates that would be an option for us to get in the studio, and I told him that I would discuss it with J and get back to him to secure our recording time.

"That sounds great, I'll be working on putting the players together in the meantime. I'm so excited about this, Jen. I really think I can help you all get where you want to be with your music career. We can talk more about marketing and promoting as we go along here, but the first step is getting a radio-quality recording for us to push. We will touch base in a few days, but I'm looking forward to meeting J as well and working with you both," he said as we ended the phone call.

I couldn't even contain my excitement. I called J and told him all that had transpired with the phone call, and it made me so happy to hear the elation in his voice. We talked eagerly about the recording and worked out our dates that we would be able to go into the studio. I couldn't wait! This was finally happening! My dreams…our dreams…were about to come true, it seemed.

About six weeks later we walked into the legendary OmniSound studio in Nashville to record our own original songs, with Dean Miller heading the production.

It was beyond surreal.

As we came into the engineering room, Dean began to introduce us to the musicians that would be playing our songs on the recording.

We stood there with our mouths hanging open as we shook hands with a group of all-stars. Our team consisted of musicians that we immediately recognized.

Our drummer was the house drummer for the Grand Ole Opry.

Our steel and mandolin player had recorded and performed with Randy Travis for over a decade.

Our guitar player had played and toured with everyone from Elton John to Tanya Tucker.

Our fiddle player had just won CMA and ACM Musician of the Year awards the year prior.

J turned to me wide-eyed as they all went into the sound booth and began to play OUR songs. *Songs that he and I had written together in a freaking barn in Bristol, Tennessee.*

He grabbed my hand and leaned over to whisper frantically in my ear.

"How did this even happen, Jen? We are so out of our league. We don't deserve

The Melody of Fire

to be here. That's a group of fucking *legends* playing *our* songs. Is this a dream? I can't understand how we got here," he said.

It was cute to watch him fangirl over the players like that, but I completely understood how he felt. He was right. We didn't really deserve to be there, but I knew exactly how this had happened. I thought back to the paper hanging on my bathroom mirror.

MUSIC VISIBILITY

NASHVILLE CONNECTION

I had called this in, and though it had arrived in a way that I never could have anticipated, Spirit had delivered *exactly* what I had asked for.

It had taken some trial and effort, for sure, but I realized that I had figured out exactly what it took to work with the energy of the Universe to manifest something.

It made me giddy with anticipation. I had managed to bring in this massive first step to the life that he and I were dreaming about, and I couldn't wait to see what Spirit would do next.

I reminded myself that I was going to have to keep practicing a level of detachment from the outcome if this was to continue. I knew it was going to be extra difficult because now I was excited and invested in this dream in a totally different way. Before Dean had contacted me, this career in music was something that I wanted for J and me, but I couldn't really see how it might happen. Now it felt real. Now we had a plan.

It was going to be extremely hard not to try and push this energetically.

I would have to make a continual conscious effort to keep surrendering this to Spirit, because that had clearly been the shift that made all of this come to fruition.

That shift in my mindset had been the thing that made it all click into place, finally.

In a way, it reminded me of something that I learned in voice lessons.

When I first began learning to sing, my voice teacher told me a truth that I've never forgotten. He said that vocal lessons were funny/tricky in a particular way: when you were working on a certain note that seemed extremely difficult to master, you would go along for a span of time and see no improvement. Teachers and other singers would tell you exactly how to place your breath or compress the note, or how to let it resonate fully to make the note easy... and you would try and try and try to do what they said, but frustratingly would keep getting the same result. But then one day you would be practicing and unintentionally do something just ever so slightly different and suddenly reach the note with ease. In that moment, EVERYTHING would just click for you about it. The progress would be instantaneous, and it would be easy for you from then on. Suddenly all of the ways that people had been trying to tell you to hit that note would make sense and you would laugh at how hard you had been making it.

179

He had been right. That exact experience had happened for me more times than I could count through my journey of learning to sing.

It seemed I had just had the same lesson occur for me on a spiritual level. I had been making things infinitely harder than they had to be when it came to manifesting and now that I had called in the thing that I wanted the most and it was solid in my hands, I had to laugh a bit at how hard I'd been making it. The plight of the overthinker is that we try to understand and anticipate all of the angles. We get so caught up in our heads that we don't allow Spirit the space to work.

I had just figured out that the key to making the Law of Attraction work is to not get so hung up on the details of *how* your prayers will be answered and just trust that they *will* be. Allowing Spirit to surprise and delight you by working in ways that you never could have come up with on your own is much more fun anyway. I could have tried to force things by reaching out to record labels and promoters on my own, but I guarantee that things wouldn't have worked out nearly as well (if they had worked out at all) as the solution that the Universe delivered to my doorstep.

I realized that when I had allowed it to happen on Spirit's terms is when the magic had happened.

Surrendering it all was the ticket.

I had just shifted ever so slightly… pressed my breath a different way…and found the note.

WITH ALL OF the success I had been having with manifesting, I began to realize that I had truly begun to build my own relationship with Spirit outside of what J had been teaching me. While it was true that J was further along on the spiritual path, our relationship itself had given me the confidence to try things right and left that were outside of his direction or guidance. I had begun working with Spirit in ways that J didn't. Alongside trying to figure out the Law of Attraction, I also began to ask Spirit for signs when I needed an answer to a question.

Right off the bat, I picked the fox as my "sign" for Spirit to give me if I was headed in the right direction. I have always felt deeply connected to foxes and latched onto them as my "spirit animal" long before I even knew exactly what a spirit animal is or how they work. For the purposes of asking for a sign, I knew that they would stand out to me in a way that I couldn't miss because of their color (and my love for them) which always made me notice when they were present. My exploration started with simply asking Spirit to "show me a fox if I'm supposed to…" – fill in the blank with whatever I wanted to know at the moment.

Sure enough, I would go into work to see a coworker holding a coffee cup with a fox on it, or I would walk into a store to see a kid's shirt with a fox stitched onto the front sitting in plain view. It started happening frequently enough that it seemed more than synchronistic to me. I told J about it, and I could tell he didn't really believe that the signs I was getting were an answer from Spirit.

"I don't know, babe. Seems awfully coincidental to me. I'm not sure Spirit actually works that way," he said.

He picked on me a little bit about it here and there until he experienced it with me one evening in a way that neither of us could write off.

We were at a show in a tiny little town near home, and I had been discussing touring with J. It was going to be tricky to pull off, we both knew. With the new Nashville album coming out, we were going to have to widen our audience a little bit, but J felt certain that Lila would never allow him to go out of town for days at a time. Especially with me. Alone.

She was definitely beginning to suspect that something was going on between J and me, though J assured me that she hadn't flat-out asked him if we were sleeping together. He told me that she had begun to ask lots of questions and to keep a close eye on the amount of time we were spending together. I could tell talking about it was painful to him, so I didn't push him too much for information. Instead, I just let him tell me his ideas for how he thought we might be able to proceed with a small tour.

We talked about it prior to the show, and then it came up again on our break after the first set. As we stepped up to the bar to grab a beer, I asked J if we should even try to make touring work if it was going to be this difficult to figure out and stressful on us all.

"Do you think we are even supposed to do this?" I asked.

He turned and flashed me a radiant smile and said, "Well, let's just ask for a fox as a sign. That's what you do, right?"

He looked up to the sky and said, "Universe, if touring is what we are supposed to do… then please show us a fox."

He then teased me a little and asked if he did it right. I rolled my eyes at him and nodded, and we headed outside to enjoy our drinks before we had to be back onstage.

We had only been out there a moment, when a kid that was standing near us in front of the restaurant suddenly shouted, "Hey!! Is that a fox???"

We both wheeled around to see, with great shock, a gentleman walking down the street holding in his arms…a *live* fox, on a leash.

There was so much excitement from the people around us, they asked if the gentleman would bring the fox closer so that we could pet it. J turned to face me with wide eyes and an open mouth.

"What the FUCK, Jen?" was all he could utter.

"Looks like we are supposed to tour," I laughingly replied.

I insisted on a photo with the fox, mostly as a memento of the way the universe is always listening.

By the time J asked for that fox that evening at the show, I already knew what would happen (though even I was surprised at the delivery of an actual LIVE fox on a busy downtown street), but I was still delighted to see J's disbelief and joy at the immediate and accurate response we received. As in tune as he was with Spirit, he had clearly never asked for a sign before, and when I think back to his face that night downtown, I have to laugh. It wasn't often that I got to witness a lightbulb moment with my boy. It was usually him educating me in the ways of the Universe, not the other way around. It felt good to have something new to add to the conversation that he was usually leading. I never heard him ask for a sign in that same way after that night, but it definitely sealed the deal for me utilizing them whenever possible.

Foxes became my little guideposts from then on. Whenever I needed a little nudge, a little reassurance, I would ask for one of my little foxy spirit guides to point the direction. If it was a bigger deal or something that I needed absolute clarity on, I would ask for a pair of foxes. I wanted something extremely specific that I couldn't write off as coincidence, because it was absolutely insane to me how my mind could look at the very thing I had asked for and somehow refuse to believe that it was an answer to my request. We are so hardwired to write off the spiritual connectivity that is available to us at all times that it is astounding.

Try it. I encourage you. Ask for a VERY specific sign about something, and then watch how, when the universe delivers it, your mind will literally tell you that there is no way that it appeared simply because you asked. It will offer most consistently to you as a reasoning that it was merely coincidence. I had a friend who once asked the universe (because he was doubting me when I told him about signs and how they work) for an octopus playing a guitar as a sign for a big decision he was trying to make. He picked something outlandish, that I know he thought would be impossible to deliver, in order to say "I told you so" to me when he didn't walk out his front door to find an octopus jamming out on his porch.

The next day, he called me, more than a little shaken, because a friend of his had sent him a photo of a folder that she had bought for her son for school that had (you guessed it) a cartoon of an octopus playing a guitar on the front. What do you think he did? Did he express gratitude to the universe for such clear and direct confirmation of the direction he needed to go? No. He wrote it off as a crazy coincidence and did the exact opposite thing. (A thing, I might add, that ultimately didn't work out for him in the way that he had hoped.)

I get it, believe me. It takes a good bit of time and a whole lot of faith to get to the place where you don't question the answers you receive. Asking for signs was one of my first experiences with talking to Spirit and though I always found it delightful when I got a response, it certainly took a while before I was confident that I was actually being guided. Over time, it became so reliable that I didn't even have to ask for the foxes anymore, they just showed up indicating the direction I needed to go. When I saw them, I always took note, especially if there were two of them. I began to think of them as my little messengers from the Universe; my little arrows helping me take the next correct steps. I had a small sense of pride that it was a way that I found to connect with Spirit that I thought of *all by myself*. It felt like a special little wink from Spirit, and to this day I always delight in the slightly miraculous feeling that I am being sweetly and very tangibly responded to whenever I asked for guidance.

I HAD GOTTEN in the habit of getting up super early to try and connect with J in meditation. To both of our surprise and delight, in the early morning hours, we found we were able to have entire conversations in the spirit plane that we both were able to remember and discuss when we were together. It consistently blew my mind (and his, though to a lesser degree) that what I first thought were conversations that I was imagining in my head were instead a shared experience that was as real as any contact that we were sharing in the physical plane. I treasured those moments together, and they were often the only thing that got me through the physical separation.

One morning, however, I had an experience that was quite unlike the others.

I got up at 5:00 am and made a cup of coffee before settling quietly on my yoga mat to try and tap in. It was a bit chilly, so I wrapped a blanket around my shoulders and groggily began to focus on my breath. I breathed in deeply, held it for a four-count, and released it slowly as I let my body settle into the present moment. I repeated this a few times, waking up a little more each time I inhaled. When I felt good and grounded – solid in my presence and awareness, I gently reached out my energy to J.

"You awake, J?" I whispered. I listened intently, but instead of hearing his familiar voice reply to me from the darkness, I suddenly felt a presence materialize in front of me that felt so physical that my eyes flew open in fear.

"What the fuck was that?! Who's there?" I half-shouted, as my eyes searched for some kind of materialization of the energy I had just felt so strongly.

As I considered what exactly I would do if some ghost or spirit DID visually appear in front of me (the answer all being some variance of screaming whilst shitting myself), I begin to get panicky.

I heard J laugh softly.

"It's me, babe. Please don't shit yourself," he said bemusedly, obviously hearing my thoughts.

"Huh? How is that even possible, J? It just felt like you were LITERALLY sitting in front of me," I replied. I was still looking wildly around the room.

He chuckled softly as he replied, "And that is how you respond to me sitting in front of you? Relax, love. Close your eyes and I'll do it again."

I narrowed my eyes, not fully trusting any of what appeared to be happening.

"I don't know, J. That was so… *weird*. I don't really like how that felt. How are you doing that?" I asked.

He sighed.

"For once will you just trust in what is happening between us without questioning it to no end? There are so many layers to this, Jen… just *trust me*, please? There will come a time when all of this will make sense to you, I promise, but for now, will you just put all of your doubts and fears aside and be present with me in this moment? You will be so glad you did," he whispered to me quietly.

The solemnness of his tone made me settle once more. I nodded in agreement and closed my eyes again.

I had no sooner done so, when I felt the almost tangible presence of him inches in front of me. I had to fight the urge to open my eyes again to look at what I was sure would be his physical body – it felt *that real*. That solid.

I felt him gently blow the baby hairs away from my forehead with his breath the way he would often playfully do. I couldn't wrap my head around how he was doing any of this, but it was so familiar, and so obviously *him* that I just relaxed instantly.

"May I kiss you?" he asked.

"You don't have to ask to kiss me, J. You should know that by now," I replied.

I felt his presence move closer to me. What can only be described as a concentration of energy so solid that it was whatever "one step below physical touch" is, brushed the side of my cheek and then gently parted my lips.

I felt myself being enveloped in the most familiar loving energy as he kissed me tenderly. There was a yearning present that I had never felt from him before. The kiss lingered longer than it normally would have.

"My God, I've missed that," he whispered in the saddest tone that I had ever heard. Something about the way he said it made me emotional, though I didn't understand why he seemed so melancholy.

"Missed it since yesterday? You just kissed me yesterday after the show, J. It's not been that long," I replied.

"Yeah, I guess you're right. What can I say? One day is too long to go without kissing you," he replied. Though he was trying to be playful, the sorrow in his voice was still present.

"Take your clothes off, Jen. Will you let me touch you?" he asked in a whisper.

"Again, love… you never have to ask permission. No matter what the circumstance," I answered. *And wasn't this a strange one?* I was entirely unclear on what was happening here, but he had asked me to trust him and so I did. I let the blanket fall from my shoulders and quickly slipped out of my pajama bottoms and t-shirt. I settled back into a seated position on my yoga mat completely naked, shivering slightly, and closed my eyes once again.

I felt him lean in to kiss me and as he did so, I felt myself being somehow supported fully as I was gently cradled and laid back onto my mat. I remember thinking that I should probably feel afraid, or more appropriately, completely and totally creeped out, but I wasn't in the least. I felt safe. Supported. Held. I had a deep inner knowing that this was real. This was actually J. It felt easy to surrender to, despite the bizarreness of the situation.

The coolness of the mat as it touched my bare back made me wince slightly.

"Cold?", J asked.

"A little…", I replied truthfully.

"Let me see if I can fix that. I'm going to come above you and try and merge my energetic body with yours. It may feel a little strange, love, but all you have to do is allow it to happen.", he said.

"I have no idea what you are talking about, for the record, but I'll just roll with this, I guess," I said. He laughed, but then went quiet again. I sensed that he was concentrating. I felt his presence strongly above me, and I became still with anticipation.

I felt the air above my body begin to vibrate and quiver. As the energy lowered down closer and closer to me, I suddenly felt my body also begin to tingle and a slow heat began to spread over my skin as if somehow a heat lamp had been turned on above me and I was beginning to feel the warmth radiating from it.

A sighed as I stopped shivering and enjoyed the warm glow.

"Better?", J asked.

"Mmmhmm. Much. Thank you," I replied.

"Let me make love to you, Jen. I want to absolutely ravish you right here and now - but I'll need for you to trust me a little deeper. This will be unlike anything we've ever done… but I promise that it will be so beautiful and magical if you can just let it unfold without fear. Will you allow it?" he whispered softly. His voice still tinged with sorrow, there was a gentle pleading behind his question; I felt as if he might cry should I decline the offer. I wasn't at all sure where this sadness was coming from, or why any of this was happening at all for that matter, but I knew there was no way I was turning down this chance to experience something so mystical with him.

"I'm in, J. Just tell me what you want me to do," I replied.

"There's my good girl," he said in a low tone. My heart skipped a beat with the phrase as he said it. I knew what that term of endearment meant. He was asking me to be completely submissive and follow his directions precisely. With my eyes still closed, I smiled slightly and nodded.

"Spread your legs for me, but then relax as much as you possibly can," he said. I obeyed, separating my legs as he asked and then becoming still again.

"I need you to breathe deeply, Jen, and try to release any tension at all that you are holding in your body as you exhale," he directed. I followed his instruction and brought the air deeply into my lungs and then tried to let go of any fear or apprehension with my exhale. I repeated a few times.

"Let go of more. I need you more open, love. You are going to be bringing quite a bit of energy into your body and I need you to make space. Release as much as you can with your exhales," he coaxed. I wasn't sure exactly what he meant, but I tried to let go of everything I could. I focused on allowing my body to become so relaxed that it felt as if it were melting into the floor.

"There. That's perfect. Now... try not to flinch or react with your body as I tell you the next step. Stay just as relaxed as you are in this moment. I'm going to penetrate you with my energy. I will start in the way that you are used to penetration from me... you will feel me enter you sexually... just surrender to me totally. Let me initiate every movement. Try and stay as receptive as you possibly can," he said.

I tried to comprehend what he was telling me was going to happen, but all my brain wanted to do was ask 1000 questions. It was as if J heard them all.

"Shhh. Stop, babe. This isn't a mental thing, it's a spiritual and energetic exchange. The quieter you can keep your mind and your body the easier this will flow," he said.

"How do you know how to do this?" I asked. Whatever "this" was, it wasn't something that he had learned with me.

"I've had a lot of practice with an incredibly powerful teacher," he laughed softly as he said it and I felt myself bristle with jealousy.

Who?

I had never heard him speak of having a sexual connection like the one we shared with anyone else...let alone a spiritual one. Had he somehow learned this from his wife? He had always made it seem as though their relationship was a fairly surface-level one. I couldn't imagine that they had been pushing the boundaries in the spiritual plane the way we had, but I also hadn't an inkling of an idea of who it might be if it wasn't her.

I was just about to ask him who this "powerful teacher" was when I felt a sensation that made me lose thought altogether.

Between my upper thighs, a warm push of energy seemed to lean into my body and caused me to spread my legs even further. It felt like J was physically between my legs and preparing to enter my body.

"Stay relaxed, Jen. Just receive me into you," he whispered. I obeyed. I didn't dare move a centimeter.

I felt the warm energy pulsating against my clitoris, moving slowly like lapping waves of sensation that touched me and then receded over and over again. I marveled at the way it felt *almost* but not quite physical, yet still causing a ripple through my body each time, in the same way that an actual physical touch would.

I then felt the lips of my vagina spread apart slowly as some sort of red-hot energy penetrated me fully. I cried out in surprise at the physicality of it. The energy filled my insides the same way that J's cock always felt – just not as solid. However, the heat made up for the absence of the hardness and I could feel every single shift that he made. As this energy began to thrust in and out of me, I began to feel as though it had somehow merged with me. My body complied as if it had no choice but to ride the waves of sensation.

Fullness, then the release.

Fullness, then the release.

The longer it went on, the more momentum the hot waves of energy gathered until it felt like my very cells were being pushed and pulled into the rhythm. My back arched involuntarily, and I felt myself opening up to receive as much as I could.

"MORE!" I cried out to J.

"Yes, ma'am," he replied.

The waves of energy then pushed up into my womb, causing the heat to spread throughout my entire abdomen. He had entered into my body deeper than he ever had. Deeper than was physically possible.

Fullness, then the release.

Fullness, then the release.

The waves were exquisite. I was writhing uncontrollably from the pleasure.

I never wanted it to end.

"Please don't stop…" I begged.

He responded by pushing into me even further on the next thrust. The warmth expanded up through my body filling me with tingling and hot heat all the way up to my rib cage.

Fullness, then the release.

Fullness, then the release.

The entire lower half of my body was ablaze with a fire that I had never felt before. Every part of me was being fucked with an intensity that I cannot fully describe. Every nerve, every vein it seemed, was at the mercy of the push and pull coursing through me in hot pulsating waves. Pleasure like I had never felt rushed through me with every thrust of energy.

"Ahhhh…. J!" I cried out in ecstasy.

"Don't come, Jen. Stay right here and don't give in just yet. I'm going to enter your heart chakra. Stay open and receiving, beautiful," he said.

I was too deep in the riding of the waves to protest or even think. Whatever he wanted to do, I was open and willing at this point. At his mercy entirely, I focused on simply not giving in to the orgasm that I was teetering on the edge of.

I felt the heat begin to push into my chest, and as it did the writhing lustful energy began to transform into something deeper.

I felt his love for me.

I physically felt in my body an explosion of love *for me* filling my chest.

I knew how much I loved him. The depth and the utterly infinite nature of what I felt for J had never been a secret to me, but *this*… this was different. This was coming from HIM, and I was being allowed to feel it in my own being. The thoughts and feelings attached to the sensation were so multi-faceted; I felt his pride for me and the way he joyfully thought of me as "his" love. I felt the overwhelming appreciation for every single quality I possessed – even character-istics that I wasn't proud of were surrounded by a loving acceptance and almost playful admonishment to let them be seen, so that I couldn't believe I had ever thought that there was reason to try and hide them. I felt so seen in my fullness that there was no part of me that didn't feel adored. Nothing left out. Divine adoration flowed over me with each warm pulse of energy.

I tasted infinity.

For the first time in my existence in this life, I truly understood what forever felt like. I had said the word a thousand times, but here in this moment, I found myself sitting in the middle of eternity with complete comprehension of what it truly meant. There was no beginning and no end to this love. It was so much a part of me that I could not be separated from it without losing myself entirely. *It was me*. I found myself shocked at the realization that his love **was me**… and therefore my love must be him as well.

I knew that it could never be lost. Never be altered. Neither time nor space affected it in the least. Physical bodies or none made no difference whatsoever.

This love could never be anything less than the perfection I was beholding. It could never be more because it wasn't possible for *everything* to be more than it already was.

There was another swell of loving heat, and I thought my chest would burst wide open. The intensity and the power of it brought me to tears, and I wept joyfully.

"I never want you to doubt again what I feel for you. You are everything to me. Do you see that now, Jen? Now that you can actually feel it for yourself?" he whispered urgently.

"Yes…", I answered. It was all I could get to come out of my mouth. I felt absolutely overwhelmed and consumed with love. Unconditional. Perfect.

It was the strongest force I'd ever felt, and it flooded through me with such tenderness that I allowed it to go wherever it liked until my entire body seemed to radiate with love.

"I love you I love you I love you I love you…" he whispered over and over. "I want you to hear it while you experience it. And should there ever be a time that you question how very loved you are by me, I want you to remember this moment."

The energy waves began to settle, though the warmth stayed all throughout my body. I felt as though he had wrapped me up in an all-encompassing embrace. I sighed contentedly.

And then my phone rang.

My conscious awareness snapped back to the present moment where I was lying naked and alone on my yoga mat. I groaned with resentment as I opened my eyes and rolled over to see who could possibly be calling me this early. Before I could get to it, I heard J say, "That's me calling, but before you answer… I just want you to know that what just happened was real, Jen. You didn't dream it or make it up. What you felt was the love I have always had for you, and it will never change or disappear. Ok?"

"Ok," I replied as I picked up the phone. I felt J's energy leave as I stared at the phone in disbelief. It was, indeed, him calling - but that wasn't what had made me freeze in shock. It was 7:45.

I had been on my mat for over two and a half hours.

The entire experience had felt like it had lasted maybe fifteen minutes.

I had gotten used to time seemingly evaporating when I was with J physically making love, but this was the first time it had ever happened elsewhere. I sat there for a moment longer staring at my phone before it occurred to me that J was likely calling to talk about what had just happened between us.

I answered the phone with, "J…what the fuck was all of that?"

"Well good morning to you too, beautiful," he replied with a laugh. "What was all of what?"

"All of that mind-blowing shit that just happened in meditation. How did you know how to do all of that?", I asked.

"Jen…I didn't tap in this morning. I overslept. I have no idea what you are talking about," he replied, obviously confused.

"You mean to tell me that we just had the most incredibly spiritual and connective love making session in what felt like another realm, and you… weren't there? You didn't feel *anything* out of the ordinary this morning?" I asked incredulously.

"Ummm… given that description, I can honestly say that I *wish* I knew what you were talking about, but no…it's been a pretty normal morning over here, my dear," he replied.

My heart sank.

I went on to relay all that had happened earlier, all the while becoming less and less certain of my sanity.

He hadn't felt any of it.

"I'm sorry, babe. I really wish I had tapped in with you this morning and somehow experienced all of that too. I believe you, though… just so you know," he said sweetly.

While I was happy to hear that he didn't think I was nuts, that didn't stop *me* from thinking that I was. I hung up the phone frustrated and fairly well convinced that I might be losing my mind. Still… how could something so powerful, something that felt as real (maybe more) as anything I had ever experienced in the physical reality of my life, be created in my head?

But if it *had* been real, and J *had* been there and basically "walked me through" the whole experience – why didn't he remember any of it at all? It wasn't unusual for him to call me right after we connected in meditation to talk about something as asinine as something I had said about work during those moments. Yet he felt and heard nothing during the most potent connection we had ever had in the spiritual plane?

I couldn't make it make sense.

I spend the next several days in morning meditation trying to call that experience back in. If it could happen once, it could happen again, right? I would sit down on my mat and try to replicate exactly the steps I had taken that morning in hopes that whatever I did that caused this phenomenon would somehow align once more.

Though I succeeded easily in connecting with J in the way I had been accustomed to prior, I never was able to recreate what happened that morning. I tried for several months before I finally gave up and chalked it up to being a once-in-a-lifetime experience that I simply needed to be grateful for instead of chasing after.

I never forgot the feeling though. I gently tucked it away in the corner of my heart, and only pulled it out to remember on occasions when I found myself feeling uncertain about J and me. When the circumstances got too rough. When the separation felt impossible. When he was unable to show up for me physically on a day when I desperately needed to feel his touch. I reached into the pocket of my memory and pulled out the remembrance of that morning lying on my mat with the feeling of his unconditional love pouring throughout my entire being. I would close my eyes once more; feel the warmth spread throughout my chest and listen to him whisper "I love you I love you I love you" over and over, with the taste of eternity on my lips and the knowledge that in some other dimension, somewhere, we were together, and he was loving me wildly beyond my capacity to understand.

Chapter Fifteen

MY SUPER-FUNDAMENTALIST UPBRINGING had given me quite a few issues to work through surrounding sex and sexuality that began to rear their head in an interesting way.

J and I began to work through mental blocks that I hadn't even known were still influencing me so much.

Growing up, whenever sex was mentioned (if it was mentioned at all) it was talked about in a manner that indicated that it was a dirty and sinful act. Married sex was the only sex that wasn't frowned upon, and the actual sex act was never discussed, only the concept of it. It was very confusing to young adults such as myself, who were inundated with purity culture in the church community. This whole attitude of "saving oneself for marriage" was of course primarily targeted at young women, and we were made to feel as if simply possessing a blossoming teenage female body was somehow causing the male population to veer off course spiritually.

When I was about fourteen years old there was a young girl in my youth group who brought a friend from school to Bible study one evening. The new girl was not a regular churchgoer, so of course she didn't know what she was walking into. She showed up for Bible study wearing a spaghetti strap tank top (with no bra, I assumed, because there were no straps to be seen) and jeans, and from the reaction that occurred within the church congregation, you would have thought she had walked into the building wearing only a thong and pasties.

I'll be honest, even I couldn't stop staring at her. I was half attracted to her, half amazed at her boldness and the audacity she displayed with just that simple act of unknowing rebellion. (*This bitch though… with her shoulders.*) After church one of the youth leaders pulled her aside and informed her that her attire was unacceptable and that she would have to wear something more modest the next time she came. That was a next time that never happened, much to the dismay of myself and the boys in the youth group. The incident was burned into my memory forever though and drew hard lines in my mind around how much (or how little) was acceptable for a female to show of her body. I wasn't allowed to wear anything that even remotely showed an inch of skin, and I had never seen anyone defy that rule until that girl walked into our church that night. My mother would never have bought me a spaghetti strap tank top. Or shorts that weren't knee-length. Or a dress that was short. Or underwear that wasn't nude-colored and full coverage.

I was shocked, but deeply intrigued.

Not long after the tank-top-girl incident, I spent the night at a friend from school's house and we were playing dress up in her big attic. Her family were performers - dancers and theatre people, and they had a huge selection of costumes that we loved to play in. This particular day, while rifling through the boxes of clothes, I found a beautiful lacy little spaghetti strap tank that had tiny little rhinestones where each strap connected to the top. I tried it on, and it fit me perfectly. I looked at myself in the mirror and felt like an absolute scandal. I wore it all evening while we played. My friend's mom noticed how much I loved it and told me that I could have it.

I wore that tank top home underneath my clothes so that my mom wouldn't see. I hid it in the bottom of my closet and would occasionally sneak it out at night and wear it around my room with just my panties on with it. It made me feel like a fucking sex bomb, but I knew that even in the privacy of my room that this wasn't allowed. I was supposed to keep my scandalous clothing item, and my sex bomb self, hidden away from the eyes of the world, that much was obvious to me; but I also had a weird sense that even feeling "sexy" by myself was wrong somehow. If anyone had caught me in this attire, I would have been so mortified I would have passed away from sheer embarrassment, which just goes to show the depth of humiliation we were made to feel for exploring our own bodies and the sexuality surrounding them.

At a time when we were naturally curious about our quickly maturing bodies, the church made sure to step in quickly and instill a sense of shame. We needed to hide away these developments of ourselves and not talk about them. Our breasts, our menstrual cycles, and even our hormones (which made us curious about sex) were all taboo topics. Christian women were modest. They didn't show their bodies. They didn't talk about sex. We could cause good Christian men to sin if we weren't careful.

I took all of this quite seriously at fourteen. Staying away from men was easy for me at the time. I wasn't attracted to them, so "saving myself" was a great excuse to not have to touch one.

My church hosted a popular class at the time called "True Love Waits," and when it was my appropriate time (around fourteen), my parents promptly signed me up for it. The course basically walks you through all of the passages in the Bible that say sex before marriage is wrong, points out all of the ways that sex can be sinful and filthy if it is not within a marriage union, and lists all of the ways that a person can stumble and fall over ungodly sex.

I don't know if it always was this way, or if it was just my particular class, but my group consisted of only girls around my age and was taught by (you guessed it) a man.

At the end of the course, we were asked to write a letter to our future husbands that we would give them on the night of our wedding. It was a gift that we would give them to indicate that we had, indeed, saved ourselves for them. We were then given a golden band to wear *on our wedding ring finger* (it looked exactly like a wedding band) as a reminder of the promise that we had made. They told us that we were to behave as if we were "married to God" until then, and that we could only take it off when we replaced it with an actual wedding band when we got married.

Of course, I never made it that far because I cheated on God with a woman.

I know, I know.

Hear me out though.

Why were we expected to make that kind of commitment at an age when we knew nothing about sex?

The church caught children (girls) standing on the precipice of adulthood and basically forced them into promising to navigate waters that were beyond our comprehension in a way that made us small and easily controlled. In fact, they were *preying* on the fact that in our innocence we didn't really know what we were committing to. They made sex sound scary, filthy, and unholy. The safest thing was clearly to avoid it at all costs. I have actually known women who were brought up in this culture who *did* wait until they were married to have sex, only to realize that they were still afraid of it and felt like they were doing something dirty even though it was biblically "ok" to have sex with their husbands.

The shaming starts at such a young age that the trauma roots run deep.

I knew around the age that I took that class and made that promise that I didn't like men. It was a wonderful scapegoat. That ring on my finger kept boys from asking me out and ended up being a neat little circle of protection that I was grateful for.

"Sorry dude, can't sleep with you. I'm married to Jesus."

It worked wonders for me during my first few years of high school.

I didn't hate on purity culture at the time, because it was honestly the best little gift that had ever been given to me. It gave me grace in a situation that would have been very difficult to navigate otherwise.

Once I realized that I was attracted to women, however, I had to rethink *everything*.

I chucked that ring out in a hurry, I'll tell you that.

Once I realized that the church's rules around sexuality weren't going to apply to me in terms of gender, I kind of felt like none of it was applicable anymore.

Gay marriage wasn't legal, so I guessed saving myself for that was off the table.

I realized that if I couldn't even follow *parts* of the expectation, then there was no point in trying to follow any of it. Christians thought that gay sex was perverted anyway, so I didn't see any reason to try to bring any kind of holy boundaries into this.

The effects of that class that I took (and the culture surrounding it) still bled over into my relationships over the years. As I said, the roots of the trauma run deep. As much as I thought I had allowed myself to step outside of that box, I still found myself dealing with issues that began there.

I had massive issues surrounding sex shame in general. I am an intensely sexual person and could never allow myself to fully express that in a relationship without feeling ashamed and exposed. I built huge walls up to keep my partners from seeing the depths of curiosity and desire that were within me.

Sex with women was a safe space for me in a lot of ways, but in some aspects it functioned as a protective mechanism to keep me from having to talk about or face the real issues underneath.

Women are really great at building up other women in bed. My partners always made me feel beautiful, and the attention that they paid to my body was extraordinary. They noticed things that only other women would notice ("Your lips are so perfect. I feel like that is what people are going for when they get collagen injections, and yours are just already like that." - an actual quote from my ex-wife) and boosted my body confidence to the max. Plus, sex with women is almost always fantastic because, well…..they are familiar with the equipment physically and at the same time they are emotionally in tune enough to know what is working and what isn't. Faking an orgasm with a woman was never necessary, and honestly doesn't even feel possible.

Women know. We just do.

I have had a few times in my life in bed with a woman where the sex just wasn't working for me for whatever reason, and I felt completely comfortable telling my partner. It was never taken personally, and we just used a vibrator together to finish. Honesty between women in the bedroom is easy.

Sex with women was so easy, and *so good* in fact, that I hadn't even realized that anything was missing at all. Or that I had built a series of walls and boundaries up to protect my innermost self.

Until along came J with a wrecking ball, and together we leveled everything.

In a way, I had worn my own wedding band in the way that I had worn my fake church one. It kept me preserved and protected in my innocence until I was ready for the actual sanction.

This had nothing to do with gender or any of that "marriage being only between a man and a woman" bullshit by the way. Just so we are clear.

I would actually argue that J had a wedding band on his hand that functioned much the same way as mine had.

This is about stepping into the highest level of spirituality and connectivity between two humans. *It is that kind of sanction.*

The physical act of union between J and me put a golden band around us both that we had never worn prior.

I began to realize that what I had been taught at fourteen was all wrong. Not only was sex *not* just a dirty physical act rooted in evil "fleshly desire" …it was the most spiritual and sacred exchange possible between two people.

There was nothing intrinsically wrong with the sex that I had been having up until J. The fact that my partners were women wasn't the reason that I hadn't reached these heights until now. I think the fact that J's partners had all been of the opposite sex and he hadn't found this connection before either is a testament that this isn't about gender/sexuality preference.

Neither of us had been here before, because we had found something in each other that surpassed everything that came prior. We were in a new place because this was a whole other level of connectivity.

I talk so much about our sex because it was both the battlefield and playground where the highest growth occurred.

Through our sex, we were able to tap into the most sacred places.

The work that we did on ourselves through each other happened in the space of sexual exploration.

We knocked down every single boundary, wall, and obstacle buried deep within each other, and we did it with *intent*.

We healed each other's scars of past gender roles and expectations. We played with femininity and masculinity, and dominance and submission until the lines were so blurred that each of us could fully embody both sides fluidly.

We cleaned the deep wounds of shame and guilt surrounding sexual desire and nursed them until they were only distant memories. For myself in particular, a voice and a presence were slowly coaxed out of me that I had been suppressing under sex shame.

I learned to ask for (demand, actually) what I wanted without reservation. I learned to give and receive completely without judgment. I learned to surrender to my own pleasure and to trust. Any time there was a flicker of shame, we pushed the kink boundary just a little. We did it over and over again until I learned that there was no need for hang-ups or humiliation between us.

Break down the wall. Break free. Repeat.

We _worshipped_ each other's bodies.

While my female partners had always made me feel beautiful, the adoration that came from J was like nothing I had ever experienced before. The way that he saw every single inch of me was staggering in its intense devotion.

I had always been made to feel pretty by other lovers, but for the first time, I learned of the sexual power of my own body.

We completely owned each other…just by existing physically.

I could bring him to his knees instantly.

He could overtake me in a second.

I became a powerful sexual goddess, an embodied archetype.

He became a god of mythical proportions when I was in his hands.

We both stepped into our power as sexual and spiritual beings.

We instilled in each other a *prowess* in those spaces that was unparalleled.

I never fully understood the concept of divinity until those moments with J.

It felt like peeking behind the veil and seeing something that we weren't really supposed to know about-like a shortcut or bypass to access the meaning of life.

Perhaps that is why the link between sexuality and spirituality is kept so hidden from us by the Christian church. That knowledge feels dangerous, doesn't it?

The power and potential of the entire universe exists in the force of sexual energy.

Life itself is created through that act.

For the first time, I understood what sex was all about, and I had a partner who grasped the concept just as fully.

Together we took a deep dive into the mysteries of the Spirit with every single touch of our bodies.

J WAS HALF propped up on my bed, naked.

I was on top of him, and we were staring intensely into each other's souls.

He was inside of me, deeper than I even thought was possible.

He was holding me steady - both of my hands in his, with our fingers tightly entwined.

We had been like this for maybe thirty minutes?

Maybe an hour.

Maybe a year and a half?

I never knew anymore.

Every single tiny movement from either one of us; a gentle leaning forward of my own body, or a slight shift of his, elicited moans from both of us of exquisite pleasure.

"I'm right against your womb, Jen," he said in a low voice.

Even the vibration from his voice radiated through him and into my own body, sending delightful ripples through my being.

"I know. Stay. Stay right where you are. I'd drawn you inside even closer if I could," I said.

I visualized bringing him into my womb, my creative space. He belonged there anyway.

Every single nook. Every curve and line and open space belonged to him.

He thrust into me ever so slightly and I thought I would die from pleasure.

More.

I wanted more and more and more and more of him until there was nothing left.

Until we just disintegrated into stardust.

His eyes were like two oceans looking up at me.

I could see the depths and infinite mysteries of the universe in either one.

I wanted to dive into them both. To explore them as deeply as he was exploring my body in this very moment.

The love I found reflected in those two luminous oceans overwhelmed me every single time.

It was like watching the stars shift in the cosmos. Always present, but each new movement brought a sense of wonder all over again.

This was a new dimension.

I thought my heart might actually explode from the love pouring out of it.

He caught every drop in those ocean eyes and mirrored them back to me.

This.

This was the meaning of life. This was all that mattered.

I had never known love before this.

"Love" didn't even seem like an adequate word. We often joked that we were going to have to come up with a new vocabulary to describe what was happening between us.

"Love" wasn't sufficient. Wasn't there something deeper than that? Some state of being that meant "greater than"? There had to be a way to say it. It was ineffable.

I have no idea how long we drank each other in like that - moving one half of a centimeter at a time and allowing every single undulation to swallow us whole together.

It finally gave way to the yearning for more.

He grabbed my waist tightly with his strong hands and rolled us over, flipping my body easily underneath him without ever slipping out of me.

I cried out in pleasure as he thrust in and out of me roughly.

It didn't take long for both of us to climax after such a long time of building up to it.

We came together, and I begged him to stay inside of me for as long as he could.

"We just *made* love. We created it between the two of us. Literally *made it* and then released it out into the world. We just uplifted the universe through our lovemaking," he said as he lay down beside me and pulled me on top of his chest.

He kissed my forehead tenderly and played with my long hair, as I pondered what he had just said.

I had never really thought about it that way.

"Lovemaking" as an actual act of creating love between the two of us.

I loved the idea of it.

He once again had shifted my perspective ever so slightly. Shown me a new way of looking at something. Gave me a new concept to consider. We were often each other's teacher - it was just another aspect of all of the ways that we nurtured each other.

This facet stemmed from the deepest of respects. It was an honoring of the wisdom that the other held. The willingness that we both had to bounce back and forth between teacher and student was what made the lessons so poignant.

We were about two years into our relationship now.

If I had thought things were deep in the beginning, they were nothing compared to where we were now.

We saw each other a few times a week, though we talked every day. It made those times together so very precious.

No second was wasted. Every moment was a deep dive.

An opportunity to grow a little more.

A chance to create something new.

A window into another dimension to explore together.

There was a sweetness to the intensity.

We took our music from the stage to the bedroom and back again. We wrote our songs through every touch, transcribing them line by line into the marrow of our bones.

We sang our lyrics to each other by passing our breath from one set of lungs to the other before releasing them into the world.

By this new definition, our "lovemaking" had taken over every single particle of our connection. We created love between us in thousands of different ways, releasing it into the universe to uplift it as we did so.

We did it through our constant reverie of one another. Through the music that flowed through and from us. Through the spiritual doorways that we held open for one another and crossed through together.

We did it through the sexual energy that continued to grow larger than we could even comprehend with our minds.

It was a spell that we had been put under instantly the first time we touched.

Now it was a magick that we had watered and fed until it became something that we could no longer control. It was much more powerful than us.

I thought back to how it started and could scarcely believe that something that had seemed so big in the beginning could have possibly grown more.

But it had.

What started as a lightning spark between the touch of our hands had turned into a twin flame wildfire that consumed us both.

Almost immediately we had begun testing each other's limits. Pushing to see where the boundaries were and putting our hands up to see if we could find the walls that must be invisible.

How much room for growth was here?

How much of this was open for exploration?

Where were the stop signs?

As it turned out, there were none.

It began as a simple desire to please one another, and to play in this new version of spiritual sex that neither of us had experienced before.

"Tell me a fantasy that you have always had, but never tried. Let me make it come true for you," we would beg one another.

And so, we would take turns becoming the genie in the bottle. The creator and the deliverer of each other's deepest desires.

We tied each other up, and brought sex toys into the bed, and tried new positions that we had always wanted to investigate.

The trust grew.

The requests got deeper.

We edged each other, physically hurt each other (just enough), used anal plugs as we fucked.

The trust grew.

The requests got darker.

He begged me to dominate him more fully. I fucked him with my strap on, and then demanded that he ride it while I lay back and watched with his dick in my hand.

I begged him to use my body like a sex doll and cried as I choked and gasped for breath as he plunged his cock down my throat.

The trust knew no limits.

We began to throw out requests that were so outlandish and taboo that at some point I realized that we were simply testing to see if the word "no" existed between us.

It didn't.

"No" never fell from either of our lips.

We had no safe word.

We didn't need one.

Our energy was so fused that we knew exactly when to stop. Wc both felt it, and the love was so immense that we respected it each and every time. We gave each other just enough to fulfill the fantasy and stopped just short of any line that would have tainted it.

Sometimes we pushed our physical limits as far as we could.

Other times, like this evening, we pushed our spiritual ones.

How high can we get?

How much physical ache does it take to reach another plane in the spirit realm?

How deep can I know you?

How much will you let me see?

Still…even here in this ethereal land…

We had no safe word.

We didn't need one.

We were free to see all of each other. Every single inch of earth and sky and sea.

Every speck of mind and body and spirit.

We longed to run our fingers over all of it. We allowed each other to do so.

"Lovemaking."

Releasing it into the universe.

We lay there for a long time together, enjoying the afterglow.

I remember thinking that I could die happy in that moment.

I had never felt so alive. This was the sole reason for existence.

I was ceaselessly captivated and enamored.

I was so in love…. not only with J, but with the Love itself.

I never wanted to move.

We were right where we belonged here: entwined in each other's arms, surrounded and held by the love that we had just "made."

Chapter Sixteen

I WAS TRYING TO fix my hair and makeup for the show at the tiny little sink at my parents' cabin and it was proving to be impossible. I scooted myself around to try and curl the back part of my hair and banged my elbow on the wall for the 17th time.

Maybe this had been a bad idea.

We were supposed to play a show at a venue that was about an hour away from our hometown. My parents owned a few cabins on the river near the music hall that they rented out on Airbnb, and I thought I had been clever in thinking ahead and booking one of them for the evening.

I knew it would give J and me a place to have some alone time before the show, and I intended to just come back to the cabin afterwards and stay the night so that I wouldn't have to drive home.

What I hadn't thought about was trying to get show-ready in a broom closet.

I picked up my contouring compact and attempted to see the back of my head with the tiny mirror. As I raised my arm up to see better, I hit my hand on the wall sconce and dropped the compact. It shattered, and makeup pieces and mirror slivers scattered everywhere.

"GODDAMMIT!" I yelled in exasperation.

I heard J laugh.

"Miss Jen! Such foul language from such a pretty mouth," he said. I hadn't even heard him come in. He was standing in the living room watching me through the bathroom door that I had left open in a feeble attempt to create more space.

"How long have you been standing there?" I asked sheepishly.

"Long enough to watch you get astoundingly angry at a curling iron," he said. "I've never seen that side of you, my dear. You're usually quite patient."

"Ha! Not when something gets in the way of my vanity," I retorted.

"Pun intended?" he asked with a grin.

203

"Of course. You're earlier than I expected. Clearly," I said, as I motioned to the bra and panties that I was wearing.

He strode over to me and picked me up roughly in his arms. I squealed with delight.

"You look gorgeous. I don't know why you would bother putting on anything more than that when you know I'm just going to have to remove it."

He carried me over to the couch, which was the closest surface available, and threw me down on it. He ripped my panties off, and the string snapped in two as he pulled it.

"HEY! Those were new!" I said as I swatted his hand playfully.

"Not sorry," he growled into my ear as he kissed my neck. He unclasped my bra as he did so, then stretched it like a slingshot and fired it across the room. I giggled.

"Listen…we have to leave here in an hour. We can't do what we normally do and let time get away from us. We have a show, remember? This is going to have to be a fast fuck," I said.

I knew how we were. It was entirely possible that we would look up and it would be midnight before we knew it.

"Challenge accepted," he said with a smile.

He stroked my clit gently as he covered me in kisses. I immediately yielded to him, allowing myself to enjoy every single brush of his lips and beard against my body.

"I couldn't wait to get here. I've been thinking about this all day…", he murmured between kisses.

"I'm dying to taste you…." he whispered. He spread my legs with his strong hands and began to kiss the insides of my thighs. I let out a long moan of impatience, and he laughed softly.

"You alright, Miss Jen? Did you need something?" he teased.

"J…I want you to fuck me first. Please? I want your cock…." I said, urgently. I too, had been daydreaming about this all day. I had been edging myself the whole evening. Touching myself in between getting ready for the show. I had been on fire for him before he even walked in the door.

"Yes ma'am," he replied. I lunged for his belt as he pulled his shirt over his head. I undid the buckle and then the button and zipper of his pants. He pushed them down quickly and I went to grab his dick with my hand and stopped with surprise.

He wasn't hard.

I looked up at him quizzically. Maybe I had just jumped the gun a little….

I didn't worry too long about it- I knew how to get him there quickly. I wrapped my lips around him, alternating sucking with my mouth and gently stroking his cock with my hand.

I tried for a few moments.......no response.

"What do you need, J? What do you want me to do?" I whispered.

He shrugged in confusion.

"I don't know....my body just isn't cooperating for some reason," he said. "Let me focus on you for a while. I'm sure that will work."

He buried his face between my legs. He devoured me until I was shaking with orgasm.

He climbed up beside me on the couch and pulled me close to him and I went to touch him again.

He was still not hard.

"What's going on, love? Are you ok?" I asked. This had never happened before.

"Yeah. I think so. I've been feeling a little off today- a little more tired than usual. Maybe I'm just getting sick or something," he replied.

"How's your tooth? Do you think maybe you have an underlying infection from that or something?" I asked. A few weeks prior at one of our shows, J had broken one of his molars while biting down on a dinner that had been sitting for too long under a heat lamp while we were playing. He had been complaining incessantly about it since it happened.

"Nah, it's fine. It doesn't really hurt that bad," he answered.

I raised an eyebrow.

"You've sure been bitching about it an awful lot for something that doesn't hurt."

He smacked me sharply on the ass. "Did you just call me a bitch?" he asked.

"I've made you mine before," I replied with a smirk.

He laughed. "Indeed, Miss Jen. And you are the only one who ever will."

"I'm sorry you don't feel well, babe. If it's not your tooth, I wonder what's up?"

I pondered what else might be the culprit, I had a sudden flicker of worry that it might have something to do with me. I wondered if maybe I had done something wrong. Was he upset with me about something? I tried to think back over our last few conversations and couldn't think of any reason that he should be upset, but suddenly a more distressing thought crossed my mind...was he not as attracted to me as he used to be? I was kind of afraid to ask. I took his face in my hands and searched his eyes. It was all still there. I could see it. But still....

"Is it me?" I asked in a whisper.

"Do you really think it's you?" he asked back, gently.

I looked away.

"Jen, seriously? My God, woman...I can't even sing onstage with you without getting hard. You know that," he said.

It was true. I couldn't count the number of times we had been performing onstage, lost in each other in front of the world, only for him to shift his guitar slightly forward so that I could see the erection he was hiding behind it. The desire between us often overtook us both whether or not it was a convenient time. It was precisely the reason why I was so surprised at what was happening this evening. He traced a finger over my cheeks, across my eyebrows, down my nose, and finally rested it on my lips.

"Look at me," he whispered.

"I want you all of the time. Your very presence is intoxicating to me. You come to me in erotic dreams, and I spend my nights yearning for you. I wake up thinking about you. I start my day getting off in the shower to visions and memories of your body. You infiltrate my thoughts, even when I don't want you to. You make me hard for you even when you aren't physically there. I will never not be aroused by you. You affect me in ways I still don't even understand. I promise you that whatever is going on with my body tonight has nothing to do with my desire for you. Ok? I want you to know that…tell that me you know it's true," he said.

I melted. I did know it. I could see it in his eyes, the same way that I always could. I felt the same way about him as well, and I knew there was no way he could turn that off, any more than I could. I had just allowed my own insecurities to bubble up to the surface because I had been so surprised that his body hadn't reacted as it usually did.

"I know it's true, J. Poetry as usual, my sweet boy. I love you so much," I replied. I kissed him softly. He stood up and pulled me up with him to stand beside him. He led me by the hand back to the bedroom.

"Can you go again? I want you to sit on my face…let me drown in you…" he said. He laid down on the bed and motioned for me to come to him. I climbed above him and steadied myself on the headboard as I straddled his face, facing the wall.

I was already dripping wet from my orgasm moments ago. I felt him slide his tongue from my clit to my pussy and plunge it inside of me. I gasped with pleasure. He pulled my hips down to him even further as he found a rhythm sliding back and forth between the two.

He removed one of his hands from my body and I felt him begin to stroke his cock to the same cadence. I couldn't see what he was doing, but I didn't need to. I knew. I wondered if he was hard now.

The thought had no more crossed my mind when he slid out from under me in a maneuver so quick that he was behind me and inside of me before I even knew what had happened. He thrust into me hard and fast; one hand roughly wrapped in my hair as he tugged it and the other encircling my waist as he pulled me closer and closer to him. He pounded into me forcefully, the slap of our skin echoing in my ears.

"YES, boy. Fuck me. Fuck me harder, J…" I begged.

The encouragement was all he needed. He pulled my head back by my hair until it was next to his. He growled hungrily in my ear as thrust violently into me, his fingers grasping at my hips.

"YES, J! Come. I want you to come inside of me. I want to feel you dripping out of me…" I told him between moans of ecstasy.

I felt the waves of energy pass through me as allowed himself to obey. It was as if his very being had exploded through us both and into me. He loosened his grip on my body as the shockwaves lessened and we tried to catch our breath.

He kissed my neck tenderly, and then playfully bit it as he laughingly said, "Well, that worked."

"Indeed," I replied with a giggle. "Stay for just a minute?"

I could feel our juices running down the insides of my legs. He leaned back onto his heels, and I relaxed into his lap with him still inside of me. He cradled my body sweetly while he whispered "I love you" over and over in my ear.

As I felt him begin to soften in me, we reclined fully on the bed, and he pulled me onto his chest.

I was so content. I began to drift off to sleep in his arms.

"SHIT! We have to leave in five minutes!" he suddenly exclaimed, startling me awake.

"Ugh. Nooooooo. I just want to stay here like this with you. Let's cancel," I said.

'That's not very professional, Miss Jen. I'm going to hop in the shower really quickly and then we've got to go," he said as he jumped up from the bed and headed to the bathroom.

I begrudgingly dragged myself out of the bed and followed him. I went to grab a broom to sweep up the compact pieces and called after him to watch where he stepped. He was already in the shower when I came in to clean it up. I then looked in the mirror and realized I needed to try and fix my tousled hair and smudged makeup. I paused for a moment to watch him through the glass shower door. My gorgeous boy. It still surprised me how attracted I was to every inch of him. I thought his long, sculpted limbs were the most beautifully created I had ever seen. I loved every hair and freckle he possessed. I had explored every centimeter of him, and I still wanted more. If you had told me three years prior that I would be so smitten with a *man* that I would worship his body the way I was staring in reverence and awe at J in that moment, I would have called you crazy.

I watched him lather himself up with soap and my heart fluttered like a schoolgirl. I hadn't been out of his arms for two minutes and I was already aching to touch him again. He caught me staring and smiled.

"Come join me," he said.

I thought about it. He slid the shower door back enough that I could slip through if I wanted. I reached my hand inside the shower and touched his wet skin. We had never taken a shower together before. It was beyond enticing.

"I can't, J. You know we will never make it to the show if I do. Plus, I don't have time to start completely over with wet hair and get ready again. Not that I don't want to," I said. I looked at him longingly. I traced my fingers down his belly to his cock and he smacked my hand away with a laugh.

"Fine. But don't think it will be like that when we are touring together. I'll just pull you in here with me and you will have to go onstage with wet hair," he said.

I sighed. Touring.

Dean had linked us up with a promotional company that had taken our new album and run with it. Our first single had just hit the radio eight days ago, and we were scheduled to start our radio tour to promote it in six weeks.

It was finally happening.

It was going to be magical. An entire life together of creating, performing, fucking, and travel.

I couldn't wait.

"Yes, sir." I responded. I was baiting him a little. It sent him over the edge when I called him "sir." He aimed the shower head at me, and I laughingly dodged the water.

"Girl. Go get ready before I drag you in here and we miss the show," he said.

We followed each other to the venue, and when we pulled in, I was surprised to see that there were only a few cars in the parking lot.

J rolled down his window as I got out of my car.

"Are you sure we got the date right?", he asked.

I pointed to the brightly lit marquee in front of the place that had our band name "The Green Rumours" beside *TONIGHT* in big letters. He shrugged and parked the car.

This particular venue was known for having its own incredible sound system, so we didn't have to unload anything. We walked in through the front door, with only J's guitar.

The place was dead. We plugged in, did a quick sound check, and then stepped to the bar to order a beer.

We normally drew a pretty big crowd. This was extremely unusual.

The owner of the venue was bartending, so we asked him what was up.

The Melody of Fire

"Well…the Christmas parade is downtown tonight, so a lot of people are doing that, but also the high school football team is playing for the state championship about an hour away. I talked to a bunch of people who were going to drive to watch it. It's not y'all's fault, but this doesn't look like a good night for live music. We'll give it a few minutes, but if it doesn't pick up there's no need for you to play for three hours if no one is here," he said.

We agreed. A few friends of mine trickled in as we began our set. I waved to them and thanked them for coming, but as I was looking out into the empty seats, I realized there were only 6 people total in the whole place. We played for about twenty minutes before the owner waved at us from the bar and told us to stop.

He walked up to the stage as we were unplugging and pressed a check into my hand.

"I'll still pay y'all for coming up because I know it's a drive. We will try this again another time. You two sounded great, what little bit I heard. I'm sorry it was such a bust tonight," he said.

We thanked him for paying us anyway. I told my friends goodbye and apologized that we weren't playing a full set. As we walked out the door and back to the cars J slipped his hand into mine.

"Hmmm. Two and a half hours with nothing to do. Any suggestions?" he asked.

I laughed.

"Want to follow me back to the cabin?" I asked.

"I'll be right behind you, my dear. For the second time tonight," he replied with a smirk.

As I drove back to the cabin, I thought about what the rest of the evening would be like. I fully anticipated us picking up right where we had left off. After all, it felt like our lovemaking had been cut short because of the show. J pulled into the drive moments after I did. I had gone into the cabin ahead of him, but when he didn't come through the door right after me, I stepped back outside to see if he was all right.

I found him leaning against his car, and he seemed to be trying to catch his breath.

"You ok, babe? What's going on?" I asked. As I got closer to him, I could see that he looked a little pale.

"Yeah. I'm ok. I don't know what happened…. when I stood up, I got a little lightheaded. I think I'm ok now. I told you I haven't felt well today," he replied.

I thought back to earlier and nodded.

"Let's get you inside so you can put your feet up," I said, as I linked my arm in his.

We walked back into the cabin together and I made him some ice water while

209

he sat in the recliner by the fireplace. As I handed it to him, he grabbed my wrist and pulled me into his lap.

"Take your clothes off," he whispered.

"I really think you need to rest, love. If I do that you know what will happen," I said.

"No, it won't. I promise. Let's just get a fire going, lay here together naked, and listen to music. Let's just have some time together. Time that we never get…to just talk and enjoy each other's company like we would if we lived together. Would that be ok?" he asked.

"Of course that would be ok, J," I said. I kissed his forehead as I stood up. He unbuttoned his shirt as he stood up after me and took all of his clothing off before he set to work building a fire.

I removed my own clothes and walked over to the record player to see what our music options were. I called out artist names and album titles to him as he worked on the fire. We settled on a Motown compilation, and I dropped the needle and walked back over to him as "My Girl" began playing softly.

He stepped away from the fire and put his hand out to ask me for a dance.

"You're supposed to be resting, remember?" I said.

"Just one, babe. This one is too good not to dance to," he said as he began to sing the lyrics to me. I rolled my eyes but took his hand. He pulled me close, and we swayed to the music.

"Do you realize that I've never told you, 'no?'" I said. "About anything? What a tremendous amount of power to have over someone, that they would literally do anything you asked them to do. In case you hadn't noticed…I belong to you, J. I am completely, irrevocably yours." Our foreheads were pressed together, and we were staring into each other's eyes as we gently moved to the music.

"I know that power intimately…because I am yours as well, love," he said softly.

I flickered with resistance. I didn't want to say it. I didn't want to ruin the moment, but it came tumbling out of my mouth anyway.

"Not entirely, J. Not the way that I want you to be. I want to be the only one that matters to you. I want to be 'your girl.'" I motioned to the record player that just played the sentiment I was echoing. "I want to be the reason why you get out of bed every morning and the last thing you see at night. I want to be able to touch you whenever I want. I want to tell the world about this incredible love that we share. I want for you to be…proud…to be with me…the way I'm proud to be on your arm. I want to stand in the light with you, J. I want you to be mine…the way that I am yours," I said.

He opened his mouth to speak and then closed it again. He took my face in his hands.

"Make no mistake, Miss Jen…I want all of those things too. Soon, babe. We are

SO close to having it all. Can you wait just a little bit longer? We are set to tour in six weeks. A decision will have to be made *very* soon, and Lila will draw the line in the sand. She and I already fight about music all of the time these days. And you. We fight about you. While we've never directly discussed what is going on between you and me, she's not stupid. She is an incredibly intuitive woman. I think we've both just been waiting on the 'last straw', and it feels like touring will be just that. If I choose to leave with you to go on tour, I have no doubt my marriage will be over officially. If she's the one that gives the ultimatum, I think I will have a little more leverage to negotiate time with my children. I know that you know they are the most important thing in the world to me. I can't lose my kids, Jen," he said.

"I know, J. I don't want you to lose them…that's not what I meant…" I began. He put his finger over my lips.

"Let me finish. I can't lose my children. That being said…you are *already* the reason why I get out of bed. From sunrise to sundown and back again you are all that is on my mind. How could you ever think that I'm not proud to be with you? I stand up in front of crowds of people and show you off. I look at you like a starry-eyed fool, and I can't make myself not. There's not a person in the tri-state area who has seen us perform together and not noticed that we were madly in love. How much more light do you need to stand in, Jen? What's brighter than the light of the truth? And we both know what the truth is…we have said it a million times. I am yours, and you are mine. It has been that way since the beginning of time….and it will be that way when time no longer exists. You can't be more mine than I am yours. We belong to each other equally. We are twin flames, remember? Two halves of the same soul. There is nothing that can break apart or lessen our love. *Nothing*," he said.

Tears were falling down my cheeks. I simply nodded in response.

"Just a little more time, love. We are talking about a few weeks at this point. It's not like I'm asking you to hold on for some undefinable date in the future. Can you give me that?" he whispered.

"I've never said 'no' to you before, remember? I can't imagine that I ever will," I answered. The song had changed, and I wanted to sit down. I motioned to the chair and said, "Will you please just sit and hold me for a while? You promised you would rest."

We snuggled back in the chair together. Touching skin to skin by the fire seemed to lift both of our spirits.

It wasn't long before we were back to our usual dynamic: tossing wordplay back and forth at each other until we were laughing so hard we could barely breathe.

I laid my head on his chest and traced my fingers gently up and down his side.

I felt his breath blow in my hair ever so slightly with each exhale.

We laid there quietly enjoying the closeness, watching the fire crackle and blaze.

It occurred to me that I couldn't hear his heartbeat.

I moved my head slightly, pressing my ear that was laying on his chest to a different spot.

Still nothing.

"Are you sure you are ok, babe? I can't hear your heartbeat. Do you think maybe your blood pressure is low or something and that's why you got dizzy earlier?" I asked.

It also might explain the erectile issue earlier, I thought, but I didn't want to bring it up again because I worried that he might be feeling self-conscious about it.

"I don't know. Maybe? Who knows? I feel all right now though…I don't think it's anything to worry about," he said.

He yawned as he added, "This fire and snuggling with you is making me sleepy though. Could just be that you aren't used to hearing my heartbeat at rest. You are usually only lying on my chest after we have been…exercising vigorously."

We both laughed.

"Good point. Do you want me to make us some coffee? We could go out on the porch swing and watch the river…that might wake you up a little before you have to drive home," I said.

He agreed that it was a good idea, so I made us some coffee. I handed him the cups to take outside while I took an oversized fleece blanket from the bed and put it over the top of my head and let it drape around me like a cloak.

He smiled appreciatively at me when I walked out to join him on the porch.

"You look like a medieval princess," he commented and kissed my nose.

"Well, it is December. Walking out here naked seemed like a bad idea," I replied as I tossed him an extra blanket that I had carried out with me. He took it gratefully and wrapped it around himself. We made a little nest of blankets and pillows on the porch swing and snuggled in together with our coffee.

We talked about the river and the land. We talked about our future together and how excited we were. We talked about music, and how well it had been going. We still couldn't believe that we had just heard our song on the radio for the first time. We were still so giddy about it.

We talked about touring again, and how wonderful our new life together was going to be. It truly felt like were about to have everything that we had ever wanted.

Several times throughout the conversation when there was a moment of silence, J would open his mouth as if to say something, but then seem to decide against it.

Knowing him as well as I did, I sensed that whatever it was that he was not saying was important. It felt big.

"What? What is it?" I asked him a few times. He simply shook his head and smiled.

"Nothing," he would reply and kiss my forehead.

"This evening has been amazing, J. It's been so nice to just have time with you. Time that isn't rushed. Time to just talk and enjoy each other. Often when I fantasize about our future together, it's moments like this that I long for. Just coffee on the porch with you, you know?" I asked.

"Naked. Coffee on the porch...naked," he said with a grin. I smacked him playfully.

"No. It doesn't always have to be sexual. Well…maybe it does because it seems like it always *is*, but you know there is so much more to this connection than sex," I said.

"Indeed, my love. It is by far the deepest thing I've ever known," he replied.

"Spiritual," he added as he touched my forehead with his finger.

"Do you know how much I love you, J? Can you really comprehend how much? Words never feel sufficient, and I always feel so inadequate when I try to speak it," I said.

"You don't have to speak it. I feel it with every touch. I know it through the wonders of the universe that I see in your eyes. I know without a doubt exactly how much you love me…because I love you just as deeply. It is like looking in a mirror. I see everything I feel for you reflected back at me when I look at you," he replied.

His words made my heart feel so full that I thought it might explode. I thought back to the morning on my yoga mat when he had made me feel his love for me by activating it in my own body. Though he still claimed to have no recollection of that incident, I felt the same feeling emanating from him in this very moment. He was right. Words were not needed. I kissed him tenderly.

We stayed on the porch swing for another thirty minutes or so before he stood up to go. I followed him back inside and watched him put on his clothes and gather his things.

Even though it had been the perfect evening, I wanted more time with him. I couldn't help it. I wondered if it would always be that way. Even when we were finally together every day…would I still never feel like I had him in my arms long enough?

He pulled me in for a long goodbye kiss. He stopped for just a moment and seemed yet again as if he were going to say something.

"J. You keep doing that. What? Just tell me," I pleaded. I kept trying to read his mind and couldn't. I felt distinctly like he was intentionally blocking me from whatever this was that he was finding so difficult to say.

"Nothing, babe. It's ok. I love you," he said.

"I love you too," I replied. He kissed me again, this time more passionately.

I began to cry. I couldn't bear to see him walk out the door. When he finally turned his back to me to walk away, I put my hand over my mouth to keep from audibly sobbing.

He stopped at the door and dropped his head.

He turned around to face me, and I could see he was crying as well.

"Jen. I don't want to leave you," he said. I watched him visibly fighting a battle between going out the door and running back into my arms.

He backed out of the door slowly. He never took his eyes off of mine until the screen door closed between us.

I collapsed in a heap on the floor the instant that I heard his car start. I cried myself to sleep on the floor in front of the fire.

I just kept thinking over and over again in my head as I drifted off to sleep that I couldn't wait for the day when we didn't have to tell each other goodbye all of the time.

Part Five

inferno – *noun*

a.: a large fire that is dangerously out of control

b.: hell

Chapter Seventeen

I WAS HAVING BREAKFAST on the porch of the cabin when my phone rang at 7:00 the next morning. My heart stopped when I saw the name on my screen. Lila.

What could she possibly be calling me this early for?

Holy shit. Had he gone home and broken it off with her?

Was that what he was going to tell me so many times last night? I remembered his face as he walked out the door. Maybe leaving me last night had been the final straw.

I quickly ran through a hundred scenarios in my head as to what could have possibly transpired in the last seven hours. None of them were going to lead to a pleasant conversation when I answered the phone.

My stomach turned over as I picked up and said hello.

"Jen. I'm sorry to call so early...but...I have some bad news..." she said. She was crying. I stopped breathing. I couldn't even formulate a word of response as I waited motionless for her to continue.

"I am at the hospital. Jason was having sharp back and chest pain this morning, so we brought him here. We thought maybe he was having a heart attack. They found that his descending aorta is torn...the damage spans the length of his body.... he is in emergency surgery right now. It doesn't look good. They...they aren't sure if he will make it through the surgery...." she broke off into sobs.

I was speechless. This couldn't be real.

I had literally just held him in my arms a few hours ago. He hadn't been feeling well, but there had been no indication that something of this magnitude was wrong.

"What? He was just fine. How could this have happened that quickly?" I was whispering in an effort to keep myself from screaming.

"I know. It seemed to come on all at once. His blood pressure was 220 when

217

we got here and his heart rate was dangerously low…they cut his clothes off of him because they didn't want him moving at all…" she said through her tears. "I'll keep you posted about the surgery, ok?"

"Which hospital are you at? I'm on my way," I said as I jumped up to find my keys.

"NO! Don't come out here. We are at the Med center…but…I don't want you here. I'm only calling you because he asked me to right before he went into surgery. There's no reason for you to come right now. There is nothing anyone can do at the moment…and I need some time alone to figure everything out. I'll update you when I know something," she said.

She hung up.

I stared at the phone in complete shock. Panic took over my body.

I couldn't breathe. I paced back and forth, as the anxiety washed over me.

Should I just go to the hospital anyway?

I needed to be near him…but Lila had seemed so adamant that she didn't want me there.

Had they fought when he got home? Is that why his blood pressure spiked so suddenly?

I tried to rationalize what to do, but I was in no state to be rational.

I called my sister.

She exhaled sharply as I quickly told her what little bit of information I knew.

"I don't know what to do, Whit. I feel so *helpless*. I need to be with him," I said through heavy sobs.

'Look, I get that you want to be near him, but if you go to the hospital right now you won't be with him…you will be with Lila. In the waiting room. For God knows how long. It seems to me that is just a recipe for disaster. You can't see him or talk to him anyway. Just wait until you hear something and then decide what you want to do at that point. But Jen…" she said.

"Yes," I replied.

"I am so very sorry this is happening. I don't know what to say, except that I love you. Let me know something as soon as you get an update, ok?" she said.

I told her that I would.

Four excruciating hours passed with no word. I literally didn't know what to do with myself. I walked the entire property anxiously. I laid on the grass and tried to breathe, only to find myself too jittery to focus. I jumped back up and walked more.

I petitioned Spirit with every exhale.

"Please. Please. Please. Don't take him from me. Please keep him safe. Please let him make it through this. Please, Spirit. Have mercy on both of us. Wrap him in your healing power. Please. Please…." I prayed ceaselessly.

Finally, around lunchtime, I received a text.

"He made it through surgery, but there have been some complications. He had a birth defect that we didn't know about - his aorta wraps around the back of his neck before it descends instead of stemming straight down from his heart. They placed a stent in the length of his body, but because of the abnormality, it is pressing against his spinal column. He cannot feel the lower half of his body, and it appears that the paralysis will be permanent. They also have cut his entire arm open, trying to find usable veins to reconstruct some of the damage. They have him stable though, and he is resting for the time being. There is no need for you to come to the hospital. I will continue to update you as things progress."

I flung the phone as hard as I could against the wall. The case shattered.

I felt beyond helpless.

My precious boy.

I imagined him lying in that hospital bed, his beautiful body sawed on and ripped open from top to bottom. The body that I had just held in my hands and worshipped reverently merely hours ago.

I couldn't wrap my head around any of it. I wondered what he must be feeling.

Did he even know what had happened to him? He must have been conscious for at least a bit if they determined that he couldn't feel the lower half of his body.

I cried bitterly.

I should be there.

I should be by his side.

Everything in me ached to just see him with my own two eyes. I just needed to know how bad it was. If I could just be near him, in his energy, I would know exactly how things stood.

The text I had just read left more questions than answers.

I went back and forth again and again about going to the hospital. I kept remembering what my sister had said. The only thing keeping me away was the knowledge that I wouldn't be able to see him. I would just have to wait this out, it seemed, as torturous as it was. My hands were completely tied.

I was only able to stand it for about eight hours, and I honestly don't even know how I made it that long.

It was about nine p.m. and I had received no further updates from Lila.

I had been a complete train wreck, and I had watched the clock every single minute hoping that one of them would be the moment that I would get some news. I finally decided that I was going to be losing my mind no matter where I was, so it might as well be at the hospital.

I grabbed my keys and walked out the door.

When I stepped out of the elevator on the cardiac floor of the hospital, I immediately saw J's children standing with his father and Lila. His brother and sister were also present. Everyone looked exhausted.

His daughter looked over and saw me walking towards them. "JEN!" she yelled as ran to me and flew into my arms.

"Hey, sweet girl." I said as I embraced her tightly.

"What took you so long? We've been here all day. Jen….is Dad going to be ok?" she asked. She looked up at me as she continued to hug me tight. Her large brown eyes were full of tears. I didn't know what to say. She probably knew more than I did about the situation at this point. What could I say to comfort her?

"I hope so. I really hope so. We are going to pray really hard for him, ok? Can you do that with me?" I asked. She nodded her head, and I bent over to kiss her forehead.

I looked up to see Lila glaring at me with a force that nearly knocked me backwards.

I swear I audibly heard, "Get your hands off of her, you traitorous bitch," but her lips never moved.

Unsettled, I let go of her daughter.

"What are you doing here? I told you not to come," Lila said loudly enough for everyone in the room to turn and look to see who she was talking to. I approached her so that I wouldn't have to yell back at her from across the room.

"It's been hours since you last texted. I just… was so worried. I didn't know what to do so I just came. How is he?" I asked.

"He's back in surgery now. They are trying to see if they can move the stent to fix the paralysis," she said.

"What? Why didn't you update me?" I asked.

"Because believe it or not Jen, you are not actually a priority of mine right now. In case you haven't noticed I have a lot going on at the moment, including caring for two children whose father could potentially be dying," she exploded. She was crying angrily. "This is too much…stay or don't. Just don't expect anything from me right now," she added. She walked back to the kids, and they all sat down close to each other in the corner of the waiting room.

I found a seat far away from them, behind some large potted plants that had been used as a divider in the room. There was no way I was going back home. At least here I would know the moment that he came out of surgery. His family came over to me one at a time and talked to me over the next few hours.

After years of playing music together, they all knew me well. None of them thought it was odd or unexpected that I was there at the hospital that night, and everyone but Lila treated me as if I were part of the family. They knew that I was J's best friend and duo partner. It made sense to them that I would be there.

I spent a good portion of that night thinking about all of the ways that I loved

220

him that they didn't know of. I could barely speak to his dad. They had the same deep blue eyes and every single time I looked at him I became overwhelmed with heartache.

It took everything in me to not say the things that I was thinking when we spoke throughout the night.

"I'm so in love with your son. He is the greatest man I have ever known. You raised him so well…you should be so proud of him…"

I managed to bite my tongue. I knew those words wouldn't be well received coming from his son's mistress, not that his dad knew that was who he was speaking to.

The minutes ticked by.

Finally, a little bit before 2:00 a.m., the doctor appeared in the doorway of the waiting room and asked to speak to Lila. We all waited with bated breath; staring at the doorway for her to reappear. When she returned, she looked tired and defeated. She looked around at all of us and simply said, "He's stable, but the surgery wasn't successful. He still can't feel anything. He's resting in recovery right now. They told us to all go home. We can't stay overnight here. If anything changes, they will call me, and I'll let you guys know."

Everyone began gathering up their things. We all dispersed a few at a time, in silence.

I considered trying to talk to Lila, but I was just too sad to formulate words.

As I walked into the elevator, I turned around to see that J's dad had been following a few steps behind me. I held the door for him.

We didn't speak until we reached the lobby. As we walked out of the door he asked if I would let him walk me to my car. He offered his arm to me, the same way that J had done so many times.

My gentleman had been raised by a gentleman, it seemed. I smiled as I took his arm.

He escorted me all the way to the driver's side of my vehicle and opened the door for me.

"You be careful now, Miss Jen. It's awfully late for a woman to be driving alone. I'll see you tomorrow?" he asked.

I nodded, and as he shut the door I looked into his blue eyes once more. All I could see was J. Hearing him call me "Miss Jen" cut me wide open. As he walked off, I laid my head down on my steering wheel and cried.

The next day I arrived at the hospital around lunchtime. I had tried to go into work but had been unable to focus in the least. My boss had gotten tired of watching me struggle, so she sent me home.

When I came into the waiting room, I saw J's best guy friend, Thomas, sitting with Lila and the kids. As soon as he saw me, he jumped up and wrapped me in a big hug.

"Hey, gorgeous! It's so good to see your face. I hate the circumstances, though," he said. He grabbed me by the hand and began to lead me away from J's family.

"Let's go down to the lobby and get some coffee and catch up a little bit…."

"Um…Thomas…I want to check on J first. Just let me talk to Lila for a minute and I'll go down with you then," I said.

"I'll fill you in. I just came from his room. Come on. We haven't seen each other in forever," he continued as we approached the elevator. I stopped in my tracks.

"What?! They let you see him?" I half-shouted. He quickly put his hand on my cheek and then moved one finger over my mouth subtly.

"Shhhh. I'll explain everything, just get into that elevator with me right now. Nod and smile and make it look like we are just having a normal and pleasant conversation. Now. Please," he said through a fake smile that he had plastered across his face. I obeyed and followed him into the elevator. As soon as the door shut, I turned to him.

"What the FUCK, Thomas? I need you to tell me what is going on this instant," I yelled.

He punched the stop button on the elevator, and it came to a halt.

"Jen… Jason is ok right now. Nothing has changed, he's stable. But Lila has been talking shit about you all morning to anyone who would listen. She's rallied the family against you, and if you walk into that waiting room you are walking into an angry bees' nest. I just couldn't let that happen without warning you. It may just be talk, but emotions are high anyway right now and I'm afraid they might even physically hurt you," he said quickly.

"What?! Why?" I asked.

He sighed.

"Look…I know about you and J. I've known for a while, and I know exactly how deeply in love you two are. There's no judgment here…I love you both and want you to be happy, ok? But Lila apparently knows too. She told the whole family that you have been trying to steal her husband and that you had no business up here at the hospital. They basically have been sitting up there all morning talking about how they were going to kick your ass if you showed up today," he said.

"I was just here LAST NIGHT. What changed?", I asked him.

"Well…I don't think she expected you to show up last night," he replied.

I leaned my back against the wall of the elevator and put my hands over my face. Angry tears were spilling out from between my fingers.

"I have to see him, Thomas. That's the love of my life in that room. I can't get to him, and he needs me…I could be losing him…." I said with despair.

"I know, Jen. Look at me.", he said as he gently pulled my hands down to uncover my face. When I looked into his eyes, I could see that they were overflowing with compassion and concern.

"I know how difficult this must be. Truly. But I also know how much he loves you. He's not conscious right now, but there is not a doubt in my mind that the minute that he is he will be demanding to speak to you. I'll do anything within my power that I can do to help you two see each other when that time comes, I promise. I'll call you for him, sneak you in past Lila, whatever it takes- you have my word. But now is not the time to fight that battle, Jen. If you aren't VERY careful here, you are going to end up unable to see him at all. We need to wait until he is awake, and then we can work this thing from both ends," he said.

He gently brushed my hair away from my tear-soaked cheeks.

"Are you hearing me? She's not going to let you see him right now," he added.

I felt completely defeated. I sat down on the floor of the elevator. Thomas slid down to sit beside me and grabbed my hand and held it tight.

"I'm sorry," he whispered.

"Don't be. It's not your fault. I'm glad you gave me a warning, anyway," I said. I wondered how long he had known about J and me? It hadn't ever really occurred to me that J might have told any of his friends, but it made sense that if he had told anyone it would have been Thomas.

"How did you find out about us?" I finally asked him.

He grinned.

"I saw you two kissing in an alleyway after a show one night…probably about a year ago. I literally couldn't believe what I was seeing. I honestly didn't think he had it in him to be unfaithful….and I thought you hated men," he said. We both laughed.

"That kiss though…it spoke volumes. I could feel the love and the passion between you two from where I was standing half a block away. Of course, I couldn't WAIT to call him out on it. He was reluctant to talk about it at first, but he ended up telling me everything. I told him that I thought he was a very lucky man to have found something so special." He squeezed my hand and looked me in the eye.

"We've known each other since middle school, and I've never seen him like this. He's crazy about you, Jen."

"I'm crazy about him, too. Thank you for understanding. And thank you for helping me," I said. I managed to smile at him, despite the situation.

"Well, he's my best friend. I'd do anything for him, but I love you as well. Thank you for making my best friend so happy," he said.

"How…how much does Lila know? Can you tell me? Just so I know what I'm up against?"

"I'm not exactly sure. What I do know is that she and J fight about you all of the time. J has shown up at my house on *many* occasions recently because being at home with Lila was unbearable. He wouldn't ever go into too much detail about the arguments that they were having because he came to my place for a break, but it was obviously really, really bad. It has been for a while," he said.

I stared at him wide-eyed. This was all news to me.

"He never told me that. I mean, I knew things weren't great between them, but I had no idea that they were arguing about me to that extent. So do you think she knows everything?"

"I'm only speculating here, but I think if she knew *everything* there is no way that they would still be together. J kind of made it sound like she never flat-out asked what was going on but danced all around it. The way he worded it seemed like Lila knew that if the affair was actually confirmed that everything would have to change, so it's almost like she didn't want to know for sure. Instead, they fought constantly about the amount of time he spends with you outside of shows, how frequently you two talk on the phone, etc.

"So to answer your question… I think that deep down she knows everything but has just been unwilling to directly face it because she didn't want to deal with what that would mean for their marriage. Even this morning in the waiting room, the way she was wording it to the family was that you were trying to steal her husband, not that you two were engaged in a relationship together. It's like if she just pins it all on you trying to be a homewrecker that she doesn't have to face the truth of her husband betraying her and being deeply in love with someone else. That story feels much easier to get the family to rally behind too. That's why I didn't want you walking into that unaware a little bit ago," he said.

"Thank you for that," I replied. This was a lot to process. While I had felt J's internal agony surrounding his home situation, I had been given very few details about his and Lila's conversations.

"J did tell me that he didn't want you to know how bad it was at home. I think he was trying to protect you from some of the guilt and pain that he was feeling by not keeping you looped in on every single confrontation with Lila. Things were coming to a head though, Jen. I was expecting at any moment to hear that they were over. That was the phone call I was *expecting* to receive…not the one that I got yesterday morning telling me that he was fighting for his life in the hospital."

"Do you think he's going to make it through this? Be honest with me," I asked tentatively. He had said that he had seen J earlier; maybe he had gotten a better read on how he really was.

His face darkened considerably.

"I don't know. God knows I don't want to lose him either, but it all feels very up in the air still. I wish I could say something to make us both feel better about it, but I just don't know," he replied. He stood up and reached down to grab both of my hands. He helped me up to a standing position and gave me a big hug.

"We can't spend all day in this elevator. What do you want to do? Go get coffee with me?" he asked.

"No…I still want to be close by. I think I'll just go back up to the waiting area and try to keep my distance. Do you think they would leave me alone if I didn't talk too much to anyone?" I asked.

"No. But I think if you sat beside me that they would be too afraid to start any shit," he said with a smile. He pushed the button on the elevator to take us back up to the cardiac floor. He grabbed my hand right before the door opened and held it tight as he walked me to where the family was sitting. Looks were exchanged all the way around, and it appeared to be clear to everyone that I was arriving with protection. They all nodded and said hello as we sat down, and then that was it. Nothing else was spoken.

Thomas put his arm around me and leaned in close to whisper in my ear, "I've got you, babe. Just stick close by for the day."

I nodded in agreement.

People came and went all day. All of the close family took turns going back to see him. My heart broke a little each time someone went back who wasn't me, but I never said a word. I knew Thomas was right, I was just going to have to bide my time.

Around 6:00, a woman arrived who I had never seen before. She came over to the family, and through the introductions to other people, I gathered that she was J's great-aunt. She apparently lived out of town, and I had never heard him speak of her before.

J's sister greeted her warmly with a big hug directly in front of where Thomas and I sat.

"Do you want to see him? Anyone can go back to see him if they want…his room is just on the other side of the women's bathroom over there," I heard her say.

I looked over to where she was pointing. The women's bathroom was located just to the right of the doorway that opened to the hallway where the patients' rooms were.

If J's room was on the other side of the women's bathroom, then it had to be the first room on the right once you went through the door.

He was just *right there*.

So fucking close to me, but just out of reach.

Then it dawned on me what his sister had said.

Anyone can go back to see him if they want.

This was my chance.

It might be the only window of opportunity that I would get.

I jumped up and followed J's aunt as she made her way towards the open doorway. I felt sure everyone would just assume that I was going to the restroom. I would just keep following her and go right into his room as she did. No one would notice, and she didn't know me so she wouldn't know that I wasn't supposed to be there.

As soon as we got to the doorway, Lila rounded the corner coming from the hallway and we stopped just short of colliding and stared at each other face-to-face.

"What are you doing?" she demanded.

"J's sister...she just said that anyone was allowed to see him.... I ...just... Please, Lila. Please let me see him," I begged.

She put a single finger up to my face.

"I CANNOT. DEAL. WITH. THIS. RIGHT. NOW." she yelled. She turned and grabbed J's aunt by the arm and began walking her away from me to J's room.

Everyone in the waiting room was staring at me.

I fled quickly into the bathroom beside me, humiliated. Why hadn't I noticed that Lila wasn't with the group? I kicked myself.

I slipped into one of the stalls and sat down on the toilet. The enormity of the whole situation overtook me and began to sob uncontrollably.

Long, low, deep wails that came from the pit of my stomach echoed loudly off the walls.

The door to the bathroom opened and closed several times as people came in and out, but I didn't care. Let them hear. I was losing the love of my life, and there was nothing I could do about it. I didn't care if the world heard my howling. In fact, it seemed only fitting.

The door opened suddenly, and I heard Lila yell into the bathroom, "Jen? Are you in here?"

I yelled back to say that I was.

"The hospital staff are doing shift change right now so there are no visitors allowed. No one can go back now," she said over the noise of the water running from one of the sinks.

"FINE," I replied, and then added much more softly, "Yeah. That's why I can't go back," as I rolled my eyes from still inside the stall.

I heard the door close back.

I commenced the wailing once more. I punched the inside of the stall repeatedly until my hand hurt so badly that I had to stop. I hung my head between my knees and wept with everything I had in me.

"I'm still in here, Jen," Lila said after about ten minutes of this display had passed.

Seriously?

I grabbed some tissue from the roll and tried to gain some control of myself. I took my time. If she could wait for ten minutes while I cried, then she could wait for two while I tried to stop.

I finally walked out of the stall and faced her. Her eyes widened.

"Why? *Why* are you still in here? You made your point abundantly clear. You won't let me see him," I said. I caught a glimpse of myself in the mirror and what I saw even scared me. My eyes were red and swollen, my makeup was all over my face, and I looked like a zombie. No wonder she had looked at me like that.

Her eyes narrowed.

"I don't understand what you need, exactly. Haven't I kept you updated on how he is? I've allowed you to stay in the waiting room, even though I don't want you here. You find out just as soon as I do when there are changes," she said matter-of-factly.

"I need to see him. I just…need to see him with my own two eyes. I need to see that he is ok," I replied.

"You don't though. You don't 'need' to be involved at all. It's not your place to be back there right now. I don't want you anywhere near him, and I know what is best for my husband," she said.

"Lila…please. I'm just so scared. I think if I could just see how he is…I would know whether or not I needed to worry so much. As it stands, I'm just terrified…. that we might lose him," I said urgently. The last few words were so painful to actually say out loud that I nearly couldn't get them out.

"Yeah, no shit. You think I'm not terrified? That's the father of my children laying in there. My high school sweetheart. The man that I've shared my entire *life* with. He's my world. I don't have to tell you that though, do I? You've known us since we got together. You were in our wedding. But that was before you were suddenly just…. *around.* All of the time. You started singing with him and I lost a big piece of Jason. I hate you for that. And now here you are, wanting to go back and spend time with him? Some of what might be the last precious time I have left with him? No. I won't let that happen. When he is recovering well, in a regular room, you can come and see him with the rest of the general public," she said. Her cheeks were flushed with anger, and she had gotten progressively louder as she spoke. The last sentence was nearly a shout.

"WITH THE GENERAL PUBLIC?! I am NOT 'general public' to him, Lila. Not to mention that you must not care too much about that time being just for you. While I've been sitting out there today you've let everyone in the whole goddamn waiting room go back and see him," I yelled at her.

"EVERYONE IN THE WHOLE GODDAMN WAITING ROOM ISN'T IN LOVE WITH MY HUSBAND!" she screamed at the top of her lungs.

As I opened my mouth to retaliate, I wondered how much of the hospital had heard her yell that. My eyes went to the wall behind her, and I closed my mouth.

J.

He was just on the other side of that wall. I thought about my sweet boy lying there unconscious. He didn't know yet that he was paralyzed permanently. If he made it through this, his life was going to be difficult in unimaginable ways.

I would likely never see him again. He would be stuck at home, dependent for his every need on the woman that stood before me.

If I said any of the things that were swirling in my head to come back at her with, it would just confirm our relationship officially.

J would wake up to find himself in a living hell in which he was unable to take care of himself physically… and he would be at the mercy of a woman scorned.

I couldn't do it.

I couldn't defend our love the way I wanted to.

I couldn't make myself say all of the things I wanted to say, because more than anything…I couldn't betray the man that I loved.

If he lived…and I hoped with everything in me that he would…I would rather die myself than make things harder for him.

I stood there silently for a long while, while the tears fell one after the other.

Part of me wanted to validate our love.

Wanted her to know that it wasn't just me who was madly in love.

Wanted her to know I hadn't just been pining away over her husband with no reciprocation.

Wanted her to know that he was just as much my world as he was hers.

The other part of me, the unselfish part of me… the part that loved him more than life itself, wanted to protect him.

It was the biggest thing I could do for him right now, though it broke my heart.

The only way I could help him now was to not make things worse for him than they already were. I knew I wasn't going to see him again, no matter which way this went.

I was going to have to love him enough to let him go.

I turned away from Lila without saying a word and walked out of the bathroom.

The sound of my boots clicking against the tile echoed off of the long hospital corridor as I half-ran toward the elevator.

I heard her call my name a few times, but I never looked back.

Through the open elevator doors, I saw her making her way after me several feet back, and I pushed the "close" button.

I stared blankly at her face until the door shut, then I burst into tears.

I had lost him.

I didn't know yet whether I had lost him to death or lost him to her…but either way I knew that I would never see my love again.

My heart shattered.

Chapter Eighteen

I WAS BACK AT my parent's cabin. Had it really only been a week since the day J had gone into the hospital? It felt like months. I had fled to the sanctuary of the cabin to get away from the constant bombardment of questions from everyone who knew us. Everyone assumed that I would be the best source of information and updates concerning J, and I didn't have it in me to tell everyone just how little I knew. I hadn't been back to the hospital since my fight with Lila. Thomas was keeping me updated on J's condition with texts and calls a few times a day but it didn't seem honest or fair for me to pass that information on to people when I was getting it secondhand.

I deactivated all of my social media and blocked all numbers on my phone that weren't close friends and family or Thomas.

I told my sister the truth of what had unfolded at the hospital. I told my parents a very abbreviated version in which I carefully left out the part of the argument about my being in love with J. I told them that Lila wouldn't let me see J because only immediate family was permitted back to his room, that I had insisted that I was "family" and should be allowed to see him, and that the disagreement had escalated into an argument that was so brutal that I felt I couldn't go back to the hospital. It wasn't exactly a lie, but it wasn't exactly the truth either. Thankfully, my parents could see how badly I was hurting and didn't press the issue by asking more questions. I knew they were very worried about J as well. The love between them had also grown deeper over the last few years since J had been more and more present in my life. They cared deeply about him too, I knew. They checked in with me multiple times a day to see if I had heard any news or updates, and I filled them in as best I could from the information Thomas gave me. When I asked to go back to the cabin as a refuge for a few days, they were thrilled to have some tangible way to help support me and told me to stay as long as I needed.

When I had arrived at the cabin that evening, I had been overjoyed to find that there hadn't been another occupant since I left it last week, which meant that my parents hadn't cleaned the cabin yet.

J's smell was still on the sheets and blankets.

His coffee cup still had his chapstick on the rim.

His hairs were still in the shower.

I changed into one of my thin lacy nighties that he loved, wrapped myself in a thick sweater, and collapsed on to the bed. I breathed in his scent deeply, and my exhale involuntarily came out attached to a soft cry. How I loved that smell. I wondered briefly how I could ever exist in a world where I never got to breathe him in again. I closed my eyes and pretended he was right beside me, and took a very long, much-needed nap.

When I woke up, it was the golden hour and the light reflecting off of the water was spectacular. I decided to go out and sit on the porch for a while, but as I walked outside, the river called to me.

It was December 15th and freezing cold. Still, she beckoned to me with her shimmery ripples. I walked barefoot down to the edge of the water and felt the cold stones beneath my toes.

The sensation was jarring, but it didn't feel like enough. I needed to be in the cold water. I needed something to wake me up from this nightmare.

I tossed my long sweater into the bushes and stood there in my lacy nightgown feeling the icy cold breeze hit the bare skin of my shoulders and legs.

I felt all of my senses come alive. Every nerve bristled to attention.

I began to tiptoe into the rushing water. First to my ankles. Then to my knees.

An inch or two at a time I eased into the river.

Suddenly, as I took a step forward, I found no place to put my foot. There was a drop-off and I couldn't regain my balance in time to keep from plunging into the icy water over my head.

I was pulled under.

I resurfaced with a loud gasp and realized I had already been moved several feet downstream just in that instant. I panicked and tried desperately to find some kind of foothold to no avail.

I felt myself being carried by the strong current, and the harder I fought, the more futile it became. I grasped for rocks and tree limbs as I passed by them but couldn't hold tight enough for more than a second as the water pulled at my body until my fingers released. Nothing was slowing me down.

I was quickly becoming exhausted from my efforts, and my fight was waning.

It suddenly occurred to me that I had nothing left to be fighting so hard to stay alive for. If it all ended now, would that really be the worst thing?

"FINE! YOU WIN! YOU HAVE DESTROYED ME ANYWAY! DO WITH ME WHAT YOU WILL!" I sputtered and screamed.

I gave in. I relaxed my body and completely surrendered.

I closed my eyes and let the water take my fate into her hands. I sent out one last prayer, pleading with Spirit that the end came quickly and that it be as painless as possible.

My body began to float over the rapids gently. When I quit fighting, I no longer banged my limbs on the large protruding river rocks and passed by them with ease instead.

I noticed that the speed with which I was going down the river begin to slow dramatically, and then I suddenly felt a multitude of tiny rocks beneath my legs and bottom as I came to a stop.

I opened my eyes.

I had been delivered gently into a small, shallow cove.

"Trust meeee..." I heard a female voice call over the sound of the water.

I sat up slowly and looked around.

There was no one in sight.

I could see the cabin in the distance. I had floated down about a mile, it seemed. I dragged myself out of the rocky cove and to the riverbank. I began the walk back to the cabin through the waist-high dead weeds along the edge of the forest in my bare feet and soaking wet nightie. I might as well have been naked for all that stood between my skin and the icy wind. I shivered violently.

I hadn't drowned.

I wasn't sure if I was happy or sad about that.

Maybe survival had been for a reason, but I sure as hell couldn't fathom what it might be at that moment.

I began to call on Spirit as I walked.

"Spirit...please... I need a sign. I need to know if J is going to make it or not. I can't live in this space of not knowing. If he makes it...maybe there is still a chance somehow that we can be together. Maybe things will all work out in a way that I just can't see right now. I know I always ask you for a fox as a sign that things will work out, but this time I need to know for sure. If I don't see a fox, I will still be wondering what that means, so I am asking you for a definitive answer, and I need it immediately. I need it before I get back inside the cabin. If J is going to live... show me a fox. If he is going to die...show me a bear," I said.

I felt a ripple of fear pass through me as I said it. I had never asked Spirit for a clear yes or no answer like that. I wondered if They would deliver. I was a little afraid that They wouldn't, but I was more afraid that They *would* answer... with a bear.

I kept my eyes peeled as I walked, scanning the tree line and the riverbank for any sign of movement. I saw a few geese, a giant blue heron, and a family of muskrats, but no foxes or bears. As I got close to the cabin, I came upon a fence that I couldn't get across. It was made of rusted barbed wire in loose rolls, and there was no way for me to go over or under it without scratching my skin.

I would have to get back in the river to make it past it.

I tiptoed back in and was surprised to find that the water now felt warmer to me than the freezing cold air had against my flesh.

I waded upstream carefully, staying as close to the bank as I could to keep from being pulled out into the rapids again.

When I got to the area in front of the cabin, I looked up with surprise to see a man standing in the front yard. As I got closer, I heard him call to me and I realized that it was my dad.

"GET OUT OF THERE! WHAT ARE YOU DOING?" he yelled.

I shook my head and threw up my hands in exasperation.

"I FELL," I hollered back to him as I pulled myself out of the water and trudged through the mud and rocks.

He ran to meet me at the water's edge with a blanket from the porch.

"It's freezing out here. You are going to get pneumonia! My heart dropped when I saw you out there in the water. You scared your Papa Bear to death!" he said.

I stopped in my tracks.

"What did you just say?", I whispered.

"I said you scared your Papa Bear to death," he repeated.

I doubled over as if someone had punched me. I let out such a foreign sound that it took me a moment before I realized it was coming from my own mouth.

A long, low, *mournful* howl poured out of me and filled up the entire valley around the cabin.

The mountains echoed back to me the sound of my sorrow, and I fell into my father's arms heaving with sobs.

"He's not going to make it, Daddy. He's going to die."

TWELVE DAYS.

He had been in the hospital for twelve days.

Carson had brought some dinner by my place because she wanted to check on me. She was a good enough friend that I had made an exception to my "no visitors" rule that I had been rigidly enforcing.

I had been talking to no one but my family, Thomas, and my three closest friends.

I had been going to work, but I was a wreck, and no one knew what to say to me to make it any better, so they all just avoided me while I was there.

I had quit eating and was living off of coffee, alcohol, and cheese crackers. I existed moment to moment, waiting with anxiety for the next time the phone would ding.

I was still spending my mornings in meditation, trying desperately to connect with J.

I was only successful in reaching him twice, and both times were very disheartening. Both conversations went the exact same way.

"Jen, what's happening? Where am I?" he would ask.

"You're in the hospital, love. You have had major surgery, and are in recovery," I replied.

"I'm in the hospital?" he asked.

"Yes...how are you, J? I've been so worried. Are you in pain?" I asked.

"I...I don't know," he replied.

"I'm so sorry that I'm not there with you, babe. I'm here though. I'm right with you in spirit. I'm thinking of you every single second. I'm wrapping you in all of my love. I need you to focus on healing, ok? Can you do that for me?" I said.

"Jen?" he said.

"Yes, my love?"

"What's happening? Where am I?" he asked once again.

And so it went, in circles of confusion. I talked to Thomas, and he told me that the doctors were keeping J drugged heavily in order to minimize his pain; that he was in and out of consciousness, and that when he did appear to be semi-alert the ventilator that he was on prevented him from communicating.

It was heart-wrenching to hear.

I kept trying to reach him. The minute that my eyes opened, I began calling out to him in the abyss. Most days I was simply met with hours of silence.

I never tried to meditate in the evening. From the very beginning of my meditation journey, it became apparent that I would struggle to connect to Source at the end of my day.

I could never settle my body well enough to allow my mind to quiet. Tapping in after a hectic day was damn near impossible; I would sit on my mat; fuss and fidget and change my body position a hundred times, only to mentally chastise myself for fussing and fidgeting each time I did so.

I had long since given up evening meditation by the time J went into the hospital. I decided that at this point, trying to go to sleep earlier was a better plan so I would typically lie down about eight o'clock in hopes that I might at the very least meet him with him in my dreams. It was a good but fruitless intention - my sleep was restless and fitful and dreamless.

Still, I kept trying.

This particular evening, I was focused on getting Carson to leave early so that I could retire once again to bed. She had attempted to raise my spirits with Thai takeout from my favorite restaurant. It smelled delicious, and I was making every effort to keep some down, despite my underlying state of constant nausea.

I also knew that if I could manage to choke down enough to satisfy her concerns about my well-being, she would be more likely to go home earlier.

We had been talking about J. Carson tried to change the subject a dozen times, but the conversation somehow made its way back to him within moments. He was all I could think about. I didn't want to talk about him, but I had nothing else to talk about. Nothing else mattered.

I got up from my couch where we had been eating and walked into my adjoining kitchen to put my plate in the sink.

Just as I turned the water on, I suddenly heard J scream my name three times.

"JEN! JEN! JEN!" he called to me in a tone of sheer panic.

It startled me so badly that I turned around quickly. The plate fell from my hands and shattered as it hit the floor. His voice had been so loud that I half expected him to be standing in the room with me. I looked around frantically.

Carson jumped up from the couch and ran to me.

"Are you ok? What's wrong?" she asked.

"I don't know…. something bad though…." I replied and sat down in my kitchen floor, trembling. I put my hands over my eyes and squeezed them shut tightly trying to quickly tap in.

Take me to him, Spirit. Put me wherever he is.

I called his name into the darkness with my entire being.

"JEN! What's happening? Something is happening…I feel strange. Jen?!! Where are you?" I heard him frantically saying.

Oh GOD. Was I losing him?

I called out to him within myself with all the strength I could muster.

"NO!!! J!! I am right here! Don't you leave me! Don't you dare leave me, my sweet boy. You STAY! You STAY right here with me. Be strong, love. I need you to fight. You fight and you STAY. PLEASE! Stay with me…" I said. I was in a full-on panic now and sobbing between words, though I was speaking none of it aloud.

"JEN…I'M TRYING… I don't know what's going on…What's happening? I love you. I love you…What's HAPPENING?" he said. His voice was loud and clear and terrifying to me.

I repeated the same things over and over and over to him. Could he hear me as well? I couldn't tell.

"Stay…please…stay with me, J. Hold on. I love you so much…can you HEAR

ME? I love you…I need you…You are so strong…BE STRONG, J. STAY RIGHT HERE WITH ME!", I said.

I had no idea how long this inward exchange had been going on, but I looked up at some point to see that Carson was on the phone trying to reach the hospital. There was no answer.

"Try Thomas! Call from my phone- he'll answer," I said.

She picked up my phone and dialed as I watched her with bated breath.

No answer.

I was still sitting in the kitchen floor, surrounded by broken ceramic.

I tried to connect once more. I closed my eyes tightly and called his name again.

Nothing.

I was now weeping uncontrollably. I asked Carson to leave. She helped me over to my couch and then began to pick up the pieces of the plate I had broken.

"Please…I'll get that later. I just need to be alone," I said.

She hugged me and left immediately.

My phone rang suddenly, startling me out of my head. It was Thomas.

I picked up quickly and answered with, "What is WRONG?"

"How did you know? I was in the room a little bit ago with him, and everything seemed fine….and then…out of nowhere he coded," he said breathlessly.

"Coded? I don't know what that means, Thomas," I said.

"He flatlined. The nurses and doctors rushed in…. no one asked me to leave so I just stood there while they all tried to resuscitate him. It was terrifying. They were able to bring him back though, Jen. They saved him. He's stable now. I came out of the room and was going to call you, but I saw that you had already called. How did you know?" he asked again.

I didn't respond. I didn't know how to tell him that I knew because I had heard J.

I also didn't know how to tell him that I knew it was only his body that had been saved.

I didn't know how to articulate why or how I knew that his soul had crossed over.

How could I explain that I had felt the other half of myself torn away; the other flame extinguished?

It was just one more wound that I would have to bear in silence. No one would believe me, and even if they did it was news that no one wanted to hear.

They kept him alive on machines for another week.

I was just as much of a vacant body as he must have been.

Christmas Day came and went. I tried to go by my parents' house to see my family for the day but wound up in the bathroom having a breakdown every ten minutes. My sister finally came in and told me that no one would be mad if I just wanted to go home.

I fled.

Two days later Thomas told me that the doctors had discovered that J was (and had been) having a series of strokes, and that he was technically brain-dead at this point. They had advised Lila to take him off of the machines. It would likely only be a matter of hours before he passed.

I watched social media like a hawk, checking every few minutes for updates from his family.

I finally saw his sister post that they had told him goodbye.

No one even called to let me know when he was gone.

I didn't attend the funeral. I knew that his family still wanted my head on a stick, and that if I had shown up there would have been a huge scene. He deserved so much more than that. I didn't want the memory of the greatest man I had ever known to be tainted because of people gossiping about a brawl between his mistress and his family at his funeral.

I hated Lila.

I hated her for keeping me from him. I hated her for being the reason that I never got to say goodbye.

I hated her for apparently knowing what was going on between us and simply allowing it. I hated her for never confronting him about it.

I hated her for trying to hold on to something that was supposed to be mine… holding on for so long that it never got the chance to happen.

I hated her for robbing me of my future. I hated her for existing. I hated her for the time that she had with him before we even fell in love. I hated her for every minute of the 23 years that she got to spend with him. I hated his last name beside hers. I hated her for having his children.

I hated her for keeping me from him.

I hated her for keeping him from me.

I hated her.

My head logically knew that none of this was her fault and that she had every right to do the things that she had done. My heart knew only that he was mine and I was his and now he was gone. She was the easy one to blame, so I made her the target for all of the rotten tomatoes that I had been handed. My anger flared brightly in the center of my grief; it flickered and scorched the edges so that the outermost part that was seen was fiery outrage. It was the place I passed through first as I entered into my heart; I waded first through spite before I crossed into despair.

As much as I hated Lila, I hated myself worse.

I knew that stress had been the cause of J's death, and it was entirely my fault.

No matter how much I tried to tell myself that this tragedy had been unavoidable, I couldn't remove myself from the equation.

I was the reason his world had been upended.

If we had not fallen so hard, this never would have happened.

Our love had put him in the most terrible position that a good man could ever find himself.

He had been in a constant state of tension between his head and his heart.

His honor and his love had pulled him in two different directions incessantly until they had finally torn him in half.

The significance of the way that he was taken was not lost on me.

The tear in his aorta had spanned the length of his body.

He had quite literally died of a heart split in two.

For that, I had only myself to blame.

Part Six

cinder – *noun*

: a small particle that has stopped giving off flames
but still has combustible matter in it

: residue of combustion; ashes

Chapter Nineteen

1/3/20 Facebook eulogy for J

J,
So many words to say, and yet you have rendered this writer silent for weeks. Probably because for a very long time, you have been the other half of my voice.

From the beginning of my journey with music, you were there. From the first big theater role to hearing our song on the radio, this journey (the journey that brought me to life, woke me up, and made me feel like I had a purpose) has been walked with my hand in yours.

You sought out the very best in me, pulled it into the light, and showed me things inside myself that I never knew existed.

Every single time I looked into your eyes, you made me want to be the version of me that you saw.

You were my best friend, although that phrase always made us laugh at the ridiculous understatement that it was. As a male/female songwriter duo, strangers always made the assumption that we were together (obviously there was no way they could know that you were married, and I was a lesbian) so we would just correct them and say, "No. Just best friends." And laugh.

Just best friends who hold one another up infinitely.

Just best friends who call out the other's bullshit; not to injure, but to force the other to grow.

Just best friends who show each other the deepest, most vulnerable parts of ourselves and then help each other write about those things.

Just best friends whose voices blend together in a way that feels deeply spiritual.

Just best friends that inspire and spark and pull out each other's best creative selves.

Just that.

You were infallibly kind. Kindness came like breathing to you. I watched you extend it to everyone whether they "deserved" it or not. Whether you knew them or not. I can't count the times I watched you jump in to help people unquestioningly. With car trouble on the side of the road. With carrying something too heavy (physically or emotionally). With learning something new or trying something scary.

You were quick with a compliment, even to a stranger. As perceptive and in tune to motives and energies as you were, you were extremely rare with a negative word toward another human. In other words - you undoubtedly saw a spade, but you would rarely call it out.

You were the most stubborn creature on the planet. I told my dad on Christmas Day that if God decided it was time to call you home, He was going to have a huge argument on His hands. I'm surprised you didn't charm Him into staying. It always seemed to work on everyone else.

You were a little vain (in an endearing way) and I must admit that I always took more than a little pleasure in calling you out publicly (especially onstage) about it. Poking at each other was kind of our schtick, but you have to admit that if the only flaw you can find to harass someone about is their man purse and essential oils that's pretty impressive. You once refused to go onstage until I loaned you my tweezers to fix your eyebrow and I told a crowd of over 100 people about it exactly 5 minutes later. You took it with great humor, as you did most things. The flip side of that is that you knew every single one of my buttons to push and could send me over the edge in 2.5 seconds. And then (maddeningly) could make me laugh when I felt like strangling you. But you never let it get too far. Whenever a fight or argument was real (not stage silliness) you went above and beyond to make sure that things were well between us… that nothing changed fundamentally.

You taught me about unconditional love in that way.

You were so good at that.

You told me that you were wrong about something exactly one time. (Well… twice actually because I pretended like I didn't hear you so that you would have to say it again. You knew and that pissed you off.) But I know you well enough to know that was a gift from you. Saying you were wrong was a rarity.

But to be fair…. you were right about most things anyway.

You despised pretense, "airs", and people treating other people unfairly/unequally. Probably because those things were so far removed from the humble and grounded person that you were. You saw the value in everyone, and because of that people loved and appreciated you in return. You made people feel seen. You made them feel heard. You made them feel (if even for a passing moment on the way into a gas station) special. Because you noticed them…listened to them (even things they didn't say out loud) and said the thing they needed to hear. And did it genuinely and wholeheartedly.

You were the ultimate supporter of humans "being".

You were always the gentlemen. "Yes, ma'am", "Yes, Sir", "Mr.", "Mrs.". All of the manners. All of the time. When you pulled me into the Bristol music scene you introduced me as "Miss Jen" so often that everyone just began to call me that. "Miss Jen" became my moniker in the music community. But you created "Miss Jen".

You built that person. Taught her how to write a song. Taught her how to find herself. Gave her a platform to share it. And stood by her like a rock while she did.

You were her music. The harmony to her melody. And the melody when she didn't have it in her.

You took Miss Jen with you.

You took the magic.

"Magic."

If we had a dollar for every time someone used that word to describe our connection, we wouldn't have had to work. From friends and family, all the way to influential Nashville musicians and promoters. It was the thing that was said so often that we joked about putting it in the album title. The "magic" of our vocal blend. The "magic" of our performances. The "magic" of the connectivity.

We laughed about it...but we never took it for granted. Not one single time.

One of my favorite things that I will always cherish is how on occasion when we could hear each other well onstage, we would find ourselves in a harmony note together that was so perfect....so vibrationally spiritual...that we would hold out the note several beats longer than it should have been just so we could live there a little longer. We never indicated to the other that we were going to do it...we just both felt it, followed it, and reveled in it. And then we would smile at each other because we both knew that we were each trying to make that moment last just a little longer. Magic.

I was always SO proud to be onstage with you. SO proud of all that we created. Proud of our songs, proud of our performances, and proud of how far we had come. (Our song was at #105 on the country charts last week!!! Not bad for a little singer/songwriter duo from Bristol.) We both wanted a career in music so badly.

I think we almost had it, J. I know you thought that too.

If there is anything that I can have some peace about, it's that nothing ever went unsaid between us. You knew exactly what you meant to me, and I knew exactly what I meant to you. We both had a huge piece of each other. There was So. Much. Love. between us. We were both always good with words, and unafraid to use them.

Two writers. Two "word people".

There have been volumes of novels of words shared between us.

Words written together. Words written to/for each other. Words sang. Words exchanged in joyful moments. Words to lift each other up in tough times. Words of love. Words of tough love. Words of trust. Words of celebration. Words of encouragement. Words about spirituality. Words of humor and banter. Words of appreciation and gratitude. Sometimes paragraphs of words that were only said in an exchange of looks. And sometimes words of knowing/understanding each other so deeply that actual words weren't needed.

And now there is silence.

Ever since we began singing together, I felt like my voice sounded empty without the fullness of yours complimenting it. Now the emptiness is all I can hear.

All of my favorite memories involve music, and therefore you are in all of them. All of my hopes and dreams for the future centered around music, and therefore you were in all of them. I talked to you every day. I lived for our shows on the weekends. I loved you fiercely, and you were the person I was most grateful for. You were woven into the fabric of my life so tightly that now all of it has unraveled and I'm sitting here in a mess of strings that can never be mended.

The world lost one of the finest men to have ever graced its presence. A kind, gentle, hugely talented, lionhearted, sensitive, hilarious, intellectually gifted, loyal, spiritual, honest, inspiring, FORCE of a human. You left a wide, gaping hole in your wake, J. You were so many things to so many people, and you were so loved. You were an incredible father, husband, family member, friend, coworker, band mate, and human and all of us who loved you are destroyed and grieving this loss in different ways and facets because we all lost something precious....but as for me....

I just lost my best friend.

My magic.

The other half of my voice.

And my entire heart.

Just that.

-Your "Miss Jen"

I CAREFULLY CRAFTED that eulogy.

I initially wrote it the way I would have written it if no one but me would read it.

Then I scrapped it and tried again. This was meant to honor him, after all. I was going to have to write it in a way that could be read by anyone.

The Melody of Fire

I rewrote it several times.

I reread it and realized that passion still poured out through every word.

I edited out anything that I thought was too revealing about our love and ended up with a piece that felt worthless to me. I reworked it endlessly.

I finally landed on the letter above. It still sounds like a love letter, but it was the best I could do. It was the most watered-down version that I could live with.

The process gave me a new reason to hate Lila. I hated her for being the reason I couldn't publicly mourn the loss of my love.

I was going to have to carry this grief in silence. That felt like her fault, though I know that at the end of the day, it was my own choices that had led me here.

I posted it on Facebook the day after his funeral and braced myself for the aftermath.

Surprisingly, there was none.

After that I felt like I had nothing else to do; there was no other way that I could honor him or our love, there was nothing else to be accountable for, and I had absolutely no purpose.

I checked out of life with no intention of returning.

I swan-dived into the darkest night of the soul, and as I broke the surface, I allowed the blackness to consume me.

I felt certain that I would never see the light again.

Chapter Twenty

THE FINAL STRAW, the thing that just completely sent me over the edge emotionally and mentally, came in utterly out of the blue and derailed any tiny scrap of a will to live that had dared to try and hang on.

I had finally gone back to work out of financial necessity, though I would have been more than happy to continue living my life as a kind of prison inmate in my little loft where meals just showed up at my door at random times and I didn't have to make a single effort to do anything but piss, shit, and cry. But alas, another month's rent was due, and oceans of tears wouldn't make the payment.

My co-workers were beyond wonderful to me during this time. They not only left me alone in my work area (which happened to be in the basement level away from the majority of the bustle), they fielded calls from friends and clients that had heard I returned and wanted to check on me, or worse: physically see me. I have no idea what they told those people, half of whom I believe were genuinely concerned about me, and the other half I think just wanted some kind of verification of the affair by the level of destroyed I may or may not appear to be should they be able to see me to assess. Either way, no one got through that front-line barrier for weeks.

Not only were my coworkers my first line of defense against talking to people, but they also simply let me grieve however I needed it to let it come out. Sometimes I would be holding what would appear to be a benign conversation with a coworker about something as meaningless as what was for lunch and tears would just be streaming down my face as effortless and uncontrolled as breathing. They simply let it happen without judgment.

No one batted an eye when they walked into my space to find me bathing a dog and sobbing, my tears falling right along with the water raining down into the tub. No one made me talk about it (though they all initially told me that they were there to listen should I want to). No one paid any mind or judged what I can only assume sounded like their very own Moaning Myrtle in the basement of the animal hospital. The amount of grace extended to me during that time was astounding.

I had only been back to work a week or so when it happened.

My stomach began to hurt in a strange way. It almost felt like period cramps, but not quite. Nausea washed over me periodically as I worked, and the pains shooting through my abdomen were hard to pinpoint. Had I eaten something bad? I didn't think so, as I was eating very little anyway. I couldn't imagine that I had consumed enough of anything to make myself sick.

I went to the restroom on a quick break and stood up to see an exorbitant amount of blood in the toilet. I had clearly started my period, but this seemed like an extremely abnormal amount of blood, and it scared me. I tried to do some quick math on when the last time I had my cycle was and couldn't come up with an exact number of weeks because suddenly my calculations were replaced with a resounding realization that blasted through my body like a foghorn:

I had been pregnant.

I hadn't known that I was. I hadn't even thought about it. In fact, even the *possibility* hadn't occurred to me in the slightest over the last several weeks because I had been completely consumed with all that had been happening with J.

To be honest though, I had been pretty terrible about paying any attention to my cycles the entirety of my life because let's be frank, pregnancy isn't exactly high on a lesbian's list of things to worry about. Having to keep that in mind as a concern had been a major adjustment for me in my relationship with J. I was so bad at it, in fact, that *he* had begun to pay attention to when I was supposed to start and would often tell me when it was coming. I began to rely on him for the heads up about it and had fallen back into my previous habit of just not paying any attention to my periods whatsoever.

However, standing there in that bathroom at work staring at a bloody wad of toilet paper, I recalled exactly when my last period had been. I remembered it quite clearly because it had ended in the nick of time. I had been worried that it was going to ruin our plans for the weekend and had been praying for it to end. The universe had complied, and I had just finished the day before our last night together at the cabin.

The night before he went into the hospital.

Ten weeks ago.

Which meant, that unbeknownst to me, we had created one more beautiful thing together in our last evening before I lost him. Up until this very moment, I had been carrying our child.

A violent wave of nausea washed completely over me, and I suddenly found myself on my knees retching into the toilet. I crumbled, pants still around my feet, into a shaking, sobbing heap on the floor.

I had never thought about having children of my own. It obviously would have required extensive planning when I was with Julia, but neither of us had expressed a desire for children so it always felt out of my awareness of possibility for my life - but even after J and I got together it was something that I never really considered. We were trying to hide our relationship, after all, and a baby didn't exactly fit into that plan. We had only talked about having children together once, after a brief pregnancy scare early on in the affair. J hadn't seemed afraid or upset in the slightest. He had, in fact, been dreamy-eyed and incredibly sweet about the possibility.

"Think about what that would be like, babe. A little Jen and J running around. I would love to be the father of your child," he had said tenderly.

Meanwhile, I was losing my mind in panic (and asking him if he had lost *his* mind) until we got SEVERAL negative test results and I finally started.

But now it was different. Now I no longer had him by my side, and the only remnant of hope that our love might live on in some kind of tangible way was gone. Gone with the bloody water that I had just flushed down the toilet.

I remembered watching him with his kids when he was alive. I had witnessed firsthand what a tremendous father he was. He also was so sweet with my baby niece that on more than one occasion it had made me teary-eyed. He had commented on how much she looked like me and once told me that he didn't think that the world could handle another Fields girl with that smile. She would go right to him every time and I always told her that was her Uncle J. Thinking about it in this moment made my heart ache deeper than I thought was still possible.

Thoughts that hadn't even occurred to me prior began to come crashing down on my head like the walls of Jericho. I wailed in agony. There would be no more chances to create a physical manifestation of the deepest love I had ever known. No chance to hold a tiny infant that had his steel blue eyes and my fiery red hair.

I mourned the child whose eyes I would never look into. The child who would never hear stories about her amazing father, or tales of how she was born from the most magical love that ever existed.

I had no logical explanation for how I knew the baby I had just lost was a daughter, but I did.

I pounded my fists into the floor until they were bruised and swollen. I wailed like a wounded animal, howling my pain to the deaf ears of the basement bathroom walls.

I mourned the loss of my J in a whole new way, saying his name over and over again until it was just ragged gasps.

For the first time, my eyes were completely opened to the realization that I was utterly alone with no hope or chance of moving forward with even a fragment of him by my side. I had been shown the possibility and the impossibility of it in the exact same moment.

From the large gaping hole in my being, I grieved our baby. Our baby that I never knew I wanted so desperately. Our baby whose loss now seemed like the most short-sighted and selfish failure that I had ever committed.

I had lost this baby with my negligence.

I had been so wrapped up in my grief that I hadn't been eating. Hadn't been sleeping. I hadn't been taking care of myself in the least, never dreaming that I was also not taking care of something that we had created together that I still could have.

It was all gone now. All lost.

No tangible proof that our love even existed.

No little Jen and J.

No little candle to carry the light from the twin flames.

It was one more wound. One more way I had lost him, and the final one before I lost myself as well. It was too much to bear, and it was in this moment that I let the last remnant that was holding me together rip like the rest of the fabric.

I have no recollection of how long I lay in a fetal position weeping on that bathroom floor. What I do remember is thinking with great clarity that death would have been a welcomed mercy. But then again…maybe it had come after all, for it was with that final blow that the rest of what had been left of myself that had been weakly hanging on to life inside my heart, died for good.

Chapter Twenty-One

GRIEF CREATES A massive sinkhole.

A deep, wide, gaping space where your hopes and dreams, and love go when you lose what is precious to you.

You find yourself down at the bottom of it with your thoughts and the ever-present, searing pain of irreplaceable loss.

Every single hour feels like a lifetime and people say horseshit things to you like,

"Time will ease this."

"You will move forward eventually."

"Everything happens for a reason."

"One day, this won't hurt so badly."

"This will make you so much stronger in the future."

"Jesus can heal this."

But all you can see in the darkness around you are the steep sides of the hole you are sitting in. Walls that lead up to the light. Up to the surface where you once stupidly lived in blissful ignorance of the depth of pain that a human could feel. You once pranced around happily up there in that light, where you excitedly planned for your future as though you had any control over any of it.

At some point, a self-righteous asshole (who lost their cat 5 years ago) will come over to the edge of the sinkhole and yell down at you that they know exactly how you feel, but that you should take comfort in the fact that it was all part of God's great plan.

As if you could feel any less loved by the Creator.

Grief is a rapist.

She will have her way with you. She doesn't know the word "no."

She'll sneak in quickly, lock step with loss. She will completely ravage your world; rape your existence by forcing herself on you despite your pleas to be left

251

alone. Just when you think she couldn't possibly destroy any more of you, you realize that while you were in shock she also broke into your most sacred places and stole all of your plans for the future that you had kept hidden and treasured.

She will leave you raw and bruised and hopeless.

She will make you question everything from your self-worth to your spiritual beliefs. She will leave you so broken and ragged that you will wonder if there actually any point in living, anyway. She will instill a fear in you that should you even think about moving forward or finding happiness again, that she and loss will come marching back through the door together again to wreak havoc and set up camp.

She will paralyze you.

She'll move her shit into the sinkhole bottom depths with you and be your roommate that eats your food, drinks your beer, and won't let you get a moment's sleep.

Should you happen to forget she's there for even a few minutes, she will quickly slap you in the face with the smell of peppermint and cigarettes, or point to the clock at the time of day when you would normally hear his voice, or stroll a happy and smiling baby right in front of you, or sing you THAT SONG. She'll slice through your very being with reminders; things that once seemed trivial or unimportant will become an unnavigable minefield of pain.

Should you be able to sleep through the night without her poking you in the eyeball at all hours, as soon as the sunlight begins to peek through the windows she will lean in and whisper a reminder that everything you wanted is gone. That this day, like the day before, will have to be endured with an absence that has left a hollow so vast that all you can hear is your pain echoing back to you off of the walls of your heart every minute.

She'll ask you why you should even get out of bed, anyway. Everything is empty down here in the sinkhole. "Just go back to sleep," she'll say.

But then she won't let you. The tears and the hurt and the memories will blend with your dreams until you're not really even sure what reality is anymore; all of it is one long continuous nightmare.

One day you awake to realize, it doesn't even matter if you do wake up. The nightmare never ends. It's the same. What used to be your worst fears are actually your life now. The person you swore you couldn't live without is gone.

They took with them everything you ever wanted.

Every place you found joy before is tainted with absence.

Everything you looked forward to has evaporated.

And now you don't even trust God enough anymore to talk to Him about it, because if the cat-less, self-righteous asshole was correct, and this is all part of His plan, then you would rather find a different "plan." Or cancel the subscription.

It's just you and Grief, sitting in a sinkhole at rock bottom, trying to find a reason to breathe.

No matter how much time passes, it feels like the indescribable loss just happened. People will ask you how long it's been, and Grief will answer for you and say, "Moments ago."

Time stopped for you that day. The world screeched to a halt in an instant and all that you will be able to remember is how things were "before" and how they are "after." It will forever be your very own "B.C." and "A.D." Before the Crisis. After the Death.

That person that used to live inside of you... the person that you were before, died that day too. They spiraled out of this dimension in the arms of the loved one lost. And what replaced them?

A shell-of-a-human, occupied by a self-centered, needy, ravaging, destructive, sleepless, rapist roommate.

Grief.

EVERY SINGLE MORNING that I woke up after that I was furious. I don't mean that I woke up angry about the loss and the situation; I mean I was literally angry that my eyes had dared to open up to face another goddamn day.

My pillow took a beating every single time my body betrayed me by not letting my soul slip off into death during the night. I would come out of a dreamless sleep to a full-on rage that slowly settled into utter despair. Every single morning with consciousness came the sickening reminder that he was gone and with him, everything I loved and wanted. All of my hopes for the future had been destroyed. Every time the dawn showed its face, I was once again bewildered at why I was still waking up when there was clearly no reason to do so. I wasn't actively doing anything to try and end my life (that would have taken effort, energy, and forethought - none of which I was capable of mustering at that time); I merely hoped that my soul would exhaust itself into expiration. It seemed not only reasonable to me that it might happen, it became maddeningly frustrating when it didn't.

I spent my evenings drinking myself into a stupor that allowed me to check out of reality and sleep. That's a fine line, and a difficult feat to manage. If you've ever tried this form of self-medicating, you know exactly what I mean. There are stages of drunk, the least pleasant of which is a mid-level phase where you are still functioning fairly well but every single emotion you feel is amplified. We all know what this looks like. It's the moment at a bar when someone looks at you and suddenly has to hug you and say something like, "I know we don't hang out that often, but I want you to know that I LOVE you. You're just, like, the BEST person, and I wish we saw each other more, but I swear you are one of my best friends. I LOVE you, man. You've always just...been there for me. Let me buy you another beer. Did I tell you that I LOVE you? Because I do......" Meanwhile, behind them, two straight girls are making out with each other because suddenly repressed feelings just popped out via purple hooter shooters, and they can't contain themselves any longer.

This phase is fun and/or entertaining when you are feeling good but let me assure you that when you are in a bad place it's hell. All of the sorrow just bubbles up and comes spilling out in the worst possible way. Everything gets amplified and what was already a sharp knife in your gut becomes a serial stabbing. Once you're this far in, the only way to get through it is to drink a lot more in a hurry because in order to reach your desired destination you have to get ahead of those pesky heightened emotions that you have fired up. If you can drink enough (and fast enough) you can reach the next phase of drunk which is what you were shooting for: not functioning well and best of all, numb to everything.

I would take this nightly journey one step further. Numb was wonderful, but sleep was best so I would stumble my way to my bed with my whiskey bottle and drink until I finally slipped off into a dreamless coma-like escape. Then the next morning my eyes would fly open in an all-out rage, and I would start the whole damn cycle again.

Rage to utter despair, into a drunken sleep, and then back to rage. My entire existence became that hamster wheel.

Meanwhile, my inability to connect with or hear Spirit in any form just plummeted me further and further into a vast sea of inconsolable hopelessness.

The divide between J and me felt deep and wide and irreconcilable. I began to feel certain that I would never connect with him again in this lifetime in any meaningful way. I tried everything I could think of.

I would still sit to meditate every morning. It was the only effort at life I was making, and I was doing it strictly because I thought I might be able to hear him again. It went the same way every time. I would be able to quiet my thoughts just long enough to realize, once again, that I couldn't find him, and I would come back to awareness on my mat to find my body shaking with heavy sobs.

It just didn't make sense to me. If I could hear J when he had a physical body (a feat which had seemed miraculous every single time it happened), why the hell couldn't I hear him when he was in spirit? Or was that even a real thing -that we became a spirit after death? What I had been told about heaven and hell growing up contrasted sharply with what I had come to believe to be true about the nature of existence in recent years. Was any of it true? The old religious beliefs or the new spiritual ones? What really happens to us when we die? Was J in some kind of purgatory? Heaven? Hell? Had he already reincarnated somewhere? Vanished into nothingness?

I didn't know where he was. All I knew was that it wasn't with me.

How could this even have happened?

How could we just be *done*?

Finished?

One day I was experiencing the deepest most profound love that consistently defied all boundary and expectation… preternatural and astoundingly magical - and the next day it just… *fucking evaporated*?

It never felt that transient – that *evanescent*, in the moment.

It felt eternal. Solid. The most substantial and immovable truth. In J's words "the most real thing – so real that the rest of existence is background noise to *this*."

I thought back to the morning on my yoga mat a few years ago when he had made love to me in spirit. It had felt so tangible. *So very real.* Where was that version of him now?

Just…gone?

I couldn't accept that.

I would never believe that we were done.

If it was going to require taking myself out of this life to join him in the afterlife, wherever the hell that was, then so be it.

As soon as I could muster the energy.

Maybe tomorrow.

But "tomorrow" looked exactly like today – which looked like yesterday and the day before… and it all felt like one big black hole that I was lost in. Where was the exit? Where was the entrance? Where was anyone or anything that had any kind of answer that made any kind of goddamn sense?

There was one tiny little gift bestowed upon me that I was able to instantly recognize as the very best thing that could have happened…and it arrived just when I needed it most.

A few months after I lost J and the baby, the universe created a worldwide pandemic just for me. At least… that's how it felt.

For weeks I had been dragging myself back to work by the scruff of my own neck, fielding phone calls from people trying to "get me out of the house" and trying desperately to hide under furniture and not breathe when people randomly showed up at my door to check on me.

I simply *could not.*

Could not anything.

My ability to interact with humans had diminished far below the acceptable bare minimum of communication by any social etiquette. I had stopped speaking to people at work unless there was a crisis-level need for it. Meaning, "crisis-level-as-determined-by-me," and my standards for that were now pretty unreachable - so unless you had one of your own severed limbs in hand upon approach or were carrying a dog with an eyeball dangling from its socket, I wasn't likely to respond with more than a grunt or nod. I also began implementing a fun new trick at home for warding off unwanted visitors in which I answered the door (if they were so insistent that they wouldn't give up the knocking and texting) without pants and gave them an opportunity to reevaluate on demand the level of crazy that they were prepared to walk into.

"Sorry. Can't shower or dress," I would say, basically daring them to come in to bear witness to more of The Nothing.

It worked.

I learned quickly that most people can't sit comfortably with someone in pain. They don't know what to say or how to act, so when confronted with agony outside of their comfort zone they will typically scurry quickly away back to their own little safe world where people take showers, and quietly congratulate themselves for making some kind of effort to check on the less fortunate pants-less. That was fine by me. I knew no one could fix my pain. Not only that, I knew no one could hold space for it. It was a galaxy-sized black hole. I sure didn't know how to hold it, and I didn't expect that anyone else did either.

Friends and family that did make an effort during that time to show up for me in any kind of capacity, all now say some variation of the same thing when reflecting back on my state.

"I thought we lost you."

"You were completely unreachable."

"There was nothing behind your eyes but pain. I couldn't find the Jen that I knew before anywhere in your being."

"I felt so helpless…I wanted so badly to help you, but I knew there was nothing I could do."

And I couldn't bear seeing my loved ones hurting over my own hurt. It just compounded the complexity of it all. I couldn't be honest with most of them about J having been my lover, which made the depth of my grief confusing to those who didn't know, and I didn't have it in me to risk being judged harshly on top of everything else. There was one morning when my mom stopped by to bring me food and I wouldn't even let her in the door. I couldn't let her see me dying like I was, and I knew if she came in and sat down that there was no way I had the fortitude to hold it together in any capacity, so I basically pushed her back to her car. She left hurt and confused. I felt terrible but I didn't know what to say to fix that. If you think that it sounds like I was being ungrateful for the support that people were trying their best to offer, rest assured that I agree. I'm not proud of the way

I pushed people away during that time, but I simply didn't know how to connect with anyone when I felt like I couldn't let my true grief be seen.

I was handling everything quite horribly. The only thing I knew for certain was that being around people was excruciating and I wanted them all to go away and leave me alone to just bleed out privately without having to babysit their feelings about my feelings. I didn't have the strength to worry about what they knew or didn't know, or how upset my pain might make them.

I loved them, but I simply could not hold anything else for anyone. Not if I was going to survive this, and I wasn't sure that I would.

As luck would have it (and it certainly felt lucky for me at the time), one day the insistent calls that I put on pants and meet people somewhere outside of my home, and the uninvited doorstep checks just…stopped altogether. COVID-19 made it completely unacceptable for anyone to ask me to do anything in person. Work dropped back to emergency-only vet appointments (i.e., not haircuts for floofs) for about six weeks, and finally…. *FINALLY*… I was allowed to die in peace. Alone.

I didn't have to pretend anymore, for anyone, that I was ok in any capacity. I didn't have to do anything else but grieve, and I was so beyond relieved. It was a full-time job anyway. I was so taken under by my grief that I was unable to see quarantine from any other perspective than a blessing. The pandemic was the biggest, most welcomed exhale that I thanked Spirit for every single day.

The entire world stopped, and it seemed rightful and just that it had done so. I couldn't fathom how it had kept on spinning as long as it had after everything on the planet worth a shit was gone anyway.

It seemed… appropriate. I felt like the earth itself went into mourning with me – as if she also knew that the most precious of loves had been severed and that things simply could not go on as they always had. There needed to be a deep retreat inward and a very long moment of silence.

For months, I was barely a whisper of a human.

"Existing" was an overstatement of my presence. I was merely a deference – a ghost of a creature made up of tears and hollowness, who was barely in response to the physical world surrounding me.

While being left alone with my own sorrow truly felt like just the reprieve I needed at the time, in retrospect, it maybe was a little *too much* free time in which to wander the hallways of my own mind. I began to have the realization that time, for all practical purposes, had stopped for me. My entire life I had been ultra-sensitive to the passage of time. I had always felt like things were flying by too fast, and that wasn't quite soaking in all that life had to offer. I had always felt perpetually behind. I had a quarter-life crisis the week of my 25th birthday that would have shamed even the most lamenting thirty-nine-year-old out of her dread of the big four-oh. I was with Julia at the time, who was 18 years my senior, and she had watched me go through my existential crisis with a mixture of bemusement and annoyance. She reminded me finally, in a not-so-sympathetic manner, that if I thought things seemed grim at twenty-five, I was in for a rude awakening.

If I thought time had flown by before J and I were together, it was nothing compared to what it had felt like afterward. Our shows came and went at the speed of light. I would get excited about time with him (either onstage or off) only to find that it passed so quickly I felt like we barely saw each other. There was never enough time together. Marathon three-to-four-hour sex sessions felt like minutes. We couldn't touch each other enough. Thousands of kisses shared never felt like enough. Sometimes he would swing by my house quickly on his way to somewhere else just to look in my eyes and kiss me for a few minutes because, damn it, there was just… Never. Enough. Time.

In his absence (and in the absence of any kind of structure due to quarantine), time not only ceased to matter, it screeched to a near halt. I felt every single second. It was like I was in one long state of marijuana high without the actual pleasantness of being stoned. I would try and busy myself with things like reading, watching a movie, or listening to music only to look at the clock (feeling like hours had to have passed) only to be horrified to find it had just been 10 minutes since the last time I looked. It was the most miserable alteration of time consciousness I had ever experienced. We all spend our lives wishing for more time, or that time would, at the very least, go a little more slowly. That wish got granted for me right when I reached the depths of hell. Though I was grateful to be alone so that no one could see exactly how bad of a shape I was in, I didn't know what to do with the endless hours.

I began to start the whole drinking/numbing process earlier and earlier in the day so that I could slip off into sleep. It wasn't so much that I wanted tomorrow to get here sooner, because I knew it was going to look exactly the same; I just wanted to check out for as long as possible each time I had the opportunity. Sleep became my only refuge.

One particular night, I checked my phone for the thirtieth time to find that time had barely moved, and I somehow convinced myself that it had to be broken or not updating correctly. My wall clock never worked properly so I couldn't use it as a reference. I called my sister and asked her what time it was, and when her response matched what was on my phone screen I burst into tears.

"I think I'm losing my mind, Whit. Nothing even feels real anymore. I've heard people talk about rock bottom…I think I might be there," I confessed.

My sister was 5 years sober. This was language that she knew well. She paused, and then responded gently, "Well, if you think you are there, then you are. If there is one thing true about rock bottom, it's that you will know when you hit it."

I heard my brother-in-law (who had gone through recovery alongside my sister) say something in the background, and my sister laughed.

"Nathan says to tell them you are with our family, and you might get a discount since we have a standing table reserved," she relayed.

I had to laugh, but then became somber again quickly. I felt so lost.

"Everything just feels so empty. It's just like my entire soul has been enveloped in this darkness that is so thick I could almost cut it," I told her.

"I know, babe. I mean…I don't know *exactly* what it feels like because my rock bottom was different, but I feel you intensely and I can't imagine how much you are hurting behind closed doors alone. So…I have something to tell you. I've been going back and forth about whether to talk to you about it or not because I couldn't decide if it is something that will help you or hurt you worse…but it seems like 'worse' isn't really possible," she said.

"Yeah, no doubt. Go ahead. There's really not anything that anyone could say that could possibly hurt me any more. I am at capacity," I replied.

I heard her take a deep breath.

"J came to me in a dream last night," she said.

"WHAT?!" I shrieked.

As it turned out, I had been wrong. Just that simple sentence sliced me open all over again. Why would he come to her in a dream and not to me? I felt the anger begin to bubble up from the pit of my stomach. I tried to rein it in so that I could hear what she would say next.

"Go on," I whispered.

"He came to me with a message for you. In the dream, the three of us were sitting in my living room. He and I were talking, but you couldn't hear us. You were watching our mouths and trying to figure out what we were saying but you couldn't. You got extremely angry at the two of us and were screaming at us both, but you finally gave up and laid your head in his lap. J rubbed your head while you cried and then he looked up at me and I realized that *he* was crying as well.

He said, 'I can't reach her right now. She doesn't remember, but we agreed upon this before this lifetime. We planned all of this out together for a reason. It's killing me as well. I didn't expect it to hurt like this once I crossed back over. It breaks my heart to see her this way. Please tell her that she will hear me again. She just has to figure it out. Tell her that I love her and that I am right with her. Tell her that I can hear and see her, and that *she will hear me again when she figures it out.'*

"I told him that I would tell you. He looked so broken, Jen. When I woke up, I wrote his words down exactly as he said them so that I could pass the message along," she said.

I was quiet for a long time.

"Figure out what, Whit? What do you think it is that I have to figure out? My purpose maybe? This lesson that we apparently planned out together? Honestly, I just don't have it in me to try to figure out anything at the moment. Or maybe ever," I said.

"I don't know. I don't have a clue what he meant by that. I do hope, at least, that you can find some comfort in the knowledge that he can hear you and see you and that he is with you. I don't think he or anyone else expects anything from you in the state that you are in. You are allowed to grieve, sis. You've been through hell. Take all of the time you need. You don't have to figure out anything right now," she said.

But I needed him.

I needed to hear him.

Why wasn't he talking to _me_?

Why was he withholding the one thing that could ease my grief?

I couldn't understand why this was all being put back on me as if _I_ were the one who somehow had the answer. If J could talk to my sister, then there should be absolutely no reason why he couldn't talk to me. He was just choosing not to for some reason.

Either that, or the dream wasn't really a message from him.

As I lay down that night it weighed on my mind heavily.

"Was that really a message from you, J? Or was it just something that came from my sister's subconscious because she is tired of seeing me hurting like this? Was it just a dream, or was it a message? I wish there were some way of knowing. I don't suppose you could validate it somehow?" I spoke out loud into the darkness.

I didn't even allow myself to hope that he might answer. I was so tired.

Tired of hurting. Tired of hoping, only to be hurt again.

Tired of all it was taking out of me to simply continue to exist.

Still, there was a little voice in the back of my mind that whispered,

"He said he can hear you…."

I awoke the next morning to three text messages, sent within minutes of each other, from three different friends of mine that lived in entirely different parts of the country.

One of them lives in Boston, one lives in Washington State, and the other lives in Nashville.

None of them know each other.

So how, exactly, was I to explain that the text messages that they all three sent said nearly word for word the exact same thing?

"Hey! I hope you are doing ok. I know this sounds weird, but I had a dream last night and J was in it. He told me to tell you, 'She will hear me again when she figures it out.' I hope that has some meaning for you? LOL. I also hope you don't think I'm crazy, but it felt important for me to tell you."

Fuck me.

He had answered.

I mean…not directly to me, but in a really big way. I stared in shock at the messages as I compared them. They were nearly identical. The actual quote from him was verbatim in all three texts.

"She will hear me again when she figures it out."

I guess that answered the question as to whether my sister's dream had actually been from J or not. I felt my heart flutter with life a little for the first time in months. I almost didn't recognize the feeling that began to blossom for what it was, it had become so foreign.

Hope.

I didn't want to feel hopeful.

I was so afraid that it would get torn from me like everything else had been.

I tried to ignore it, but it was there. Hope. Gently making its presence known as I read and reread the texts from my friends.

I knew it…I knew we weren't done.

If I could just figure it out. (Whatever *it* was.)

He was telling me that I would hear him again.

Wasn't that at least something to hold onto?

I tentatively placed my fingers around that promise.

I didn't fully trust it, but it was more than the nothingness that I had been holding.

It made me shift my focus ever so slightly. If I could figure out how to hear his voice again, the thought of living might just become a little more palatable.

I wasn't entirely convinced that it was going to happen, but I found myself entertaining the possibility. That alone was much more than I had ever thought I would have been capable of again.

Chapter Twenty-Two

I BECAME RESTLESS.

LIKE it or not, the idea of talking to J had lit a little spark of life in me.

I wanted to "figure it out," but I didn't know where to even begin. I wanted answers and I didn't know how to get them. My existence became one of day after day of frustration. It was like being in a padded room in a psych ward. I was screaming, yelling, flinging myself against the walls, and barraging my surroundings with a never-ending line of questions. I was also fairly certain that I was being heard, but not acknowledged. I thought back to the dream messages from my sister and my friends. J had told me he could hear and see me then, and I had no reason to believe that had changed.

I certainly believed that Spirit could hear me.

Yet here we were. Or rather, here I was- psych ward dwelling, straitjacket-wearing, mad-woman pointlessly screaming into the abyss.

I imagined J and God (I always reverted back to the masculine title "God" when I was pissed at Him) sitting behind a two-way mirror in another room watching my behavior and discussing the deterioration of my mental health between themselves. I assumed that as I yelled and pleaded for answers, they replied only to each other. I asked for directions while the map sat between the two of them. No one buzzed an answer through the intercom into the other room. No one sent a nurse in to up my medication. They just popped some popcorn and propped their feet up while they watched me lose my mind.

Since petitioning the Divine didn't appear to be working, I began to read again. As I tore through book after book on spirituality looking for answers on how to connect to the other side, I was deeply disappointed to discover that "meditation" was the all-encompassing prescription.

I had already been trying this, to no avail. There had to be another way.

In the past, I at least felt like I was being met halfway. I had heard J (and Spirit)

263

all of the time. Now it felt like I was the only one putting in any effort here and it was maddening. With this in mind, I tentatively started down a new path.

If God and J wouldn't come into my room, I would have to find a way to get into theirs.

If they wanted me to "figure it out," then I was just going to have to fucking figure it out.

No matter what it took.

I walked over to the two-way mirror and stared deeply past my own eyes, searching for signs of life on the other side.

"Boys…I'm coming over there so you might as well put some coffee on and pull me up a chair."

THE FIRST BIG move I made was the only stab at sobriety that I had ever attempted in my adult life.

It wasn't my idea, it came from Alice, my longtime therapist who was pretty woo-woo herself and had been delighted to hear about the telepathic connection between J and me when it first began (and all throughout the relationship up until his death). She knew that I had stopped hearing him after he died, and that it was one of the biggest pieces of my grief. I never had to convince her of the truth of mine and J's connection, which is not to say that the magic of it all kept her from busting my balls over every other facet of the relationship (particularly my role as a paramour) when J was alive. While at least I always knew without a doubt that she believed me, sometimes I wished I had a therapist that was a little softer – and by that, I mean I wish I had one who could be charmed into allowing me to wallow in my own bullshit and Alice was not the one. I remember once throwing a complete tantrum in her office over the unfairness of my lack of time with J to which she simply responded by raising an eyebrow and saying, "Well that was cute. Are you done with that now so that we can actually look realistically at your expectations?"

Can't get by with nuthin'.

Our most combative argument had begun right after my miscarriage and was still running hot on this particular day as I sat in her office in a chair by a large bay window that felt entirely too bright. We were arguing about antidepressants. She wanted me to take them. I wouldn't.

By now she knew my argument well. Every single person in my life that is on antidepressant medication, which I will point out is a significant percentage of the people I know, has ended up in a mess. It started out the same way with each of them: a simple prescription for one antidepressant with the lowest dosage possible. As time passes, the drug doesn't seem to be working as intended, so the doctor increases the milligrams. The next thing you know, they have to change medications because that drug no longer works. More time passes, and then at some point, I have a conversation with my friend that reveals they are now on two or three medications (because supplemental drugs have now been added to boost the effectiveness), the levels are impossible to regulate, and they are in a less stable state than they even were to begin with. I even have one friend whose doctors have resorted to shock therapy (LIKE THEY USED TO DO BACK IN THE DARK AGES) on her brain because the cocktails of medications have amplified the problem instead of fixing it and she is now in a state of high anxiety with suicidal thoughts 80% of the time.

Call me crazy, but I'm going to pass on that rollercoaster ride, if at all possible.

"I might be the lowest of the low right now but fuck, at least my depression is predictable," I told my therapist.

I absolutely believe that clinical depression exists, and perhaps for people who have that, antidepressants can alleviate that pain. I also know that I am not one of those people. My depression was not stemming from a chemical imbalance in my brain. It rode in on the same horse as grief when I lost my baby and the love of my life. I didn't believe for a second that throwing a substance at situational depression was going to fix anything, which is why when Alice looked at me during this argument and said sharply, "Well, if you refuse to take an antidepressant, then you CERTAINLY don't need to be taking a depressant," I listened.

I dropped my head, ashamed. I hadn't really thought about my drinking in that way, but she was right. In my attempt to numb everything, I had been consuming mass quantities of a substance guaranteed to do the exact opposite of what I was longing for. I couldn't meet her gaze.

"While we are on the subject, I have to tell you that I honestly believe that one of the reasons you can't hear J any longer is your drinking. Alcohol lowers your vibration, Jen, and right now that is the last thing you need. You are going to have to meet him in the middle a little bit here if you have a chance of reconnecting. Grief is a thick vibrational curtain for him to push aside if he were trying to reach you. Adding alcohol on top of that would likely make it damn near impossible. If you are going to take attempting to communicate with him as seriously as you say you are, I suggest that you start by reaching for clarity. Through sobriety," she said, piercing me with her eyes until I met them.

I felt the tears spill out when I looked up. I nodded wordlessly in agreement to indicate that I had fully understood. She was right that I wasn't doing myself any favors on any level, but I hadn't even considered that I might be unintentionally blocking the thing I wanted more than anything.

I whispered, "I would do anything…ANYTHING. I have to get it back, Alice."

"We both know there is no guarantee here. But I don't think you have a prayer of hearing him again if you don't quit clouding your senses with alcohol. I will say that I don't think that is the only issue. I think you have some subconscious blocks going on as well, and I'll do everything I can to help you work through those if you will begin pulling your weight and start by laying down the bottle," she replied.

She had softened her tone at this point. She had watched me cry a thousand oceans on this couch, but I suddenly realized this was the first time she had explicitly told me to do something. As ball-busting as she had a tendency to be with me, she still had only in the past "led me to the water," so to speak. She had always trusted that I would follow through in the direction that she pointed me, without having to make me drink the water forcibly. This time she was actually handing me a glass. I took it from her without question, grateful to have something I could control in my hands.

"Done. Consider it done. I won't touch it again until I die if you actually think it will help," I said, between sobs.

She rolled her eyes. "Unnecessarily dramatic, as usual," she said. I had to smile.

"I'm not saying never again, Jen. How about 30 days? Can you commit to that? If you don't feel any different at that point then we can reassess," she said.

"Yes. Absolutely. But can I ask…what did you mean when you said I had other blocks? What else am I doing that I need to change?"

She sighed.

"I haven't talked to you about this because I wasn't sure that you were ready to hear it, but if you are dead set on starting down a path of doing everything you can to try and connect with him again, you need to be aware. I don't know if it is something that you can intentionally change. Our subconscious knows how much we can or can't handle. Sometimes, your subconscious will try and protect you by repressing things or blocking them entirely. *Especially after a trauma.* I know you think you want to hear J again, but you may not be able to handle it. If that is the case, it's very likely that even if he is trying to connect with you, your subconscious isn't allowing it. It's a defense mechanism, and a very strong one at that," she said.

I stared at her blankly. "Well, how the fuck am I supposed to fix that? And are you telling me that this whole time I've been blaming him for not communicating with me, and it's been my fault? Do you honestly think I wouldn't be open to hearing him? Of course, I could handle it. I would literally, willingly give up my life to connect with him again! There is no way I am blocking him!" I was nearly yelling at this point.

"Jen. Think about it logically for a second. Hasn't he reached you with messages repeatedly since he crossed over?" she asked.

"Yes, but always through someone else. Never directly to…" I stopped short.

Never directly to me. The sentence I couldn't finish held the answer to the entire problem. He had never stopped talking to me. He had, in fact, gone completely the long way around the barn to make sure I heard what he had to say – and wouldn't he only have to do that if he couldn't get through to me directly?

Talking to me would have been infinitely easier than tracking down my friends and family with a message and turning the volume up so loud that they couldn't ignore it. Usually, by the time they reached out to me to pass the message along, the push was so strong that they were almost annoyed.

It *was* me. It had to be. I had been blocking it.

And J had been so persistent that he had found ways to reach me anyway.

I had been looking at this all wrong. I began to sob uncontrollably.

"Now you see why I hadn't mentioned this to you prior?" Alice said.

"Yes…but…I could have been trying to somehow get past the blocks this whole time. I could have been trying to fix it…you just let me live in the belief that it was him. I wish you had said something sooner," I said. I was so dejected. I also felt like a complete asshole for all of the things I had said out loud to and about J in regard to "ignoring" me.

"You needed, very much, to heal a great deal before this conversation. I know you, and you would have just jumped into what would have been a very painful effort to move blocks that I am not sure you are able to remove on your own anyway. It wouldn't have done anything but put you in a worse head space, and we both know that you didn't need that. Whether you realize it or not, there has been a great deal of forward movement in the last few months. I honestly wouldn't have even tried to talk you out of drinking until now either, as I felt like you numbing out enough to sleep peacefully was the thing that was keeping you from actively trying to take your own life," she said.

I let that sink in for a minute. She was definitely correct that the ability to sleep soundly had become my only form of escape. Having a place to run to had made living bearable. Who knows what I would have done for that sweet peace if I hadn't had that as an option? As usual, she was right.

"So, what now? The drinking I can stop, but you said you don't think I can remove these blocks on my own. What do I do?"

"I'm going to send you to an appointment with a friend of mine. He's a healer, and he normally does chakra alignment, but I have had a few of my clients have tremendous success with him working through subconscious blocks. Think about it this way…when you are stressed you hold tension in your body, which restricts the flow of energy. Energy work with a gifted healer can help restore the natural flow of what has been stagnated. It may not fix the problem entirely, but it should help begin the process and I definitely think it's worth a shot for you. Are you open to trying it?" she asked.

"If you told me that you thought drinking rat poison would allow me to reconnect with J and Spirit, I would buy a bottle on the way home," I responded.

"Well, it would…but I would like to keep you around to hear about the reconnections so let's not take that route," she replied with a laugh. She took a card out of her desk drawer and leaned forward to hand it to me. I took it and read the services underneath her friend's name: "Reiki, Chakra Alignment, Energy Work."

It reminded me of Bobby Drinnon's business card so many years ago, and how I had read it with a mixture of intrigue and amusement. I had long since let go of any hang-ups I had about "woo-woo" spiritual practices that I knew nothing about. After my awakening with J, I had begun to just be open to whatever because it was continually proven to me that there were many powerful truths that I knew nothing about. Just because I hadn't heard of it, didn't mean it wasn't meaningful or useful in some way.

The problem now was that I had lost my faith in Spirit.

When I had gone to see Bobby Drinnon, I knew nothing about the ways of the Universe and was closed-minded out of ignorance. Now I was afraid to surrender for a different reason.

I felt like I had gone through a breakup with Spirit.

I didn't trust Them anymore. Spirit had taken everything from me, or at the very least, hadn't stopped that from happening.

Before the trauma, I would have taken this referral as a Divine sign. A nudging toward the direction that I needed to go for my highest good.

Now I was dubious, at best.

How could I make myself have faith again that Spirit had my back?

I reminded myself that I had been searching desperately for answers and direction on my own for months and that it had gotten me nowhere.

Today, for the first time, I received information that might actually prove to be helpful. My therapist had at least given me options that I hadn't thought about.

Sobriety. Energy work.

These were actionable things that I had a little control of that could make me feel like I was at least *doing something*.

They were worth a shot I supposed.

I had no idea what energy work or Reiki consisted of, but if it meant that it would help me talk to J I was willing to find out.

As for the drinking, I told myself that I could lay it down easily.

Boy, was I wrong.

Chapter Twenty-Three

BEING SOBER PROVED to be much more difficult than I ever could have imagined, partially because I then had no escape from the all-consuming grief, but also because I fucking love alcohol.

Love. It.

It started with a penchant for wine in my early twenties, escalated into a love of craft beer and brewery hopping in my late twenties/early thirties, and finally settled into a deep love affair with fine bourbon and whiskey as I approached my mid-thirties.

My friendships, social activities, and even my marriage were all centered around alcohol as a unifier.

"Having fun" meant finding the next neat place to drink together; on our pontoon boat, at a concert, at a fun new brewery or distillery downtown, at a ballgame or tailgating, camping, at my own shows, even on foodie tours of towns we would vacation in.

Julia and I had even gotten into the habit of going to our favorite local Mexican restaurant and meeting with friends to drink beer every single Sunday night. All of our friends knew we would be there on Sunday evenings so we never knew who would show up, but it was guaranteed to be a party on the patio if it was pretty, and inside if it wasn't.

Every. Single. Sunday. Night.

I started off every single Monday morning dehydrated and hungover for years, because I'm classy like that.

The problem with all of that (or rather, the biggest of the problems - I'm aware that there are lots of problems with all of that) is that for years I wasn't actually present in my own life….and I didn't even realize it.

What I thought was just a "hunt for the next good time" was hurting me far more deeply than I ever could have imagined.

I was literally squashing every emotion that needed to be processed, halting any healing or growing that I desperately needed to be doing, and drowning out any little voice inside that decided to whisper, "Hey! We aren't ok in here!"

Though this had been going on for decades, after losing J and our baby, those voices went from a whisper to an all-out scream.

It got really noisy inside my head and my heart with a whole lot of uncomfortable truths being shouted about when I was sober, so I had been doing what I knew would work. I used alcohol as a tool to silence them.

Depression? I need a drink.

Anxiety? I need a drink.

Grief? I need a drink.

Fear? I need a drink.

Despair, agony, or even mild inconvenience? You guessed it.

Alcohol was so entwined with my life by this point that I actually hadn't even realized how much of a problem it had become.

That is, I didn't realize it until I tried to extract it.

When I attempted to remove the numbing mechanism, I crumbled.

The pain was so unbearable that as much as I had thought I wanted to die before I tried to quit drinking, the desperation to do it was amplified by a hundred when I wasn't.

That is not an exaggeration in the slightest.

I had to face the depths of my heartache over and over, and I simply wasn't strong enough to do it. I made it through a few sober days at a time, only to relapse.

I realized just how bad it was when it got to the point that I was literally talking myself through entire days by repeating this phrase over and over:

"Just make it the next ten minutes and then you can kill yourself."

That was my coaching method.

Just wait ten minutes.

If it still hurts this bad, you can end it all.

Ten more minutes.

Ok, five.

I know, I know...I said that ten minutes ago, but let's do ten more.

Ok - how about if you make it ten more then you can have a shot of whiskey. That's better than suicide, right?

And that's the path I would take that led me to being drunk and passed out in my bed, once again.

I never heard J any better, but I also was able to recognize that I wasn't clearing my system for long enough spans to help anything.

I wanted to hear him desperately. I wanted that to work so badly.

But I also couldn't survive without a break from the hurt.

I felt like such a failure.

Here I had thought that I would be able to "figure out" how to hear J, and I couldn't even do something as simple as not poison myself. I couldn't bring myself to tell Alice that I couldn't do it. Not only could I not be sober for thirty days, I couldn't even manage three.

I canceled my next few therapy appointments so that I wouldn't have to face her.

I did, however, go to the Reiki session with the healer that she referred me to.

I had no idea what to expect as I pulled up to the building. The place was an acupuncture and healing center, and though it was located only one street over from my apartment I had never really paid attention to it before. It was a beautiful Asian-inspired building, and I admired the landscaping as I parked.

A very tall, extremely mild-mannered man with sandy blond hair and glasses met me at the door and introduced himself as Alice's friend Stephen. I followed him back to a room that had a massage table in the center of it. Surrounding the table were all kinds of drums, bowls, and chimes. Long tables and shelves featured an astounding array of crystals and herbs.

I uneasily wondered just how many of these items were going to be used on me?

Was he going to ask me to take drugs or something?

This felt weird already, but I sat down on the table anyway.

"Alice told me that she had referred you to me, but she didn't really go into any detail. What brings you here today?" Stephen asked.

When I opened my mouth to try and speak, I unexpectedly burst into tears.

Every time I tried to formulate a word nothing came out but sobs. It took me forever to get myself together enough to speak.

I felt so humiliated but couldn't stop. It dawned on me that this was the very first time I had been asked by a perfect stranger to tell them what had happened. Everyone in my life already knew at least some version of the story, even if they didn't know that J and I were lovers. I was struggling to know even where to begin. My emotions just came pouring out ahead of any words that I tried to say, so I just gave up and let the tears have their way with me until they finally slowed enough that speaking felt like an option.

Stephen waited patiently for what felt like an eternity until I was able to regain my composure.

"My God. I'm so sorry…I had no intention of doing that, it just came spilling out. Jesus, how embarrassing," I said when I could finally utter something that sounded like language and not just guttural sounds.

"It is completely fine. Please take your time. There's no judgment here," he replied.

"Shew. Ok. I'm sorry again. So…I am here because I have suffered a tremendous loss. The love of my life passed away about eight months ago, and then I miscarried shortly after. I've been grieving terribly, as you just witnessed, and I am trying to heal from all that has happened. But I also feel like I have lost my connection to Spirit through all of this. Alice seems to think that I have some blocks energetically that are hindering that connectivity, and she thought you might be able to help," I explained.

I toyed with telling him about J, and how I used to be able to hear him but couldn't anymore. After all, that was really the reason why I was here. Only a few people knew about that though, and I always felt like it sounded crazy when I said it out loud.

I could always talk to Alice about synchronicities and mystical experiences because she was very attuned to those things as well. It was one of the reasons why we had lasted so long as a therapist/client partnership. I never hid anything from her because I knew she believed me without question.

That was also one of the reasons why I was sitting on this massage table even though I was completely out of my comfort zone. I trusted Alice's knowledge of the spiritual realm enough to follow her guidance.

Stephen, however, was a stranger.

Though I felt certain that anyone who considered themselves a "healer" would probably have knowledge of telepathic communication or even mediumship (was that the term for what I was seeking at this point?), I couldn't help feeling stupid every time I opened my mouth to tell him.

I just let it go.

I figured that restoring my connection to Spirit would naturally help with the J situation as well, if any of this even worked at all.

Stephen listened with compassion as I told him about losing J and the baby and said that he would do all that he could to help me. He explained to me that I would lie on the massage table while he performed his energy work while he would be listening to the guidance of Spirit for what to do. He also warned me that sound healing would be a big part of the experience so that I wouldn't be startled by the drums or chimes when I heard them.

I felt relieved to hear that he wasn't going to give me any of the substances or herbs that I had seen on the table when I walked in. I have always been wary of unknown food and medicine, partially due to my long list of allergens to avoid, and partially because I am chickenshit and a lightweight when it comes to drugs. (Seriously. Even marijuana. My sister had brought me an edible to try and help me sleep during this whole "lay down the alcohol" period, and I ate a quarter of what she told me to eat and ended up stoned out of my mind for hours - making time that had already felt halted somehow feel even slower. No, thank you. Hard pass.)

The Melody of Fire

I lay on my back on the massage table and closed my eyes.

I heard Stephen begin to whisper what sounded like a prayer, though I couldn't make out the words. Was it even in English? I couldn't decipher.

He then began to use the instruments around me to make various sounds around my body. At first, it just sounded to me like a giant racket. The musician in me cringed as I listened to notes and drumbeats that seemed to have no relation to each other echo around me. I'm not going to lie, even though my eyes were closed and he couldn't see them, I rolled them a few times.

However, a few minutes into this cacophony I began to notice something peculiar happening. When he would strike a chime or play one of the bowls, I began to feel the vibration in my body match what I was hearing.

It started lightly, in a way that simply made me curious. Different sounds seemed to reverberate in different places. I would feel one in my head more, and others in my gut or chest. How strange this was.

As it went on, the vibrations got stronger and stronger.

My body began to respond as if the sounds were coming from inside my very bones instead of the instruments. It became so intense that my other senses got involved with the interaction. When certain sounds were struck, they would resonate through my head in such a way that it was as if I could *see* the sound instead of merely hearing it. My heartbeat seemed to be pulled onto the drumbeats that were played.

In fact, it was so intense that it almost felt as if it were the other way around - as though my heart was dictating the drumbeat.

The vibrations layered one after another became almost unbearable to me. My body felt as though it were at the mercy of this man and whatever sound he decided to create next. I felt like a live wire. Every single nerve seemed to be responding.

It was extremely uncomfortable. I opened my mouth a few times to ask him to stop, but each time talked myself into trying to tough it out.

Just when I felt as if I couldn't take any more, he stopped.

I lay there on the table, feeling like I was buzzing with vibration from head to toe though the room was now silent.

Stephen leaned down and whispered in my ear, "I am now going to work on each chakra to open them up. Once they are flowing well, I am going to come up above your head and send the negative energy that has been blocking and hindering you through your body and out your feet. It will go into the earth where it will be transmuted into light."

I nodded.

I had no idea what that meant, but whatever.

As I lay there feeling him work above me, I felt something heavy being placed on my body at various places. I quickly remembered all of the crystals that I had seen on the table when I walked in.

That was exactly what it felt like. Rocks.

He must have been putting crystals on each of my chakra points.

The weight was heavy and hot at each section.

I once again was uncomfortable and prayed that this would be over soon.

I lay there, still vibrating from the sounds moments ago, and now all down my body the heat and the heaviness at each chakra point seemed to sink down into the center of my body.

I felt Stephen move back behind me and above my head.

He began whispering again and I felt the air around me move as though he were gesturing with his hands above me.

The hot energy began to make its way down my body. I felt it first in my head around my third eye. It seemed to gather and almost roll its way down my chakras. I felt it around my throat, and then my heart.

I then felt it push in a wave to my upper abdomen….and stop.

He must have picked up the crystals that he laid on my lower three chakra points because suddenly the weight lifted.

The energy continued to sit at my solar plexus, though the heat and movement halted.

I thought that was strange. (As if this wasn't an exceedingly strange experience all the way around already.) Didn't he say that the energy would flow down my body and out of my feet? Maybe I had misunderstood.

I felt him place his hands on the side of my head and they felt cool and steady in comparison to my body.

"You can open your eyes, Jen. We are all finished," he whispered to me.

Wasn't he going to move the other crystals he had placed on me? I opened my eyes. and looked down at my body. There was nothing there.

How was that even possible? I had felt the dead weight of rocks on my body just as surely as I had heard the sounds from the instruments earlier.

"Didn't you put crystals on my chakra points? I was certain I felt that," I asked him.

He tilted his head to the side slightly. He seemed a little surprised by the question.

"No…I didn't physically touch you with anything until the end when I put my hands on your head," he replied.

"Huh. Weird," I said. It was the only word that I felt like summed up the whole session. I wasn't sure how helpful it had been, but it had certainly been… weird.

I slowly sat up.

I felt a little nauseated.

The Melody of Fire

I thanked him for his time, and quickly paid him. I practically ran out of the building. I was feeling extremely strange and couldn't wait to just get home and rest. My stomach hurt where the energy had seemed to stop when I was in the session. It was now churning uncomfortably.

When I walked through my door, I went straight to the bathroom.

I threw up instantly.

What the hell had happened on that table? I had been physically fine when I walked in. Now I felt heavy, and the nausea that had washed over me seemed to settle deeply into my body.

I tried walking around my apartment. I tried lying down. I drank some soda. Nothing seemed to alleviate it.

I threw up again.

This can't be normal, I thought.

After a few hours of this cycle, I decided to call Stephen back and ask him what in the world was happening to me.

When he answered, I relayed to him the state that I had been in since I got home.

"Hmmm. That is very strange, indeed. When you were on the table, were you able to feel the energy that I was pushing go through your body and out of your feet?" he asked.

"Not exactly. I felt it roll down my body in a big wave, but it stopped at my upper abdomen. Then it just kind of went away," I answered.

"Oh wow. It stopped at your solar plexus? Why didn't you tell me that when you were here?" he asked.

"I mean… I didn't really know if that was normal or not. I've never had anything even remotely close to that done to me. Hell, I thought you had put rocks on my body and there was nothing there. I didn't mention it to you because all of it was so foreign," I said.

"Ok. I understand. But you will need to come back. Apparently, you have one hell of a block in your solar plexus. It halted that energy from being sent out and transmuted. That is what is making you so sick. All of that negative energy that was supposed to be carried out of you just got stuck and gathered in your center. I need to try and send it through again. Can you come back?" he asked.

"Yeah. I only live a street away. I can be there in a few if that works for you," I said.

The thought of going through that sound healing and energy push all over again seemed exhausting to me, but I also couldn't deal with the nausea. I grabbed my purse and headed back over to his office.

I had never realized that energy could be so tangible. Honestly, I hadn't known what to expect from my session, but I kind of thought it was a crock of shit at the beginning. I had been willing to try it, because I had been willing to try anything, but I had never expected to physically feel anything in the slightest.

I certainly had never expected it to affect me the way that it had.

It was hard to deny that *something* had happened, though I still didn't understand exactly what.

When I lay down on the table for the second time, the session went nearly verbatim the same way. When it got to the point where Stephen was to send the energy out of my body through my feet, it once again seemed to stop and settle at my upper abdomen.

This time I told him the moment that it happened.

He tried a few more times to send it through, but all I felt was I slight movement (almost like a breeze) that seemed to continue past my solar plexus.

He finally gave up trying and told me I could sit up.

"I think this is just going to be a process. I want you to come back once a week if you can, and we will continue to work on this block. Think of it as a stone in water. We will repeatedly run the energy across it and eventually, it will wear down enough to allow a flow to happen around it," he said.

"I'm I going to be sick like this until then?" I asked. The thought was excruciating. I already was finding it difficult to get out of bed in the mornings. I would never make it through if I was constantly nauseated on top of everything else.

"I think…that you may be sick for a few days, but that things will eventually resettle as they were before, and you will be ok. As ok as you were, anyway. Once we get things finally moving you should feel considerably better if you can just hang in until then," he said.

I nodded, reluctantly. It kind of seemed like I didn't have a choice. If things were stuck, they were stuck.

I was used to that feeling by now.

I could make it through as long as the nausea subsided.

I considered what he said.

"As ok as I was."

I hadn't been ok at all when I walked in the door, but I had become accustomed to my not-ok-ness.

I could tough it out.

I would come back again if I knew there might be a chance of fixing me. After all, I had felt *something* move, hadn't I? Some movement was better than none. I agreed to come back in a week.

It was a commitment that I ended up being so glad I made because it turned out that something had indeed shifted that day of my first session.

When I went to sleep that night, I had contact with J for the first time since he died.

The Melody of Fire

I was in a dimly lit room, standing in front of a giant map of the world. It was massive and brightly lit. I noticed that the map was incredibly detailed. As I was inspecting it carefully, I suddenly felt a presence approach me from behind.

I turned to see J standing before me.

I flew into his arms, sobbing.

"*I've missed you so much...where have you been? How could you leave me like this?*" I murmured into his chest through my tears.

He took my face in both of his hands and when I looked at him, I could see that he was talking, but I couldn't hear anything.

"I can't hear you, J. What are you saying?" I asked him. I tried to read his lips, to no avail. God this was *maddening*. Was I never going to be able to hear him again?

He kept trying emphatically to convey what he was saying, but not a single sound reached me. His head dropped in defeat.

Then it seemed as though an idea occurred to him, and he moved with purpose.

He took me by the hand and turned me back around in front of the giant map. He opened my left hand and gently placed something in it.

I looked in my palm and saw that he had handed me a small pin.

I picked it up with my other hand and looked at it closely.

"I don't understand, J. What is this?" I asked.

He wrapped his own hand around mine and we held the pin together.

He led me closer to the map, and I noticed that we were standing in front of South America. He then guided my hand to a section of Peru, and we both pushed the pin into a tiny dot on the map.

As I felt the pin insert, the map in front of me dissolved and I found myself standing in the edge of dense foliage that gave way into a clearing.

I looked before me and could see a bustling camp of indigenous people. Some were cooking around campfires; others were working together with their hands on various tasks and talking to each other intently. Children were happily running and chasing each other with laughter in between all of the commotion.

I noticed a small group of women walking towards me, talking amongst themselves. Suddenly, one of them looked up and saw me.

"She's back!", she exclaimed with joy. The rest of the women looked to see who she was talking about and before I could move, they had all run to me and enveloped me with excited hugs and a million questions.

"We have missed you so much!"

"Where have you been?"

"How did you get back here?"

They bombarded me from all sides with such genuine warmth that it made me teary-eyed.

These women knew me.

I was one of them.

I looked at my hands and saw that my skin was a rich brown that matched the color of the beautiful complexion of the people before me. I understood their words, though they were clearly not English. As I looked closer at their faces, I suddenly remembered their names. I laughed out loud at the familiarity and the sense of homecoming.

I tried to explain how I got there, but I realized I didn't really understand it myself.

No one seemed to care. They were just overwhelmed with joy that I was with them once more.

One of them suddenly called to a man standing at the edge of the camp and frantically motioned him to come to us.

"He is going to be so happy you are home. He tried to take his own life when you passed," one of the women whispered to me.

As the man approached, I looked carefully at his handsome face and chiseled body. He carried himself with an air of confident strength. This man was clearly a warrior. When he got close enough for me to look into his eyes, recognition and love washed over my entire body.

J.

The women stepped to the side to make way for him as he ran to me and scooped me up in his arms. Though he physically looked nothing like he had looked in this lifetime, I still knew unquestionably that it was him.

My love. My J.

"Oh, my beloved, how I've missed you……" he said to me. He looked deeply into my eyes and kissed me passionately. I closed my eyes and let myself feel all of the love pouring from him.

When I opened my eyes, I was staring at the map again.

J was standing at my side and smiled at me tenderly.

He took my hand, and we pulled the pin from the map. He then walked me carefully to the right until we were standing in front of Africa. He guided my hand with the pin and together we pushed it into a spot along the Nile River.

Egypt.

Again, the map dissolved.

This time I found myself someplace dark and cavernous.

I was being escorted by a group of men in strange armor through a long corridor and our footsteps echoed off of a damp stone floor.

I looked to my right and my left as we walked, and I suddenly realized this was a prison of some sort. Men were being held captive in cells made of stone all along the path that we were walking.

I realized that the group of men I was following were guards. They finally stopped in front of one of the holding cells and waited for me expectantly.

What was I doing here? I turned to look into the cell that we had stopped in front of, and the captive that was chained to the stone wall turned his head to meet my gaze.

Though his body was emaciated, and his features looked unfamiliar, I still knew instantaneously that it was him.

J.

I dropped to the ground on my side of the bars that were between us and cried out to him.

I turned to the guards that had walked me to him.

"Open this door. Let him go this instant," I yelled at them.

No one moved, but one of them answered sternly.

"We can't do that, princess. Your mother has ordered that he be put to death in the morning. You are to say your goodbyes and then we must leave," he said.

"What?! No!", I exclaimed. I looked into J's eyes. He looked resigned to his fate, though tears fell from his eyes. I slid my hand through the bars until I could grab his. Our fingers barely clasped but I felt the same familiar electric buzz that I knew so well pass between our skin as we touched.

"It's ok, love. There's nothing you can do. I love you. Please know that. I have always loved you…and I will love you for eternity. Nothing will ever change that. I will find you again somehow. I promise," he said.

I wailed mournfully as he said it.

Not again.

I knew this hurt. Losing him was as familiar to me as loving him. With my fingers still linked to his, I lay face down on the damp stone floor. I said his name over and over as I cried and closed my eyes tightly.

When I opened them again, I was in front of the map once more.

J was staring at my face with deep concern.

He nodded once, knowingly.

We had been through this all before, hadn't we? He was showing me the lifetimes.

My God.

How long had we been repeating this pattern? Were we just destined to lose each other over and over again for all of eternity?

"Have we been torn apart every single time, J?" I asked him.

He nodded his head yes.

I began to cry. What a miserable existence.

"Has it all just been shit then?" I asked.

I saw him laugh, though I couldn't hear it. He rolled his eyes dramatically and shook his head for me to see.

He pulled the pin from the map and handed it to me once more.

I took it from him and let him guide me farther to the right on the map.

He guided my hand toward a spot in India that had no dot.

Together we pushed the pin in.

This time as the map disappeared, I found myself alone on a riverbank.

I had a basin filled with berries in front of me. I was holding fabric in my hands.

It appeared as though I had been dyeing the silky material a dark purple.

As I looked to my right and my left, brightly colored fabrics that must have been hung up to dry fluttered in the breeze all around me.

I suddenly saw movement behind some of the fabric and laid down what I was doing and walked towards it.

As I stepped behind the curtain that was swaying there stood before me a massive elephant who looked at me expectantly.

I was overwhelmed with emotion as I recognized her.

This was *my* elephant.

Memories of her came flooding back to me.

I ran to her, and she wrapped me in her trunk as I cried tears of joy.

"I thought I would never see you again. I can't believe you are still here!" I said.

"I have been here, dear one. It is you who left and came back.", she replied. Her voice was light and airy and seemed to come not from her mouth, but her entire being.

"I've missed you so much. I need your help. I am so confused. I have been revisiting lifetimes…I think I must be dreaming," I said.

She was quiet for a moment.

"You are not dreaming. You are waking up," she replied.

I pondered this. Perhaps she was right.

I saw her begin to wade into the river. I took some of the fabric from a branch and followed her into the water. I began to sponge her off, carefully washing her wrinkled and dirty skin.

"Thank you. You've been neglecting and ignoring me," she said as the water dripped down her body.

"I'm so sorry. I didn't mean to. I didn't remember you, or know how to get back here," I said. The sadness weighed heavily on me. I wanted to make it up to her. I walked back to the bank and took some of the brightly colored fabric down. I braided it carefully into a circle.

The Melody of Fire

From the edge of the water, I picked the most brightly colored flowers that I could find and carefully wove them into the braided silks. When I walked back to my elephant, I showed her the crown I had made her. She picked me up with her trunk and raised me up to her head where I placed the beautiful headpiece between her large leathery ears. I kissed her forehead gently.

"There. You look beautiful," I told her as she lowered me back to the water.

"Thank you, sweet child," she said.

I looked up to see a man walking toward me on the riverbank. The sun glowed behind his silhouette, and he appeared to be on fire.

The pull was undeniably familiar.

I knew it was J.

"I think I have to go," I told my elephant.

"I know," she said.

"But I'm so afraid…I keep losing him. Every single lifetime. I've just done it again, actually. It just happened in the lifetime that I came from. I don't know how to break the cycle. What should I do?" I asked her.

"There is so much magic to be experienced. Grab on to that every chance you get. Don't be so afraid of losing him that you don't allow the love to happen. Look…there he stands, waiting on you. Go to him. *Don't miss out on that*," she said.

I saw him beckon to me through the bright fiery light that seemed to radiate from him.

I longed to run into his arms.

Could I do it again, I wondered?

It had been worth it, hadn't it? The love had been so profound that I could never regret it, but still…. could I go through the pain of losing him once more?

"You've never lost him, dear one. Not one time. When you finally realize that… the cycle will be broken," she replied.

"It's time to wake up. Wake up, beautiful girl……*wake up*."

Part Seven

pyriscence -

: an adaptation to an environment in which
post-fire conditions offer the best germination
and seedling survival rates

Chapter Twenty-Four

To MY DISMAY, it was the only dream that I had of J, though it certainly gave me much to think about over the weeks that followed. I may not have fully reconnected with him, but the message was powerful enough that it fueled the fire for me to keep trying.

Figure it out. Wake up.

I continued to go to Stephen week after week.

I sat in my meditations for longer, instead of giving up quickly when I couldn't hear J.

Nothing else seemed to shift for a while, but I no longer thought about suicide every waking minute and that seemed like a big victory.

If nothing else, I kind of wanted to stick around just to see what else (if anything) might happen.

Things were uneventful for a few months. But then one day, Spirit came through, as Spirit does, in a most unexpected way.

A strange computer glitch set things into motion once again.

A friend of mine texted and told me that she had emailed me a link to a YouTube interview with one of my favorite authors that she thought I might be interested in. She said she had tried a few times to copy and paste to send it via text but just couldn't get it to do so.

When I got home, I settled in for the evening and decided to try to pull it up on my laptop. I opened the email and clicked the link, but when it pulled up, the video was not for the interview that she had told me about. Instead, it appeared to be a documentary about a word I had never seen and didn't know how to pronounce. I tried to sound it out.

Ayahuasca.

Ay-uh-hoo-asca? Spanish had been my minor in college, and I felt certain this was a Spanish word, but it wasn't one that I was familiar with. I read a few of

285

the comments in the video as it began to automatically play. A few people talked about how "Mother Ayahuasca" had changed their life by helping their addiction or depression. Other people said they hoped to get the opportunity to experience a ceremony one day.

What was this? Some kind of female shaman or healer that met with people to help them work through their problems? I was intrigued, so I decided to watch the documentary.

What I found out was that Ayahuasca is not an entity (in the human sense), but rather a psychotropic tea that is made from a combination of two different plants: chacruna leaf and ayahuasca vine. When brewed together, the combination activated one of the most powerful psychedelic substances known to man: DMT.

The people in this documentary had traveled to South America for the opportunity to sit with trained healers in a ceremony to drink this "medicine," as it was referred to in the film.

The video showed very little footage from what actually happened in these ceremonies, so I was still confused as to what exactly they were "doing" physically. There were interviews before and after the sessions, but not much footage from the actual ceremonies. As far as I could tell, there was just a bunch of lying around on mats in a circle while the shaman sang indigenous songs. However, whatever it was that was going on here must have been pretty powerful because when the documentary ended, I took away one very important impression.

Each of the individuals came with specific issues they wanted to heal. Their intentions varied widely between them as far as what they came to fix in their lives. As far as I could tell from the documentary…. the ayahuasca worked.

It worked for each one of them.

I was fascinated.

How could one medicine treat such a varying array of illnesses, traumas, and pain? Furthermore, if such a wide range of healing was available through one substance, why had I never even heard of it before?

I thought about my own pain. There had been a woman in the documentary battling deep grief from the loss of her mother. She claimed that ayahuasca had shown her things that eased her sense of loss tremendously. I couldn't help but wonder if this (whatever "this" was exactly) might help me. I was still in the very bottom of the depths of depression and grief. Things still felt beyond hopeless each and every day. I had resigned myself to the conclusion that nothing could pull me out of this. I had accepted it as my fate.

Still… some of these people in this film had battled lifelong depression or anxiety. I felt sure that they had felt the same way at points in their lives, yet here they sat at the end of the documentary in follow-up interviews six months later saying that their lives had been changed.

The Melody of Fire

It was clear that I needed to research this more.

I stayed up all night that night watching every single thing I could find on ayahuasca. I started on YouTube, and then ended up purchasing a subscription to Gaia Network because I saw an ad for a documentary that I wanted to watch. This led to a self-guided crash course on psychedelics in general, because as I learned that night, there are an array of psychedelics that can connect you to Spirit. Who knew?

Certainly not I.

I had simply listened wholeheartedly in D.A.R.E. as a child when they told us all drugs are bad and to "Just Say No." I honestly never gave it another thought. (Drugs are bad, don't do them. Got it.)

Yet here I was thirty years later (never having even taken a single recreational drug in my life, save marijuana on a small handful of occasions and I don't think that counts), ordering books off of Amazon about psychedelics and spirituality.

I was even amused at myself in that moment.

I will barely even take the full recommended dose of Tylenol when I have a migraine.

One day prior to watching that documentary, I would have described myself as vehemently anti-drug, though I didn't know the slightest thing about them except that I wasn't "supposed" to take them. Now I was ordering books about them.

I remembered back to my apprehension when I had first walked into Stephen's office and seen the herbs on the table. If he had suggested that I take any of them that day, I would have undoubtedly declined, and probably left.

Hell, I wouldn't even take a prescription antidepressant when my therapist repeatedly told me she thought I needed to.

I also knew myself to be very sensitive to substances. I don't handle prescription drugs well, and normally only took half of the prescribed doses when I was forced to by illness or infection to minimize the side effects. I had a food allergy list a mile long.

What was wrong with me?

Was I actually considering psychedelics?

I was surprised to realize that I was indeed contemplating this as a viable option.

I took the fact that I was even interested in this subject as an indication that my current mental state was much worse than even I had realized. I was a little amused (and let's be honest, concerned) with myself but I continued my research.

The more I learned, the hungrier I became.

In another ayahuasca documentary I watched, a girl was able to reconnect with her dead grandmother in one of the ceremonies and talk to her about events that had happened before she passed. As she spoke about it, I could tell in her

287

expressions and tone that whether or not this actually physically happened or it was all in her head, she believed it to be true.

The film went on to explain that ayahuasca is known as "the vine of the dead" or the "vine of souls" because it was able to connect you with the spirit realm and those who had passed before you.

I immediately thought of J.

Were they saying that it was a possibility that I might actually be able to talk to my precious boy again if I drank this tea?

That was it. I was sold.

I kept reading, kept researching, but I knew my mind was already made up. I would have swum the entire Atlantic Ocean or died trying if you told me that doing so would reconnect me with J. I would literally have done anything for even a chance that I might be able to talk to him again…and here was the discovery that a magic potion existed that might bring me the very thing that I desired more than anything?

Sign me up.

Or so I said…until I looked up the cost of flying to South America to participate in one of these ceremonies.

The cheapest option I could find (and seriously, when it comes to personal safety when consuming mind altering substances…is the cheapest option really the one that you should go with?) would have set me back around $5000 by the time airfare was factored in. It would take me forever to save up that much money. Not to mention, at the time that I had decided that I HAD to do this, the COVID-19 virus had virtually shut down the entire world. Many of the retreat centers were not open at the time, and air travel in and out of the U.S. had been halted.

I wanted to scream. It was like the universe was dangling a huge carrot in front of my face, only to pull it away from me. I couldn't see a way to grab it, and it was maddening.

One day during meditation, it occurred to me that in my frustration about my seeming inability to get to an ayahuasca ceremony, I had basically thrown everything I knew about manifestation out of the window. Over the past year, I had simply been existing moment to moment through my grief. I had forgotten about setting intentions and working with the laws of the universe because I had ceased to care about the future. The only thing I wanted was my old life back. Now, suddenly there was something enticing in front of me. I had begun to write it if off as unattainable, but I realized that I should know better. Hadn't I manifested exactly what I wanted dozens of times before I lost J? I knew how this worked by now. This ayahuasca ceremony could happen for me if I would just take my power back and call in what I wanted.

I went down to the river on my parents' land. I sat on the dock and let the sound of the water quiet my mind. I brushed my hair back from my face as the wind off of the water tousled it gently. I called out to Spirit across the shoals in a confident and determined voice.

"Beloved Spirit, if you are calling me to plant medicine…if you brought the messages of ayahuasca to me for my healing…then I need for you to make it ACCESSIBLE and AFFORDABLE for me to reach it. I will take the next step if you will just provide a way for it to happen. Thank you, thank you, thank you…." I said.

I closed my eyes. I released any and all expectations of how or when my request would come forth. I washed my hands of worry and made myself let go of any attempt to control the details of my request in any fashion. I laid it all down by the water.

I spent time imagining what reconnecting with my J would feel like. I allowed myself to revel in the joy that hearing his voice once again would bring to my tired soul. I thought of the things I would say to him, and how happy I would be to be back in his presence. I allowed myself to completely embody the emotions that reuniting with him would bring. I let myself live there in my mind for a long while.

When I finally came back to my senses, I opened my eyes once more.

"It is done," I whispered across the water, and I knew that it was.

As I sat there quietly, Spirit gently reminded me that we are all in an infinite partnership with the divine. Had I not figured this out before my world crumbled? Indeed, I had…but in my pain, I had forgotten about the tools at my disposal. I had been an absentee in participating in my own life creation for the last year. In my grief, I had hit the "pause" button.

In that moment of sending my request out into the universe, I had just hit "play" again.

I felt the shift. Movement had stirred beneath the ashes. Signs of life had kicked up the dust a little. I felt Spirit lean down and take my hand once more.

Ahhh….so you are ready to move again, dear one? Wonderful. Let's go.

The next day, Carson called me out of the blue to check on me. She wondered how I was doing in my grief and healing processes.

I told her that nothing had changed. I still was raw, hurting, and barely existing most days.

"I wish I had better news about the state that I'm in, believe me. I would have thought that I would have been so much further along a year in, but I'm just not," I told her.

"Well…that is part of the reason why I called. I thought of something that might help you, but I'm not really sure whether or not you would be open to it. At this point though, it sounds like you are open to help in whatever form that may take. Have I ever told you about the 'Journeys of the Heart' that I have done with my friend Kat?" she asked.

I thought back and felt certain that I had never heard her use that phrase before. I told her that she was correct about my openness to help at this point and that she had not told me about these "journeys."

"Ok. Well...Kat is a healer and spiritual teacher. She leads these ceremonies called 'Journeys of the Heart' where you take medicines that put you in touch with your subconscious and connect you to the spirit realm. Kat guides you through them and helps you through whatever difficulties arise and she is amazing. I think I have done seven or eight journeys with her over the years, and they have helped me so much, with so many different things. It is kind of like having years of therapy in a single evening. They are so healing, Jen. I've been thinking about you a lot lately, and how much pain you have been in. I really believe that doing a journey with Kat would help you so much. I would be happy to go and do it with you if you wanted to. Is that something that you would even consider?" she said.

I smiled. Sometimes Spirit is so much fun.

They always deliver what you ask for. They never deliver it in a way that you see coming.

Carson and I had been friends for fifteen years and she had never breathed a word of this to me prior to this moment.

I had been exactly one person removed from a plant medicine facilitator for nearly half my life and hadn't known. For almost fifteen years that information hadn't mattered, but the very second it became relevant Spirit swung the door wide open.

I put the call out, and less than twenty-four hours later, Spirit connected the wires.

Even though I already knew what the answer would be, I had to ask….

"You said that she gives you "medicines." What exactly is it that she gives you, just out of curiosity? I'm not asking to judge; I am definitely open to trying this. I would just like to know exactly what I am signing up for," I said.

"I'm not sure what all she uses, but I do know that she chooses what she gives you based on what you are coming to work through. Medicines that she has personally given me are San Pedro, psilocybin, and ayahuasca," she said.

I laughed with delight.

"What's so funny?" she asked.

I couldn't wait to tell her the synchronicities that had just unfolded.

"It's just so funny that you called me today. You aren't going to believe this……."
I began.

Chapter Twenty-Five

AFTER OUR CONVERSATION, Carson contacted Kat to set up a time for us to come to a journey.

It just so happened that she was facilitating an upcoming ceremony that was a week away and had a few open slots.

Doing a journey in seven days felt terrifying to me. I didn't feel prepared enough in the least. I needed more time to research.

I needed more time to come up with reasons to be afraid was really the issue. I hadn't sufficiently exhausted myself with things to worry about. I quickly realized that more time to think about it would likely mean that I would back out. I just needed to do it.

After all, what in the world was the point of waiting? Hadn't I specifically asked for this to be accessible and affordable to me?

I told Carson to book us.

My stomach turned as soon as I said it.

Things fell seamlessly into place. The trip quickly worked itself out; travel, food, etc. all just took care of themselves effortlessly.

It felt like a good omen, but I couldn't shake the apprehension.

I tried to busy myself all week to keep from drowning in nervousness.

Was I just being stupid for trying this? Was it just a desperate attempt to connect to my love that was doomed to fail?

What if this didn't work?

What if it did?

Something deep inside of me was telling me that everything was about to change.

I tried to think about the last time I had felt this strange deja vous-esque sensation. It was familiar in a way but took me a while before a could place exactly the last time I had felt it.

Suddenly I remembered.

It had been at my first theatre rehearsal. The night that J had asked me to start a band with him. I had felt exactly like this. As if my soul knew something that my mind didn't, and my entire being felt the anticipation of something huge about to happen.

That had worked out all right, hadn't it? Maybe I should just trust.

Trust and surrender. Trust and surrender. Trust and surrender.

How many times was Spirit going to have to ask this of me before I did it naturally? It was beginning to feel as though it would never come easily to me.

I kept trying to find things to do to fill my time before the journey. I sent Carson about a hundred texts asking questions about her past experiences with the medicine. I desperately searched each one of her replies for something that would make me feel better. I wanted her to fix the fear that was overtaking me about it.

Apart from overall fear for my well-being during the journey, there was one other overwhelming concern that kept popping up over and over again like a deep nagging from the back of my mind. If something happened to me and I died (either at this ceremony or otherwise), no one would ever know what had happened between J and me.

I had been working on writing down our love story over the last several months because I didn't want to forget a single moment of it.

I had a huge fear that I would look back years from now and wonder if I had made it all up in my mind. By writing it down exactly as I remembered it, I was trying to document all that the experience had been while it was still raw and fresh in my mind.

I had been finding it exceedingly frustrating.

Not only did I not know what my actual intent had been in writing down…I felt like I wasn't even remotely capturing what the connection had been like.

With the journey approaching though, I had a sudden window of insight about why I had been writing it all down. I hadn't been documenting it just for me.

I wanted people to know.

I had this extraordinary love. This huge thing that I had never even heard another person speak about experiencing. This earthshaking, supernatural connection with another human being.

And no one knew about it.

If something happened to me, the story would just disappear along with my crossing over. I had been writing it down so that somewhere, some kind of documentation existed that once…between two otherwise ordinary individuals, the most mystically aligned and profound unconditional love had existed. It is why it had felt so important to me that I had been making an effort to write it even through grief so consuming that I wanted to die.

I wanted it to be a book.

I wanted people to read our story in its fullness.

I didn't know how the story would end, or if it had ended already...but I knew it needed to be told.

I went back and reread all that I had saved on my computer, and I realized that I had written our love story as well as I could. It wasn't polished, but it was on paper.

It was complete unless something major happened at the ceremony. If it did, then I would keep writing when I returned.

If I didn't return, it was enough.

I saved what I had written on a jump drive and put it in an envelope with my sister's name on it along with a note that said,

"If something has happened to me, will you please make sure this story gets read somehow?"

A few nights before the journey I sat down and wrote a letter to J.

J,

My love.

I miss you so.

I'm writing so much these days, trying to tell our story. I don't even know why I'm doing this most of the time, except that it feels too special to just live in the void of us. It feels too important somehow to carry to my grave, in only my own thoughts and memories.

Too powerful to hold in just these two hands alone.

Throughout my life, I never thought I would ever get to have what we had. Had I set out on a journey to find it, I would have missed it because I wouldn't have even known what to look for. The immensity of what ultimately found us was far beyond my wildest imagination. I never knew depths like that even existed.

It was truly uncharted territory.

How could I have known that what I could conjure in my mind as the ultimate connection would pale in comparison to an entirely new land, with a new set of rules, that would make any other relationship look like "playing house". What once was desired has forever become obsolete. My best-case scenario was always fairy tale love. Getting swept off my feet and living happily ever after with a princess in a tower. God, did you ever turn that on its head. I'm sure your Leo self is quite proud of that.

You taught me so much, my sweet boy. I didn't know that love could consume you, teach you, grow you, and show you the universe and your connectivity to it,

293

all at the same time. I didn't know it could set you in front of a mirror and turn you inside out and show you every single facet of yourself. That it could show you the ugly and make you want to work on it, show you the beautiful and make you want to exalt it, and all the while making you feel so perfect and so loved *just as you are* that it doesn't matter if you do neither. I never knew that someone could know you deeper than you know yourself. That they could nearly breathe your own breath and share your own thoughts. I never knew I could exist and be so perfectly surrounded by another's existence that I never had to explain or justify a thing.

I never knew that I could reciprocate a love that deeply either. What we found together always just seemed like something too good to be true. I guess, in the end, it wasn't so much that it was too good to be true, but maybe that it was too true to be good.

Not that we didn't have our share of good, boy. What we had puts other people's "good" to shame.

What we had was a meteor. It destroyed both of us, in different ways. But God…that ride was magical, wasn't it? Astronomical. Preternatural and perfect.

A comet with a wildfire tail.

I've got a goddamn hole in my being the size of Asia, but you were worth it.

We were worth it.

I keep trying to tell it. I'm trying so hard to put the unnamable into words.

I can't seem to get it right, J.

I'm not doing us any justice. In fact, the more I put pen to paper, the more I worry that I may be just making us both sound insane. That it will never connect the way I hope that it will. That I'm just putting this story out because it's screaming like a banshee to be released in my every waking moment, but that its futile to try and tie it to pieces of paper through words.

I also wonder if perhaps it was just always and forever meant to be only ours. Maybe the rest of the world is like the two of us before this happened. We talked about it so much…how we both would have thought this was crazy if we hadn't actually been living it. We would have written it off as woo-woo and ridiculous and called other people liars if they said they had found it……until it actually happened to us. We felt moved like two chess pieces in a game we never knew we were a part of.

Perhaps I will be resigned to a life of people looking at me like a lunatic. Maybe our story will be discounted, misrepresented, and misconstrued. If that's how this goes down, I'm so sorry. Your legacy means more to me than my own, but against my will, you've left me alone to decide how to proceed with this story.

I'm sorry, love, but I think I have to try and tell it.

The problem that I keep discovering is that it needs your flavor. That's what's missing. Like the songs we wrote together, singing them without you feels empty.

It's why I keep thinking that I can't get it right. It should be both of us recapping this tale, but now I have to bear that torch alone.

I just wish I could play a reel from my memory to show everyone.

I wish I could just make it come to life the way that it lives in my mind.

No one would ever second guess *if they could have just seen.*

The times when you looked at me and sent me through the wall behind me with the *knowing.* The times we sang together, and it felt like we were sexually entwined in front of hundreds of people. The actual sex, that felt like praying and getting all of the answers all at once.

The deepest existential conversations when I thought you were so intelligent and your wisdom took my breath, but then you would look at me and tell me that you thought that I was smarter.

The appreciation and awe that we held for each other. Always and irrevocably.

Writing together, which always felt like giving birth, when we talked each other through the tough parts and then gazed at each other with wonder when we held our new creation in our arms together.

Meeting together in other planes of existence. Dreams. Meditation. Sex. Music. All of which felt simultaneously surreal and hyperreal.

The oceans of tears that were shed together for this thing that we couldn't grasp yet put every single other thing on the line for.

The opening. The vastness of the knowledge of creation, and the universe, and love in its purest form that was gifted to us both through this indescribable thing that we shared.

The inability to exist without the other.

Yet now here I am, expected to exist without you.

We said we wouldn't. We actually promised each other that we would never do that again. But here we are. Or rather…. here I am.

I haven't died. I'm still breathing.

I'd rather not, if we are being honest. Life without you has, without question, killed the magic of living for me. It's supremely unfair. I wonder if John, after receiving his visions of heaven when writing Revelation, felt the same way?

If he ever just thought, "All of THIS exists? And now I'm just supposed to have experienced it firsthand, go on with that knowledge for the rest of this lifetime, and be fine with that?"

I wonder if it was ever too much for him? If he ever saw the shortcut to getting back there and thought of taking it.

I know I have.

"Enter through the narrow gate. For wide is the gate and broad is the road that leads to destruction, and many enter through it. But small is the gate and narrow the road that leads to life, and only a few find it." Matthew 7:13-14

Saint John and I …we somehow stumbled upon the road and found the gate open; we saw the splendor, and the meaning of all of that is. We found the life. And then we got bounced back to the other side.

I don't know how he did it.

I don't know how I am doing it.

Perhaps we both were only meant to be messengers. Sometimes people are just gifted things that are bigger than them, and they have to tell the story no matter what destruction occurs in their own heart.

The sacrifice is for the greater good.

It's one individual life.

One grain of sand in the desert.

Some stories aren't for those who got the vision. They are for those who will hear the retelling.

Maybe that's all our story was meant to be, my love: a ray of hope that heaven actually does exist.

But I'm afraid, J. In a few days, I am going to try to make it back through that gate. I don't know how this story is going to end, other than that one way or another I'm making my way back to you.

By journey or by death, I know not yet.

All I do know with any certainty is that you, my only boy, will always be everything to me. Everything that existed before, not just in this life, but in all of them. From the moment we held hands, you were everything that mattered in this lifetime to me, and you will be all that matters to me through whatever lifetimes may follow. My own alpha and omega. The light unto my path. The gospel that you wrote to me the day that our soul was born, and our being was split into two.

We found our way back together here on Earth, as was written in the stars. Two halves of a whole can't stay segregated forever. Apparently, we signed up for more than I ever could have bargained for.

I was mad about it. The ripping away. I'm not now. Which is not to say that I understand. I don't. Maybe I will never get to see that point of all of this loss until I cross over myself.

There are so many mysteries about this that I can't comprehend.

I don't know how something could awaken me and destroy me at the same time. You made me experience God in a way that I never had prior, and then you left me cursing His name for tearing it away. You made me feel the most alive that a human could feel, and then you killed me. All I thought I knew prior to us was smashed to bits, and then all that you taught me was torn to shreds as well.

Why?

That can't have all been for naught, right, J? There was so much truth there… so much extraordinary…I'm writing this all down trying so hard to believe that perhaps it has a rhythm and a rhyme. Hoping that perhaps the melody will come through the hammering of these keys and the song will start to take shape.

I'm simultaneously praying desperately that you weren't my only purpose, and still deep down believing that you always were.

If I died right now, people would say it was from a broken heart. The truth is… if I die in thirty years, it will still be from a broken heart. Should I live, no matter what I do or who I love in this lifetime…nothing will ever hold a candle to the twin flame that still burns inside of me.

I am one half of a whole that is no more. I have two lips, once part of four, that changed everything that has ever existed for two souls with the words that passed between them. I am a divided universe that was completed in your arms. I am one half of a double flame that at one point, lit the entire cosmos.

Now I am just a solitary, lonely, broken human being.

I'm still searching desperately for the lesson.

Maybe we *were* given something that other people don't get for a reason.

Maybe this has a bigger purpose than the two of us.

Maybe there is some point in all of this that I just haven't found yet.

Maybe Spirit really does have a bigger plan.

Maybe I'm being selfish by focusing only on the loss instead of all of the love that we had.

Maybe I should just be deeply grateful.

Sometimes I am.

Most of the time, I just yearn for you. I look for you in every pair of eyes that I encounter. I listen for you on every breeze. I feel for you in every ray of sun and every raindrop. I search for you in every waking moment, in every existing form, and in every place that I can think of. I refuse to believe that something so powerful could simply evaporate. I'll never believe that we are finished.

As a wise man once said to me, "I am yours and you are mine. It has been that way since the beginning of time, and it will be that way when time no longer exists."

Your "Miss Jen"

Chapter Twenty-Six

I WAS SCARED SHITLESS. I had worried that waiting longer than a week would have given me too much time to think, but as it turned out even seven days had been too much time to think. Plant medicine is known to strip away the ego (not the ego as in "pride or arrogance", ego as in the baseline survival mechanism whose job it is to keep us alive and safe), and apparently, my ego heard this through the grapevine and freaked the hell out. I began going over scenarios in my head of all the possible things that could go wrong in such a grand manner that it became humorous.

I started the fear dialog with my allergies. I was allergic to so many foods and derivatives of foods, my mind immediately went down the path of what anaphylactic shock to an illegal substance would look like. I had an EpiPen in my purse at all times in life in general, but whenever I used it, I had to follow up immediately with emergency services in case more was needed, etc. How could I possibly get the care I might need if the cause of the reaction wasn't legal?

This became the lake that kept treading water in; fear of allergic reaction, fear of inability to get help, and fear of dying. I came up with some amazingly creative ways in which I might die from this experience, and if I ever doubted my ability to write fiction, my ego proved to me that week that we are a quite capable team when it comes to creating outlandish and implausible scenarios out of thin air.

Stephen King had nothing on me when it came to horrific death stories.

On more than one occasion I found myself bemused at the fact that someone who didn't much care if they woke up every morning was fundamentally so afraid of dying. After all, I'd spent the last year desperately wishing something would happen to me that would take that decision out of my hands and now I finally had my chance.

I tried to logically have talks with myself about how it wouldn't really matter if I did die because then I would for sure be with J again, and hadn't I already come to the conclusion that death would almost be a relief at this point, and can we please get it together for the love of God?

My ego wasn't having it.

A few times I found myself physically shaking at the thought of even leaving my house to make the trek.

I had other concerns, about I how would feel during the actual journey, how "out of control" of my faculties I might or might not be, the possibility of seeing things that terrified me, etc. but the most prevalent fear was definitely dying. My ego and my logical mind were clearly not paddling in the same direction, or it seemed, even paddling the same boat.

The day before we were to leave, I had struggled so much that I was in tears by the time I left work. I had almost called and backed out a thousand times. I decided that I had to let it go somehow, and the solution I always eventually come to is to surrender it to the universe.

Trust and surrender. Trust and surrender. Trust and surrender.

(Again.)

You would think at this point that I would just go ahead and start there since it always ultimately ends up being where I end up, but no...I have to wrestle everything to death in a controlling vise grip until the universe finally slaps my hands with a ruler and I let go. It's my least favorite lesson. It's my algebra class in the school of life. I suck at it, it's my last resort, and it comes as naturally as deep breathing underwater to me.

Something deep inside me said very loudly, "Something has got to give. Why are you so afraid of this? It's not like what you have been doing has been working so well. The only way to go is up. Surrender this to me and let me guide you."

As soon as I heard those words, a wave of nausea washed over me from pure, undiluted terror.

I felt like Dorothy in *The Wizard of Oz*, standing at the fork and listening to the brainless scarecrow babble on about which direction to go. I felt so confused. Was that advice coming from me or Spirit? I wasn't even sure if I could trust either one anymore, but I was going to need a clearer nudge than that.

As I sat trembling in my car, I said out loud to Spirit, "I can't do this. I need a direct push because I literally can't feel which way I need to go here. If I'm supposed to do this journey, I need a 'DO IT' loud and clear. Somehow. However, you need to get it to me: a billboard, on a car bumper sticker, on the radio...I'm listening, but I need it to be clear and unmistakable. If I get this message from you by the time I get home, I will stop questioning or wavering and just face the fear and go. If I don't get the message by the time I pull in the driveway, I will assume that I'm not meant to do this, and I will stay home." I started the car and began my long commute home. It felt good to leave it up to the universe to decide because I had been starting to drive myself crazy.

About 3 minutes into the drive, I heard my phone ding and glanced over just to see who it was and there, on my display screen, was a text from my sister. It simply said,

"Jen, I really think you need to do it."

I began to laugh. I was more than a little in awe of what I was seeing, but also delighted to have a clear and unmistakable response. Relief washed over me as I thanked Spirit out loud, "Thank you, thank you, thank you. I'll listen, as promised. No matter what, I'm getting in that car tomorrow, and I will let go of the wavering. Thank you for listening to me and always providing what I need, when I need it."

I called my sister and told her what had happened, and we both laughed together, delighted at the ways the universe works.

"Would you like to hear this side of the story?" Whit asked. I told her yes and listened as she went on to tell me what had transpired that day for her.

"All day long, there was a voice in my head telling me that you were thinking about backing out. I just kept hearing and feeling that I needed to encourage you to go and that it would be exactly what you needed. It was such a strong message that it was almost distracting from everything else I tried to do today. Right before I sent that message it was almost a yell in my mind that said 'Send her a message right now and encourage her. Tell her to do it!' so I did. You know I don't typically question guidance when it is that loud," she said.

God forbid then, that I ignore it. I thanked her for her openness and willingness to always be the messenger. I told her I loved her dearly, and that if I died to please make sure that she took the envelope on my countertop with her and followed the directions inside. Otherwise, if I made it through, I would call to fill her in after the journey.

That night the fear tried, again and again, to sneak in, but I held tight to my resolve.

In moments where I felt like I might back out, I simply read the text from Whit again and reminded myself that Spirit was pushing me hard to do this, so I needed to trust.

Even if I couldn't sleep and wanted to puke every time I thought about it.

Carson picked me up bright and early, and as I heard her pull in the drive, I grabbed my things to head out the door. I got halfway down my stairs when I suddenly remembered one last thing that I wanted to bring. I ran back to my

dresser drawer and pulled out the leather bracelet that J had made me and carefully fastened it around my wrist. It made me feel closer to him whenever I wore it, and I certainly wanted him near me now.

I took a deep breath and headed back out the door.

The whole trip there I felt my fear growing stronger and stronger. I recapped the last several months of my grief to Carson, as we hadn't seen each other physically in months. I cried nearly the whole way there as I tried to put into words the depth of my sadness. I felt so disconnected, I told her. From my boy, from Spirit, from everything. Until the previous week with her phone call, I hadn't received a single sign that I had asked for in months.

We were about halfway there, and I was playing DJ; on a whim, I decided to play J's favorite artist. As soon as the song started, I looked out the window, and amidst a patch of dense trees, virtually in the middle of nowhere, I saw a sign that simply said, "Red Fox."

No town, no river, no actual fox. It seemed to be marking nothing.

I thought back to how I used to frequently ask for a fox, or a pair of foxes when J was alive to indicate that I was on the right path. I hadn't asked for that in so long that it felt like a lifetime ago.

Carson knew about the foxes and when I looked over at her I realized that she had seen the sign as well, and we both just burst into laughter.

"What was that sign even for?? Besides me?" I asked her through the laughter.

"I think that's it. I think it was just for you," she responded emphatically.

An ACTUAL sign….as a sign. That was new.

I hadn't asked for that this time; it had just appeared, I assumed, as an indication that I was heading the right way. I wavered a little though. This journey felt like the biggest step I'd ever taken in my life….my biggest leap of faith. The fact that there wasn't a pair of foxes made me wonder if maybe I wouldn't receive what I needed on this trip. Perhaps I would be safe, as indicated by my little guidepost, but it wouldn't be as monumental as it I had hoped. I decided to just latch on to the idea that I would be safe on this journey and put all of my focus there. I was just grateful to have any reassurance that I was heading in the right direction.

When we arrived at our destination, Carson and I unloaded the vehicle and came inside to sort out the sleeping arrangements and get our bearings a bit. There were a few people who had arrived before us, including Carson's friend the healer/facilitator, Kat. I found myself looking into the face of a woman who could have been my sister. She was tall like me, and strong of build. Also, like me, she had cascading red curly hair and pale skin. What differed between the two of us was that Kat's presence took up the entire room. There was a strong, peaceful energy around her that was almost tangible. Her powerful serenity collided harshly with my nervous anxiety that had, by this time, essentially taken over my body. Her eyes were deep and knowing, and I remember thinking that the last time I saw eyes like that I was searching through the mysteries of the universe in my beloved's eyes. Carson introduced us and Kat enveloped me in a warm hug.

"Welcome, I'm so happy that you came! I'm Kat, and I will be facilitating the journey this evening. I am a healer, spiritual facilitator, and my totem is the red fox," she said.

My eyes widened. I heard Carson giggle, and I turned to look at her.

"I forgot that Kat is a fox until just now. I'm actually so glad I forgot, that was a much better way for you to find out," she laughed.

Kat looked at me quizzically.

"The fox is my spirit animal," I explained. "I always trust them to guide me in the direction I need to go. Like a marker or an arrow."

She smiled warmly at me. "It will be an honor to help guide you on this journey tonight."

One of the other girls in the room, who had been listening, passed by us on the way to the kitchen and playfully tugged my long red hair as she brushed by me.

"Looks like we have TWO red foxes here today," she said with a wink.

Two red foxes.

My pair. My ultimate sign that I was on the right path. And I finally realized… this whole time…. I had been instrumental in guiding myself right where I needed to be.

Trusting my intuition, despite my fear. Listening to myself. Following the arrows from outside myself and following the nudges from within.

Spirit and I were a team.

I was the other fox.

Chapter Twenty-Seven

I MOVED TO THE living room area of the cabin and saw Carson warmly hug the only boy that was there for the journey that weekend. I could tell there was a sweet comradery between the two of them, though prior to arriving I had no idea she would know anyone here besides Kat. His name was Chrystopher, and I instantly found his energy delightful. I couldn't help but eavesdrop on the conversation between him and Carson, as they were just across the room and the dynamic between the two of them was captivating.

As they talked and caught up a little, suddenly Chrystopher stopped mid-sentence as if he were listening to a noise outside of the cabin that we hadn't heard.

"I'm sorry. They won't shut up. There is a very persistent male who wants to talk to you, and he's not going to let it go. May I?", he said.

I watched Carson nod her head, and Chrystopher became very still as he appeared to listen even harder.

Huh?

"What's happening over there?" I whispered to the stunningly beautiful blonde girl who had sat beside me on the couch. She and Chrystopher had walked in together and appeared to be close friends.

She giggled.

"Chrystopher is an extremely powerful medium. That's actually how we became friends. We worked together and one day he walked up to me and grabbed his head and started giving me all of these messages from a dear friend of mine who had passed away from a head injury. We've been close ever since," she said.

"Seriously? That's incredible! I kind of want to pop some popcorn and watch that show over there with Carson. I think that's so fascinating," I said. I was enthralled.

"Move closer, if you want," she said. "He won't mind at all, especially in a space like this where everyone is spiritually open and supportive."

305

She didn't have to tell me twice. I relocated to a chair closer to the two of them to listen.

"This gentleman is of thicker build, kind of muscular. He has a beard. He's an intellectual…very well-spoken," Chrystopher began.

"My grandfather, maybe?" Carson offered.

"He says he's not your grandfather. He's telling me that you work with your hands for your career, but that you are a very talented writer.", he said, as he looked at Carson for confirmation.

"I write poetry…I'm not sure if that's what he's talking about," she answered.

I was riveted. This was so unexpected and cool. I was pulling for her so hard to figure out who it was.

"He says you have a podcast?" he quizzed.

"Actually, Jen and I were working on a podcast," she answered and waved a hand in my general direction. Chrystopher looked at me and I nodded back a hello.

"He says he died suddenly. Something to do with his chest," he said.

Carson shook her head, confused.

"I just don't know. I'm sorry. I have no idea who that would be," she said, a little sadly.

"It's ok, there is a lot of energy in this room so maybe it wasn't meant for you," he said. "I'm going to go grab a water out of the car, I'll see you in a few, ok?"

They embraced again, and he left the room while Carson came and sat beside me.

"I was rooting for you so hard to figure out who that was," I said to her.

"Yeah, me too. I'm still wracking my brain trying to figure it out," she replied. "The last time I was here, my grandmother came through and had some messages for me. It was so spot on. He's a very gifted medium."

I thought back to the last experience I'd had with a psychic/medium. It had been nearly twenty years ago with Mr. Drinnon, and he hadn't given me any messages from spirits from the other side. Maybe that wasn't in his wheelhouse, now that I thought about it. His messages were more predictive of the future and felt less like a "channeled" message. Perhaps my concept of psychics was uneducated and off base. It's not something I ever really researched or looked into after that initial meeting with Mr. Drinnon. I always just assumed if I ever wanted that kind of guidance again, I would just go back to him. That meeting had changed my life though, and I was intrigued and delighted to find a spiritual counselor of a different breed here in our midst for this weekend's journey.

Chrystopher had come back in and sat beside Carson. One of the other girls asked him something about her astrology chart, and he began to give an in-depth explanation of the cosmic energies that were aligning at the present moment.

He was clearly very bright and very well-versed in astrology; something that the others in the group appeared to be aware of prior to this meeting. Everyone took turns asking him questions about their own charts and sun/moon placements. He told us how to look up a more extensive personalized chart online if we were unsure of ours.

I typed my birthdate and time into the site that he suggested on my phone and examined it closely.

I might as well have been looking at the daily stock market update. I had no idea how to read either of those configurations.

Chrystopher noticed me studying it, brows furrowed, and laughed.

I looked up and grinned.

"You know I'm going to ask what this means," I said laughingly.

He held out his hand and I gave him my phone to look at the chart.

He had barely taken it from me when he exclaimed, "Oh my God…it's YOU!"

I looked at him very confused. Everyone in the room had turned to look at me confusedly as well.

"YOU'RE the one that the spirit was trying to reach earlier. He knew you were listening to me talk to Carson," he said emphatically.

My jaw dropped, slightly. Chrystopher leaned forward slightly and tilted his head to the side as he appeared to listen intently to something I couldn't hear.

"Ok, Ok. Slow down… you're throwing a lot at me here," he said, seemingly to no one.

"He's very excited and extremely assertive. He's giving me a ton of information, and a lot of it feels very private, but he said that you like to just be told things straight up. Is that true? Is it ok if I just relay all of the things he's saying to you as he says them?" Chrystopher asked as he looked at me with eyes filled with compassion.

"Y… yes. You can say whatever, it's fine," I stammered.

Surely not.

Surely this wasn't J trying to communicate to me through him. I suddenly felt excited and scared about what was happening. What if it really was him? If it wasn't him, then who was it? It had caught me so off guard that I just felt a whirlwind of emotions all at once with no time to process any of them because Chrystopher then looked at me and said probably the only thing that he could have uttered in a single sentence that convinced me without a trace of doubt that he was actually talking to my boy.

He held out one arm and took his finger and thumb from his other hand and wrapped them around his wrist like a bracelet.

"Does this….and dancing…mean anything to you?"

I felt the tears spring hot to my eyes. I pushed my sweater sleeve up to reveal the leather cuff on my wrist. The memory of our naked slow dance the night that he unknowingly measured me for it came flooding back. I saw his thick fingers wrapped around my wrist, the same way that Chrystopher was demonstrating now, as we danced together.

No one knew about that. *No one.* No one but J and I. It was one of the most private and intimate moments of my life.

"He made me this…" I said, through the tears that were now falling down. "He measured me for it like that…while we were dancing."

Chrystopher nodded, "Yes, he just confirmed that's what he meant. He's so intelligent and well-spoken, but he has a slight country twang in his accent. It's a very pleasing voice. He says that you sang together?"

I nodded yes.

"He's telling me that he actually has a good voice, but most people didn't realize that because he played harder rock music when he was younger. He also says he doesn't like the music playing right now," he said with a gesture to the Bluetooth speaker behind us that was playing soft acoustic music.

I laughed. "Yeah, he was in punk bands before we started playing together. He definitely likes harder music."

"You're sure it's ok for me to say whatever he tells me?" Chrystopher asked again.

Shit. I had no idea what J was telling him, but there was no way I was going to get shy now.

"Absolutely. Please continue."

"He's showing me a violent relationship that you had when you were younger. I'm seeing a moment of physical abuse, and he is protecting you," he said.

I paused. It took me a minute to realize what he was talking about. It suddenly clicked as a memory that had long been buried flashed into my mind. It was from when I lived in my first apartment with Molly, which was directly below J and Lila. Right before we split, Molly and I got into a nasty fight. It began with an argument in the apartment and escalated into a screaming fight outside as I tried to leave. She pushed me up against the side of the house roughly with her forearm under my neck. The next thing I knew something moved her off of me as quickly and easily as if she had been made of paper. Sputtering and confused, I suddenly found J standing inches away from me and staring into my eyes.

"Are you ok?" he had asked gently. I could only nod.

He turned to Molly. "Get the fuck out of here, and if you ever lay another hand on her you'll answer to me. Understood?"

"I LIVE here Jason," she had retorted.

"I don't give a shit. You need to leave RIGHT NOW, or I'm calling the police," he said through clenched teeth.

The Melody of Fire

She walked away, muttering to herself, and got in her car.

He had taken me upstairs to their apartment and sat with me until I calmed down and felt safe enough to let him walk me to my car.

"Are you sure you're ok?" he had asked.

"Yeah…I'm just going to go to my parents for the night. Let her calm down a bit. Thank you so much for what you did. though. I'm not really sure how far that would have gone if you hadn't stepped in," I said.

He had nodded in acknowledgment.

"Yes ma'am," he had said in that sweet way that he always did, as he backed away from my car.

It was something that I hadn't thought about in years, but even now the recollection shook me. How could I have been so blind, for so long? The love of my life had literally lived above me for 4 years, and though I always liked him a lot, how is it possible that I never saw him for what he was? I was so wrapped up in my lesbian warrior mode that I hadn't even seen what was right in front of me. The universe had just kept trying to put us together, and I had just kept ignoring it.

My attention came back to Chrystopher.

"Yes, I remember what he's talking about now," I confirmed.

"He wants you to know that just as he was your protector then…he always has been, and he always will be. I get very fatherly energy from him towards you," he paused to listen.

"He says he's actually been your father a few times in other lifetimes."

This information touched me deeply.

We had loved each other in all of the ways possible, it seemed.

"He says that he brought you here tonight. He sent you the messages about Ayahuasca. He felt certain that you would know it was from him because of his interest in Native American traditions. Wait…how long ago did he pass away?" Chrystopher asked, puzzled.

"A little over a year ago…why?" I answered.

"Because he just said, 'Not to culturally appropriate,'" he replied.

I burst out laughing. Of course he said that. That was a very J amendment, always the respectful gentleman.

"He's very charming, but I don't think he realizes he comes across that way," Chrystopher said. He grinned at me.

About the time I started to say, "Oh, he knows," Chrystopher laughed and said, "Never mind, he just said he always was aware that he came across that way, but just pretended not to know." We laughed together.

"He's such a damn Leo," I said.

"Did he have a hairy chest? Because he's showing me *his* chest and his arms.

That might be because I like that…I'm not sure if that was for you or for me," he continued.

I rolled my eyes.

"It's definitely for you. See? His Leo is showing again. He is SUCH a flirt and loves attention. From men AND women," I said laughingly.

"Was he bisexual?" he asked.

"No…just… open-minded and confident," I replied.

I thought back to one of the last shows we played where a group of young gay men sat at a table right in front of us. One of them ordered meatballs, and J spent the entire evening flirting and asking the boys how their balls were.

I laughed and shook my head. Of course he would be showing Chrystopher his strong arms and broad shoulders. He was always less hung up on sexuality than I was. I remembered what he told me the night that we had been discussing my sexuality. "People don't fall in love with genders, they fall in love with people, Jen," he had said.

"Do you…like men?" Chrystopher asked me, tentatively.

I sighed. What a loaded question. I still didn't know how to answer that.

"I don't know. J was the first guy I was ever with. It was long-term relationships with women prior to that. I was madly in love with him, but I'm not sure that it means that I like other men," I answered.

"He says that you do. He says that you like men, and he wishes that you would just accept that about yourself. He says he understands that you fought really hard when you were younger with your family, and that it was really difficult, but that there is no need to struggle over your sexuality now. You don't have to be so hard on yourself. You were designed to be his. You couldn't have fallen for him the way you did if there were no attraction to men whatsoever," he said.

I stared at him wide-eyed.

That was a lot to take in.

"He also just told me that you miscarried?" he asked me very gently. "A little girl?"

I gasped. The tears began to pour down my face uncontrollably now.

I hadn't been sure. Well…my heart had been, but there had been no way of knowing the gender of our baby for sure until now.

He just said it. It was true.

It was a daughter that I had lost.

I couldn't even answer, I just nodded my head as I sobbed.

"She is with him. I just saw her. He says that you should still be open to having children. To being a stepparent or adopting. You would be an amazing mother. He said that he just sent you a new four-legged baby?" he asked.

At this, I couldn't help but smile through the tears. Leo.

Six months ago, a tiny little puppy had shown up on my doorstep on the day of the full moon in Leo season. He was barely even five weeks old. I look him in, and instantly fell in love with him.

I knew that J had sent him to me, from the first moment I held that little angel.

I had, of course, named him Leo in honor of J.

Chrystopher appeared to be listening hard again.

"He's telling me that you two were about to move? He is showing me an RV? Does that make sense to you?" he asked.

"Tour. Yes. We were about to start touring together. We hadn't done that yet, but it was upcoming," I said.

"Tour with your music? That's cool. I kind of get the sense that maybe there was some uncertainty surrounding that? Why is that?" he asked.

I sighed heavily.

"He was married…to someone else. We had an affair for a long time," I answered sadly.

Chrystopher's eyebrows shot up in surprise. "Oh! I mean, I'm not judging you or anything, that just surprised me because…" he said.

A confused look crossed his face. "Wait. He wasn't divorced when he passed away?" he asked.

"No," I responded.

He listened again, and shook his head adamantly as he said, "He was about to be. It was over with her."

My jaw dropped slightly as he continued.

"He wants you to know that this wasn't supposed to happen. If he had more control it wouldn't have. He was going to be with you. Things just got cut short and it was out of his hands. He also says to tell you that he's so very sorry that he didn't express his emotions or keep you looped in with what was going on at home like he should have. He says there is a lot he should have told you," he said.

Tears slipped down my face as I tried to absorb this new information. I couldn't even speak.

He continued, "But he's so happy that at least you two can still have this."

"This?" I asked. "Meaning?"

"This right now. You can talk now. And he is telling me that he will guide you through your journey in the ceremony tonight. He wants you to know that when you hear him tonight, that it's really him. He doesn't want you to doubt that, ok?" he said.

"I….ok." I stumbled trying to find words. I was finally going to hear him again?

Just as I was about to ask more about the journey ahead this evening, Kat came into the room and asked if she could speak with me for a minute before we began the ceremony.

311

I didn't want to leave this moment. There was so much I wanted to ask Chrystopher while I had J here with us. I was so torn.

"Yes, of course - you need to go with her. I'm so glad I was able to do this for you and with you," he said as he reached to embrace me. "Thank you as well, J," he added.

He then laughed loudly and told me, "He just said 'Oh, we're not finished talking.' "

It was exactly what I needed to hear to be able to stand up and walk away from that space. I felt like I had finally gotten my boy back and tearing myself away from it felt impossible.

But there would be more. We weren't done.

I already knew that though, didn't I?

Chapter Twenty-Eight

K AT TALKED TO me a bit about why I had come. I filled her in as best I could with a brief summary of all that had transpired. I told her about the love and the loss. I told her about the messages I had suddenly begun receiving about ayahuasca and the trail that had led me to this very moment.

I told her how terrified I was.

She told me that I wouldn't be human if I weren't at least a little afraid but assured me that I would be safe in her hands.

She double checked my medical chart. Went over my allergies. Made sure I had fasted all day.

She asked if I was ready to begin, and I lied and said yes.

We walked back to join the group who was already sitting in a circle waiting for us.

There was an opening prayer for the ceremony that I barely heard a single word of because the panic mode had been pressed down again inside of my mind.

I held the pill that Kat had handed me for a good solid five minutes. I could feel it vibrating in my hand, and that unsettled me deeply. Everyone else had taken theirs already. I felt Carson watching me intently, though she was trying very hard to not appear as though she was doing so. I finally looked over at her helplessly.

"I can't make myself take it," I whispered.

"Jen…J told Chrystopher that he was going to guide you through. Trust that. Isn't that what you want more than anything? Go get your boy," she replied.

I thought about J's face, and all of my what-ifs began to slip away. Carson was right. I hadn't come this far only to hear that he was waiting for me and turn and leave. My love had said that I would hear him again tonight. Wasn't that more than enough to give me the courage to leap? I took the pill quickly before I could think about it any longer.

"No turning back now," I said to Carson after I swallowed it. She nodded solemnly.

She got up and gave me a hug and told me not to hesitate to call for her if I needed her, and then went outside.

Everyone else had scattered. I was alone in the cabin living room with Kat.

"Why don't you come over to the couch, Jen? You can get comfy and settled while your medicine drops in," she said. She made me a nest of pillows and blankets on the couch, and I moved over to it and let her cover me up and arrange pillows until I was comfortable.

"You good?" she asked. I replied that I was.

I closed my eyes and talked to J in my mind.

I wish you were here to hold my hand, J. I'm so afraid right now. If you could just hold my hand until this kicks in, I think I would feel so much better.

Kat sat down in the floor beside me and grabbed my hand.

"It's not him, I know…but I'll stay here until you're not afraid anymore," she said.

I turned to her wide-eyed.

"I didn't say that out loud," I said.

She half shrugged.

"Jesus. Is everyone here psychic but me?" I said. Kat laughed.

"Sensitive people naturally gravitate to this work. Should you continue to do this after tonight you will find that most people in these circles are very tapped into the spirit realm. They can hear, see, and know things that the majority of the population can't. The medicine helps with that too - it brings you into the spirit plane. It changes you and enhances your sensitivities every time you work with it…and that part never goes away. You'll see. And though you may not know it at the moment, you are psychic as well. Your lover wouldn't have said you would hear him tonight if you couldn't do it. I think…that you are going to be surprised at just how powerful you are," she said.

"Why do you think that?" I asked.

"Just a feeling. I know things, remember?" she said with a wink. I smiled back at her.

Suddenly, my vision went wonky. It only lasted for a second; everything seemed to go diagonal and a bit blurry, and then it righted itself quickly as if it had never happened.

I looked around the room to see if anything had changed. Everything looked a little brighter, a little more defined, and clear, but otherwise the same.

I felt a warmth in the center of my chest that began to spread throughout my body. It was pleasant and I allowed myself to simply feel and enjoy it.

As the warm sensation took over my body, I felt a sense of well-being settle in. My fears slowly dissipated, and I began to feel safe.

"What did you give me, if I may ask?" I said to Kat.

"It's called a heart opener. There are several different medicines that work that way, but this particular one comes from Africa and the tribesmen take it before they hunt so that they can literally hear the forest. It enhances all of your senses. It also feels like happiness," she said.

"Is this still scary to you, Jen…. or do you feel safe now?"

"I feel safe. I feel really good actually," I replied.

"Great. That means you're officially in the field, so you can just relax and let go and trust that you are safe. You know what it is going to feel like now. You can see that there is nothing here to fear, so just breathe deeply and listen to what Spirit has to tell you. I'm going to leave you alone for a while, but why don't you start out here in the field by telling Spirit all of the things that you are grateful for. I'll check on you later, ok?" she said as she let go of my hand and stood up.

I nodded.

I began to go down the list in my head of all of my blessings.

Thank you Spirit, for my family. Thank you for my health. Thank you for Leo. Thank you for my job…………

So, I was "in the field."

I felt unbelievably clear-headed.

I had expected to be not in control of my faculties in the least. Coming in the door, I had fully anticipated that when the medicine kicked in that I would simply be inebriated and unable to even function or go to the bathroom without assistance.

This sharpness of perception…. this was not at all what I had expected.

I felt the most present I had ever been in my life.

Time felt like it had just ceased to exist. It reminded me of the way time used to feel when J and I were making love. That thought seemed to confirm what I had always known. We had been on a different plane together. I had no idea how long it had been since I took the pill, nor what time it was in general. It also didn't seem to matter.

All that seemed to matter was right now. As I let my thoughts go from one whisper of gratitude to the next, I thought about each thing that I was listing in a whole new way.

Thank you for my niece….

As I offered my gratitude for my precious two-year-old niece, I thought about how much joy she had brought into my life. I truly saw the bigger picture of the gift that she was to me. Every little nuanced way that she had changed me for the better; the way that she opened my heart to children in a way that it wasn't before, the way she awakened my maternal senses the minute that I first held her, and all of the ways that she reminded me of what a magical place the world is through a child's eyes. It was as if, for the first time, I was given a bird's eye view of the web of goodness that she had woven into my life with just her presence. I felt gratitude in a way I had never felt before. All-encompassing and pure thankfulness poured from my heart.

And so it was… each time I uttered something that I was grateful for to Spirit, I was shown every single way that it had blessed me. It began to register with me for the first time how very loved I must be to be given all of these wonderful blessings. Who deserved so much goodness in their life? I certainly didn't feel as though I did, but Spirit reassured me that They loved me so much that they were happy to bring these things into my life.

I became so caught up in all of the gratitude, and all of the wonders that I had been gifted with that for the first time in a year I gave not a single thought to all that I had lost. I simply radiated thanksgiving for all of the things that I had and appreciated the way they touched my life in so many different ways. I sang the praises of Spirit with each new moment of clarity.

Kat was suddenly kneeling down beside me again. I turned and smiled at her and saw that she was offering me a piece of chocolate.

It smelled and looked delicious with my newly heightened sharper senses. As I took it from her, I gave thanks to Spirit for chocolate out loud, and Kat and I both laughed.

As I chewed it up, I detected a very foreign and bitter taste and I quickly realized that she had not simply given me a piece of chocolate. This was another medicine of some kind.

"What is in this chocolate?" I asked her.

She leaned close to me and smoothed my hair back off of my forehead.

"It is the teacher that called you here. The Grandmother of the plants. You asked for her by name when you arrived, so she is who you are meant to work with. Mother Ayahuasca," she replied.

"Oh shit. Here we go," I said.

"There is nothing to fear. This will just be a bit of a pivot. You have been very in your heart energy with the first medicine. This will shift you to the south and bring you into the realm of the spirit. The Grandmother will guide you. Surrender to her wisdom and let her lead your journey now," she said. She placed a finger on my forehead, and I felt what must have been my third eye pulse beneath it. I closed my eyes and felt Kat leave the room.

Miss Jen? I thought.

What a strange thing to think. I pondered on this for a moment. Why had

I just said my own name out loud in my mind? In the way that J would say it, nonetheless?

You aren't saying that, my dear. I am, I thought.

This was so curious. My senses still felt so clear and so heightened, and I heard these thoughts very plainly in my own voice…yet…they didn't feel like they were originating from me at all. If anything, since I had taken the medicine, I had felt a step ahead of my own thoughts in a way I had never experienced. When I was giving thanks earlier, it was almost as if I saw the entire concept of what I was expressing gratitude for as I said it out loud in my head.

These last few sentences I hadn't seen coming and I hadn't even seemed to formulate them. They simply appeared. As if someone else had spoken them.

"What do you mean, you are saying that? This is my mind. That's my voice. Who else could possibly be speaking other than me?" I said.

"*This is J, my love.*" Again, it just seemingly popped into my mind out of nowhere.

"I don't understand why you sound like me. If that is even really you. That's confusing, J,", I replied. I tried to completely quiet my mind as if I were going to meditate. I would just silence all of my thoughts so that I could prove that this was coming from me. I dropped down into the center of my being and began to focus on my breathing. I released all thoughts from my mind, in the same manner that I always did when I was in meditation. It only took a moment to bring myself to a place of absolute stillness and quiet.

I'm still here, Miss Jen. It sounded extra loud this time. Persistent. It shook me out of the stillness.

"I don't know, J. I'm still not buying it. It sounds like me…I think this is just coming from me. And the medicine," I said.

How can I prove to you that it is me?

Hmmm. Good question. What would it take for me to believe these thoughts weren't originating in my own mind? Maybe if there was some knowledge given that I didn't previously know. Something that I knew couldn't have come from me, because it wasn't in my memory or realm of things I knew about.

"I need something novel. Something that I couldn't possibly know. That is the only way I could believe that this isn't coming from my own mind," I replied.

"*Ok. That's fair enough. Candace, the beautiful blonde girl that you were talking to earlier, is about to walk in here and get her water bottle that she left on the end table beside you. You know nothing about her, but I will tell you something to ask her. She has had a very successful career in modeling, and her photos have actually been featured in Playboy. She is now making a major shift and is beginning to work behind the camera as a photographer. She came to journey tonight to find guidance for this next step. Ask her about it. If she confirms what I just told you, you will know that you are actually talking to me.*"

Well, that would certainly be news to me. I didn't really have much time to think about how that information had been conveyed because almost immediately I heard the door open and in walked Candace. She walked over to the table beside me and picked up the water bottle sitting there. She smiled at me.

"Sorry…didn't mean to disturb you. I forgot my water," she said as she held it up for me to see.

So far so good, I thought. I wouldn't have known she was about to walk in at all, let alone to get her water bottle.

"No worries, you aren't bothering me. I hate that we didn't get much time to talk earlier anyway. I won't keep you long, but I was just wondering…if you don't mind my asking- what do you do for a living?" I asked.

"Oh…well…that is kind of changing for me at the moment. I have been a professional model for a long time, and I have really enjoyed it…but lately, I've been doing some photography work and I just LOVE it. I'm thinking about trying to move in that direction more. It's actually why I'm here tonight. I was hoping to get some answers about how to go about making that happen," she replied with a smile.

"Ask her about the magazine," I heard.

"Oh wow! That is so cool. Good for you. I hope that you get everything you are seeking tonight. I bet modeling is a really fun career though. What is the biggest shoot you ever worked on? Anything nationally published?" I asked. It occurred to me that I was going to feel like an intrusive asshole if she told me that she had only done local work.

She blushed slightly and smiled.

"I actually had a spread published in *Playboy* last year. It was definitely a career highlight," she responded. "We can talk more about it tomorrow if you want. I'll let you get back to your journey. Time is precious here and you didn't come all of this way to talk to me. Enjoy and I'll see you later," she said. She patted my shoulder sweetly as she walked past me on the way out the door.

So, there it was. Novel information that had been given to me from this voice, confirmed.

Was it really possible? J was communicating with me via my own thoughts? Had this been going on the entire past year, and I just hadn't realized it was him because it came through in my own voice?

"This is how you come through, J? Has it been happening all along, and I didn't know it was you?" I asked.

"Yes. Do you remember that I told all of your friends that you would hear me again when you figured it out? You actually heard me quite a few times, but just wrote it off immediately. You thought you were just imagining what I might say to you in those moments. Especially in your deepest moments of grief," he replied.

I thought back to one particular instance immediately. I had been lying in the floor of my apartment, curled up in a ball, and wailing at the top of my lungs. This particular moment of breakdown consisted of me screaming questions into the abyss that I never expected an answer to. "Why couldn't you just be with me before you left? Why wasn't I enough for you? You didn't make the move in time, and now it's all gone. Why? Why couldn't we have just been together?" I asked over and over and over.

Suddenly in a very loud and very clear thought pattern (just as I was experiencing now) I heard a rush of responses. "Oh, Jen...you were so much more than enough. It was never about choosing you. I chose you a thousand times. You were all I wanted. It was just terrible timing, my love. I am still right here. I am right here with you..." I heard in my thoughts.

"Well, it's official. I've lost it. Now I'm just creating responses in my head that I hoped he would say," I thought to myself. It concerned me enough that I got up out of the floor, dusted myself off and went and took a shower.

So, I had known even then that there was something different about those thoughts. I just hadn't realized what it was exactly.

"I do remember that happening...at least once, J. It felt exactly how it feels right now. But this is so confusing...how will I ever know what is coming from you and what is coming from me? It all sounds the same and it's hard to determine whether I formulated the thought, or you spoke. It's very frustrating," I said.

"That's why I had to get you here. You were so very low, my sweet. We had to raise your vibration quite a bit so that you can hear me better. Ayahuasca lifts you into the spirit plane and allows you to see everything more clearly. It's sort of like tuning a radio...you were only getting a crackling signal that was hard to make sense of. Now you're in the exact frequency. As a matter of fact, I believe that the medicine has dropped in fully now. Notice anything different about this communication?" he asked.

I began to cry as it dawned on me.

I was no longer hearing this as if it were my own thoughts.

It was him. I could hear his voice now.

"Oh, J. I've missed your voice so much. I've missed everything about you...I've felt like I was dying without you. Like my very soul got ripped out of me. I felt like I would have so much to say if I could just talk to you again, but now that I am talking to you, I don't even know where to begin. I just want to listen to your voice and feel you near me forever...." I said.

"I know, love. I know exactly how much you have suffered because I've been right with you this entire time. It's broken my own heart to see you in so much pain. It's been killing me all over again to watch you in the depths of grief and despair, knowing that you believed that we were separated forever. I couldn't reach you. I couldn't do anything to lift your spirits…until tonight. I've been working so hard to get you here. I had to talk to you again…I had to make you see that you never lost me. It was I who lost you. You gave up. I had to get *you* back, Jen. Not the other way around," he said.

I hadn't thought of it that way, but I realized that he was right. There were many nights that I had lost all hope of ever reuniting again.

"I did give up. I couldn't see how I could ever connect with you again in this lifetime. My entire world was empty. Everything was silent. It all seemed lost. I felt so alone, J," I told him.

"How could you ever have thought that I wouldn't be doing every single thing in my power to be next to you? If the roles were reversed, wouldn't you have been tearing at the veil between the realms as hard as you could to get to me?" he asked.

"Of course I would have…I just…didn't even know what was possible for you to do to get to me. I still don't. This is blowing my mind that we are even here right now, talking to each other. I've never heard of someone reconnecting with their loved ones after they passed in this way," I responded.

"Well, neither of us had ever even heard of a love like we had from the very beginning, remember? We always talked about how it was powerful beyond our wildest imagination. A fire like that can't be extinguished, Miss Jen. You should've known that," he said.

"I think that deep down, I did know that…but after you passed, I just began to feel like maybe I had made it up somehow. Or…not really made it up…but built it up in my mind to be more than it was. The more distance I got from it, the more I just began to wonder if I was remembering it accurately. It didn't help that I couldn't talk about it to people, or even really allow myself to grieve the way I needed to. It just became this overwhelming secret that I had to carry…. both the love and the loss were too big to talk about, so I just shut down. On top of all of that, I couldn't hear you the way I used to when I would try to tap in. It didn't make sense to me. How could something be so earth-shatteringly strong, and then just be gone? I'm sorry that I didn't have more faith in you…in us…I was just so very heartbroken," I said.

"I'm not chastising you, babe. You don't have to apologize to me for anything. I just want to make sure that you know that the whole time you thought that I had left you, I was right beside you and trying everything I could think of to make you realize it. I never left you, but there was a brief time after I crossed over that I had to get my bearings. This realm is obviously completely different, and I'm still figuring a lot of things out…or rather… I'm remembering them. But everything

I've learned, I've used to try and reach you. I love you endlessly. I have loved you that way from the very beginning. I could never let you go."

I sighed with contentment.

He had never left me, and we were back together again here.

Wherever "here" was.

I opened my eyes and looked around. Everything in the room appeared as normal. Time still felt irrelevant and suspended, but otherwise, it could have just been any other evening I had spent at a cabin on a long weekend. It was as if I were simply talking to my boy on the telephone before I went to bed, exchanging our "I love yous" and "I miss yous."

I was hearing him that clearly. It was exactly the way we used to connect in meditation before he passed away.

I thought about that for a moment. The term "passed away" makes it sound like our loved ones are gone for good. I realized that up until now I had fully believed that was what happened when someone died.

"Where are you, J?" I asked.

"I'm still right here."

"No… I mean… in general. Where are you existing? Are you in heaven…but you are being allowed somehow to talk to me right now? Do you have a body? I have so many questions…." I asked.

He laughed. "I'd rather not spend this entire evening explaining all the mysteries of death and the universe to you, if that's ok. All this time of painful silence between us, and you want to know how it all works instead of just reveling in this beautiful reunion? That's not the girl I know."

I grinned. "You're right. I'm sorry. Curiosity just got the best of me. Plus, I just didn't want to be keeping you from anything that you'd rather be doing. I hear heaven is pretty magnificent."

"Yes, she is," he whispered.

"She?"

"You are my heaven, Jen. We get to choose how we spend our time in the afterlife. Where we go and who we are near is entirely up to us. I check on my children and my family, and make sure they are safe and protected. And then I come back to you. Over and over and over again. I'm by your side nearly all the time, and when I can't be, I keep an ear out for your voice should you need me. You are the heaven I will always choose, in any lifetime or in-between. Hell would be an afterlife where I couldn't reach you. I would never want to exist in an eternity that didn't have you in it," he said.

I melted. "You know you already have me, right? You don't have to go so hard with the wooing, anymore. I just took an illegal substance that I was terrified of just to hear your voice again."

"Just wanting to make sure I say all of the right things since I kind of dropped the ball the last go-round," he replied. I could actually *hear* the smile in his voice.

"'Kind of' is… one way to put it. Not the way *I'D* put it but…"

"Ok, ok, ok. Geez. Can't a man even get a break when he jumps through a realm to make amends?" he said.

We were both laughing now.

"Forgiveness is under consideration, given the current circumstances."

"Oh. Well, that's very kind of you, Miss Jen. I'll consider continuing to speak to you the rest of the evening."

Our laughter died down into a moment of quiet.

"Hey… you were kidding right? You're still here?" I asked. I felt a little bit of panic begin to sneak in.

"Oh my gosh…yes! Yes. I was totally just playing with you. I'm so sorry… it was so easy to just fall back into our old dynamic – I didn't think about that scaring you. I'm not going anywhere, I promise. I wouldn't miss a minute of this."

"Ok good. I thought so…" I said. "Just…maybe it's a little too soon for jokes about not hearing you."

"Agreed. I'm so sorry again. No more jokes about that. Listen… do you want to go outside by the fire for a while? We can continue our conversation under the stars. Kat is the only one out there at the moment," J asked.

I thought that sounded nice, so I pulled myself out of the couch nest that I had been nestled in and went to the restroom on my way outside.

I was still beyond amazed that I was perfectly in control of my body. All of the horror stories that I had heard about psychedelics had made me believe that I was going to be incapacitated for several hours, but I was walking around better than I would have been if had drunk my usual nightly pint of whiskey. I didn't even hit my elbow on the wall when I sat down on the toilet, which usually would have been a given if I had been drinking.

I looked at myself in the mirror, reluctantly.

Warnings echoed in my mind; I had heard repeatedly that you shouldn't look in a mirror when on psychedelics. I was pleasantly surprised.

I looked the same except for my eyes. They looked brighter…clearer. There was a spark there that I hadn't seen in over a year. Happiness.

I had almost forgotten what I looked like when I was happy.

"Do you know how beautiful you are to me? I'm still so smitten with you. I watch you with awe every hour of every day. I lie beside you and stare at you while you sleep. I still want you with everything in me…that never went away, Jen. Still. *I still want you,* my gorgeous red-haired girl," J said to me as I looked at myself in the mirror.

"I still want you too. I can still picture your face…the way that you would look at me like you wanted to tear my clothes off," I said. An image of him standing behind me and looking at me with that very expression appeared in my mind. It looked so real that I actually turned to physically look behind me, half expecting him to be standing there.

"I'm looking at you like that right now. Did you see it?" he said.

'I did! How did that happen? Did you send me that image somehow?" I asked. He laughed softly.

"I did. I wasn't sure that it would work, but now we know it does. You are open enough to receive images from me now. That's going to be fun," he said.

I suddenly got bombarded with a slideshow of sexual imagery. I began to see a series of ten-second video-like clips of us fucking - one after another.

They were all from his point of view. I was watching myself be ravished in every conceivable way and in every position imaginable. Some of the images were from instances that I remembered; most were not. He showed me things that we had talked about doing and never got the chance to. They got raunchier and more taboo with each passing vision.

"Dirty boy. I want to see you, not me. Can you flip the perspective?" I asked.

"No. I want you to see and experience every single thing I want to do to you," he responded in a deep tone. The primal growl in his voice made me weak. The images intensified and became zoomed in on details that I could never have seen from my own vantage point when he was alive. I saw his cock sliding in and out of my body the way it must have looked to him. I saw his fingers pressed into the flesh of my thighs as he pulled me closer and closer to him. The longer it went on the filthier the acts became.

It was delightful.

"My GOD, boy.... you have got to stop. You are killing me. This isn't even fair considering I can't touch you," I finally said. I had sat back down on the toilet seat with the lid down to steady myself. I was trembling with desire.

He laughed heartily.

"Not sorry. I must say though...it's nice to know that I can still do that to you," he said.

I tried to get myself back together so that I could go outside. I didn't want it to be all over my face that my lover had been fucking me with images in the bathroom.

As I walked out into the hallway and made my way out the side door, I still felt the flush on my cheeks. I smiled sheepishly when Kat looked up from the fire as I approached.

"Well, hello, foxy. Looks like your journey is going well. Come sit and tell me about it. The G-rated parts, anyway," she said knowingly.

Well, damn. So much for trying to hide anything.

"I can hear him again, Kat. I know that Chrystopher told me I would be able to before the journey began, but I still can hardly believe that it's happening. You have no idea how much this means to me. I'm so happy…I feel so much lighter. I got my boy back," I said with tears in my eyes.

"I don't think you ever lost him," she said. Her eyes were full of compassion. "I wish I could have seen the two of you together when he was alive. Even tonight, the energy is overwhelming. I can't imagine what that must have been like. I'm going to go back inside so that you can have time alone together by the fire. I know you have a lot of catching up to do. Enjoy the journey, you two.", she said as she stood up and headed back toward the house.

Suddenly she stopped and turned back to us.

"And J.…." she said.

"Yes ma'am," I heard him reply.

"There are only two rules in this space, and I need you to abide by them no matter what side of the veil you are on. Understood?" she asked.

I heard him laugh and then he replied, "I'm not sure that what you are insinuating is possible, but I'll try to behave."

"Try?" Kat said impatiently.

"Fine. You have my word. I'll follow the rules," he said.

"Thank you." she said as she turned to go inside.

"What was that all about? What 'rules'? What did you just agree to?" I asked.

"The two rules in a ceremonial journey space are that you can't hurt yourself or anyone else. And….no sex between participants is allowed. I'm guessing that she wasn't worried that I would hurt you, so she must have been talking about the second rule," he said with a chuckle.

I felt a thrill run through me at the thought.

"Could we…even do that?" I asked. I tried to imagine what that would even be like.

"Honestly, I'm not sure what all is possible with you this far into the spirit realm. I don't think that we could physically touch, but I don't know. Either way… she wasn't happy with the imagery I was sending you. I'll have to back off a little. I don't want to be put in time out," he said.

I laughed at the idea of J's ghost being put in the corner until he learned his lesson. He gave me an image of myself looking like a librarian and smacking his ass with a ruler.

"Unless it's like that," he said. We cracked up.

"Well….do you want to sing together a little out here, then? Since we have to behave?" he asked.

"I don't know, J. I'm not really in the mood to sing but I would love to hear you. Would you sing to me?" I asked.

The Melody of Fire

"Play me a song, J." he said sarcastically. I gasped and then burst into laughter. I knew exactly what he was referring to. Nearly every morning since he had passed, when I got in my car, I had asked him to play me a song. I would then turn on the car and listen to see if the first song that came on seemed like a message from him.

"Don't you dare be mean to me about that! It was all I could think of at the time to get a response from you," I said with mock hurt.

"Yeah, but then I would scramble around before you got in the car to make sure that the first song that came on was a love song or something that would cheer you up, and then you would hear it and be like 'Was that really from him or just a coincidence?'. It was maddening. I've rarely been annoyed with you, Miss Jen, but I swear I could have strangled you over that," he said. We were laughing together so hard. It felt wonderful. I marveled at how we had gone right back to how we were as if nothing at all had changed. We had always picked on each other constantly; even onstage it had become known as part of our dynamic. It was always good-natured, and even when it sounded mean we both knew it wasn't. We strictly did it for the laugh.

I hadn't realized how much I had missed the teasing.

We were us again.

My heart was so full.

"While we are on the subject of things that are annoying, why do you keep cock blocking my guitar players? Do you realize I've tried to work with five different musicians and something strange has happened each time to make them not work out? I know it's you. Why are you doing that?" I asked exasperatedly.

"Because none of them have been good enough for you. Or they have had their own agendas and I realized they were just trying to use you to get more visibility…OR get in your pants, so I put a stop to it. I promise you that when the right one comes along, I will help it move forward the way it should. But I will always protect you, and if that requires me running off a few more guitar players then so be it. You'll just have to trust that I can see more than you can right now. Believe me…I want you to sing again. Apart from auditioning guitar players, I haven't heard you sing at all. You wouldn't even sing with me just now when I asked. I miss your voice, babe. Why have you stopped?" he asked gently.

I felt the emotion welling up from deep within. It was true. I hadn't been singing. How could he not know why?

"It hurts, J. Every time I hear my voice without yours accompanying it, I feel like I've been shot through the heart. Do you remember when I quit the band years ago and you told me you weren't even sure if you wanted to do music anymore if you had to do it without me? That's how I feel. I've been making extremely half-assed attempts to get back into singing in hopes that it might cheer me up, but each time it just makes me realize that I don't really care about music when

325

you aren't a part of it. Every time I sing, I feel your absence. I remember all of the spectacular nights we had together writing and performing…and it is excruciating to know that it will never be like that again. All it does is remind me of what is forever gone. I just…can't bear the hurt," I told him.

I heard him sigh.

"It won't always be like that, love. There will come a time when singing will bring you joy once more. You are going to have to try a whole new approach though. Do a new genre, or a new style of writing that is entirely yours. It's the only way you are going to be able to get past hurting when you sing and hear me when I say that *you need to be singing*. It will bring you more healing than you know. I know you're afraid to try and pursue it without me, but I promise you that you can do this on your own. In fact, you will. I've seen it," he said.

This surprised me a little, although that was becoming harder and harder to do as this evening progressed.

"You can see the future?" I asked.

"Parts of it. I'm not really sure how much is set in stone though. I get the feeling that what I see are just possibilities, or maybe things that are just highly likely. But I knew that this was going to happen tonight. I saw you and I talking. I also know that you and I will be in this space many more times. This is the first journey of many for you, and I will always be right beside you," he said.

Relief washed over me. I had been wondering if this was going to be the only night that I would ever get with him. It was nice to know that I was going to be able to come back to the spirit realm periodically and have time with him.

"Oh no, my dear. You will hear my voice and receive images from me from now on, even when you aren't on plant medicine. Ayahuasca permanently rewires your brain. The sensitivities that you have now won't go away, they just won't be quite as strong as they are when you are in the field. That is what Kat was trying to tell you earlier; the medicine has increased your vibration and ability to sense things. It's opened you up in new ways. You won't close back up because you are forever changed. I didn't mean that you had to come back here just to be with me…you will come back here to learn and grow and heal…and I will be with you to protect you and guide you each time. You're never going to feel like you lost me again. We are together forever, once again. You might not always hear me as clearly as you do right now, but you'll always hear me," he said.

I was weeping. Could this be true? Would I always be able to hear him after tonight?

I felt the sense of urgency to ask him a million questions ease off a little. There was no need to hurry here… I could simply enjoy what was left of my time with him tonight.

"That being said…because you *can* hear me extremely clearly right now, there

The Melody of Fire

are some things I want to tell you because I want you to hear them word for word. So, I just want you to listen for a bit before our time here is up, ok?" he said. I agreed. I stared into the fire while he began to speak.

"First of all…I'm so very sorry about the position that I left you in. We had this massive and incredible love, and I forced us to keep it a secret because of my marriage. That was my fault, and I carry a tremendous burden of guilt because of it. I know that the situation robbed you of steps that you really needed to go through in order to heal. You didn't get to tell me goodbye- you didn't get to go to my funeral, you couldn't talk about your miscarriage, you didn't get to write my eulogy that you posted in the way that you really needed to……I saw how much those things destroyed you on top of what was already an unbearable loss. If I had just made you mine before I passed…if our love had been publicly known…I think it would have softened the loss a little. At the very least, it wouldn't have added insult to injury. So, I want to apologize to you with all of my heart that I didn't make that leap in time. I also want you to know that I wanted to do that for you and that I had every intention of being with you. I just…thought I had more time. I'm committed to redeeming myself now that we are able to communicate. I will make this right, I promise you. I was, and am, so deeply in love with you.

"It was all real, Jen. It still is.

"Please stop doubting the magic and the fire that exists between us. Everything that you remember about our love actually happened. It was every bit as strong as you recall. Hell…look at what is happening at this very moment. We are communicating across realms that should have divided us. If that doesn't prove to you that this was a love like no other, then I don't know what possibly could. No matter what the future holds, I want you to look back and know without a shadow of a doubt that I love you just as much as you love me… I always have, and more importantly, I always will.

"I also want you to know that we are in an entirely different era of our relationship now. That fire between us is eternal and will never lessen or change in the least, but by necessity, the dynamic will have to shift. You have an ally in the spirit realm now, my love. In many, many ways I can love you better from here than I could by your side in the earthly realm. Think of the possibilities, Jen. I can help you achieve your dreams because I can help things run smoothly. I can be your messenger and the extra assistance you need energetically to help move you where you want to go in life. I can protect you INFINITELY better because I can see what is coming.

"Most importantly, I get to be with you all of the time now, my precious girl. I go everywhere you go. I hear all of your thoughts and feel all of your desires. I am as close to you as your breath. We never have to tell each other goodbye again- not even for a second.

"Of course I would like to have had more time with you in the physical, but I'm thrilled to be able to be with you in this way. I hope that you can see that my crossing over isn't a bad thing entirely - if you will be open to the changes in the dynamic, I think that in time you'll find that this is simply a whole new way to love each other. We have always tested and pushed the limits of all of the different dimensions we could explore each other in. Think of this as what it is- newer, higher, more powerful levels that we can reach together. We've never seen heights like these in this lifetime together. What an amazing opportunity to learn each other's souls in a way that most people never get the opportunity to do. Are you beginning to see what we can have together now? All is not lost here, my dear. In fact, it's just the opposite - we have been given an incredible gift," he said.

I had been listening intently to him, without interruption. His words made me feel hopeful for the first time after such a long season of loneliness and despair. I could see that he was correct; our relationship had once again shifted into a deeper level. This was going to be new territory, and one that seemed guaranteed to be difficult to figure out how to navigate.

We may not have ever been to this particular land before, but we had certainly explored other realms with the sole purpose of knowing each other better.

I knew that no matter the difficulty, we were going to be ok because this new journey was something that we were embarking on together, and together we had always been magical.

Chrystopher and Carson came out of the house behind me. They pulled chairs close to the other side of the fire. Carson was looking at me carefully and trying to assess how I was holding up.

"I'm good, my friend. I hope you haven't been worrying about me too much," I said to her before she could ask.

"Kat told me that you were doing wonderfully, so I had let it go for the sake of my own journey. It's good to see you with my own eyes though. You look so happy. Have you been in contact with J?" she asked.

I grinned.

"Constantly. We've been talking all night, it's been incredible. I can't thank you enough for bringing me here. Have you been having a good journey?" I asked.

"I have…mine has been a little emotionally difficult this time…but it feels good to be working through all of it," she said. I nodded in acknowledgment. I knew we would tell each other all of the details on the way home tomorrow. We all fell silent, and I could tell that everyone was going back into their own experiences. I closed my eyes once more.

"I have so many things I want to ask you, J," I said.

"I know that you do, but Kat is about to come out with food for everyone and close the ceremony. I have a million things I want to tell you as well, but we will have to save it for another time. The good news is, now you know that I hear every single thing you think and say. You will be able to hear me again as well, just remember that it won't be as clear as it is right now…yet. Over time, as your gifts open up more you will get to the point where the way you hear me now is normal for you. Will you do something for me, love?" he asked.

"Anything. You know that. I've never told you no, remember?" I replied.

My heart had sunk a little when he said that the ceremony was closing soon. I wasn't done here. We had so much to catch up on still -I wasn't ready to let him go again. Though he was promising that I would hear him when this was over, I loved the way that talking to him in this space was exactly like talking to him when he was alive had been. I was afraid of how much I would or wouldn't be able to hear once the medicine was out of my system.

"Will you watch the sunrise with me? We never got the chance to do that together. I would have given anything to have watched the sunrise with you in my arms while I was alive. Will you let me make that up to you in the morning?" he said.

"You wouldn't have done that when you were alive. You hated mornings," I said with a laugh. I thought back to how I used to avoid calling him in the early mornings because he was such a grump. We had a few early morning shows over the years for various events and he was impossible to deal with until he fully woke up and had several cups of coffee, which was usually when we were halfway done with the gig. Though I loved the idea of spending the night with him at the time, watching the sunrise together was never something that I thought he would want to do.

"That may be true…but *you* love mornings, and I would have done anything to see you smile. Even watch the sunrise. I used to fantasize about that often. If I could hold you while we watched the sunrise, that meant that you would have been in my arms all night. I know you always said that you wanted me to be yours all of the time, but I don't think you realize how badly I wanted those things too, Jen," he said.

Tears were streaming down my cheeks again. I had forgotten how romantic he was. How I had missed this man. The last year I had been reliving all of the memories that I had of all of the beautiful things he had said to me. Hearing him captivate me with new words in this moment touched me so deeply. It reminded me once again of how easy he was to fall in love with. It was a damn good thing I couldn't see his face right now, or I would be lost all over again to him.

Or… could I?

"J? Is there any way that I could see you right now? Not just in my mind like how you sent me the images earlier…but with my eyes?" I asked.

"Hmm. I'm not really sure. I can try to come through. I don't know if I can do it though, and I'm not sure if you will be able to see me, so no promises, ok? Don't get upset if it doesn't work," he said.

"I won't, I promise. Just please try for me," I said.

"Ok. Look to the left of the fire from where you are sitting. I'm going to try and come through the smoke and heat waves because that energy is thin and easy to move," he said.

I rested my gaze where he told me, to the left of the fire which was only a few feet away from me. I began to see a green shimmering light that almost looked like a vapor coming off of the fire. It flickered and moved with the smoke, and I watched it with curiosity as it intensified in color and concentration. The dancing color began to move into an outline, and I could see the forming of a silhouette that was very familiar to me. His strong shoulders and long limbs began to become more defined, and everything shifted so quickly that it took a second for me to realize that his face had materialized fully through the bright green aura. I was staring into his beautiful eyes once more.

"Oh, J…." was all I could manage to get out. He gave me a devastating smile, blew me a kiss, and then disappeared instantly.

"That's all I've got, babe. I'm sorry. That took so much energy and concentration," he said.

"Thank you, thank you, thank you! Please don't apologize…. that was so wonderful! You did so well! I could see you so clearly there for a second!" I said giddily.

He laughed.

"I'm exhausted… but it was worth it to see you this excited," he said.

"You are still the hottest thing I've ever seen, by the way," I said.

"You're only saying that because I literally just came out of the fire," he said. We both laughed.

"No… seriously though. I don't know what I thought happened to us after we die, but I definitely didn't expect it to be like this. I guess I just still kind of thought we became 'angels' and were suddenly transformed into these higher spiritual beings that lost the human qualities that we had when we were alive…at least to a degree. But being with you tonight has shown me that it's not like that at all. You haven't changed a bit. Everything is the same. You have the same sense of humor, the same desire for me, the same protectiveness, and the same qualities that I loved about you that you always had. You were even flirting with Chrystopher earlier like I know you would have done if you were here physically. And now I know…you look exactly the same as well. Except you have more hair," I said.

"Well, that's really the only thing I would've changed about my looks, so I did," he said.

I rolled my eyes.

The Melody of Fire

"Of course you did, my vain Leo. I guess that's just one more thing that is exactly the same," I said. I couldn't help but giggle. His vanity was one of my favorite things about him because it gave me an easy button to push to tease him. If I wanted to poke at him jokingly, attacking his vanity was the easiest route. It was a surefire way to get a rise out of him every time. I was actually glad that he hadn't lost even the personality quirks that were less than positive. I had gotten him back in his entirety, flaws and all, and I wouldn't have wanted it any other way.

I hadn't heard her come out of the door, but Kat suddenly appeared behind the chair next to me. She knelt down beside me with a cup of hot vegetable broth and a small plate of fruit and crackers.

"I know you don't want this to end…but unfortunately, it's about that time. Can you eat a little for me? It will help you start grounding into the earthly realm once more," she said.

I took the broth and food from her and stared at it sadly.

If this was the anecdote for the medicine in my system, I didn't want it.

I wasn't ready. I wanted this night to last forever.

"It feels like we only just began. I don't want to lose him again, Kat," I whispered.

"You won't. What have we been telling you all night? These shifts are here to stay. Funny that you were so afraid to take this journey, and now you don't want it to end, isn't it? Spirit works like that sometimes. We have to face our biggest fears in order to get the biggest rewards. Eat," she said as she gestured to the untouched food I was holding.

I reluctantly drank some of the broth. I don't know if it was because my senses were still heightened from the medicine, or if it was because I had been fasting since early in the day, but that broth was the absolute best-tasting thing I had ever put in my mouth. The flavors exploded on my tongue, and I savored every sip.

"I passed behind you two frequently tonight, just to check on you and make sure you were still doing ok. I couldn't hear what you were saying, but I heard you two laughing and talking constantly. It was a joy to witness. You have such a beautiful energy as a couple - it was magnetic even for me. I had to resist the urge to come closer and eavesdrop. I didn't want to intrude, I just wanted to be a part of it for a little bit. You are very lucky to have a love like that….in whatever form it may take now. I hope you realize that," she said. I had been eating the berries and crackers on my plate as she spoke. I stopped and looked up at her.

"One thing that I can say about J and me…we never took our love for granted even a single second. We knew what a rare thing we were holding in our hands. It's what made it so hard to lose. It's also what makes it so sweet to get back," I said.

She smiled at me.

"Come inside when you are ready. I think the others are already heading to bed," she said. And with that, she was gone.

"J?" I called out softly.

"I'm still here, Miss Jen. She's right though, it's time for you to go to bed. I'll be right there with you though, and we'll watch the sunrise together, I promise," he said.

"Ok. 'Thank you' doesn't even feel sufficient to say to you but I will anyway. Thank you for tonight. Thank you for all you did to get me here. And thank you for loving me so much that you didn't give up on me. I love you so very much… and I'm so happy to have you back," I said tearfully.

"Lifetimes, Miss Jen. Remember? This love spans hundreds of lifetimes. I could never give up on you…on us. We will still be standing together when the world crumbles away. Nothing will ever separate us. Nothing ever has. It only appeared that way for a bit. Go to bed, sweet. Rest well in the knowledge that our love story isn't over…not by a long shot," he said.

"Babe…. Wake up."

"Hmmm? What is it, J? What…." I murmured sleepily. I was still half asleep and confused. Where was I? Oh…that's right…the ceremony was last night. I was in my bed in the cabin. I groggily tried to remember how I got in here.

"Get up, Jen," I heard J say again. I rolled over and in my half-sleep state expected to find him in bed with me.

"I'm so sleepy, love…. just a few more minutes?" I asked with my face pressed into the pillow.

"You need to go to the bathroom and come outside…we are going to miss it," he replied.

The sunrise! I suddenly remembered that we were supposed to watch the sunrise together. I sat up in my bed and looked out the window. It was still pitch-black outside. I had no idea what time it was, but it looked too early for the sunrise.

"GO. Go pee and then come outside. Quickly!" he said.

"FINE," I said grumpily as I swung my legs over the side of the bed and stood up. I went to the bathroom, as directed, all the while complaining that it had to be too early for him to wake me up.

When I came out of the bathroom and walked through the kitchen, I noticed that someone must have set the coffee pot on a timer because it was just finishing brewing. I poured myself a cup and walked out on the porch.

The second that I sat down on the porch swing the first rays of light began to burst forth over the horizon.

"Just in time, love," J whispered.

The Melody of Fire

"Mmm… thanks for waking me up. I would have missed it," I said. "Hey! I can still hear you!", I exclaimed as it registered that his voice was just as clear as it had been last night.

"The medicine is still very strong in your system. I'm going to settle in behind you with my energy and wrap you up in it. It's the best I can do to hold you right now," he said.

I suddenly felt a warmth surround my entire body. I leaned back into it blissfully.

It felt just as he described……he was wrapping me in his energy. It felt strong and familiar. I was overcome with happiness.

I sipped my coffee as the sunlight slowly began to creep over the tops of the mountains.

"Our love never got to live in the light. It felt like trying to hide that sun forever behind those mountains, didn't it?" he said.

"That's exactly what it felt like. Trying to smother or cover up the most radiant light that ever existed. I always felt like little rays peeked out no matter what we did to try and hide it," I said.

"They did. It's impossible to bury something that powerful. I want you to know that I was ready to walk away from that exhausting effort. I was ready to just let everyone see the explosion of light between us. I want to do that with you now if you're willing?" he said.

"I don't see how, but I'd do anything for you," I whispered.

"This is for you, my love. Not me. Drop the blanket that you've been trying to cover up the sun with. Let go of the shame and uncertainty. Secrecy has no right to try and diminish a light that bright," he said.

"How, J? It feels too late. You want me to tell the truth without you standing beside me? That is so frightening," I said.

"Baby steps, my dear. I want you to simply walk away from the futile battle of trying to keep it all a secret. Just lay that down. Step away. It was always pointless for us to try and hide anyway…it's absolutely irrelevant now. Allow yourself the freedom from that burden. We are on a new journey together now. Let's not start this one out the way we did the one before. Let's walk in the light together from now on," he said.

I nodded. I could do that. I could release the grips of the shovel I was using to continually throw dirt on top of a wildfire.

In fact, just the thought of inaction…of simply walking away from that constant fight and worry, brought me overwhelming relief.

I watched the sun get brighter by the instant, its rays reaching further and further across the morning sky.

"How had we ever thought we were hiding that?" he said with amusement. I smiled.

"Watch the light as it touches each new section of the earth. It all just explodes with color the moment it is seen. That light is our love, Jen. Let it spill over into every single part of you. Let it pour out of everything you create. Let the rays of it explode out of your fingertips and toes and touch every part of the world around you. What is the sun, but an unstoppable ball of fire in the sky? We know the ways of the flame intimately, my love. The melody of fire is our love song.

"Fire only gets stronger as it spreads. As it grows it ignites, consumes, and purifies everything it touches.

"Fire is unstoppable once it is no longer contained. Step back from the firewalls, dear. Lay down the wet blankets. Let fire do what fire does, and watch the power burst forth just like that sunrise before us.

"The strongest fires put out the most light…. and my sweet girl…. our fire puts that sun to shame," he said.

I leaned back into the warmth that was now not only surrounding my body but spreading throughout it. The melody of fire, indeed.

In my grief, I had stopped singing it. It was time to raise my voice again.

I would once again offer my lyrics to this song. With my love beside me I felt ready to reunite with the chorus of the heavens.

I would allow the fiery love song to spill out of me once more, but this time it would be different.

This time I would let it touch every inch of the earth that surrounded it. I would allow it to brighten and purify the landscape as it pleased. I would let it float uninhibited over the mountains and the valleys, until all who heard it knew that this song was different. This refrain…this composition of flame and smoke…. this melody of fire, was an unstoppable love song.

And it was mine once more.

Chapter Twenty-Nine

WHEN I GOT home the next day, I was exhausted. The lack of sleep from the journey, alongside the lengthy drive hope had wiped me out. I decided to take a long hot bath and go to bed early.

I ran my bath water, and as I eased myself into the tub, I realized exactly how tired my body was. I leaned back into the water and closed my eyes for just a moment, enjoying the warmth and the peace.

When I opened my eyes, I found myself staring face-to-face with my grandmother.

It startled me so badly that I nearly came up out of the water.

She was standing before me, just outside of the tub, in an orange aura.

"*What the fuck*! I'm not on medicine anymore," I said to her. I was demanding an explanation with my tone.

"It is still very strong in your system, my dear. I didn't want to disrupt the beautiful journey you were having with your boy last night, but I did have some things I wanted to tell you," she replied.

My grandmother had passed away when I was ten. I had very few memories of her, but she looked so much like my mother (or visa-versa) that I had immediately recognized her.

It scared me, not only because she was standing beside the bathtub unexpectedly, but because I suddenly wondered if this was how my life was going to be now.

Were spirits just going to pop in and out of my awareness from now on?

"Yes, and no," she responded to the question that I had thought.

"Clairaudience is your strongest sensitivity…for now. You will hear spirits. And the Great Spirit. You won't always see them like you see me right now…yet. There is a lot coming for you, child. You can't fathom the door that you unlocked with that journey last night. That is part of why I needed to talk to you. I have been one of your guides since I crossed over. I've been watching over you and

335

protecting you in this realm for the last thirty years. I'm so very proud of you, Jen. I'm especially proud of you for not taking your own life last year. We all heard how much you thought about it. I'm proud of you for staying. There is so much good in store for you, I want you to know that," she said.

"Well…that's encouraging, for sure. I'm happy to stay now that I have J back," I said.

"He's a good one. I like him a lot…he loves you more than you can even conceive. We all do, but that one is special. He's been a wonderful addition to your guide team," she replied.

"Don't you all go falling in love with him over on that side of the veil. I know he is unbelievably charming, but he's still mine," I said.

She laughed.

"Believe me, we know. We've never seen anything like it. I don't think you really comprehend the lengths he went to in order to get you back. He did some things that we are all quite impressed with. He's very powerful…. but so are you," she said.

"Which brings me to what I need to tell you. You have walked into a plane that you know nothing about. You are in a completely foreign land, my dear one. There will be a lot of information thrown at you that will be difficult to comprehend and situations that will be hard to navigate. You will have mystical experiences that will be hard to relay to other people. It may get lonely in that way at times. You also may be afraid sometimes. Nothing can hurt you in this realm unless you allow it to. I just wanted you to know that I am always here, and so are the rest of your guides. If you come up against something frightening or confusing, all you have to do is call out to us and we will help you. The rule is that you have to ask though. You have to be the one to initiate it, we can't just step into your life and alter anything without your permission."

I pondered this information.

It frightened me to think about it. I was going to be in another realm frequently enough that I would need help and guidance? Was I even going to be able to choose my experiences or were things just going to be thrown at me the way they were at the moment with one of my ancestors standing by my bathtub while I was trying to rest?

My grandmother laughed.

"Sorry about that. I just knew I needed to talk to you before you went to bed, I didn't really mean to intrude. We don't really think about things like that on this side, which is why you are going to have to learn to set very clear boundaries. It's a good place for you to start. You can say when you are open to talking with us, and you can tell us when you need to be left alone. We have to respect it," she said.

"I have one more thing to tell you, and then I will leave you for the evening.

The whole lesson…the main reason why you incarnated this lifetime has to do with your Father and your Mother. There is a major fracture there, particularly with your Father that you have got to figure out how to heal. Loving and losing J was instrumental in bringing it to light. While you are rebuilding and healing and trying to figure out how to move forward…start there," she said.

I opened my mouth to ask a hundred questions, but as I did so she vanished.

"Thank you. I think?" I said out loud to the empty room.

So much for being able to interact on my terms.

I lay there in the warm water thinking about what she had said. Things had never been the same between my parents and me since I came out, but I didn't really think they were still damaged that badly. We had sort of fallen into a space of not discussing my sexuality, but I didn't really feel any animosity surrounding it anymore. I guess we could have another conversation about it if need be, but things had changed so dramatically that I honestly didn't see the point. They didn't know about J. I had never told them that we were anything more than musical partners because I didn't want to open that can of worms. I didn't want the backlash from them over him being married. More importantly, I didn't even know how to answer the questions that I knew would arise about what loving him meant about my sexuality.

I didn't even know how to talk about those things with myself, let alone prepare a multilayered defense about the subject against an inquiry from someone else.

"You sure seemed unbothered by my gender when my cock was in your mouth," I heard J say.

I laughed out loud.

He appeared in front of me, sitting at the other end of the bathtub naked and stroking himself.

"Mmm… very nice, sir. Look at you, coming through visually so easily for me," I said to him.

"I watched your grandmother come through and figured out what I was doing wrong. I'm so glad you were in the bathtub when it happened though. Now we can take a bath together. We never got a chance to do that, remember?" he replied.

I sighed happily. If seeing and hearing spirits was going to mean that I got this, I was just fine with it.

"I do remember. Keep touching yourself, I want to watch you," I said.

He smiled at me with a look I knew well. We were about to push the envelope a little. There was a cocky glint in his eye that meant, "I dare you…."

"Only if you do it too. I may not know how to physically touch you yet, but that doesn't mean we can't get off together," he said.

"I'm so happy you said 'yet,'" I said.

"Oh…I'm going to figure it out, don't worry. But in the meantime, know that this energy is still ours, Jen. Did you ever wonder why sex between us felt so important? That exchange is rooted in divine energy. It brought us to the spirit plane each and every time. We can still meet there, love. That sexual explosion of energy that we have always had is exactly the same. I want you to tap in and connect with me every single time you touch yourself…even when you can't see me like you do right now. Call me in, and we will be right back in that space together with the same vibrational connection. I'll send you images. I'll talk to you. Until I can touch you again, it will be the next best thing, I promise," he said.

We were both touching ourselves now, eyes locked.

I was reminded of times that we had done this very thing when he was alive. Watching each other. Edging ourselves until we couldn't take it any longer and someone caved and touched the other.

What had been a beautifully torturous game to play before now seemed like such a waste. I should have held him in my hands every moment that I physically could because now watching each other was our only option.

Still….it was more than I expected to ever get back.

"You're so gorgeous, love. Seeing you looking at me that way again still drives me crazy. I want you to say my name like you used to…say it when you come…." he whispered between moans.

Hearing him aching with pleasure sent me over the edge. I could feel myself teetering on the edge of climax. It had been so long since I had even had the slightest interest in sex. Having him here with me again was delicious. My body easily slipped back into responding at the mere sight and sound of him.

"That's my good girl…come for me…. I can feel how close you are…." he said as we both increased the intensity of our stroking.

I suddenly felt the wave of orgasm wash through my body, and I yelled his name as it did so. I closed my eyes and let the ripples of pleasure continue for a moment.

When I opened my eyes, he was gone.

"Remember, that is *always* ours. I love you, Miss Jen," I heard him say.

I wasn't sure why I couldn't see him anymore.

Was the medicine finally wearing off enough that seeing him wouldn't be possible now?

"Something like that. But also, there is someone else who wants you to see her face before you go to bed," he said.

"Can I get out of the bathtub first, please? I didn't mind you being in here, but the rest of this ghost parade feels a little intrusive," I said.

"You won't mind her being here either," he replied.

A pink glow at my breasts suddenly caught my attention and I looked down to see a tiny and perfect newborn baby nursing on my nipple.

My daughter.

I began to weep as I looked at her little face.

She looked so much like my niece that they could have been sisters.

Sweet pouty lips. Eyes shaped like mine. J's nose.

"Oh, J. *She's so beautiful.* She's perfect," I said between sobs.

I couldn't stop staring at her.

I felt a wave of guilt and grief wash through me again. I could have held her just like this if I had only known. If I had just taken better care of myself.

"I'm taking good care of her, Jen. She's with me. I love her just as much as I would have if we had all been together as a family in the physical. Please let the thought of her in my arms be some comfort to you," J said.

She faded slowly from my sight.

I sat in the bathtub and had a very long ugly cry, which no one from either side of the veil dared to disturb.

When I finally had exhausted myself, I got out and made my way to bed.

I lay down and snuggled in, grateful to be back home in my own bed with my own pillow.

I closed my eyes, and as soon as I did so I was assaulted with a slideshow of images unlike anything I had ever seen before.

Grotesque creatures - half human, half god-knows-what began to appear one after the other. I also began to see gory, violent images of mangled and bloody human and animal bodies interspersed in the mix.

I would open my eyes to make them go away, but the minute I closed them the slide show would begin again.

It was terrifying.

I couldn't make it stop.

I finally screamed out into the darkness for J and my grandmother.

It was J who answered.

"They are just low vibrational beings, Jen. They know you can see things in the spirit realm now so they are trying to get your attention. Don't give it to them. Attention grows their power and makes them stronger - otherwise, they are extremely weak and can't really do much of anything. They won't hurt you. Try and clear your mind like you do when you are meditating. When one of them appears, just let the image go like you would any other intrusive thought in meditation. It's going to be ok, love. You are safe. You are just lit up like a Christmas tree to them right now because of the door you have opened. They will be drawn to you for a while but will move on when they realize you won't pay them any mind," he said.

I lay there trembling.

I tried to do what J told me, but the bombardment continued.

I was afraid to get up to even go to the bathroom, for fear that one of these horrific creatures would materialize before me.

I asked J to sing to me and he did. I tried to meditate and that worked on and off, but it took me nearly all night to get the hang of it.

In between trying everything I could to get some sleep I just kept wondering what in the world I had done. Was it going to be like this from now on?

What in Pandora's hell had I opened?

OVER THE NEXT few weeks things settled considerably, though I definitely had interactions with the spirit realm frequently.

As promised, the terrifying creatures stopped coming through.

In fact, most visual interaction ceased. The contact I got from the other side was nearly exclusively audible. I could still hear J, though not as clearly. I would get single sentences, or one-word responses from him and anything else sounded muffled or too distant to hear.

A new voice came into my awareness, and I began to realize that it was the voice of Spirit. It sounded genderless to me and was the only thing that came in as loudly as what I had experienced the night of the journey.

It came in during moments that I needed direct guidance.

Apart from those brief interactions, my life pretty much went back to normal except that I talked to J frequently now because I was delighted that we were reconnected. Even though I couldn't hear him as well as I would have hoped, I knew he could hear me, and I knew he was with me. The journey had at least reassured me of that, so I just spoke to him all of the time in my mind and aloud, trusting that even when I didn't hear an answer that he still was listening.

In the journey I had been shown that the reason why I couldn't hear J after he passed was that my vibration was so low from my grief that he had been unable to reach me. I kept trying to incorporate ways that I might be able to lift the heaviness enough that I could hear him more clearly. I had some mildly successful moments, but it quickly came to my attention that I was doing one specific thing that was consistently inhibiting my connection.

I was still drinking.

I hadn't really thought it was a big deal at the time, but it was definitely in my awareness that alcohol lowers your vibration. Hadn't Alice tried to get me to lay it down when I was adamant about figuring out how to reconnect with J?

Through the readjustment period after the journey, I learned something interesting about alcohol and Spirit.

You can't hear two "spirits."

You have to pick your spirit.

One drowns out the other.

When I would drink, it felt like I literally put earplugs in my spiritual ears. Not only could I not hear J...I couldn't hear the guidance from Spirit clearly either.

It reminded me of how it felt before I went to the journey.

I hated it, but apparently not as much as I hated the idea of not drinking.

Naturally, Spirit took the opportunity of this newfound awareness to ask me to be sober.

Literally ASKED me.

"We can't reach you when you are in that state. You need to keep your vibration high so that we can connect. Will you lay down the alcohol, please?"

I said no.

For the record, I wouldn't recommend declining a request from the most powerful entity in existence, because the next step wasn't as gentle as "asking."

A month or so had passed, and I got the opportunity to prove yet again that I'm foolish (and persistent!) when it comes to drinking. One evening I got a wild hair and got drunk at a Mexican restaurant for no good reason other than that swimming pool-sized beers were $3 and I love a bargain. I had drunk a little here and there since I had been back, but this is the first time that I had truly been intoxicated.

I came home and went to bed.

About 3 am I woke up out of a dead sleep in a panic. Head reeling, I stumbled to the bathroom. I felt extremely strange. It was like my mind and my body were disconnected. It felt as though I were not in control of my thoughts. I was confused and absolutely terrified.

My hands went numb, and my mind began frantically racing. Was I having a stroke?

I considered going to the hospital, but I heard a voice say, "Drink some water and lie back down. You will feel better by 6:00."

I drank a large glass of water and tried to lie back down, but my thoughts felt manic, and I spiraled into a full-on panic attack.

I lay there, gasping for air and trembling from head to toe for what felt like an eternity. My heart was racing so hard it felt like all I could hear was the pounding in my ears.

I began to cry. Apologize. Swear off drinking. (We've all been there, though usually, I reached this lowest of moments whilst hugging the toilet the morning after a binge.)

This was a new set of circumstances for me to be making promises to God about not drinking that I would typically break the next day.

This was a new terror, and I meant it this time.

"I swear if you will just make this go away, I will quit drinking. I promise," I finally pleaded out loud.

"For a year," the voice commanded.

Shit. There were going to be stipulations? Fine.

"Fine. Yes. For a year. I won't drink for a year. Please just make this stop," I replied.

"Glad we are on the same page, finally," the voice replied.

My heart slowed a little, and I felt like I was finally able to get a good deep breath. I slowly felt myself stabilize. Warmth and feeling began to return to my extremities. Clarity stepped back in, and the cloudiness and confusion began to lift.

I took another full breath and exhaled in relief. I was beginning to feel like myself again.

I rolled onto my side and looked at the clock.

6:00, on the dot.

And that, my friends, is the story of how Spirit scared me shitless and into sobriety.

I had been drunk countless times before and that had never happened. It was as though after I told Spirit no when they asked me originally to quit drinking, they decided to clear their throat and say it a little louder for the people in the back.

(It's me. I am the people in the back.)

Message received.

I talked to a healer friend of mine about what happened to me that night, and she explained to me that alcohol intoxication literally takes your spirit out of your body a little. She can see energy/auras and told me that though the spirit and the body are still attached by a cord, she can see a separation when someone is in that state.

This explained the disconnect that I felt during that episode. Then, of course, my ego panicked (because that seems to be the thing it is best at) and sent me into a spiral.

She also explained to me the origin of the word "spirits" for alcohol. It literally pushes your own spirit out a bit and resides in its place. If you think about it, it makes perfect sense. People behave in ways they would normally never behave sober. Inhibitions are dropped (as well as morals, often) when a person is intoxicated because the alcohol pushes their own spirit and sense of self to the side a bit and steps into its place.

The more I thought about it, the scarier that thought got. I had been allowing, for years, my true and authentic self to be pushed to the side and numbed down because the spirit of alcohol gave me an escape from my own body.

My own body where all of the fear and trauma and feelings resided.

I didn't have to deal with them, because alcohol pushed me just far enough out of myself that I couldn't hear them anymore.

And now, it was pushing me just far enough out of myself that I couldn't hear the voice of Spirit anymore either. That's why I had to lay it down.

That's why Spirit was so insistent, and as usual, had to show me first-hand why it was important.

Sometimes I wish that Spirit was a little easier on me when it comes to how the lessons get delivered.

But then sometimes, They tell me that it wouldn't have to be like that if I was less stubborn and just listened when guidance was given the first time. It's like the omnipotent version of "this hurts me more than it hurts you" while you walk to the woodshed.

I have to say, I'm getting really tired of the woodshed, and picking my own willow switches out for my own thrashings.

I know I keep talking about it but surrender always has been, and maybe always will be my biggest stumbling block.

I eventually get there, but only after I'm on the ground with a bloody knee.

I'm still working on it.

At least now I'm working on it with clarity and presence, and without a bottle for a crutch.

When I laid down the alcohol something unexpected happened.

Fear began to ooze out of every single pore of my body.

It was almost like a detox, except that I had to feel the toxins pass through me in waves as they exited. I became afraid to even make a move at all. Scared of the voices that I was hearing in my head (even J's). Terrified and untrusting of the whole shift that had occurred, I tried to close myself back up.

I didn't want this anymore. I didn't trust the unknown.

I gave every effort to shut it all out and return to "normal."

I was at work one day, grooming dogs, as I had done at the animal hospital for the past several years. Once you work for that long in a service profession you have built a clientele that is around ninety percent returning clients. This makes for a fairly predictable schedule (albeit slightly boring) even for a job working with creatures who have a mind and agenda of their own. At this point, I just knew what to expect most days. Bella, my 10:30 appointment was going to poop all over herself the minute that I finished her haircut, so I needed to allow time for two baths. Max, my 12:00, was going to spend the majority of his groom trying to turn my fingers into sausage meat with his teeth, so he would take twice as long as other grooms. Sophie, my 1:00, was precious and perfect and I wanted to schedule in an extra ten minutes to kiss her nose between working on her.

You get the idea.

However, one day not long after I quit drinking, I had this one dog that came in that I had never seen before. He was a goldendoodle, (because do they even make dogs anymore that don't end in "oodle"?) and had the cutest face ever. However, he was about two years old and had never been groomed before. I normally recommend that a dog (particularly a doodle, as their hair is difficult to manage/ maintain) begin their grooming experience at 12 weeks old and come every 7-8 weeks afterward. I spend a great deal of time that first groom showing them the ropes, while they are still tiny enough to easily handle and move; teaching them that the dryer and clippers are loud, but nothing to be afraid of, teaching them how to stand on the table, rewarding good behavior with treats and affection, etc. I have just found that once a good foundation is established, the dogs are happy to come in and enjoy the process (a process that will be necessary for the rest of their life) from then on. It makes for a better experience for both the dog and myself.

This doodle, we will call him Baxter, had not had any experience with any of the grooming process and now weighed around eighty pounds.

Baxter was terrified of EVERYTHING.

He was literally shaking all over and trying to melt himself into the ground to get away from me from the get-go.

I picked Baxter up and put him on my table, which was no small feat considering he was eighty pounds of unwilling beast, snapped him into a neck restraint, and before I could get his rear restraint looped around him, he made a suicide move and tried to jump off of the table (which would have hung him, had I not been there). I caught him and tried to settle him down a bit, but he wasn't having it.

I decide to just move him straight to the bathtub and start there.

He was quivering with fear from head to toe.

I carried him to the tub, and he immediately tried to jump out.

I got him safely restrained and the minute that I cut the water on he began flailing and screaming as if I were pouring acid on him instead of water.

He even tried to dodge the shampoo bottles, which are noiseless (obviously), and ended up hitting his head on the side of the tub.

When I cut the dryer on all hell broke loose.

He screamed and howled in terror. Pissed and shat everywhere.

I had to cut the dryer off nearly immediately after I turned it on, and we had to do that whole bath process AGAIN because in his terror he had run a few circles through his poop and now had it all over him.

I decided that I would just comb through his hair while it was wet and put him under a low dryer. It was quiet but would take about 4 hours for him to dry. Then I would try and cut his hair.

I began to comb through the tangled hair and found a large mat behind one of his ears, so I decided to just take my clippers and shave it out so that it wouldn't be painful to him like trying to brush it out would be. I didn't need him any more afraid than he already was.

When I turned my clippers on (which, really, are quiet as far as clippers go) and went to shave behind his ear, Baxter lost his shit again and turned and flailed wildly right when I got near his head. I almost ran the clippers straight into his eyeball.

Up until now, I had been talking to him sweetly, trying to calm him with my every move and breath and trying to soothe him out of this over-the-top reactionary anxiety.

However, nearly cutting his eye with a blade scared the hell out of me, and I threw the clippers down and grabbed either side of his head with my hands and made him look at me as I yelled,

"BAXTER!! Listen to me. I'm not going to hurt you!! But if you don't calm down YOU ARE GOING TO HURT YOURSELF!!! I can only do so much. BE STILL AND TRUST ME!!!!!"

In retrospect, I realize that screaming at a terrified dog for them to trust you isn't exactly the best way to go about calming them down, but it's just where we were.

Standing there with Baxter's head in my hands, looking deeply into his troubled and untrusting eyes, I heard as clear as day, the voice of Spirit.

"Do you see how difficult it is to do anything when fear is all-consuming? This is what working with you is like right now. I can't make a move because of the state you are in. Be still and trust ME. Let ME do my job. I would no more hurt you than you would hurt that dog, but you have to surrender and trust that I know best. Let the fear go," it said.

I felt myself well up with tears. Compassion flooded over me, and I kissed Baxter's nose tenderly.

Spirit was right.

I had been behaving just like Baxter. Freaking out over any little shift of the wind.

Zero trust in any move that placed me in unknown territory.

I had just gotten a crash course in exactly how frustrating it is to try and help a creature who was in sheer panic.

I called Baxter's mom to come and pick him up because I was afraid that pushing him further would cause him to injure himself.

I wondered how much more of my own flailing and terror Spirit would put up with before they gave up on me the same way.

In the prologue, I discussed the opposing forces of fear and love. I also highlighted how the Southern Baptist faith that I grew up in was centered around fear, and how that focus on fear as a tool to manipulate people to the Lord by playing on their deepest fears was counterproductive at best.

What I didn't realize was how deeply that fear had shaped and affected me to the very core of my being.

When I quit drinking and was sober and clear consistently for the first time since my early twenties, I was shocked to find that what bubbled up through the cracks of my soul most frequently and caught me off guard was not depression or grief. It was pure, undiluted fear.

There was a period of time after I got sober that I would be driving to work, or settling in for the evening, and the minute that my body got still I would find myself suddenly in the grips of panic. It would just wash over me suddenly, and I would have to get up and move, or take a walk outside just to feel like I could breathe again.

It was deeply unsettling to me that just below the surface there was something inside of me ready to run for the hills in terror at any given moment.

It is said that "healing" something (whether that something be an emotion, or a trauma) is not to get to the point in your journey where that something no longer bothers you; instead, true healing means getting to a point where that something no longer runs your life.

I thought that something for me was my grief. As it turns out, my something was much deeper and had been much longer present than that.

Fear was my something.

Fear had been imprinted in my very cells. It had been bred into me in a lineage passed down from my mother, grandmother, and who knows how much further back. This fear was ancestral, generational, and felt much deeper than the religious trauma that reinforced and engrained it.

Deep beneath my skin lay a network of synapses firing off, constantly reminding me that I was in danger. It had been so present, for so long, that my body now did it on its own without my conscious direction or reaction. I hadn't even realized it was present until I removed the protective coating of alcohol.

I felt SO raw. Like an exposed nerve, any little brush of the wind sent me into a frenzy that felt beyond my control.

If there could have been a window into my conscious thought at this time, it would have been hilarious to look at all of the crazy things it occurred to me to be afraid of or worry about. That is, it would have been hilarious if it weren't so deeply pitiful.

My body, soul, and mind were in a constant cry for help.

It's no wonder I was exhausted. My fight-or-flight switch was stuck on flight, and I've never been big on running. (I mean…I'll DO it…but can't I just sit on the couch and drink beer to calm my nerves instead?)

I knew there was only one way that I was going to unearth this deeply rooted fear and get to the cause of it.

I was beginning to understand that our subconscious holds the key to all of the ugly parts of ourselves, and the only way to overcome it was to meet it face to face and see it for what it was.

You can't heal what you can't see.

I called Kat and scheduled another journey.

A private one.

This time, I was going in alone.

348

Chapter Thirty

I WENT DOWN TO the river and sat on the dock the night before the journey. I sent out my intentions through my breath and my words as I listened to the rush of the water.

My river.

So many important moments of magic had happened here that I was beginning to think of her as my own. It was as if all I had to do was send my energy into the flow of water and it got carried right to Spirit.

Show me what this fear is all about.

Take me to the source of it.

Teach me how to heal it.

I whispered my prayer over and over as I hung my legs over the dock and dipped my toes in the icy water.

Suddenly, I heard a rustle in the brush beside me and I turned my head to see a raccoon pop out of the weeds not four feet from me.

He didn't see me and was busily scuttling along the water's edge toward me even closer.

"Umm…hi," I said very gently to him, trying not to scare him.

It didn't work. He jumped back in terror, his eyes huge, as he looked at me. He quickly ran back into the brush and out of sight.

I felt bad. He was so cute. I hadn't meant to startle him so badly.

I turned my attention back to the water in front of me and resumed my talk with Spirit.

Suddenly, I saw something in the water directly in front of me that I thought at first was a log floating in the water.

As it registered what I was looking at I burst out laughing.

It was the raccoon, allowing the water to carry him down the river to the other side of me.

349

I apparently had ruined his plans to walk down the bank, and swimming was the option he had chosen to make it to the other side of the dock that I was sitting on without getting too close to me.

I watched him get out of the water on the other side of me and shake off and continue on his merry way. I was still laughing when I heard the voice of Spirit.

"There is your guide for this journey. We are going to take off the mask. We are going to show you how to work around the fear."

I became solemn as the gravity of what was said sunk in.

Last journey the foxes had been my guide.

This time it was a playful raccoon.

Except that suddenly he didn't seem so light-hearted.

Had I been wearing a mask? I wasn't so sure, but I was certainly willing to follow this little creature to safety if it meant learning to navigate my fear.

Tiptoeing around the bank wasn't going to cut it, it seemed.

I was going to have to dive in willingly.

I tried to brace myself for the icy plunge that loomed ahead.

When I got to the journey space, I was nervous. I hadn't been as afraid of the actual medicine this time. It was more of a fear of what I was coming here to look at.

I placed a few crystals on the mantle of the cabin, and then carefully placed a photo of myself and J that I loved dearly against the stone of the fireplace.

It rested still for a moment, but then to my absolute horror, suddenly shifted and fell between two cracks of the stone and disappeared.

I frantically looked for a way to retrieve it, but it was out of sight completely with no way to get to it.

"No. This time it's just about you," I heard Spirit say distinctly.

"Well, fuck. That's fine I guess, but did you have to take my picture?" I asked with exasperation.

There was no answer. Both the loss of the photo and the silence unsettled me. I was beginning to feel more and more alone here.

Kat and I sat together cross-legged in front of the fireplace. I had written her a lengthy email a few days prior to that told her about my intentions in coming to this journey. I needed to dig out the root of the fear that had been consuming me. I had to have some clarity about why I was the way that I was.

I wanted to know how to fix myself.

Since Kat was already up to speed on the goals here tonight, I didn't go over

The Melody of Fire

them again. Instead, I told her about the raccoon incident that had happened the night before. She smiled and showed me a card she had pulled for the journey ahead from a spirit animal guide oracle deck that was lying on the hearth of the fireplace.

A raccoon.

I shook my head and smiled.

"Spirit likes to beat me over the head with things in case I don't listen the first time. They know I'm stubborn," I said with a laugh.

We said an opening prayer, and she handed me my pill.

There was no hesitation this time; I took it instantly.

We both lay back on the pillows in the floor and began just talking like friends do. We caught each other up on the things that had been going on since the last journey. It was a pleasant and sweet interaction, but I suddenly noticed an odd sensation passing through me. I just ignored it in the beginning but then I started to become very uncomfortable in my body as we spoke.

It crept over me slowly at first.

I got extremely hot, then it eased off and I gradually found myself feeling cool.

What started as a little red flag for attention from my body began to escalate, the more I tried to ignore it.

My extremities began to feel ice cold, and I started to feel numbness in my fingers and toes.

I knew this feeling.

It was what almost always accompanied a panic attack.

The thought of that alone began to send me into one.

My breath quickened.

I freaked out, feeling my body respond to the familiar mental loop that I fell easily into.

"I feel weird," I told Kat urgently.

I saw her raise an eyebrow.

"You remember why you came here, right?" she asked half-jokingly. I could tell that she was trying to assess what I meant by that declaration. The fact that I didn't laugh made her get up and move behind me. She had me lay my head in her lap as she spoke softly to me.

"Ok. What is happening right now is that we have been just talking and connecting, but your medicine is trying to drop in, and you are fighting it tooth and nail. You can't back out now, Jen - it's too late. Will you simply allow it?" she said.

I was struggling to get a good breath. Fear gripped my heart like an icy hand. I literally felt the coldness around my heart, and it made me physically start to shiver.

351

I had changed my mind. I didn't want to do this.

I was strong enough to keep my mind tight, surely. I could keep the effects of the medicine at bay if I just fought hard enough.

The panic attack became full-blown. I lay there in Kat's lap trembling and gasping for what felt like eternity.

I began to hear a voice yelling at me loudly, "SURRENDER! SURRENDER!"

I knew it was Spirit, asking me to drop the resistance.

I just couldn't do it.

The thought of losing what little bit of control I had terrified me more than anything. I pushed back even harder. While my mind tried harder and harder to keep from giving in, my body freaked out more and more.

Suddenly, I physically saw J appear to my left. He knelt down beside me in the floor and put his hand on my forehead.

"I swear woman, I know I said it to you all of the time before, but *you are the most stubborn person alive*. Let it go, babe. You won't feel safe until you do," he said to me.

Kat responded from above me as well.

"He's right, Jen. You are doing it to yourself. Just surrender," she said.

My heart was beating out of my chest. I was pouring sweat now, which was making me shiver even harder. My mind was reeling. Was I going to die like this? It felt like a possibility. What in the name of God had possessed me to want to come back here and do this alone? But then I realized that I was alone anyway. No one could rescue me from my own mind. Not Kat. Not J. No one.

Spirit's voice boomed above me.

"*We would not bring you here to hurt you. You can trust us. Please, PLEASE, SURRENDER*," They said.

I was becoming exhausted physically. My will began to wear down.

I suddenly remembered the night that I had fallen into the river, and how it had quickly worn me out to the point of giving in. Hadn't I heard a similar voice then?

I recalled that when I had finally let go that I had been gently brought to a safe place and was finally ok.

That memory was exactly what I needed in this moment.

I struggled against my panicking body to take a large inhale.

"FINE," I said through a long, exhausted exhale.

As I released my breath, I handed over all of the fight.

Let the medicine drop in.

Let Spirit speak.

Take me wherever.

I'm so tired.

"Good girl," J leaned over and whispered in my ear. Kat rubbed my shoulders gently and talked me through slowing my breathing until my body finally quieted. She stood up and went to get something.

"I'll be right here if you need me, love, but Spirit has an agenda this evening so I'm stepping aside for now, ok? You can talk to me any time you want though, I'm coming with you on this journey in support. You don't have to do anything. Just rest, and let the unfolding happen," J said to me gently as he slowly vanished from my sight.

Kat reappeared beside me with a piece of chocolate and a cup of hot tea.

"Aya?" I asked her tentatively as I eyed it suspiciously.

She nodded an affirmative.

"And the tea has indica oil in it…for anxiety," she said.

It hadn't even occurred to me that she might be dosing me with something in the tea that I had now drunk a few swallows of.

I laughed.

"There she is," she said with a smile.

"Shew. Yeah, that was terrible, I hope we are done with that part," I said. I ate the chocolate that she had given me, even though I silently prayed as I chewed it up that it wouldn't send me into another panic attack. I lay back down in front of the fireplace.

"I think you are done with that for tonight. Sometimes in journey you have to go through what you are working on in the moment to learn the lesson. I know it felt like it was your body that revolted, but it was your mind that was causing all of that. Now you know if you need to get out of that place that you have to surrender, and also to breathe to calm yourself. So if it arises again…anytime, not just tonight…you know how to navigate it now," she said.

She tenderly wrapped me in warm fuzzy blankets as she spoke. She placed pillows under and around me until I felt like I was enveloped in a cloud.

I was cozy and content.

She smoothed my hair from my face and asked me if I was ok now. I told her that I was.

"Good. Just close your eyes now, and let Spirit talk to you. I'm right beside you if you need me again," she whispered.

I obeyed.

I closed my eyes and settled into the darkness, allowing my tired body to melt into the softness surrounding me.

It wasn't long before I heard Spirit.

"I wish you would trust me. I would never bring you to the spirit plane to hurt you. You want to connect, and I want to connect with you. This is the best place to do it," They said.

353

"I know. I'm so sorry. I don't know where that fear comes from. It feels beyond my control in a lot of ways. It simply bubbles up and out of me and I don't even know why. I can feel it so much more now that I'm not drinking. I guess I had been pushing it down with alcohol for so long that I didn't even know it was there. I know that you know it is the reason why I came here tonight," I replied.

"Why is fear so stitched into my being? How did that even begin? I can't remember…."

I trailed off because out of the darkness came a glowing shape. At first, I thought it was a snake. (It crossed my mind briefly that maybe I had gotten snake bitten at an early age and hadn't remembered it, in which case, I could totally understand why I was scared to death of everything.)

As the shape got closer, I could see that it wasn't a snake.

It was a belt.

My father's belt.

I suddenly remembered how terrified I had been of that belt. My dad was the disciplinarian in our house and getting spanked with the belt was the punishment of choice for any missteps my sister and I made growing up.

Looking back, I'm not even sure that he chose the role of the punisher. It very well could have just been handed to him because my mother didn't want to do it. If we misbehaved when we were with Mom we always heard, "Just wait until your father gets home….".

Sure enough, Dad would walk in from work and be bombarded with the tales of the crimes we had committed according to Mom, which he was expected to punish by spanking us.

I was a pretty well-behaved and quiet child, and actually only got spanked a handful of times (unlike my sister who was forever getting whipped it felt like) because I very quickly learned to keep my head down and stay in line to avoid it. It scared the hell out of me. As I looked at the image of the belt in front of me even now, I felt myself tremble with fear.

How curious.

The image faded.

As I was pondering the belt that I had just seen and all of its implications, I noticed a silhouette of a person begin to emerge from the blackness.

A small-framed man with dark skin and large expressive eyes was walking toward me.

I scanned his face carefully, trying to see if I knew him. I had no recollection of this man. I felt certain that we had never met before, but I still decided to ask him just to be sure.

"Hello. Do we know each other?" I asked.

He nodded yes and smiled at me. His eyes seemed to overflow with compassion.

The Melody of Fire

I felt like he loved me tremendously. The feeling was radiating from him, and it poured into my heart the closer he got to me. It made me sad that I didn't know who he was.

"Please forgive me for not remembering you…what is your name?" I asked.

"You know me as Jesus of Nazareth", he replied in the most soothing voice I had ever heard in my life.

I stared at him dumbfounded.

"Oh my God. Am I that fucking racist that I didn't recognize you because you aren't *white*?" I asked, horrified. I then realized that I had just sworn in front of the LORD AND SAVIOR, and I wanted to die.

To my relief, he laughed heartily.

"It's not your fault, dear one. My skin color was just one of the many ways I was misrepresented to you," he said.

"What do you mean? Not about the race thing, I get that, and I can see how I got bombarded with white Jesus images constantly. What other ways were you misrepresented to me?" I asked, puzzled.

"So many ways, beloved, but I will share with you the most important one. You are afraid of me, aren't you? And of God?" he asked.

I considered this. My initial gut reaction when he had said his name had indeed been to fall to the ground in front of him and cower. Who was I to be having this conversation with God incarnate? Surely, He was about to punish me for all of the things I had done wrong.

With this thought, I realized he was correct.

I was afraid of him.

Deeply, fundamentally terrified.

"Yes. I am. I am very afraid of you. You are an entity and a power that I am not worthy of standing before. I've done so many terrible things…the latest of which consists of breaking one of the Ten Commandments by falling in love with J… and…." I stammered. He cut me off gently.

"Shhhh. You were taught my message all wrong, my child. As you were growing up, I was misrepresented to you as full of wrath and anger, awaiting the moment that you made a mistake so that I could punish you. Or rather, so that God could punish you. You believe that we are the same entity, and that is a conversation for another time. What is important for you to know right now is that I do not want to make you suffer. In fact, nothing could be further from the truth. No one wants to punish you. No one eagerly awaits your misstep. No one wants to condemn you. You are so loved. *Sooooo loved.* Loved beyond your comprehension. My message as a Teacher here on earth was all about that love. It got twisted and turned because of money and power - the same two demons that twist and turn all good things. You internalized those teachings as a child, and they have influenced your entire life. You have been terrified of me… and terrified of God. Two entities that consist entirely and only of love in the purest form. You have such fear and animosity surrounding the Divine that you don't even use the word "God" anymore. You say Spirit," he said.

It was true. I had spent my young life scared to death of what would happen if I went against the teachings of the church. When my sexuality came into play, even though I turned my back on God and spirituality as a whole I was still deeply concerned that I was hell bound. I was convinced that God hated me and that I would be punished. It's not what I wanted… I just didn't think there was anything I could do about it.

"So, all of this fear in me…all of the anxiety and repressed emotion that has been coming out of me lately….it all goes back to that? I was afraid of God as a child, so I'm afraid of everything now?" I asked.

He tilted his head slightly.

"Not exactly. It's more specific than that. Can you see the connection between what you've been shown thus far this evening and the overall course of your life? Are you able to connect those dots yet, child?" he asked.

I shook my head no.

They had shown me my dad's belt, and Jesus. Two things I was deeply afraid of as a kid.

I just couldn't see how that got me to this point or what he was referring to as far as my life path.

"I'm afraid I'm a little slow, I'm sorry. Could you help me?" I asked.

"You are terrified to the core of masculine energy," he said as if it were the most obvious thing in the world.

I froze. Maybe it *was* the most obvious thing in the world, but it certainly had never occurred to me in that way.

"You were afraid of your dad, because he was the physical bringer of punishment to you. He was bigger, stronger, and you had no choice but to submit to him. The same with the God that you were taught about. Big. Scary. Full of wrath and fire. You felt powerless against that. Those two beings were the only present male forces in your life as a child, and that was very frightening to you. When you blossomed into womanhood, you subconsciously chose to be with women because they felt safe to you. You think you fought your family and your church over your sexuality, but you actually fought so hard for that because it was the only space that you felt truly able to express yourself and be seen safely. You put that mask on and never looked back because it served you well. You didn't have to cower to feminine energy. You understood it and clung to it. It gave you a place to hide from the masculine," he said.

I stared at him with my mouth hanging open.

I tried to process this, and I realized that it made sense. Except for one thing…

"But neither one of those things were really that scary, in the scheme of things. It shouldn't have been so traumatic to me that I took on a whole persona with my sexuality just to hide from that. My dad is a teddy bear, most of the time. I have always been afraid to tell him things, or mostly, to disappoint him…but I know that deep down he is a sweet and compassionate man. I know that he loves me more than anything. He's the best father I know, and he has always just done the best he can. As far as God goes…yes, I have been afraid of the wrath of the Almighty for as long as I can remember…but I also felt like I stood up to that fear, in a way, when I chose my own path that went against what people told me was His 'will.' So, I couldn't have been *that* afraid, or I wouldn't have done it. Why did those things trigger such a reaction from me?" I asked.

Jesus sighed.

"I'm afraid that what I am about to tell you may mess with you a little, in regard to what you fundamentally believe to be true about the nature of things.

"That fear is lifetimes deep, dear one. You incarnated this time specifically to heal that wound. Your soul, which has always been feminine in nature, has suffered such horrors at the hands of men in other lifetimes that the fear is in your very DNA. If anything more traumatic had happened to you in this lifetime… say… sexual abuse as a child, or being raped as a teenager…. you would have shut down and never been able to work through the fear and mistrust that you came here to conquer. As it stands, the somewhat mild trauma that you suffered merely triggered you intensely enough that you ran from men for the first half of your life. Your soul remembered what had happened to you, even though your mind did not," he responded.

"But J…." was all I could squeak out.

"Ah yes. Your beloved. He is your masculine counterpart in every sense of the word. The two of you agreed together before this incarnation to work through this together. What you tried to apologize for earlier…the 'breaking of a Commandment' was divinely put into place, my dear. Earthly commitments and decisions could never have hindered what the two of you came to do. Falling in love with him was never an option. It was the whole point of living this lifetime," he said.

I was crying now.

"I knew. You said all of that might mess with what I thought was true about the nature of things….and there is a lot that I'm not sold on…. but that part I knew. Our love runs through my being just as surely as my blood does," I said.

It was true. Outside of my and J's relationship, I had a very difficult time wrapping my mind around reincarnation and soul contracts and making it gel somehow with the religious ideas that had been instilled in me as a child. When I was in his arms, however, there was no doubt to me that we loved and knew each other far more deeply than was possible from being together in this single lifetime. Hadn't he and I both had very clear memories of loving each other in other times and places? That had been impossible to deny no matter how it had clashed with my preconceived notions of the way things "worked" spiritually.

I thought back to my sister's dream that she had in which J had told her, "She doesn't remember, but we agreed on this…."

Now Jesus was telling me that all of this had been set up for my growth before I was even born. No wonder I had been pulled to J like a magnet. Even though I had been afraid at first, I had stepped around that fear to be with him because everything in me felt like it was the right thing to do. It was all that mattered to me.

Of course it was. I had been right in believing that no human being could have walked away from that connection.

In fact, we never had a choice.

"So, the fear that seems to emanate from my being…that fear has always been a fear of the masculine?" I asked. I still needed some clarity here. I felt like I wasn't fully grasping the lesson that was being conveyed. After all, though it made sense that I was afraid as a child of that energy, I was still dealing with quite a bit of anxiety and fear *recently*. Even after being with J, which to my mind should have eased those fears if I was understanding this correctly.

"It is all about the balance of Divine Masculine and Divine Feminine energy, dear one. Do you remember your grandmother telling you that you needed to heal the relationship with your mom and dad? She wasn't talking about your earthly parents. She was referencing The Divine energies that exist within us all. You have been extremely imbalanced, and it has spiraled nearly out of control. You have been living in a very juvenile and unawakened state. That is where the fear is stemming from.

"The juvenile feminine lives in a constant state of fear. There is not trust enough in the masculine to protect her, so she tries to fight the battles herself. You stepped into the masculine role to try and feel safe, but you weren't meant to carry that as a predominantly feminine soul. It never felt right to you, and you did it poorly because you weren't made for that. You were never able to embody the nurturing and the creative *force* that you are until you were able to surrender and complement a divine masculine energy. J opened you up to that. You trusted him, didn't you?" he asked.

I sighed heavily.

Boy, did I. I would have willingly placed my very life in his hands.

"I trusted that man with everything in me. There was no place inside that I didn't allow him to go," I answered.

"Exactly. For the first time in this lifetime…indeed, for the first time in MANY lifetimes… you not only allowed yourself to be held in the Divine Masculine energy, but you also stepped fully into the truth of who you are at your core. You are a Divine Feminine entity, my child," he said. He came closer to me and wrapped me in a warm hug. I felt the love flood my system and allowed myself to accept it deeply.

I began to cry into His shoulder.

"But Jesus…why am I so afraid now? I feel the most terrified I've ever been, and I don't know how to overcome it," I said between my sobs.

"It is because you thought he left you. You felt the powerful connection of Divine wholeness and then you believed yourself to be torn away from it," he replied.

My tears came in great streams down my face now. I knew he was correct. I felt so alone. I missed the safety and ability to just BE that had been present in J's arms.

"Your work is to balance those energies in yourself, my child. The Divine Masculine and the Divine Feminine are present in all beings, though each human leans slightly one way or the other. Stepping fully into your Divine Feminine means growing her up quite a bit, Jen. It *requires* surrender. It *requires* trust. And for you, that is even deeper of a necessity because you have been so askew. You have got to make peace with the Divine Masculine in order to fully bloom. You know what it feels like when it's in perfect balance, remember? You had to fall in love with J in order to get a taste of that. And then you had to lose him in order to figure out how to do this on your own because it is *all inside of you*. It has to all be healed *inside of you*," he said to me tenderly.

"But I just want him back. Can't I just have him back? It would heal everything for me," I cried.

"It wouldn't. I know you think it would, but it wouldn't. In fact, it would hinder it because you would be relying on an outside force to fix it for you. But I will say this…you have him back in all of the ways that matter. You were gifted something more than most people ever get after losing a loved one to death. You are connected to him in a way that many people would die for. Can you see that, and give gratitude for it?" he asked me.

I nodded my head.

"I am so deeply grateful for that. I wouldn't have made it through if that hadn't happened. If we had never reconnected, I would have taken my own life. May I ask though…why I was given that gift? I have often thought about how many people long to talk to their loved ones on the other side and it never happens. I get to continue this journey of my life, this lifetime, with him still by my side in many ways that I never dreamed possible. I can hear him now. We have this space of journeying to spend time together. I feel him. I see him sometimes. Why? Why me?" I asked sincerely.

"You just said it yourself. You would have taken your own life if it hadn't happened. You haven't completed the lesson that you came to learn yet, dear one. You were given what was necessary to keep you here in order to do so," he replied.

I pondered this. The answer only led to more questions.

"Forgive me if I'm overstepping here...but why does it matter in the scheme of things? Why does one single human's life lesson matter so much that such a gift was given? Why...and to whom...does it matter if I live or not?" I asked.

Jesus smiled at me with amusement.

"You aren't overstepping, and I promise that those answers will be given to you in time, but right now I just need you to trust that we will bring you that information when you have ears for it. I will give you a very brief answer to what you just asked for the time being. You are on a path to enlightenment, my child. Each soul that reaches enlightenment raises the vibration of the collective consciousness. So, each soul matters. Every single one. It is like adding sugar to lemonade. Each granule makes the container a little bit sweeter. Each awakened soul sweetens the lemonade," he said.

I stared at him blankly. I wasn't sure I was grasping what he was trying to tell me.

He laughed at the face I was making.

"I think that's enough for now. We will revisit these questions, I promise. Right now, just focus on the healing part of your path. There is no need to cut corners or try and take a shortcut to knowledge. It can only be understood when you come to the portion of your walk that requires you to receive it," he said, still chuckling softly.

The sweetness of his tone and the love that I still felt radiating from him allowed me to laugh at myself along with him. It was fine that I didn't understand. I wasn't meant to yet, clearly.

I thought about all that had been shown to me this evening. I wanted to make absolutely sure that I walked away with all of the knowledge that I *had* been able to comprehend.

"So... just to reiterate...because I don't want any of this time to be wasted or forgotten...I came here this lifetime to heal a wound from the masculine. J and I planned out our love so that I would be willing to fix this, and I lost him because I have to do it internally? I have to learn to step into my truth, which is a Divine Feminine essence....and the only way to do this is to trust and surrender to the Divine Masculine? Right?" I asked.

He nodded.

"All correct except for the part where you said you 'planned your love.' You planned the *lesson*. The love between you has existed as long as your soul has. J IS your Divine Masculine. He just resides in you now. When you can reach a balance within yourself of the masculine and feminine, you will understand Divine wholeness. One thing leads to the other. A microcosm and the macrocosm, if you will. It's a path to God…assuming that you are ok with that title now?" he said with a wink.

"I still like 'Spirit' better, but I don't hate the name as much now," I replied.

He laughed.

"Such a stubborn child. I have to leave you now, your journey is coming to an end this evening," he said.

It made me sad.

Turns out all of the years of professing my disdain for Jesus had been in vain.

I loved this man standing before me.

He, without question, loved me too.

"One more piece of advice, if I may?" he asked.

I nodded for him to continue.

"In the same way that you had to let yourself be completely broken into a million parts before you could begin to put yourself back together……you are going to have to completely let go of everything in order for it all to be given back to you." he said.

Huh?

"That feels more like a riddle than a nugget of wisdom," I replied.

"It's not. It can be summed up in one word, my beloved: Surrender. Keep surrendering, Jen. When you don't know what to do, simply let it all go. When you are hurting, surrender everything. Trust in Spirit with all of your being. When you think you have surrendered it all, surrender even more. Then sit back and watch all of the goodness flood into your life," he said.

And with that, he was gone.

I slowly opened my eyes and begin to orient myself back into the space that my physical body occupied in front of the fire.

I blinked several times and then looked to my right to see Kat perched on the couch above me, drinking tea and looking at me quizzically.

"You ok down there, foxy?" she asked.

"Yeah…I…met Jesus," I said. I didn't even try to hide the disbelief in my voice.

"Oh? Did he have anything interesting to tell you?" she asked with a bemused smirk.

I thought about all that had been said. It was so much. I was still trying to wrap my mind around all of it. I didn't have words for it all yet.

I chose to simply say,

"Yeah. He told me I was…. straight," I said in the same tone I would have used if I had just discovered a hair in my food.

Kat burst out laughing so hard I couldn't help but join her.

361

I lay there laughing so hard with my friend, my teacher, my guide. I realized that I was so beyond blessed to be in this moment.

I told her I loved her. I wanted to make sure that she knew.

I found myself in the deepest gratitude for the gift of this work with the medicine.

The experience I had just had felt like it had accomplished what years of therapy hadn't been able to do.

I knew how to work with or around the fear now because I knew where it came from.

I knew the root cause of it all.

It was as if the camera had zoomed out and I could see the bigger picture of my whole life, if only for a moment.

Healing this finally felt doable, because now I knew that the fear and loss and the heartache all had a purpose.

I hadn't been stripped of everything I loved for nothing.

I hadn't been randomly destroyed for no reason.

I had simply been disassembled in order to be rebuilt differently.

The caterpillar has to disintegrate into an unrecognizable blob of goo in the cocoon before it can emerge as something different altogether.

The phoenix burns to ash before it rises.

I had a map now. This whole entire time I had been longing for something to hold on to that would make it all make sense.

It had finally been given to me; folded neatly and wrapped up in a pretty bow with the instruction "surrender" written across the top.

Spirit was taking care of it all.

The weight of an entire lifetime seemed to lift off of my broken shoulders.

For the first time in my life, I felt like I could breathe.

Part Eight

chimaira : *noun*

a.: mentioned in the *Iliad* of Homer and called,
"The Fire Which Never Goes Out"

b.: an eternal flame

Chapter Thirty-One

I BOOKED A WEEKEND retreat with Kat before I left her place. My parents' cabin, the cabin where J and I had spent our last evening together, had an open weekend in eight weeks. I decided to bring Kat there and try and get a small group together for a two-journey weekend. We put it on the calendar, and I came home.

The Jesus journey (as I had been referring to it) had mentally, emotionally, and physically exhausted me.

Integration is the hardest work of plant medicine. The journeys themselves are often full of mystical and magical insights, as well as downloads about your patterns and behaviors and how they are affecting your life.

It's a lot of information to absorb, and it's even more difficult to apply. Typically for weeks after a journey I'm solemnly trying to process what all took place and trying to integrate the lessons into my life. There is also an emotional kickback that leaves me feeling raw and exposed.

After this particular journey Kat warned me that integration would likely take even longer, as I had been working with fear that had been present since childhood as well as other heavy information that affected my entire thought processes surrounding my very identity.

I had braced myself for several rough weeks.

Oddly, that is not what happened at all.

From the moment I got home, J was distractingly loud in my ear about the upcoming journeys that I had scheduled at my parent's cabin.

"I have things to tell you."

"Let me make it right for you, my love."

"It's the last place we were together…let me redo that night."

"Let's go back in time together."

"I want to make things right."

365

I found it curious.

When I asked him what he thought he needed to "make right," he wouldn't answer.

But he persisted over the next few weeks so strongly that it was not only impossible to ignore, it was nearly all-consuming in my awareness. Each time my thoughts drifted too far from the subject, J turned up the volume even louder.

He then began to ask me to invite Chrystopher, the medium that I had met at my first journey, to come Friday night to the cabin.

"I want you to ask Chrystopher to come. I have things that I want to say to you that I don't want you to hear inside your head. I want them to come from someone else's mouth so that you never doubt what I am going to tell you.

"Write him, Jen. Write him and ask him to come," he pushed me.

"I want him to let me use him as a channel. Ask him, please."

I didn't know what to think.

A good portion of the time I still questioned whether or not I was actually hearing J, but this was so loud and so clear and so insistent that I knew it wasn't coming from me. I finally decided to give in. A sat down and wrote Chrystopher a letter, wondering if I was so far off base with what I was hearing that he would think I was nuts.

Chrystopher,

I have something to ask you.

This is a very vulnerable place to be, and a very difficult thing to ask.

I'm aware that you may not be able to work this out, and if not that is ok, because I firmly believe that Spirit lines things up and works things out in the exact way that they are meant to happen. That being said, I keep hearing that I need to ask you this. (Frequently and loudly enough that I am writing this letter.)

When I got back from my last journey, I expected to be processing through the very hard work that I did that night. But from the minute I got home, J has been talking to me earnestly about the August first weekend journeys that I booked with Kat. I have a small group of women coming Saturday night, but as of right now, I am the only one journeying on Friday night.

So it's just me. On a solo journey. At the cabin where J and I spent our last night together.

He somehow orchestrated this, and I think it has been the intent from the beginning.

When I got home last week, he asked me for a redo.

All I've heard, over and over and over....in my head, and on the breeze, and coming off of the water is

"Let me make it up to you."

The Melody of Fire

"Let me make it right."

"Let's go back in time and redo that night."

"There were things unsaid that I need to tell you."

He also told me that he really wanted to get you there, because he didn't want me to hear what he had to say in my head. He said I still doubt that too much, and he wanted me to hear it come from the lips of someone else so that I would never, ever doubt the things that he told me. He said he wanted me to hold them in my heart from now on, and never look back and wonder if they came from me or from him.

So that brings me to the question.

I don't know if you have ever channeled a spirit…. I know you converse with them…. but I wondered if you might be willing to try in this case? He seems to be asking for this.

That is a big ask, I am aware. If that makes you uncomfortable, I understand and would be content with just letting him talk to you and you relaying the messages.

I do remember at that first journey, where you and I met that Kat came in and asked to talk to me privately. You said to go on and told both J and me that it was nice talking to us….and then you laughed because he apparently replied, "Oh, we're not done talking."

I can't help but think this was what he meant.

Whatever you decide or can/can't work out I know that I will still get everything I need at that journey, no matter how it comes in. Just let me know if this feels right to you.

Love,
Jen

Chrystopher called me a few hours after I emailed him.

"Of course, I will help you, Jen. I'm so honored that you even trust me enough to ask me to do this," he said.

I was relieved and overjoyed.

"Oh, Chrystopher. Thank you so much. I wasn't sure that you would be comfortable with that, but J was so insistent," I said.

"Actually…direct channeling is something that I have always wanted to try, but it just requires so much trust with the spirit that you are working with that I haven't ever been comfortable doing it. But I absolutely trust J. This will be beneficial for everyone involved. He gets his message delivered, you get to be in his presence again for a while, and I get to try something new that I probably wouldn't have gotten the opportunity to do otherwise," he replied.

"That is so great. I'm so excited now! What do you think it will be like? I don't even know what to expect…." I asked.

Chrystopher laughed.

"J just gave me the image from the movie *Ghost* where Patrick Swayze is dancing with Demi Moore…but it's Whoopi Goldberg's body. Do you know that movie?" he asked, still laughing.

"Ummm…I have loved that movie since I was a little girl and J knows that," I said as I laughed along with him.

He got quiet for a moment. I sensed that he was not waiting on me to speak, but instead listening to something else.

"Oh wow. His intention for this meeting is very interesting….do you know what it is concerning?" he asked.

"Not really. He keeps saying that he wants to 'make things right', but I don't know what he means by that. He also says he wants to redo our last night together at the cabin…but I don't really have any regrets about that night. I actually feel like I got the most perfect goodbye that a person could ever ask for. Our last night together was beautiful…and the last thing he ever said to me was that he didn't want to leave me. I don't know what could be redone that could be better than that, honestly," I said.

Chrystopher paused.

"Ok. He doesn't want me to tell you what he just told me, but just know that there is one thing that he thinks he can do to make it up to you. He wants to bring this in on his terms so I'm going to comply. I'll be there on August first! I'm so looking forward to this. It's going to be awesome. We will talk soon, my friend! I love you!" he said.

We said our goodbyes and I sat for a long time pondering what in the world J could possibly be orchestrating with all of this.

Suddenly I heard him again.

"Don't try and figure it out. Just let me love you. Trust me, please."

I thought back to the last night together at the cabin. If there was one thing he knew to be true without question it was that I had never been able to tell him "no". It seemed that even now (in fact, perhaps now more than ever) I still would do whatever he asked.

"All right, love. I'm following your lead here," I said out loud to him.

We confirmed the journey with Kat.

It would just be Kat and Chrystopher and me on the first night.

The second night would be a small group of women that included Carson.

I didn't even know where to begin with setting intentions, as it seemed J had an agenda all his own this time.

The Melody of Fire

"*Let me love you*".

"*Just receive it.*"

"*Stop trying to figure out what I'm going to say and let me surprise you. Clear your mind of any expectation.*"

"*Let me love you.*"

"*Let me love you.*"

All week prior to the journey weekend these were the whispers that I heard from J.

That, and so many love songs that I lost count.

I would be driving, and listening to a playlist on Spotify or Pandora, and I would hear,

"*Can I play you a song?*"

"Of course," I would respond.

It was a guarantee that the next song that came on would move me to tears and I would have to pull over. Usually a song I didn't know, by an artist I'd never heard of. It was as if every single lyric was from him to me.

He was romancing the hell out of me, and yet…I was still afraid.

I had two major fears about the upcoming journey that I couldn't seem to settle.

The first was that he was bringing me there to tell me to let him go. That I was going to have to move on in order to properly heal. I feared that it was a goodbye, and the very thought of having to lose him again tore my heart to pieces every time it popped into my mind.

The second fear was a very persistent trap that I had repeatedly fallen into since he died. What if time and distance had somehow escalated the intensity of everything in my mind? It had been about six months since our first journey together where we had been able to talk extensively. What if he had just tried to "patch things up" for me because I was hurting so badly? Was the relationship really as powerful and magical as I remembered? What if he never did feel the way I felt about him? Maybe I had just projected all that had been pouring out of me onto him in some way. I always thought we were on the exact same page (in fact, even the exact same word on the exact same page), but maybe I had romanticized it into something that it wasn't. I was afraid that maybe that was going to be the message. After all, though he told me frequently how he felt when he was alive (and I saw it all in his eyes), at the end of the day he didn't choose to be with me. I never truly felt validated. Maybe I was about to find out why. It broke my heart when I thought about it that way.

I wasn't sure what "healing" was supposed to look like. Did it mean I would have to be in a place where I was ok without J in my life in any form? Was that the agenda of Spirit? Jesus had talked about the balancing of the masculine and

369

the feminine within myself…was I expected to get to a point of feeling whole without J? I didn't trust anything as "solid" anymore. I was still fighting a very strong knee-jerk reaction to anything that appeared to bring me the joy and happiness that I had felt with J in the physical. My entire being seemed to wince in fear at the prospect of happiness because of what horror might follow it. While this restored psychic connection was beautiful, I was so sure that it couldn't last - that the reconnection would be ripped violently away from me once again. I was bracing myself to have my teeth kicked in should I dare to smile for too long. I felt like the very best thing I could do to protect myself was to try and anticipate the direction that the blow might come from.

These were the thoughts that were reeling in my mind. I was trying to let them go, but they were persistent. And then J would come in once more with what was beginning to feel like a mantra.

"Let me love you."

I did my very best to surrender to it fully by the night before the journey.

I went to bed that night with some peace about the whole thing and had begun to allow myself to have flutters of excitement. I was about to have a whole night with my love again, just to be in his energy fully and talk and laugh with him. I would have paid any amount of money or gone to any lengths to have that one more time, and it was about to happen. I decided to just try and put my fears aside and rest my focus on that.

That night I had a very vibrant dream about the Saturday night journey.

I was with the group of women that had arrived at the cabin, and we all gathered to hold the opening of the ceremony together. The women were sitting in the field in front of the cabin, but the cabin was a stage. We were all wearing white (and each person was wearing the color in the version/style that they would wear in real life), including me. There was singing and someone was drumming and there was a tambourine that one of the girls was playing.

I looked around at the scene before me. There was nothing on the stage yet, but we were clearly there to witness an event. The energy was lovely, and the music filled up the night sky. It felt so beautiful. I was a little sad when I woke up, only because I wanted to be in that place a little longer. I realized that I had been so excited about Friday night's promise of time with J that I had given almost no thought to what Saturday's journey might hold. The dream felt very feminine in its message.

Whatever we were being gathered to witness felt like it revolved around connecting to the Divine Feminine, surrounded by my sisters. I felt a tingle of excitement.

I got out of bed looking forward to experiencing what would unfold over the next two days. I couldn't wait to see what Spirit had in store. I made myself some breakfast and sat on my mat for a few minutes to try and tap in. After meditation, I was staring out the window with a cup of coffee in hand, watching the river flow by when suddenly, I saw a flash of bright color so close to my vision that it took a second for my eyes to adjust and my mind to register what I was looking at.

To my delight, a tiny hummingbird hovered directly in front of my face, wings fluttering so fast I couldn't even make them out.

He cocked his head this way and that, as if trying to make out what I was.

His joyful playfulness made me laugh out loud. As I did so, he flew backward just a little, but then back close to my face just on the other side of the window.

"There is your guide for this weekend," I heard Spirit say to me as I continued to be amazed that this happy little creature wasn't the slightest bit afraid of me.

I marveled at his long beak and bright feathers.

He stayed engaged with me for about five minutes before my mother's flowers seemed to call to him. I watched him drink the nectar from them, flying in all directions. He had such freedom of mobility. It had been so long since I had seen one in action; I had forgotten that they could maneuver with such ease.

Hummingbirds exude such happiness and freedom. I found myself whispering a prayer of gratitude for this tiny spirit guide. If this was my path leader for the weekend, I couldn't wait to see what was in store. I would follow this little guy wherever he wanted to go.

I knew he was a very good omen.

When I arrived at the cabin Friday evening, Chrystopher was already there. He hugged me warmly when I walked in, and we began to talk almost immediately about the evening that lay ahead. I could tell he was excited too.

We sat in the living room of the cabin and while we were listening to music and catching up, I noticed his eyes flicker to the right a few times as if something had caught his attention.

"J is standing right there," he pointed to his right, where I had seen him look. He described him in great detail, including what he was wearing. 'He's wearing a hat…not like a ball cap. I don't know how to describe it. It's gray…and flat?" he said.

I knew exactly what hat he was speaking of -J's gray newsboy cap that he wore nearly every day. I nodded, and he continued.

"He is wearing jeans…but they are a grayish color, and a button down. He is wearing skater shoes, but not name-brand. He is very specific about that?" he said as if he were uncertain as to why that was a detail included.

I knew why. He would have been that specific when he was living. He cared a great deal about his clothes and appearance. His Leo was showing, even as a ghost. Chrystopher described his hair, a light brown that now had some salt and pepper in it, and how it curled out from the back of his cap gently.

Chrystopher laughed suddenly and said that J had opened his mouth wide and said, "Well if you are going into that much detail here… you can look in my mouth and tell her about my broken tooth."

I cracked up, but it really was extra validation for me (not that I really needed it at this point) that he was really talking to him. Until that moment, I had completely forgotten about J's broken tooth. No one would have known about that except me (and his family), but he had complained about it quite a bit in the few weeks leading up to his death. I remembered that I had even called him out about how whiny he was being about it the last time we were together in this very room. I realized that J was making sure that I knew with absolute certainty that Chrystopher was hearing and seeing him perfectly clearly.

"Now he's telling me that he wants to sit down, because his old knees hurt," Chrystopher said, rolling his eyes. "As if I am the one who is making him stand right there while we talk. He walked up to ME."

I laughed again.

"He was only 42 years old when he passed, but he always made jokes about being old. Especially about his knees and the gray in his beard," I said.

I loved that Chrystopher was getting to see a little window into J's humor. It was one of my favorite things about him, and this little preamble was reminding me how very much I had missed just his general state of good-natured playfulness. We were already being enveloped in his energy.

"Sit down then, I'm not the one making you stand there," Chrystopher said, looking at the spot where he had told me that J was standing. I watched his eyes follow what appeared to be nothing physical and settle on the couch to my left. I pointed to the spot where his eyes had landed.

"He's here now?" I asked.

"Yes, and rubbing his knees and groaning about them dramatically." He laughed.

"So ridiculous. You are truly getting a taste of my boy," I said.

Chrystopher's face became solemn suddenly.

"I just saw you going through some very heavy stuff this journey. Spirit just showed me an image of you, and you were wailing…deep, heavy sobs," he said.

My stomach dropped. I felt my fears bubbling up to the surface.

Losing him again. Finding out it wasn't the same love that I thought it was.

My mind began to spiral.

"Can you give me a little heads up regarding what it is about?" I said. my voice shaking a bit.

"It's your grief. I see you dropping into the depth of your grief, and I see you being taken back to the exact moment," he replied.

"The exact moment….?" I asked. What exact moment?

The Melody of Fire

"The exact moment when you heard that he passed," he said.

I thought back to where I had been when I heard he was gone. It was such a strange moment for me. His best friend had told me they were going to take him off the ventilator and machines the day before, so I was expecting it. But no one even told me exactly when it happened. I had received no call or text letting me know it was over. I had simply watched for a Facebook update to confirm that he was, in fact, gone.

It had hurt me badly, but it didn't feel like the worst portion of my grief. I was intrigued, and a little afraid…but at least I knew it wasn't a goodbye from J tonight that was going to bring on the wailing.

I nodded at Chrystopher.

"Thank you for warning me," I said.

He stood up and said that he wanted to change clothes and freshen up a bit.

He gave me a hug on his way to the bathroom, and I decided that I would set up the space a little.

I had brought fresh sunflowers, partially because they were my favorite and partially because it was Leo season and sunflowers are their flower. I arranged them in vases on the table and outside on the porch. They were huge and lovely. It made me happy. I imagined that I was decorating to welcome J back to our space. A homecoming for a night together. I found myself smiling the whole time.

I came back inside and out of my bag I pulled out the things I wanted to put on the "altar." I designated the fireplace mantel as the sacred space.

I carefully placed a few crystals that were special to me, including a selenite sphere that reminded me of the moon, at either end. I had a small ceramic square painting of a fox that my sister had gifted me. I always want my animal spirit guides close by for journeys. Then, carefully, one after the other I placed seven pictures of J (and of us together) in a layered collage-type fashion across the fireplace. I was extra careful this time, because of the photo I had lost at Kat's cabin. Then at one end, I put an oracle card with a painting depicting a woman with her eyes closed and her hands on her heart. It was titled "Surrender" and I knew that I would need the reminder this weekend. On the other side, I placed a print of one of my favorite twin flame paintings.

I stepped back and switched and adjusted a few things, and was admiring the layout (and, not gonna lie…J's eyes) when Chrystopher walked up behind me and shrieked, "Oh my GOD. That's him???"

When I turned, he had his hand over his mouth and looked more than a little taken aback.

"That is so crazy. A spirit will often tell me or show me what they look like but that is exactly what he gave me. That's the only time I've ever seen a photo and it was exactly what I had seen in my head. THE HAT even…I didn't know how to describe that, but he showed me that hat. Also…he is HOT. I would have been all about him," he said.

We both laughed.

"Yeah, I actually have a strong feeling that is one of the reasons why he chose you from the get-go. I think he knew that and wooed you a bit. He likes you too," I said. I felt very confident in saying that. He always did love attention from either gender. As I have said before, he was very confident and comfortable in his sexuality.

Kat arrived about two hours later than what she had originally intended. She walked in the door in a whirlwind of bags, blankets, and wild red hair. She said she had gotten lost, ended up somewhere in another state, and had no GPS signal. She told me had been afraid and that she had asked J for help. He guided her back to where she needed to be.

My boy had had a busy day, it seemed. Getting us all where we needed to be safely.

Kat gave us both hugs, put her stuff down, and asked where we wanted to go to begin the ceremony.

"Let's walk down to the dock that I always sit on. It's beautiful and I'd love for you guys to see it. We can watch the sunset," I suggested. They both thought it was a good idea, and we all began the walk down.

The light was just starting to get pink and glimmered off of the water, as we found a place to sit on the small dock. We all just took in the gorgeous scenery and the flow of the water for a bit before Kat began the opening of the evening.

"This is a very unorthodox journey. The whole situation is just totally different from any other journey I've led before. But I'm excited to be here and bear witness to what is going to unfold tonight. I'm intrigued and feel honored to get to see Chrystopher use his gifts, and to hear what healing message comes through for you, Jen. Chrystopher, do you want to talk a bit about why you are here?" she said.

"Well, as you know I am here to help Jen. I'm honored and excited as well to see what happens tonight. I just pray to be a clear channel and bring in the messages that she needs to hear, and that J is trying to deliver, in the way that they need to come in. I'm trying to release myself of the pressure of wanting to perform well and asking to only say things that are meant to be said without flavoring them in any way by trying to piece things together for my own clarity. As long as things make sense to Jen, that is all that matters. I feel good about it. I'm excited to be here to help," he said and smiled sweetly at me.

"I'm here for it. Jen, we know that J brought you here, but do you have anything you want to add about hopes or intentions for the journey tonight?" Kat asked.

I took a deep breath. I didn't really want to tell them about my fears of this being a second ending for J and me. So, I decided to talk about my grief.

The Melody of Fire

"You know, I still am grieving SO hard. Some days it is still debilitating. I can cry at the drop of a hat…the pain sits just below the surface at all times - just looking for a place to pour out of. I just feel like I can't get over this. If I could just get over the other side of this mountain of grief, maybe I could start moving forward a little. I'm hoping that maybe tonight I can be shown how to get a little relief from the constant presence of pain. I'm so tired of hurting like this all of the time," I said. I was sobbing now, tears rolling down my face as I finished speaking. Kat reached over and held my hand. She had me take a few deep breaths with her and calm down a bit.

She reached into her pocket and pulled out 3 tiny capsules.

She said a prayer of deep gratitude. She asked Spirit to guide us and protect us through the journey, and for the highest good of all involved to unfold. She gave us each a capsule and we took them together.

I was about to pee on myself from being outside so long so I suggested we go back to the cabin. Chrystopher walked a bit ahead of Kat and me, and I could tell he was in deep contemplation. He would later tell me that on his way back he was in conversation with J, asking him to help him say what he wanted to say to me. He was settling into trust with him, opening up to allowing him to come into his body and speak.

While I went to the restroom Kat pulled fuzzy blankets and pillows down next to the fire pit and made a lovely little nest for us to relax in. I sat on the porch watching the river and the fire for a bit, waiting for the medicine to kick in. By now I was used to the telltale sign and when my vision went slightly wonky for a second and then settled back into place, I knew I was in the field.

I walked down to the blankets and pillows where Kat and Chrystopher were sitting and talking. When I sat down next to Chrystopher he pulled me close and then we lay down together and he held me tight.

"Are you in?" he whispered.

"Yes," I replied.

"Ok. I am too. When I speak, I am probably going to use 'I' and the first person a lot because I am just going to let it come straight from him. If he doesn't come straight through my mouth, I am going to relay it that way. I'll try and make a distinction between when I am relaying or paraphrasing something, and when he is directly speaking, ok? I'll try my best to make it crystal clear for you to know who is talking at all times. He says he has a lot to say….and that we have all night," he said.

"Ok. Thank you," I said.

As it turned out, he didn't even need to preface the evening with that. I was afraid I would be confused about the mechanics of the channeling, but the entire evening I would find that I had zero issue discerning when I was talking to J and when I was talking to Chrystopher.

I heard a clear distinction in the change of who was "driving the car" so to speak, and I could tell in Chrystopher's eyes when he was present and when he wasn't. We would talk after it was all over and find that there were big pieces of conversation that Chrystopher couldn't remember at all.

I will do my best to relay it here as it was told to me, and to make it easy to follow, I will tell you when J is speaking and when it is Chrystopher.

The switch flipped almost immediately, and J came through with an intensity and passion that was unmistakable.

"Why are you trying so hard to get over me? Why are you in such a hurry to heal? This was *everything*, Jen. It is such a beautiful love. I would be so pissed if you were able to just lay that to the side and walk away as if it wasn't what we both know it was," J said.

"I...don't really want to get over it...I'm just so tired of hurting like this," I replied.

"Jen, the loss of a great love can't help but bring great pain. But you can find a balance...a way to hold happiness and joy in your heart and still honor this tremendous loss. I will help you, but you need to realize that this wound is so deep...it deserves the time and attention it takes to heal it. I hurt being separated from you too. It's why I brought you to the plant medicine from the get-go. I had to reconnect with you again. That first journey together was so beautiful, but I still have a lot to say. Your job tonight is to listen, and like I have been telling you all week...let me love you. Let me do it in the way I want to and let me try and make things right for you. Can you do that?" he said.

"Yes," I whispered. My stomach fluttered a little. So, it wasn't a goodbye. He didn't want me to let him go. I allowed myself to release that fear.

Chrystopher popped back in. "He says that he actually really wanted to start this way...he intended to until he heard what you said at the dock. He wants me to sing this to you...." he said.

He began to sing "Unchained Melody." I laughed softly as tears rolled down my cheeks. Always the romantic, he was playing me the song from the movie *Ghost*, before he came back in like my very own Patrick Swayze to have a channeled dance with his love. It was *so* like him. He knew I loved that scene. Forever the charmer, my love. I lay in Chrystopher's arms and listened to the words with new ears.

J came back through.

"I wanted to be with you. I thought about leaving a hundred times. There were so many logistics that came into play on my end. I financially carried the household. My children would have suffered terribly if I had left them unstable like that. I had planned on putting things into place to support them as much as I could and then making the leap. I'll be honest…I also took advantage of the fact that you were allowing me to let it take longer. You never really pushed me to leave, so I let it ride along as it was because of that. But I never really thought that you doubted so much that I really did want us to be together. I'm so sorry that you never felt validated. I was working you into my life…did you not see how I was introducing you to the people I loved the most…bringing you in slowly so that they would know and love you already when that transition finally happened? 'This is Jen'…I would say…and proudly introduce you. I knew they would love you. I just had to get you around them. That all had a purpose, love. I was making the move. Just not fast enough," he said.

"I just always felt like maybe I wasn't enough for you," I was crying heavily now.

"You were sooo sooooo much, Jen. Too much, really. I often couldn't believe that you loved me the way that I loved you. I always thought you would find someone better and move on without me. I feared that, but I expected it. I didn't think I deserved *you*.

"I was so deeply in love with you. I can't believe I ever left room for doubt in your mind about that. I let you down in that way, love. I should have told you every single day how beautiful and how wondrous you are to me. I'm going to spend the rest of your lifetime making that up to you. I promise you that you will never again doubt my love for you. I'll find a million different ways to show you, and you will live the rest of your life knowing without question the depths of my love for you," J said.

I sighed, contentedly.

"I think I just took for granted that because of the telepathic connection, and the overwhelming sense of oneness that happened every time we made love…that you just knew beyond any shadow of a doubt how I felt for you," he said.

"Well, let's not downplay the sex. If there was any time that I *did* feel absolutely certain about the connection, it was definitely in those moments," I replied. "My God, I miss that, J."

Chrystopher entered back into the conversation.

"He is showing me so much sexual imagery. He wants to have rough, very animalistic sex with you. It's so primal and hot, the visual he's giving me. He wants me to tell you how much he LOVED your body. Your legs and your feet. Your hair…he loves how red it is and he is showing me his fingers tangled in it. He says that he loved pulling it and feeling your reaction," he said. I gasped slightly upon recalling how it had felt.

"Perfect. He says your breasts are perfect. He just showed them to me, sorry…" he said. We both laughed.

"It's ok. He used to tell me that I had 'comic book tits' because he thought they were so round and even that it looked like someone drew them," I told him as I chuckled at the memory.

"He made me feel like the sexiest creature alive."

"*You are,*" J whispered to me in my mind.

"He says he tried to love you through your insecurities. To love them so hard that you could let them go. Your inexperience with men, your belly, your height… those things that he sensed you were self-conscious about - he tried to just shower them with extra love. He never wanted you to give them a second thought. He wanted you to see yourself the way he saw you," Chrystopher continued.

"He *worshipped* your body. He's showing me just burying his face below your stomach and between your legs. He's going on and on about how much he loves the way you taste. He just said he was addicted to you," Chrystopher said.

I sighed. "I was addicted to him too. Our sex was fire… and I loved his body just as much as he loved mine," I said.

"Oh wow. He had a nice dick. He just showed me…" Chrystopher said.

"Well… I'm not very well versed in dicks, but I thought so," I said.

"Well, I am, so trust me, it's nice. It's so…."

"Thick," we both said together at the same time. We laughed with surprise that we said the same exact word.

Chrystopher leaned into my ear and J growled through him. "It was made for that pussy."

I felt a jolt of response go through my body as he said it, and I had to remind myself that he wasn't there physically and to keep my hands to myself. He must have made a similar move on Chrystopher because he began laughing and said, "Oh, really? He just informed me that if he were here physically, we would be having a threesome tonight and that it would be so hot."

"Undoubtedly. See, I told you he was flirting with you," I said. I was zero percent surprised at this information. I suddenly heard J in my head, the way I had gotten used to hearing his voice. "We always talked about bringing another person into the bedroom…he would have been perfect."

"He's not into girls, J." I replied.

"No…but he would have loved me…and you know how the two of us were in bed. It would have been delicious. He would have *loved* it," he said.

I giggled as he gave me my own series of images to view like a movie in my head of the three of us in bed together. I wouldn't tell Chrystopher about it until the next day.

Chrystopher continued, "He is showing me with a dog collar around his neck and you holding a chain. He says he loved for you to dominate him. I see you fucking him with a strap-on, and he is submitting to you and enjoying every second of it."

I was a little caught off guard that he showed him that. I had been wavering on how much of our sex to include in my book as I was writing it because I wasn't sure if he would want me to relay that to the world. He was so strong. SO masculine. I loved it when he dominated me, but I loved it more when he submitted. I just wasn't sure if he would want me to talk about it. He of course read my mind, and through Chrystopher he said, "Tell it. Tell all of it. You were so sassy and such an alpha, and as much as I made you feel safe in masculine energy, you allowed me to feel safe in feminine power. It's important. Tell it."

He then went on to remind me of things that we had done, and to very graphically tell me all the things he wanted to do to me again while I was lying there on that blanket.

Thankfully, this was one of the portions that Chrystopher would not remember.

"Naughty girl," Chrystopher said out loud. I wasn't sure if it came from him or J, or how much Chrystopher had seen.

"He wants you to know that over the next few weeks, there will be intense sexual energy. You will have very vivid dreams of the two of you having sex. He wants you to know that when that happens….it is really happening. You are meeting on that plane to have that together again. It's real, ok?"

"Oh my God…THANK YOU. I've wanted that for so long. Ever since he passed, I have been hoping that would happen.", I responded. I thought about how much I had longed to touch him again. Longed for the sex. Ached for it. I was excited to feel him again, on whatever plane it needed to happen.

"He said he knows you have been, but that you also, deep down, wanted this night with him. You called it in. You manifested it, and you have manifested the dreams," Chrystopher said.

"He just told me that Kat and I are playing with fire when it comes to you. Your healers have been trying to coax all of this power out of you and have been asking you to step into it. He just said we have no idea how much is underneath there. *Playing with fire.*"

I marveled at this. I hoped it was true.

I had no idea what it meant, but for the past six months my new healer friends, including Chrystopher, had been telling me that my gifts were about to explode. That I had merely scratched the surface of what was to come. I was intrigued.

"He is giving me songs that he wants me to sing to you… so I am going to just follow what he gives me," Chrystopher said.

He began to sing love song after love song to me. J always did speak to me through music. On stage. Writing together. Singing together. Sending me songs (as of late). It was no surprise that he would sing to me right now.

I just lay there and listened in awe of how he wove the songs together. He would stitch sections of different songs together in a way that flowed together perfectly but said the most beautiful parts of each. He was romancing me through song, yet again.

"Girl, he is putting on a show for you," Chrystopher said in between lyrics, and then suddenly he stopped.

"Oh my God. Ok. I thought that was where this was going......he was clowning around and putting on a huge display and singing....and he just stopped, dropped to one knee, and is proposing to you with a ring in his hand," Chrystopher said.

"WHAT??!!" I squealed with shock.

"That is why he brought you here. That is how he wants to make it right. He told me that earlier in the week, and I thought you might have known. Clearly, you didn't. Did you all ever talk about getting married?" Chrystopher asked.

I was sobbing.

"We talked about our future as a couple often. It all felt like it was heading in the direction of marriage. I felt so robbed of that opportunity when he died...it just destroyed me that I would never get to know what being his wife would feel like..." I said. Tears were streaming down my face.

"He wants you to call him your husband when you refer to him. You are to say, "I lost my husband" when you talk about him to other people. He loves that verbiage, and he wants you to own it," Chrystopher said.

I looked at my left hand. There was a silver, rustic metal band with a white stone in the setting that had a rainbow veining running through it. It sparkled and shone like the moon.

"Is it moonstone?" I asked him.

"Opal," J replied.

It was beautiful. I was still in shock.

"I had it with me. Carried it with me. I intended to give it to you as a promise. I almost gave it to you that last night at the cabin. Do you remember how I almost said something to you a hundred times that night but backed out every time? You asked me about it, remember? That was what I was going to say. I was going to give you the ring finally... and promise you that you would be my wife one day.

"I wanted to marry you, Jen. I intended to marry you," J said. "I had planned out asking your dad- I had gone through the whole scenario in my head of what I was going to do the minute that I got divorced. I still want you to tell your parents, babe. I loved them, and I want them to know about our love. I want them to know what a beautiful thing we had."

I felt fear run through my body at the very thought of telling my parents the truth.

Chrystopher chimed back in

"He says that is part of the reason why you are here this weekend. You need to tell your parents. You need to tell your friends. You need to tell your story. He WANTS you to tell it. He says that you have *the most beautiful love story,* and that you need to let it be heard. But he also says that you need to tell it because no one truly knows what you lost. You have been carrying a mountain of pain. *Alone.* You've been dying in private, putting on a mask and walking out into the world trying to pretend you were fine. You need to let people help you carry this. Let them see your pain…and if you say it the way that is true, people will shower you with compassion. 'I lost my husband. I lost our baby.' Do you see how much deeper that resonates? It's not 'my best friend passed away,' or even 'my lover passed away.' Call it what it was. Stand in your truth," he said.

"He says he wants you to finish the book that you are writing. He will help you, and it will be received in a more loving way than you can even wrap your mind around. He wants the world to know your love story. He wants you to tell it all. Stand in the light with your truth and your love. He's right there with you. He says the secret ends now," he continued.

"I've been so afraid of that book. I didn't want to tell things that he didn't want shared. I was afraid he wouldn't want his children, especially, to find out all of that," I said, with deep sadness.

J came back through.

"Tell it, Jen. Seriously, I want you to tell all of it. My kids will read it one day, and I want them to. I want them to know about the love we had. I want them to see the human side of their father. They will look back and remember all of the 'dad' moments, but there will come a time when they will yearn to know who their father was as a person. They loved you, you know. Especially my daughter," he said.

"I loved them too, J. I really thought that I would be their stepmother. I was preparing myself for that," I said.

"I know. I was too. I kept trying to bring you into that role more when you were around them. Making sure they connected with you and had a chance to love you before I made a move. There will come a time when my daughter will reach out to you to reconnect. You know, she is very musically inclined…I think you two might sing together a little. She misses you. My son does too, though he was a little less aware of my affection for you. I need to warn you also, that Lila will read the book. There is a confrontation coming between the two of you. It may happen before the book comes out. She will yell and scream at you, and it will be very painful for you…but I need you to hold your peace and just let her say what she needs to say, Jen. There is nothing that you can say that could soften or smooth it over, but you could injure her even deeper if you retaliate. You already won the war here…there is no need to destroy her. Just let her express what she needs to so that she can move on and begin to heal this. She is angry at you the way that you are angry at death, because you took me away from her long before death ever did. You know that feeling, so please honor her loss. Let her have her say. You did that when I was in the hospital, under even worse circumstances when everything was so up in the air. You can do it again. Hold your tongue and give her that. It will help ease your guilt for the pain you caused as well," he said.

Nausea washed over me at the very thought of that confrontation. I agreed to do what he was asking. I was grateful for the warning, and the guidance on how to handle it. I had spent a year and a half kicking myself for all of the things that I felt I should have said to her in that hospital bathroom. I knew with certainty that I would have just taken this second confrontation as an opportunity to say all of the things I wished I had said then. It's a good thing he was stopping me now.

I agreed that I could hold my tongue. Or rather, that I would try. That was a lot of undoing of thought patterns on my part…but I could see how she neither asked for nor deserved what happened. And I could understand why all of her anger would be directed towards me. But most of all, I felt deeply sorry that I had been part of her hurting. I knew what losing him felt like too, and though it was very different in a lot of ways…. it also wasn't. Though the relationship had manifested differently for the two of us, we both lost the deepest love and the most special man we had ever known. We each wanted the parts that the other one had. She wanted the soul-deep connection that he had with me. The layered and spiritual and creative intimacy that we shared. I wanted to wake up in his arms in the morning and have coffee and time with him day to day. I wanted to be the mother of his children.

We were sisters in this grief, like it or not.

I tried to let it go. This was clearly going to be something that was going to require a lot more internal work on my part. I couldn't fix it now, and I felt like I was ruining time with J by stewing on it in this moment.

I tried to change the subject.

"Are you ok with me using your real name in the book?" I asked.

"You'd better," he said, and we both laughed.

"I'm fine with the world knowing how in love with you I am. I was so proud to be with you, Jen. That's not changed at all. I loved to show you off at shows. I could have looked at you for all of eternity. I *am* looking at you for all of eternity," J said.

Chrystopher nudged me gently. "He wants you to turn and face the fire- he wants to lie in front of you and stare into your eyes," he said.

I rolled over to face the fire. I saw J appear in my mind's eye, and we held each other's gaze tenderly.

"He wants me to sing to you again," Chrystopher said, and he began to sing Prince's song "I Would Die for You" softly behind me.

The Melody of Fire

He ended with his own words:

"I DID DIE FOR YOU."

The last words were spoken aloud, and I knew they came from Chrystopher's mouth, but I heard it in J's voice.

I began to sob as the words resonated and soaked into my soul.

I heard J whisper softly to me in my head, "Greater love hath no man than this…"

J began to speak through Chrystopher again.

"I'm ok now… but there was a moment in the hospital that I knew that I was going to die. I was so afraid, Jen. I had let the stress take over and my body just shut down…but I want you to know that even if I had known ahead of time what was going to happen, I could never have let you go. My love and desire for you mattered far more to me than anything -including my own well-being. I should have been taking care of myself, but I couldn't bear to walk away from you. I hadn't realized things had gotten that far gone with my health, and my biggest fear when I knew I was going to die was that I was going to lose you. You say I didn't choose you, but I actually chose you over everything. Every single day I put everything I loved on the line because you were first in my heart. I jeopardized every other thing, including my physical health, in order to hang on to you. Can't you see how very much I love you? What greater sacrifice can be given than my own life?" he said.

I was still weeping. The greatest love, indeed. Chrystopher pulled me back into him to hold me and when he did so, I found myself surrounded by the most familiar energy. So strong, yet so tender. Extremely masculine, yet with a softness that I recognized instantly. J had taken over the energy of his body fully, and as I buried my head in his chest, I knew I was back in my beloved's arms again. I felt myself melt into that embrace almost without thought. I was home. He wrapped me up and held me tightly as I murmured his name softly.

Divine masculine energy. J had been the first in my life to show it to me, and I had surrendered to it so willingly. Memories came flooding back to me like a river as I felt that tenderness overtake me again. I recalled fully as it enveloped me the safety that I always felt in my love's arms. This powerful force of a human, both physically and energetically, somehow was able to gently rein in all of that power when he touched me. He held me in his hands as carefully and tenderly as he would a delicate flower. Nestled. Nurtured. Worshipped. Safe. Protected from the harshness of the world, when he held me between his fingers.

Chrystopher fully embodied all of it as he allowed J to hold me through him. I could even smell him. I closed my eyes and surrendered, in bliss.

Safe for the first time since I lost him.

Held for the first time in a year and a half.

Appreciated, supported, and deeply loved.

I had almost forgotten what home felt like.

He held me for a long time without words.

Finally, it felt like a lifetime later, Chrystopher popped back in.

"He's showing me clocks and calendars…something about a child? Have you thought about trying to have a child?", Chrystopher asked.

"No. I never even really thought about having kids until I lost my baby.", I replied.

"Our baby.", J corrected me gently. "I wanted so badly to be the father of your children.", he said.

"I wanted that too." I whispered back. "I didn't know how badly I did until the chance was gone. I'm so sorry that I lost her, J." More tears. More heavy sighs.

"Oh, love. You couldn't have carried a healthy child in that state, it's not your fault at all. She wants to come back through though. If you have her, Jen, she will still be energetically our child. I'll still be the father. I can make sure she will have a strong father figure on earth, but she will be sooo loved and protected by me as well. But you need to decide if you want to…time is running out on that. Will you think about it?", he asked.

I paused. I was going to have to know more details about it. I would never even have hesitated if he were alive. I just wasn't sure to what degree I would feel that this child really was ours. And honestly, the thought of carrying, delivering, and raising a child alone at forty years old was very scary to me. However, in the same breath - here he was, holding me tight and asking me to consider it. If I thought I could even have a piece of him back through that child, I would do it. I told him I would think about it, but I wanted to talk to him more about it as well. He agreed.

"I just wish we had been allowed to have a little time, J. Just a little time to live fully in our relationship together…like a real couple," I said. It was something that I had said often to him out loud.

"If we had had more time, we would have had a lot more anal sex," J retorted.

Chrystopher and I cracked up.

"One track mind. Some things never change… but yes… we definitely would have. Wait. Are you talking about fucking me or me fucking you?" I asked.

"Yes." he replied.

We laughed again.

"In all seriousness, I wish that too…that we had more time. I wish it more than anything. We were so very close to having it, my love. So close," J said.

"I can't decide if hearing that makes it easier or harder.", I whispered.

"I know, believe me. I know," he answered.

Chrystopher and I lay tangled up there on the blankets for another hour

The Melody of Fire

or so…just laughing at things J would say, or at the banter that was happening between us all.

It was exactly like having him back in the flesh. The laughter. The discussions. The sexual energy. The overwhelming love.

I was so happy.

After a while, I heard J inside my head again. "My love… can you go inside for a bit? I'll meet you on the couch and we can talk just like this. I just have some work I want to do with Chrystopher tonight. Man stuff. Are you ok with that?" he asked.

My heart melted a little. I loved that he was going to work with Chrystopher, who had given so much to me tonight. I felt J shifting a little into father energy. It reminded me of when I used to watch him with his kids (or anyone's kids, really). He would drop into this side of himself that I rarely got to see. It was a teacher mode for him. He was always gentle to explain things and used nearly every moment as a teaching moment. It always made my heart explode to witness. I was always so proud to be with him, but none more so than when he was guiding and nurturing children.

It was fiercely attractive as well. Not even in a sexual way…more like in a "please be my baby daddy" kind of way. Coaxing a desire for children out of me that I hadn't even known was inside of me, lying dormant.

"I would love for you to do that. Thank you for that, sweet boy," I replied, also inside my head.

I kissed Chrystopher gently on the forehead and told him I was going inside for a bit.

He nodded wordlessly, and I knew J was already in his ear.

I came inside, went to the bathroom, and then nestled in on the couch in the cabin. The exact spot where I had sat naked in his lap in front of the fire on the evening of our last night together. I got comfortable and the images of that night came flooding back to me, not from my own memory, but through images that were from J's perspective.

He was showing them to me.

All of this sexual energy was almost unfair. I was reveling in it, but I was so turned on that I couldn't even sit comfortably. I was loving reliving it all, but I was more than a little mad that all of this had surfaced, and he wasn't physically here for me to touch.

"Hey!" J suddenly exclaimed inside of my head.

I jumped out of my skin a little, it startled me so.

"What??!" I replied slightly wide-eyed.

"You never said yes. Will you marry me, Jen?" he said much more gently.

I laughed. Silly boy, as if he didn't know.

"Oh my God…YES! Yes, yes, yes, yes, yes. With all of my heart, J. I would love to marry you. Thank you, thank you, thank you," I said.

I just kept repeating it over and over. The thank yous and the yeses. Gratitude and love spilled out of me.

He showed me the ring on my finger once more, and I felt him kiss me again and again.

"My Miss Jen," he whispered.

"My Missus."

He wrapped me tightly in his energy.

"We are the same soul, you know," he said.

"We got that part right. Twin flames. That really is our origin. We are two halves of a whole…in full union now."

He showed me in my mind a ring of fire. The circle in the middle was split between masculine and feminine energy, with a bit of each in the other side. Like a yin yang.

The balance was perfection.

"That's us now," he said.

"We were never meant to be apart. Our energy completes each other, and now you hold that entirely within you. I am within and around you. We are a unit again - merged back into one for all of eternity. Hieros gamos – the sacred divine marriage. It is all within your heart now."

I smiled dreamily as he spoke. It felt so true. I felt at home because I was home…. or maybe it was he that was home again finally. Nestled beneath my breastbone, for good this time. Stitched into my very cells.

Joy, which had become a stranger, returned to live in our house beneath my skin once again.

I drifted off to sleep that night amidst flashes and pictures of our last night together, and words of love from this night together still echoing in my ear.

Sex and passion merged with home and stability and validation.

We were one, again.

This time never to be severed.

Chapter Thirty-Two

I WOKE UP EARLY the next morning, before anyone else, and made coffee. I took it out on the porch to enjoy the river in the early morning hours. I was in a love bubble.

The last time I had been this happy was when J was physically in my arms. It felt so good to have that back again.

It felt good to have *him* back again.

Though I had been talking to him since that first plant medicine journey, I hadn't been able to tap into the layers of energy in the way that I had just received it.

He had been right to bring Chrystopher here. I would never doubt the things that were said to me last night. I would always look back and remember the way J's entire presence wrapped around me as I received the words that had touched my heart so deeply.

If it had all happened inside my own head, as I had grown accustomed to hearing him, I never would have believed it. Hearing it from the mouth of someone else and feeling it through someone else's touch made it undeniable to me.

I had never felt so very loved.

Heaven and earth had been moved to reunite us. I couldn't help but feel like there must have been some cosmic "rules" broken for this to happen.

As I pondered on it, I decided that I didn't really care if heaven itself was somewhere crumbling because of some breach of spiritual code that we had manipulated.

We were together again.

That is all I cared about.

Everything felt right again, finally.

I heard the porch door creak and Kat came out to join me, coffee in hand. She sat beside me on the swing. The previous evening her presence had been nearly undetectable. She had only interjected to make sure Chrystopher and I were comfortable and hydrated. She had merely stayed in close enough proximity to listen to us and tend to the fire pit – on hand should we need her for anything else.

"I don't know how you're feeling this morning, but I can only imagine. I feel like I just watched a Disney movie," she said.

We laughed.

"I got my prince back, that's for sure," I responded.

"Seriously though, what a beautiful fucking love story. I'm so happy for you! I'm in awe myself, and I was just an observer. I'm so honored that I got to witness that. It has renewed my belief in unconditional love and the power of the divine," she said.

I was touched.

It all felt unbelievable, even to me. Though I had never truly doubted our love, it certainly had been tested to the brink of all that was holy. Trials and tribulations while J was alive. Death tearing us apart. (In reality, all of the "laws" of the universe stated that it should have ended there.) Navigating the spirit realm…a new place for both of us. Coming back together in all of the beautiful ways, to merge back together in our love. Overwhelmed and overjoyed didn't begin to describe how I felt.

Part of me couldn't grasp what had happened.

The other half of me had always known that it couldn't have been any other way.

The human side was shocked. The eternal soul had known it was only a matter of time.

We never gave up on each other. Not really.

He came into the spirit realm like a goddamn tornado hell-bent on moving anything that stood in his path to get back to me.

I had clung tightly to the few messages that he sent me early on, and the undying belief that nothing could stop a love like we had.

A love that was so powerful, even death had to step aside.

I didn't understand why it had been gifted to us, but I certainly wasn't going to ruin things by dwelling on that.

Gratitude spilled out of me from every pore.

"What do you think tonight's journey will look like? Kind of hard to top that.", Kat said.

I felt a flicker of fear as I remembered what Chrystopher had seen. My wailing. My grief. It hadn't happened last night, so it must be coming during this journey.

I told Kat about the vision that he had seen when he first got there.

As I was relaying it to her, I heard Spirit in my head. "It's nothing that you

The Melody of Fire

haven't felt before. It's not any deeper than the grief you hold all of the time. But it needs to be seen. You need to allow yourself to be seen. It is important."

I had stopped talking to listen because the message was so loud. I told her what I had just heard.

"Mmmm. Yes. I see. Have you ever cried like that before? Full body wailing? Just to release all of that? Have you let yourself go there?" she asked.

'Oh, yes. I go there frequently when I am at home alone. I can't help it, really, it just washes over me and takes over. I have spent many an hour in that state,' I replied.

"But have you allowed yourself to go there in front of anyone else?" she asked.

I thought back. I hadn't. The circumstances surrounding my and J's relationship had made me feel like I had to hide all of that. My sobbing was done in the floor of my home, surrounded by the safety of solitude. I screamed, cried, and banged my fists on the floor in the peace of my apartment. The minute that I stepped outside it was with a mask on to cover that depth. Everyone knew I was not fine. No one knew exactly how not fine I was.

"No. Not even a little," I replied.

"I'm seeing a recurring theme here, Jen. Validation. J proposed to you to validate the relationship in a way that he hadn't done. He wants you to feel and express outwardly the love that you two had. He asked you to tell your parents… more validation. If they know why you are hurting so badly, it will make so much more sense to them. Also, if he hadn't passed you two would have eventually told them and it would have been honored and recognized by your parents at that point. You didn't get that experience. You were holding the entire universe in your hands, and you had to try and hide the light radiating from it. Show them. Allow yourself and your love to be seen by those who love you most. And now, the grief is surfacing to be seen. You have been carrying the weight of the world…alone. *Alone*, Jen. You don't have to do that, and no human being alive would be expected to. You lost your husband, as he so adamantly asked you to call him last night. You lost your child. If that had happened to any one of your friends, you would have been devastated for them. You would have held space to help them carry that grief in any way that you could, right?" she said.

"Of course. Though I now know that there isn't much, if anything, that anyone can truly do for someone who is in that state of grief," I said.

"You're wrong about that, because there is one thing that you haven't tried to do for yourself. You haven't allowed yourself to be seen. Your parents, your sister, your friends that love you, and the women coming here this evening- at least one of which loves you so very much…they can do one very powerful thing to help you. They can honor and behold the magnitude of your loss and your pain. They can offer to help carry some of it by simply being a witness to the depth of hurt. There is a grace that comes from that that you haven't experienced because you haven't allowed it. Let them shoulder some of the weight for you. Let them VALIDATE your loss, by letting them see it. You don't have to carry any of this in private anymore," she said.

I heard J remind me gently in my mind what he had said the night before.

"The secret ends now. Tell it. Tell it all. Let the world see."

I nodded, wordlessly as I processed through the guidance.

She was right. It was the one thing I hadn't tried. And it was feeling more and more like J and Spirit also knew it was the one thing I desperately needed.

About this time Chrystopher came out onto the porch, coffee in hand, looking like he was still half asleep.

"Good morning. You two seem awfully intense already. What's going on?" he said with a yawn.

"We were just talking about the vision you had of me in my grief during journey. It didn't happen last night, obviously, so I feel like it's on its way this evening," I replied.

He nodded solemnly.

"I have to leave here shortly, but just know that I am still holding space for that as well. I can take some of that off of you as an empath. Let me do that for you. I can lighten the load by taking some of that pain into my own body for you. Send it to me. I was made for that, and I would be honored to do it," he said.

"Thank you, Chrystopher. You've already done so much for me. I don't even know where to begin to thank you for last night," I said.

"I am so very grateful to have been a part of it. It was something truly beautiful to witness. Thank you. And thank you J. And Spirit," he said.

We sat on the porch for an hour or so, integrating the happenings of the night before. There was a sweetness about the connection this morning. It was evident that we all felt that we had witnessed something very special together. We were deeply bonded because of it.

Finally, Chrystopher stood up to head back in to get ready to leave. I felt a sudden pressing urge for him to hold me again, the way he had held me the night before. I felt like it was my last chance to feel just a little bit more of J's energy physically.

"Chrystopher…before you go…can I ask you a favor? Would you be willing to lie down with me on the bed for a bit and just hold me? Is that all right?" I asked, tentatively.

We were no longer in the field this morning. I didn't want to be intrusive. I wondered if the urgency I felt to ask him this was just my ego grasping to hang on to last night.

"Of course, I will do that," he said.

We went back to the bedroom that I had slept in last night; the bedroom that J and I had had our last amazing sex in that final night that we spent together. I had dozed off to sleep here last night amongst vivid recollections of the last time I was in that bed. I wondered as Chrystopher lay down with me, if J was giving him those images. I felt myself blush slightly as I eased into his arms as I thought about how he had been shown probably far more than he ever wanted to see of J and me over the last 24 hours.

He wrapped me up tightly, and I nestled my head against his chest. I could no longer feel J's energy through Chrystopher's body. I began to cry quietly.

"The physical separation is so unbearable at times. I know I have him back… but I miss his touch so much," I whispered tearfully.

"I know.", Chrystopher said. He pulled me in even tighter. As he did so, I felt a different kind of energy emanating from him. Not J's…but familiar somehow. I allowed myself to lean into it and be enveloped by it. His embrace was strong, but so tender. An anchor for me through these emotional waves…yet yielding to allow me to flow as I needed.

It dawned on me.

It was Divine Masculine energy.

I remembered J sending me into the house last night to work on "man stuff" with Chrystopher. Had he been gently coaching him to step into his own divine masculine? I had not felt this energy from him previously. As a matter of fact, Kat and I had spent both last night and this morning referring to Chrystopher as "the young one," or "the little". He was only about 10 years younger than the two of us, but he carried such a boyish energy that it had felt appropriate to refer to him that way.

There had been a shift last night, somehow. I was curious about it.

"J sent me in the house so that he could work with you alone last night. Did he do that? Were you aware of it?" I asked.

Chrystopher's eyebrows raised, and he laughed softly.

"Oh yes. I felt his presence the rest of the night. Almost like a father energy holding me steady," he replied.

I smiled. J had been helping find his legs. I had a vision of a boy on a bicycle for the first time with the training wheels off. Wobbly, but with J right behind him to help keep him upright should he need it.

"Thank you, J. Thank you for helping him grow through this experience as well. I can feel the change in him already. You did well, babe," I said to him in my mind.

"He was ready. He just needed some nudging, and to be able to feel it himself. He felt my energy pouring through his own body all night last night as he held you. It served as an arrow pointing in the direction that he could take as well. A little taste of what is already within him. He took it from there. He's so brilliant, Jen. He puts things together so quickly…all it took was shedding a little light on it for him to grab it and call it his own," J replied.

I sighed deeply as I thought about my two boys working together last night. My men. My heart felt so happy that not only had last night benefitted me, but that it had brought them together as well.

What a beautiful experience for all of us. Gratitude consumed me.

How had I ever thought that I didn't need this energy in my life?

I felt like I had grown up in many ways as well.

Receiving, nurturing, surrendering to the divine masculine.

I felt my own divine feminine energy blooming and bursting forth in colors I hadn't known were inside of me.

I thought back to the circle that J had shown me before I went to bed last night.

There had been an unfolding in me that had been happening so slowly that I hadn't realized it.

From the first moment that J and I touched, the divine feminine had been awakening from her slumber. The first little crack in the seed that had been giving way to a little green shoot pushing upward toward the sun.

It had been happening so slowly, that I was now shocked to see the bright blooms coming forth from me, coaxed out in full color under the rays of the divine masculine.

Receiving, nurturing, surrendering.

What a beautiful gift from a love that just continued to keep on giving. Unconditional. Strong. Whole within me.

The sun and the flowers. Forever delighted by and in love with each other. Giving and receiving beauty and warmth for all eternity.

Hallelujah and amen.

Later, as Chrystopher got up to get his things together to depart, I asked him if he would ask J if he got to say everything that he wanted.

Chrystopher did so and then laughed.

"He says no. He says there was nothing unsaid in particular, but that he could talk to you and tell you things for the rest of eternity," he said.

I knew the feeling.

I had so many questions and things I wanted to say, but I also knew for sure now that we would never be separated in our contact ever again.

There would be time for all of that.

J of course heard my thoughts, and Chrystopher added, "There is nothing else to say *through me*. He knows you will trust what comes through from him now. It was mostly the proposal that he wanted you to never doubt -that's what needed to come through me."

The Melody of Fire

I nodded and thanked him again.

I certainly would never doubt what had happened last night.

I finally showered and got cleaned up for the upcoming ceremony. I had brought a lacy white shirt to wear tonight that felt a little dressy for the occasion, but I had packed it with my dream that I had about this journey in mind. All of us women had been wearing white in that dream. I didn't want to be the only punk that didn't follow suit. (Even though I knew the others didn't know about the dream, it still just felt like the right thing to do.)

When I stepped back outside, I almost collided with a hummingbird that was flying across the open porch. I jumped back, and he flew backward simultaneously. He hovered in front of me briefly and we both stared at each other in surprise.

I laughed out loud, and he flew on his merry way just as quickly as he had arrived.

I had forgotten about my little guide.

My tiny joy-bringer.

He had worked overtime last night in the spirit realm it seemed. I couldn't wait to see what magical winding flight he would lead me down this evening.

Chrystopher left shortly before the women began to arrive. Carson was the first to get there, and I was so excited to see her. I filled her in a little about the previous night's journey and caught up with her about her family while everyone else arrived and got settled. I thought about how my friendship with her was one of the longest in my life, and how very grateful I was for that continued blessing. The fact that she was the one who connected me to the group of healers and the plant medicine work that I was now studying under only endeared her to me more.

She is an amazing human being. Stoic and serious, but also witty and charming, her presence has always been both grounding and uplifting to me. I was so happy to be back in this medicinal space with her. I hadn't a clue as to what the night would hold, but I knew that having Carson there would make it extra special.

When we did the opening of the ceremony, as usual, we took turns stating our intentions for the evening. When my turn came, I told the group about my dream that I had two nights prior. How we were all in white, and how joy and music had abounded. I told them how it had felt like we were there to witness something special together. (I explained my too-dressy shirt to them at this point, because I was of course the only one wearing white.) I also gave them a heads-up about the grief that Chrystopher had seen coming.

"I've been warned, so I feel as though I should, in turn, warn you that Chrystopher foresaw me sobbing with grief at some point during journey. I don't know when or how that will pop up, but I just didn't want you all to worry for me or not know what was happening. I don't really think there is anything that you

393

can do to help me if that happens, but just know that it is something that I always carry with me…I just don't normally let anyone see." I exhaled. Just saying that out loud felt so heavy.

The group thanked me for giving them a heads up, as they all would have undoubtedly worried if I hadn't. Especially Carson.

We said a word of thanksgiving and prayer and took our medicine together.

Everyone dispersed to find a comfy spot to relax until the medicine kicked in. I went back out onto the porch and enjoyed the summer breeze.

I am normally the last person in the field. It takes anywhere from thirty minutes to an hour and a half for the medicine to drop in for any given individual. I am typically an hour and a half-er.

It couldn't have been twenty minutes before my vision slanted suddenly and I was in the field. This time when I went in, I went in deep immediately.

I have no doubt it was due to the medicine already being in my system from the night before, and also because I had eaten very little even before the fasting "cut-off" time of 2:00pm.

Everyone was still chatting and giggling together outside of the cabin. I turned to Kat slightly wide-eyed.

"I'm already in…I'm going to go lie down for a minute," I told her.

She nodded her head.

"I'll come check on you in a few," she said.

I went in and lay on the couch for a while. I talked to Spirit about my fears.

I bet Spirit gets really fucking tired of hearing about my fears.

Like…for real.

I drive myself crazy when I'm in that space, I couldn't even imagine if I had to listen to someone else whine about how scary the wind blowing, or a piece of paper rattling was all of the time. I know I wouldn't be as patient with them as Spirit has been with me, yet here we were again.

I told them that the impending meltdown that Chrystopher had seen was scary to me.

They told me (again) that it wasn't any deeper than what I had already been feeling, but that it had a purpose.

I asked if we could side-step that part.

They said no.

I felt the anxiety bubbling a little below the surface, but then suddenly my heart felt strange. Almost as though the beating got harder for a few beats, and then back to normal, and then it did it again.

Of course, because I'm me, I panicked.

"What's wrong with my heart?" I asked.

"Ephemeral," Spirit replied.

Had heard that word before? I didn't think so. Was it a medical term? I started scanning my memory for heart conditions or illnesses that had the word "ephemeral" in front of them. I couldn't come up with anything and made a mental note to look it up later.

Whatever it was, it went away quickly.

I didn't recap that whole instance to set up that joke.

I'm using it to illustrate to people who might be doubtful that you are actually talking to a consciousness (God/Spirit) other than yourself when you are working in the medicine, that you are in fact tapping into something greater. I did indeed look that word up the next day, only to find that I hadn't actually known what it meant. Ephemeral means "lasting for a very short time."

Spirit gave me that word. A word outside of my vocabulary.

This is only one small instance of something that has happened several times in journey, and why I have no doubt at all that the things I hear are not just me talking to myself.

Even J from time to time has come to me with something novel. Something that I know didn't come from me. It's how I know that I am in fact talking to him as well.

As my heartbeat returned to normal, I tried to change the subject in order to settle my fears a little.

I asked about the Divine Feminine. I told Spirit that I didn't really understand that energy in God-form. We revisited how I had been taught that God was a man (and a scary one at that), and that my concept of femininity in general had been skewed. That much I knew from the Jesus journey a few months ago.

Though I now felt that I had a much deeper understanding of the Divine Masculine, particularly after all that I had witnessed the previous evening, I needed clarity around the Divine Feminine.

I told Spirit that I had been taught that we were the weaker gender, and that had been reinforced so frequently that "powerful feminine" seemed like an oxymoron to me on many levels. Anytime a female had any sort of power, I watched her be discredited in every way possible. She "slept her way to the top," her husband was really "running the show' behind the scenes, her family has enough money to put her in that position, etc. So even earthly feminine power didn't feel real to me. I truly couldn't grasp the feminine aspect of God. I knew I was being called, repeatedly, to step into my own Divine Feminine energy. I wanted a role model, an example to follow.

I knew that I had tasted it here and there, and even just this morning could see it bursting forth in me in different ways. I just wanted a deeper understanding.

"Get up," said Spirit.

I obeyed.

"Go outside and walk down to the river," They said.

I pushed through the screen door and waved to the girls as I passed them to head down to the riverbank. I stood on the rocks right beside it and listened.

"Put your feet in the water," They instructed.

I hesitated slightly. I remembered the last time that I had dared to wade out into the river what had happened. The power plant located upstream was generating this time of day, which meant that the river was several feet higher than it is in its normal state. What would have barely covered my feet early in the day was now almost to my knee. Still, I knew I had to obey. I climbed in and the force of the water nearly knocked me off of my feet. I held tight to a tree to steady myself and I stood there, again listening.

"The Divine Feminine is quiet in her power. See how quiet the river is to your ear? Yet she could easily pull you under and carry you away, as you have experienced before. This is why you have been missing the power of the Divine, or you don't feel like you know Her. She is a quiet force.

Make no mistake, she is no less powerful than the loud, action-oriented Divine Masculine. She is simply a different kind of powerful. She is flow. She is emotion. She operates cyclically. She is creativity. She is found in surrender. All of these characteristics are crucial to the human experience…. but you have to get quiet to hear them. The vast majority of humanity has scoffed at or overlooked the Divine Feminine because of this. Juvenile masculine energy runs this planet, manifesting in egocentric power struggles using the name "God" to manipulate through fear-mongering.

"Divine Masculine energy is not comprehended, and Divine Feminine is overlooked and undervalued. It takes a perfect balance of the two to create what you call 'Spirit.' One cannot exist without the other. Indeed, for harmony in any microcosm or macrocosm of energy there must be a balance of the masculine and feminine- be it the earth, a relationship, or a single human.

"Reacquainting oneself with the Divine Feminine often starts right here, just like this. She can easily be found by immersing yourself in nature. It's not that you have never met Her, you just haven't listened to Her. Be still. Feel Her power around your legs in the rush of the water. You are familiar with Father God. Embrace Mother Earth. Let her be your teacher and your guide to tap into your own Divine Feminine energy even deeper."

I stood for a long time, feeling the quiet power surging all around me. Connecting. Grounding. Welcoming Her into my heart.

"Open me up more. Let me be your student. I am willing and ready to know you in all the ways that you want to show me," I whispered to Her.

I savored the time for a while longer, but then I heard J calling to me to come back by the fire. The sun was setting and the orange glow from the dying rays and the light from the fire glistened on the water spectacularly.

I watched with awe as the sun faded in minutes, and the stars began to peep through the night sky.

I suddenly had the image of J standing before me, in a suit and bowtie. He looked devastatingly handsome. It pulled all of my attention to him.

"Wow, love. You look gorgeous. I don't think I've ever seen you in a suit except for…"

I stopped suddenly. Except for his wedding.

I had been in his wedding. I was one of his wife's bridesmaids – a recollection that felt super fucked up, even now. Maybe *especially* now.

I suddenly saw the wedding from his point of view. His bride stood before him, yet he was looking past her….at me.

"I didn't know it would be you, Jen. I had no idea that we would end up having all that we had, but I was in love with you even then. I loved you always," he said to me.

I was watching myself giggle and whisper in the line of bridesmaids behind his wife. My long hair was pinned up, and I looked about twelve years old to myself, though I know I had been in my early twenties.

"I didn't really want to get married. Lila and I had just been together for so long, and we had just had our first child. She put so much pressure on me about getting married. I finally just gave in, because I felt like her family and my family were all wondering why we weren't married. It was something she wanted badly. I never could articulate why I didn't want to, but it just never felt like the right move to me. I finally gave in, because there wasn't a good enough reason not to do it that I could offer anyone, and I got tired of being pressured from all directions. Once we went through with it though, I was committed. I loved her, make no mistake about that. That was never the issue. I really thought that was where I was going to be for the rest of my life. A husband to Lila, and a father. I was content and happy where I was, for the most part. I never in a million years would have guessed that you would even have given me a shot at being with you. I certainly couldn't have known how deep it would go if you ever allowed it. Honestly, it was the only thing that could have made me leave where I was. It took something as powerful as our love to shake me awake – make me realize that I there was something so much more that I had been missing out on. Once I experienced that, I couldn't live without it. I'm not telling you anything you don't know. Except maybe that part about always being in love with you," he said.

I was still watching baby bridesmaid me from his point of view, through his eyes. I looked up at him and caught his gaze briefly. I blushed and looked away quickly.

397

Had I known even then? I had obviously felt some kind of energy between us, or I wouldn't have reacted like that.

I tried to think back and couldn't remember. I had always liked J, but he was never on my radar in that way. At least…I hadn't thought he was, but here was a memory from him of baby 23-year-old me looking like she just got caught staring at her middle school crush. How intriguing to me this was. Perhaps I hadn't been as stupid as I thought that I had been. I had been beating myself up this whole time for not realizing the love of my life had been in my life (my whole life), and I had been too stupid and blind to see it.

Maybe I had picked up on more than I realized.

Whatever it was that had been passed between the two of us with that look exchanged had made me uncomfortable and a little…. giddy? Or so it appeared.

"What was that look, J? I couldn't see you, but I saw my own reaction. Were you flirting with me at your own wedding?" I said with a laugh.

"Not flirting. Just…appreciating, I think. I don't really remember, but I certainly remember what you looked like in that dress," he said.

The perspective shifted and I was now watching the wedding from my own eyes again. I watched J repeat back his vows to the pastor. The exchange got to the end, and I heard him say, "Until death do us part."

The image went black.

"That contract is over. Fulfilled. Complete," he said from somewhere in the blackness.

Coming forth from the darkness, I saw a figure in white.

As it approached, I was shocked to see that it was myself in a beautiful wedding gown. The dress was sleeveless and fitted, with lace detailing and a long train. Half of my long red hair was pinned up with a veil, the rest cascading down my shoulders and back in gentle waves. I held a bouquet of orange and yellow sunflowers. I was laughing and was absolutely radiating joy.

I turned and joined hands with J, who was now in a different suit and was older. No longer the baby-faced boy from the previous wedding scene, this was the J that I had fallen in love with. He looked distinguished and remarkably handsome, with his full salt and pepper beard and a little more age around his eyes. My heart melted all over again, seeing his sweet face smiling at me.

He was looking at me the way he had always looked at me - as if I had hung the stars and moon in the sky.

My God, how I loved this man.

We took our own vows. We promised to love each other through eternity. We swore that we would be together through the rest of this lifetime and all of the ones to follow.

Nothing would ever tear us apart again. This love would never die.

We recited the lines from a poem he had written me when we first got together, that was now stitched beneath my skin in a tattoo on my arm that I had gotten right after he had passed.

"Smoldering eyes of earth and sea, the way they meet mine...it's eternity.
It spans across time and crosses all lines. It's you and me."

He kissed me deeply. The sweetest, most passionate kiss that felt like making up for all of the kisses we had missed out on since his death.

As we turned, I was shocked to see a crowd full of people that we knew and loved cheering as we made our way down an aisle.

Both sets of our parents were there. Our friends. The girls from the journey.

It suddenly hit me that *this* was the event we were all gathering to witness in my dream. We were all coming here tonight for my wedding. I thought about how I had ended up being the only one who had worn white, and I laughed with glee.

I yelled to J over the noise of the crowd, "You put this all together! Even the DREAM!"

He nodded with a huge smile.

Rice and confetti showered down on us as we laughed together.

We were then at a gorgeous reception with candle-lit tables and chandeliers. He pulled me in close and we slow danced just as we had done so many times together.

He wouldn't even let me get an inch of distance from him. I laid my head on his shoulder as he murmured, "I love you, l love you, I love you…" over and over into my ear.

"My wife," he said.

It sounded like the most wonderful word in the English language to me as he said it.

"Oh, J. It's all I ever wanted. To be yours…in front of everyone. I'm so happy… and I love you so much," I said.

Tears of joy were streaming down my face, and when I looked at him, I saw that he was tearful as well. We couldn't contain ourselves.

There was champagne and cake. More laughter and joy. More dancing. My heart felt like it would explode.

The scene began to get quiet.

People waved goodbye and trickled out. We found ourselves alone again.

J took off my veil and ran his fingers gently through my hair.

"What a beautiful bride you are. My bride. My Mrs. Jen," he said.

We murmured "wife" and "husband" back and forth to each other amidst I love yous and giggles of delight. We kissed again tenderly, and I leaned into his chest and let him wrap me in his strong embrace.

After a long year and a half of separation…we were finally in blissful reunion.

"I could die happy right now, J," I whispered.

I felt him sigh deeply.

"That's something that we need to talk about, love. I have some things to tell you. It's another part of why I brought you here this weekend. Do you have ears for it right now?" he asked.

I felt disappointment rear its head a little. I didn't want to leave this moment. I had everything I wanted right here in my hands again finally.

"I don't want to lose this. I'm not ready to lose you again," I said.

He pulled me close to him again and held my face in between his strong hands.

"Never. Never ever ever ever again, Jen. We will never be separated again. Remember our vows that we just took? Infinity, my dear. Those were promises born from the greatest love that has ever existed. Not even death was able to split us apart. What makes you think anything else ever could?" he said. He kissed me gently. When he pulled back, he searched my eyes in the way that he had always done.

It was as if I were a clock, and he would just open me up and look at the way things were ticking to see what was going on inside. It was that easy for him, always. *Just look in her eyes and I'll know all that she's thinking and feeling.*

I nodded, and he knew I was agreeing to listen.

He held my hand as we walked back to the fire and the group, but then he disappeared from my side.

"I'll have to talk to you like this again now, I'm sorry," he said.

"I know. It's ok," I replied. The girls all appeared to be deep in their own journeys. Everyone was lying on blankets and pillows around the fire, and no one had their eyes open except for Kat. She nodded and smiled as I settled back in a chair close enough to the fire that I could prop my bare feet on the stones beside it to warm them.

I covered up with a blanket, nestled in, and closed my eyes.

"Ok, babe. I'm listening," I said.

"You know how I told you yesterday that at some point when I was in the hospital, I knew I was going to die?" he asked.

"Yes. How did you know? I tried to reach you so many times through meditation during that time, J. SO many times. You seemed confused, always. I was chalking it up to the medication that you were on, because you would ask me the same things over and over again," I said.

"I remember a little of that. There is a lot that I am unclear on surrounding that time, honestly. When I was coherent in the beginning, they had me on a ventilator, and I couldn't speak. It was maddening. I tried to pull it off/out several times and they strapped my arms down. Then there was a time period of just being in and out of consciousness. I don't really remember much of that. But at some point, I knew that I was going to die. I can't explain it really, it's just as if the knowledge was given to me. I knew it with certainty, and I was so afraid Jen. I couldn't get to you to tell you, and I was so terrified," he said.

My heart ached to hear this. I don't know what comfort I could have brought him at the time, but it hurt to know that he was so afraid and that I couldn't get to him. It hurt all over again. I thought back to the night he coded…the night I thought he crossed over.

I remembered hearing him yell my name in a panic three times.

I remembered it being as loud as if he were in the room with me.

I thought back to how I sat down and tried to tap in immediately that night, and how I heard him asking with panic over and over again, "Jen what's happening? Jen what's going on, I don't know what is happening to me…Jen….?"

I remembered sending him, with every ounce of intention I could muster, pleas from the depths of my soul. 'STAY! J…don't you leave me…you stay…you can do this. Hang on for me, my sweet boy….my love…please….'.

"Did you hear me that night, J? Was I able to reach you the way that you reached me?" I asked.

"Yes. I heard you too," he said.

And then I heard something from him that I had never heard before.

In all of the times that we had cried in front of each other and with each other, I had never heard it in his voice. He had always managed, through our entire relationship, to keep his voice steady even when his eyes were betraying him with tears.

As he spoke his next words, his voice broke. He spoke through a sob.

"I…didn't want ….to be separated from you. My last thoughts as I crossed over were that I didn't want to leave you. I knew my wife and kids would have each other, and they would make it through together…. but I knew…you only had me and I couldn't protect you from the heartbreak. I knew it would destroy you… but more than anything…. I just didn't want to be apart from you," he finished. His voice had cracked and wavered as he spoke. I could hear the absolute pain in his voice.

It was more than I could bear. I began to sob, uncontrollably.

The thought of my sweet boy's final thoughts being that he didn't want to be separated from me was like a fresh knife in an already gaping wound.

As the grief washed over me, I thought, "Oh there you are, old friend. I knew you wouldn't get too far gone…"

I allowed it to take over, once more. I felt the deep sobs start from my very core and make their way to my lips in body-shaking heaves. I felt the depth, once again of the wound.

Empty. I felt the emptiness swallow me whole, my agony echoing off of the chambers of my rib cage. I became one long, gasping wail.

I suddenly became aware that I was not alone.

I opened my eyes, and to my horror, Kat was standing in front of me, watching with compassion in her eyes.

I tried to rein it in. I put my hands over my mouth to try and dam up the sound that was exploding out of me.

"NO. YOU STAY IN IT," Kat commanded.

She knelt down beside me and placed her hand on the tender spot of my chest above my heart where I felt certain she could physically see the giant gaping wound of my grief.

As she touched it, I writhed in pain. There was no stopping the agony that was pouring out of me now.

"Let us see you, Jen. Let us know and acknowledge this pain you have been alone in for so long. We can carry some of it. Let us," she whispered.

I looked around to see that the women had each taken a place near me on the ground. Pulled from their own journeys to come and hold space in this moment for me.

Each one quiet, eyes closed, tapping into the depths of my pain.

I surrendered.

I wailed in great full body heaves. The sounds pouring out of me were those of an otherworldly pain. I felt like one giant and raw open wound, yet again. As I cried out in anguish, I noticed the deep place from which those cries came. It felt as though there was an endless reserve. A bottomless sea of grief.

I flung my grief out into the open, no longer ashamed or reserved. It became a cry for help. Without my saying the actual words every breath seemed to cry out for validation.

"DO YOU SEE??? DO YOU SEE HOW BADLY I HURT??? LOOK AT THIS! THIS PAIN HAS CONSUMED ME! CAN YOU FEEL THE DEPTH OF IT ALL?"

I cried until there were no more tears…until I lay there shaking with deep rattling breaths in sheer exhaustion.

"You did so well, love. So, so well. The secret ends here, remember? You don't have to be alone with this anymore," J said softly to me in my ear.

I felt the love and compassion pouring into me from the women around me. Wordlessly they nurtured me with their energy. The murmurs of their thoughts surrounded me.

We see you, Jen. We are so very sorry that you are in so much pain. We honor what you have been carrying. We are here to bear witness. We hold space for you in the knowledge that there is nothing anyone can do to fix your broken heart, but you don't have to hide it anymore. What a beautiful thing to have loved something so very much that it caused such a canyon of grief in the wake of its loss. We see it. We see you. We love you.

I allowed the love to tend my wound. It was still raw and oozing from the exposure. They began to bandage it tenderly. Not to cover it up, just to protect it from the burn of the wind a little. I let them mother me in that moment. It was the very first time that I had let anyone see what had happened to me. There I lay.... broken and battered and bruised. They had seen it now with their own eyes.

They knew they couldn't fix it, but what they could do was try to make me a little more comfortable. Just a little. I felt them set to work quietly around me. A kiss here, some gauze there. A warm cup of tea. It wasn't much in the scheme of things, and they knew it, but it was more than I had allowed anyone to give me before and it felt monumental in that moment. Just the acknowledgment of the shape that I was in felt like the biggest gift. The overwhelming, unifying thoughts from them over and over eased the heaviness a bit.

We see you. We see the pain. We love you.

My ragged breaths slowed back into a normal pattern. I gently began to uncurl myself from the tight fetal position I had clenched myself into. Kat was by my side instantly with pillows and blankets and helped me onto a reclining position on my back. She laid beside me for a bit, holding me tight and rubbing my shoulder tenderly with her open hand, almost as if she were applying a healing salve.

"I'm so proud of you," she whispered, so softly I could barely hear it. And then she added just as quietly, "Warrior."

My face was soaked with tears and snot. Kat began to help me clean up. I indeed looked and felt like I had been through a battle. This war that I had been fighting in had seen many battles, but this one felt significant. It seemed to me that it would be the Gettysburg of my own civil war. The turning point.

For as I cleaned myself up, wiping the caked-up snot and tears off of myself, wrapping up in clean blankets, and nourishing my body with tea and medicine, I felt something new begin to touch me ever so slightly.

Peace.

She brushed gently against my cheek at first. She checked my temperature with her cool hand on my forehead.

"Lay down, my child. Close your eyes. We have one more thing to show you, and then I will be back to rock you to sleep," She said.

I felt exhaustion taking over my entire body. It felt like it came physically through me, but not of me. It wasn't just exhaustion from the battle I just fought, it was a deep depletion of all that had been sucked out of me over the last twenty months.

Kat was still tending to me sweetly.

I caught her gaze, and realized for the first time this evening, that there was worry present in her face.

I had scared her a little. Or rather, the depth of pain that she had witnessed had done so.

I let myself ponder on it briefly. What would that have looked like to me five years ago had I seen someone in that agony?

I knew it would have scared the shit out of me.

If I had seen that from another human being it would have made me instantaneously realize that hurt like that existed, and I would have spent the rest of my life praying that I never had to feel it intimately.

Some wars are better fought when you can't see what you are walking into.

There is no way to prepare for that kind of battle wound anyway.

Best if you don't know it can happen to you.

I knew Kat had seen a lot through this work that she does. She is a professional space holder. I knew it hadn't scared her shitless. But I also knew enough to know that if it had even slightly rattled her, it was something. She had been on the battlefield with many a soldier.

It was oddly comforting to me for some reason that my pain unnerved her a little. I didn't feel like I was being overdramatic all of this time when I was wailing alone, but I had often wondered if in the scheme of universal grief if my pain was actually that large and frightening…. or if it were only that large and frightening to me.

I found the answer in her eyes.

"I'm so tired, Kat. So. Very. Exhausted. It feels soul deep. Like…every cell in my body is wiped out, but so is my spirit. I could just let it all slip away, I feel like," I said to her.

"With good reason, Jen. I can feel that emanating from you. Just lay back and rest," she said. She appeared to stop and listen for a moment. She looked slightly confused.

"What color were J's eyes?" she asked.

"Blue. Steel blue," I replied.

She nodded and smiled knowingly.

"He's looking for you," she said as she backed away from me.

I let my eyes close.

"J?" I asked.

"I'm still right here, love. I just wanted your attention back. I'm so proud of you. I'm going to let you rest very soon, but I have one more thing to show you," he said.

"What is it, my love?" I asked.

The Melody of Fire

"Remember how I told you that I was so afraid of dying? How when I knew that I actually was going to go that it terrified me?" he asked.

"Yes," I said.

"I know that is your deepest fear as well. Of all the things that unsettle you, and of all of the things that you are afraid of…that is the biggest one. I would like to ease that for you if you would let me?" he asked.

"Of course. How?" I said.

"I want to walk you through what dying is like…with a simulation right now, if you are willing?" he said.

My eyes flew open.

"What?" I gasped.

It scared me. I couldn't help it.

I heard J laugh softly.

"I knew you were going to freak out. Will you just trust me? Let me talk you through it?" he asked.

I wavered with uncertainty. After all we had been through this evening, now he was asking me to face my greatest fear head-on? I didn't know if I had it in me.

"I know you're exhausted, Jen. This will be so healing for you though, if you will let me guide you through this," he said.

"Ugh. Fine," I replied with resignation. I'd been in these types of conversations with him before. He wasn't going to let it go, I knew. I might as well give in now and save the argument.

He snickered.

"Stubborn girl. Thanks for not making me fight all night with you about it," he said.

I opened my eyes again, exclusively so that he could see me roll them before they closed again.

"I saw that," he said.

"Good," I replied.

He laughed.

"Ok. So, I am just going to remind you again that this is a SIMULATION and that you are not, in fact, dying this very moment. I know how you are, and I don't want you flipping your shit halfway through this thinking that you died during journey tonight," he said. I could hear him trying to hide the amusement in his voice. It would have pissed me off if I hadn't known he was right. That is exactly where I would have gone in my mind without that warning.

I became very still and waited.

Everything was pitch black. Slowly, a violet light appeared above me. It started as a soft dark purple that was lighter at the center. I watched it with curiosity as it widened and got brighter and brighter as I stared at it.

"It begins like this. That light is the only thing you see. See how it keeps getting brighter? It's captivating, isn't it? Doesn't it feel magnetic in the way that it pulls you towards it?" he asked.

It did. I found myself drawn to it like a moth. It was beautiful, and though it had started as a twinkling violet firework-esque display, it was now a presence that was quickly becoming more and more all-encompassing.

"That's the bridge, Jen. I'm waiting on the other side of it for you. The instant that you step through I will be right there to catch you," he said.

I stared at the bright light as it got closer and closer (or was I the one getting closer and closer?) I began to notice two blue orbs in the very center of the light. It was as if they were coming to the surface from the depths of whatever was beyond the violet. I watched them intently as they began to deepen in color, and little darker veins of color began to appear in them radiating out from the center.

They approached closer and closer as the violet light surrounded me and brightened. I was in the middle of it now, and everywhere I looked it was all I could see. Just wavering light all around, except for the two blue orbs directly in front of me.

The edges of the orbs began to define, and I noticed a dark center where the varying rivers of color seemed to originate from.

As they got larger and larger before me, and became more and more defined, I suddenly recognized them for what they were.

'Your eyes, J!! I can see your eyes!!' I exclaimed.

"Yes, love. I can see your outline in the light. I am going to reach out my hands to you…when you see them, grab tight," he said.

I felt them before I saw them. A pull of energy, grasping for me through the light. An energetic yearning that was tangible. When I finally saw his fingers stretching before me, I reached forward and grabbed them as firmly as I could. In an instant, I was in his arms.

He covered me with kisses as we both laughed.

When the giddiness subsided a bit, I looked around. We appeared to be in a long dark hallway. Alone together.

There was a doorway at the end of the hallway that I could see, and there was a bright white light that outlined the door. Whatever was on the other side was so bright that it couldn't be contained.

I looked at it for a while, and then back at J.

"What now?" I asked.

"Now, I will throw you up against this wall and fuck you," he said, as he put his hands roughly around my waist and pushed me against the wall of the hallway.

I cracked up and swatted him away playfully.

"Thanks for making this lighthearted…I haven't been afraid at all," I said.

"Yeah, well. I'm not really kidding about that. I know when I finally hold you, I will want to have you all to myself for a moment before I have to share you with the others," he said. He wasn't laughing. He took my face in his hands and kissed me.

"I've already missed touching you so badly since I passed. The time until today has been brutal. I can't imagine what it will feel like when I finally fully get you back in my arms the day you join me," he said solemnly.

"I know. I'm already looking forward to it," I said. And then, "J…what 'others'? You said you weren't ready to share me with the 'others.'"

"That's right. Come with me, love," he said. He reached out and took my hand in his, lacing his fingers between mine, and then led me down the hallway.

I followed behind him, alternating between looking at him and the door with the glowing outline. It was apparent that we were going to open that door.

J reached forward and as the door opened I was blinded by the brightest light I have ever seen. I squinted and put my hands over my face trying to shield myself from the intensity, but it didn't help at all. I couldn't make out anything for a moment, but I heard J yell out,

"HEY EVERYONE!! MY WIFE IS HOME!!"

There was such excitement and pride in his voice. It made my heart explode with joy.

I heard cheering and suddenly was surrounded by beings whose features I could only make out parts of through the blinding light.

Both of my grandfathers.

My dear friend who I lost to suicide years ago.

Both of my grandmothers. ("Joyce is here now too," J whispered in my confusion.)

Apparently, this was a scene from when I actually do cross over, because she was alive and well when I started this journey.

Suddenly my daddy stood before me, and then enveloped me in the tightest embrace.

"Welcome home, my girl. I've missed you so," he said.

It went on for a long while. My vision became accustomed to the light the longer I was there. I was reuniting and laughing with all of those that I had loved. I looked up and J had backed off a bit to give others space to hug me and welcome me.

I was overjoyed and felt completely surrounded by love from every angle.

J finally stepped forward and began to send them away a few at a time.

"Alright, alright everyone…I know we are all excited, but I technically still have her for the rest of this night. Can we have some space?" he asked. He was laughing good-naturedly as he shooed them away. The light began to fade.

I found myself lying back on the blanket by the fire once more.

"I don't want you to ever...*ever* be afraid of that again. I've got you, babe. You don't have to be scared of crossing over ever again. It will be just like that, I promise," J said softly as I watched the fire dance in front of me.

I sighed with contentment.

"I'm not afraid anymore. What a beautiful gift. Thank you, J. Thank you so much. I love you," I whispered aloud.

I closed my eyes once more and found myself surrounded by greenery and a gentle breeze. I was lying on my back and looking up at the stars in wonder. J was lying beside me, holding my hand.

"Where am I now?" I asked.

A soft feminine voice replied across the breeze.

"Peace. You are in the middle of peace. I am surrounding you and holding you. Relax and rest, dear one. You deserve it. And remember...anytime you want to, you can come right back here. Just remember how this feels. Let yourself come back here often. This place is in the deepest, truest part of your heart. You can find it anytime you wish."

As I lay there quietly, soaking it all in, I realized that this place was different than any place I'd ever been.

There was no time. Nothing to worry about. Nothing that I had to do in particular.

My fears were gone. All of them. Even the scariest one. Especially the scariest one.

I had no regrets about the past.

My love was right with me, holding my hand.

I wanted for nothing more.

This moment was the only one that mattered.

Then the next moment was the only one that mattered.

And so it went, as I simply enjoyed each moment as it presented itself....and slowly drifted off to sleep in the tender arms of peace.

Chapter Thirty-Three

I AWOKE THE NEXT morning feeling the most rested I had felt in ages.

A little dehydrated and ravenously hungry…but rested.

We had breakfast and integration all together that morning on the porch, where I shared my story of the unfolding of the night's journey. I thanked the girls for not only being a part of my wedding, but for holding space for me in the throes of my grief.

I listened intently to each of their own tales from their individual journeys.

Plant medicine continues to amaze me every single time I journey with it.

As if my own experiences hadn't been mind-blowing enough, hearing the way it moves differently in each and every person's story floors me every time.

Every single person got their intentions met.

Not one single person got their intentions met the way they thought they would.

Spirit astounds me with how it meets our needs so perfectly in that space, yet never in a way we could anticipate.

Take my own journeys that weekend, for example.

I wanted to reconnect with my love in a way that would ease the pain of my grief.

What Spirit brought to me was validation.

They knew that the thing I needed most was validation of the love that I held in my hands and lost. I never received it fully from J (in the public eye) when he was alive. I never let the world know what had happened. In fact, to an outsider, it was as if it never happened it all.

The most powerful thing I had ever experienced felt like it got buried with the love of my life.

Erased.

All I wanted, in the deepest parts of my being, was for the world to know that I had a love like no other. That I was his and he was mine. Validation.

That was the thing that was keeping me stuck and feeling like I was drowning continuously, though I really hadn't seen it that way at the time.

Spirit saw it though and brought it to me in all of the ways that I didn't even know I needed.

It reminds me of part of the work of Dr. Joe Dispenza, and his take on how the quantum field works.

He teaches that Spirit has to serve us from the vast unknown. We limit Spirit when we try to anticipate (or especially control) how we get what we need. We limit it so much in fact, that Spirit has to find a way around those parameters. "The Generous Present" moment, as Dispenza calls it is a place where all possibilities exist. Spirit can bring us our desires and fill our needs best when we are open to those solutions arriving via the path of least resistance.

In other words, Spirit works best and most effectively when you just surrender completely and let it serve you. After all, it knows what you need even more intimately than you do.

To me, plant medicine is a powerful example of this theory working in a very fast way.

You can observe an intention being set, and witness how Spirit meets that need all in the same evening.

It's utterly fascinating.

It's like looking at Their methods in fast forward.

In fact, plant medicine feels like a shortcut to me in a lot of ways when it comes to working with and in Spirit. Or rather, letting Spirit work with and in you.

I'm not naive enough to think this is always a good thing, nor do I believe that plant medicine is the solution to everyone's problems. In fact, I know from experience that ten percent of the work is done on the night of a ceremony, and the other ninety percent is done through integration and very difficult work afterward.

This path isn't for everyone, nor is it for the weak of heart or the lazy.

Especially not the lazy.

As a matter of fact, if the thought of deconstructing every single facet of yourself and committing to your healing on a daily basis sounds like too much work to you- it is.

Don't even start down the path of plant medicine journeys.

You would be wasting time (your own and your facilitators') and resources that could be used to serve someone who could benefit more from it.

But to those of you who feel the call - those of you who are willing to sit with the ugliest parts of yourself, in the darkest places, until you can claim them as your own and love them wholly…there is something special there for you.

For those of you who long for a deeper connection to the Divine and intimate relationship with your Creator as they work to align you to your true purpose…. you can find it through the plant teachers.

To those of you who want to better understand the cosmic forces of the universe and truly be shown how you are a part of something much bigger than yourself… miracles await.

Prepare yourself to be astounded at what you uncover.

Ready yourself to sing the praises of the Almighty.

Open yourself to receive the praises They sing back to you.

Plant medicines are the great teachers of Mother Earth.

I feel like they are a direct phone line to Spirit.

If you hear that phone ringing for you, by all means, pick it up. Your life will never be the same.

I know mine won't be.

This story has been about my love with J on the surface, but there is a deeper and more ancient love affair that has surfaced into my awareness through all of this.

My love affair with Spirit predates all of existence.

My soul may have been split in two at my creation, and J has been the other half since that moment, but it was Spirit that did both the creating and the splitting.

Spirit has adored me and wooed me at every turn, and when that didn't work for me to turn my eyes to Them, They humbled me and took me to the lowest of rock bottoms to shake me out of my slumber.

Spirit showed me the spark of Divine love through my love with J, and then took it all away (or made it appear so) so that I would seek it out again like a dying man in the desert looking for water.

And when I did…when I finally surrendered in all of the ways a human possibly could…. Spirit lovingly scooped me up and made me new.

They not only restored all that I had lost, They surpassed it.

My love was returned to me in a way that allowed us to be together in a far greater way than I could have imagined. Validated. Held. Loved unconditionally across realms and timelines. He is now not only my husband, but also my greatest ally in the Spirit realm.

(So basically, don't mess with me is what I'm saying. I have a guardian angel that loves me more than the sun and moon and will cut a bitch.)

I am a new being. My old self is dead forever. That clingy, fearful, control freak that used to be the ringmaster stepped down from running that circus where the animals were running rampant, and we were struggling with ticket sales. Spirit stands in the center of that ring now, and this sideshow that I was calling a life has been transformed into something more akin to Cirque de Soleil in Vegas. I want front row seats every night. I can't wait to see what They come up with next.

It's The Greatest Show on Earth and I'm beyond happy to just hand over the reins, pop some popcorn, and simply show up for the action.

I know it won't be all sparkle and glamour. I'm aware that there will still be heart-stopping, death-defying feats that leave me shaking in my seat. I know that the lions could still take your hand off if they wake up on the wrong side of the bed on any given day. The difference is that I now know that the Master has it all under control.

At the end of the day, the most frightening things I will ever encounter live behind the eyes that stare back at me from the mirror.

We create our own hell. All of us. We torch our own circus tents.

It's just how we are built.

There is nothing that truly exists outside of us, yet we all go running around trying to find water and firemen and wet blankets to extinguish the fires that we started ourselves. All it really takes is going within, asking the Ringmaster to take over the shitshow that you have put into motion, and help you find the matches that you've hidden within yourself so that you don't do that again.

Spirit is never exasperated with us.

Trust me.

If Spirit could be exasperated with *anyone*, it's me. I've been pulling matches out of my asshole every time They turn around.

My favorite change in my life, the part that was given to me in abundance where I had only seen glimpses of it before, has been the surge of moments of delight.

Prior to losing J, when I was just finding my feet in the spirit realm, small synchronicities and/or psychic hits seemed like tiny miracles to me every time.

To my delight, that sense of awe has not only never lessened….it now surrounds me in great magnitude on a daily basis.

It never gets old. It's as if Spirit loves showing off to me because They know I will appreciate it. I laugh at the spectacular way things line up at least once a day. I stand at the feet of God in awe of the magic that They surround me with.

I went from not caring whether or not I woke up every day, to rising in the morning with excitement to see what new wonders that Spirit will bring into my life that day.

Do I have it all figured out?

Hell no.

But I'm actually kind of glad that I don't. It leaves room for Spirit to dazzle and amaze me without ceasing. Each time I think I have some sort of grasp on the infinite power or the way that Spirit works, They make some sort of spectacular move to prove that I don't know anything at all.

I love it.

I love Spirit.

I am *in love* with Spirit.

I couldn't be happier to have my J back by my side. There is a sweetness and a newness now to this ancient love story. All of the circumstances have changed, but the love is still the same.

I'm still so in love with him it hurts. I'm still so amazed that heaven, earth, and even death moved out of the way to make sure we found our way back to each other.

I'm so happy that he is home, and that I can feel the love between us every single day until I die. And then every single day after that.

Every single lifetime after that.

Until the earth disintegrates and the only thing left standing in the universe is us.

In love.

He was never lost. He was never more than a breath away. He was never not loving me.

The more I rejoice and give thanks for that, the more I see....it is the exact same way with Spirit.

One love story begat the other.

They have circled together and back apart again since creation.

The tiny flames will ignite and draw us into the holy fire again and again and again. They will continue to do so until the end of time.

The spark of divinity within us will always find its way back to the hearth.

The smaller love always leads to the greater Love which then deepens the smaller love all over again.

love is Love is love.

May it consume us in its fire forevermore.

1 John 4:19: We love because He first loved us.

I HAD ONE thing left to do after the journey.

I had to tell my parents about J and me.

I didn't want to, but J reminded me every five minutes that I had agreed to do it. The thought made me physically ill, and I barely ate the entire day that I had decided it finally had to be done. Or rather, the day J decided it had to be done. I would have put it off indefinitely if given the option.

No option was given.

I sat on the dock for about an hour prior, watching the river and drinking marijuana-laced chamomile tea (sweed tea, as I like to call it) from an indica oil that Kat had given me for anxiety, trying to calm my shaking hands before I started the walk back up to their house to tell them.

I stopped about halfway there.

"Please don't make me do this, J. *Please*. It's fine if they don't know, really. It's been a year and a half…. what's the point now anyway? I'm really not sure I can handle anyone being mean to me about our relationship right now. Please let me off the hook on this one?" I pleaded.

"I can't believe I have to ask you again to trust me. Will you though? You will be surprised at their reaction, Jen," he said.

"Yeah. Well. I was also surprised when my mother started flinging dishes in the house when I told her I was gay, so that's not exactly comforting," I said.

He snorted. "*Pleasantly* surprised. You can do this, love," he said.

"Can you send me something physical - a sign to let me know you are there with me? I mean…I know you are right here, but I'm gonna need a little more than the voices in my head by means of support if I'm going to get through this, J," I asked.

"Hmmm. Yes. Like what?" he asked.

"I don't know. They are sitting on the porch so it looks like that's where it will be happening. An animal guide would be good. A squirrel or butterfly or something?" I said.

'Yes. I can do that. I'll support you however you need me to. Now go. I'll be right with you. I love you endlessly, and I can't even begin to tell you how proud I am of you," he said.

I walked the rest of the way to the porch muttering under my breath about how I didn't see how he could be proud of me for doing something he didn't really give me a choice about. He sent me an image to my mind's eye of himself rolling his eyes in response.

Mom and Dad were sitting in the white wicker chairs on the porch, and they brightened up when they saw me. I said hello to them and gave them each a kiss on the head, but I couldn't look them in the eye.

My stomach churned miserably.

I sat on the porch swing across from them and we began small talk about the weather and work. The lump in my throat got bigger and bigger. I almost cried twice over completely unrelated questions that they asked because the emotions were already bubbling up to the surface. Things got quiet and everyone was looking out at the river and enjoying the sunset.

I took a deep breath.

I tried to speak, but nothing came out.

I couldn't do this.

"WHOA!! LOOK AT THAT HUMMINGBIRD!" my dad suddenly exclaimed while pointing at me.

I heard it about the same time he said it. I looked immediately to my left and there…directly beside my face was a tiny, brightly colored hummingbird hovering next to me. He cocked his head slightly, looked me in the eye, and then buzzed off happily towards the river.

"I'm right here. You can do this," J whispered.

It was the break in the quiet that I needed. I gave it no more time to think, lest I back out again.

"I…need to talk to you all about something. It's something very difficult for me to say…and I want you to know that I'm not looking for approval or acceptance about it…it's just something that I need for you to know," I squeaked out hurriedly, trying to get it out before I changed my mind.

I looked up at them as I finished. They both had solemn expressions.

"What? What is it?" my dad said instantly.

Ugh. Here we go.

I took a few more deep breaths, and the tears already began to fall before I even could speak.

"J and I…we were more than just friends. Much more. We were together…as a couple… for nearly three years. He was, without question, the love of my life. That is why I have been dying from grief since he passed. I lost the greatest love I've ever known.

AND….it feels important for me to tell you that not only did I lose him…I hadn't known that I was pregnant when he passed away, but I was. I miscarried a few weeks after he died.

I've been trying to carry all of this alone and in silence- mostly due to the nature of the circumstances surrounding the relationship. I didn't want to hurt anyone any more than I already had. But I just can't do it anymore. I have to speak about it… so I needed you guys to know," I said. I finished in full-blown sobs, and when I finally dared to look up at their faces, I was surprised at what I saw.

I had expected to see dumbfounded stares, and more than a little judgment in their eyes as they processed through this bomb that I had just dropped.

Instead, I saw deep compassion and sorrow.

No one spoke for a while.

Finally, it was Dad who broke the silence.

"Well…honey…I have to say…this makes everything make a lot more sense to me. I knew you were grieving much harder than someone who had lost a close friend. I couldn't figure it out. I knew that J was in love with you. I had picked up on that long ago. The way he looked at you…. I could just tell that he had fallen deeply in love. But I also knew that you were gay, so I just figured that it would be something that you would never be on board with or that you didn't feel the same way about him," he said.

Mom chimed in at this point.

"I know that is why you didn't tell us this sooner, Jen. The way we reacted when we found out that you were gay wasn't good. I know that probably scared you from telling us anything else about your life that you thought we wouldn't receive well. I'm so…*so sorry* that we made you feel that way. It absolutely breaks my heart to know that you have been grieving all of this alone," she said. Her voice was tearful.

I nodded my head in agreement.

"That is a big part of why I didn't tell you, but also…the situation with his wife was very difficult. I nearly told you when he was in the hospital, because I knew you thought it was strange that I wasn't visiting him. Lila wouldn't let me see him. So I almost told you what was going on at that point when you asked me for updates. I just couldn't do that to him, though. I really thought at that point that he was going to make it, and I just didn't want him to have to deal with all of that on top of the physical recovery that he was facing. Then when he passed, I didn't want his memory to be dishonored in any way. I just couldn't bear for you to think less of him because of our relationship. He was such a great man…" I said, dissolving into tears once more.

"We don't think any less of him, Jen. Of either of you, for that matter. Love like that knows no boundaries. The connection was obvious to everyone, even though the details were unclear. I know Jason was a great man, and I know how very much he loved you. I would have been honored and blessed….and…proud…. to have had him as a son-in-law. I loved him very much too," Dad said.

I thought about Dad and J's relationship. There had always been a sweet comradery between the two of them. I knew that he meant what he was saying. He would have welcomed him into the family with open arms, no matter how he got there.

"He loved you too, Dad. It was very hard for me to not share this with you when he was alive. We were so in love that I wanted to shout it from the rooftops but couldn't. Of course, I never saw what ended up happening coming. I always thought that the day I told you two about us, I would be telling you with a wedding announcement and a ring on my hand," I said.

"You just did," J whispered happily in my ear.

I felt the joy well up inside of me when I heard it.

The Melody of Fire

He was right. I just did.

Mom had been listening intently and I could see the sorrow on her face.

"I'm sad about that too, Jen. I'm sad for you, of course, and the pain of losing that love…. but I'm sad for us as well. I'm sad that we lost our future son-in-law. It hurts to know that we missed out on a wonderful relationship with him in a whole other way. I feel like I am grieving the relationship I didn't have as well," she said.

"Two relationships," I added. "There was a grandbaby that you didn't get to spoil rotten as well."

Both of them hung their heads in sorrow.

None of us had words.

Finally, Dad was the one who broke the silence.

"I'm just…so very sad for you, honey. I wish we could go back in time somehow and be there for you more than we were. The more I think about it, I'm not really sure what we could have done for you…but at least you wouldn't have had to go through it without knowing how much we love and support you. We could have just been there for you," he said.

"I know, Dad. But part of me is glad in some ways that I did wait until now to tell you. I think if you had seen me at my worst, in the first few months after all of this happened, it would have terrified you both. There would have been nothing you could have done to help, and you would have just had to watch me struggling to even breathe. It would have been more of a burden to me in that moment to know the worry I would have been putting you through as well," I said.

"Well. We were already worried. It honestly would have at least made more sense if we had known what all you were grieving," he replied.

Mom had been fairly quiet the last little bit. Turns out she had been formulating the question that I had feared the most about this whole conversation.

"So…I have to ask…. you made it quite clear to us over the last twenty years that you liked girls. Fought us hard over it until we accepted it, actually. What changed? What does this mean?" she said.

There it was.

I had thought about how I would answer this question from the moment that J and I kissed the first time. What came out was nothing like what I had practiced.

"Mom…. honestly… it wouldn't have mattered if J was a boy or a girl. Or a dinosaur, or a unicorn. I loved him in a way that was far beyond physical reality. What we had was deeply spiritual. I never truly understood what people meant when they spoke about their 'other half' until him. It was otherworldly, magical, and so…so special. That is why at the end of the day, his gender didn't matter. The fact that he was married didn't matter. We had to be together no matter the obstacles that appeared to be between us. It was that powerful. It shook both of

417

us awake to what love actually is. There is nothing that could have come between us," I said.

Not even death, I thought. There was so much more to this story that I longed to tell them now that the cat was out of the bag. I didn't want to overwhelm them though. I knew I had given them a lot to think about today already.

Mom nodded knowingly. I had known that the most vocal of the criticism about my sexuality would come from her. I waited uneasily to hear her response.

"I can understand that. You are correct...nothing comes between true love. You know, I never told you this, but I actually tried to stop loving you several times after you came out. Tried to turn off the depth of the way that I loved you. I couldn't do it. I was SO angry at you, but at the end of the day, you were my child, and nothing can sever that love. Not to mention that you truly are one of the best people I know. I didn't want to see that or honor it at the time, but there was no way around it. I had to come to terms with the fact that the problem surrounding that situation.... was me. Well. Us," she said as she pointed at Dad and herself.

"Gee thanks, Mom. I didn't know you tried not to love me. I mean, it felt like that to me, but I tried to convince myself that you weren't really taking it that far," I replied.

"I'm not telling you that to hurt you. I'm telling you that to show you how we have grown, and to give you an example of how I know personally that true love is not something that can just be turned on and off. It truly is unconditional. I know it's not the same relationship...a parent/child versus a love relationship... but fundamentally love works the same. I can see that you and J couldn't have stopped loving each other no matter what, any more than I was able to stop loving you. And if feels important for me to say this - I don't think any less of you or love you any less than I did ten minutes ago before you told us all of this. The only thing I feel that is different is grief and sadness for all that you have lost and all that we have lost as well," she said.

I was more than a little shocked.

I had been mentally preparing my rebuttal for what I was sure was about to be an argument about my sexuality, or a dissertation on adultery and the Bible.

To my delight, I didn't have to say anything.

There was nothing to defend. Nothing to argue. Just pure gratitude for the words that had just been uttered.

There was only one thing for me to say, and I felt humbled as I spoke it aloud.

"Thank you," I said.

"See," J whispered in my ear.

Not to be outdone, Dad spoke up again.

"Not only do I not think less of the two of you...I actually admire the courage that it took and the willingness to surrender to love in that way. I truly believe that God had his hand on bringing the two of you together. I am so deeply sorry that you had to lose him, honey. But I also am so happy for you that you got to experience a love like that. Most people never do," he said.

"Thank you for saying that. And thank you for not chastising me about the whole situation."

"Well…you know…when one of your children is hurt, you aren't supposed to yell at them. You're supposed to love them and hold them and tell them everything is going to be just fine," he said.

We locked eyes and I nodded wordlessly. I was overwhelmed.

I was crying, yet again, but this time with gratitude.

I could physically feel the weight lifted off of me.

My and J's love felt validated. Seen. Understood.

Most importantly, it felt honored for what it had been and what it was.

And after a very, very long road, I was standing in a place that I never thought I would see -

I felt loved and accepted by my parents for exactly who I was, instead of in spite of it.

We talked for an hour or more on that porch, wading through questions about the whole relationship and about his death. And my miscarriage.

I was delighted to find that they were so curious about how it had all come about. They wanted to know details that they had missed out on when it had been going on.

We laughed about moments when they had seen interactions between us that had made them raise an eyebrow, and about how they had just written it off as not possible because of my sexuality.

Mom even made the statement that she would like to go back in time and know what she knew now and just watch the two of us trying to hide it. She thought it would be quite entertaining.

I'm sure it would have, indeed.

From all accounts from friends, we had been spectacularly terrible at hiding our love, particularly on stage. My sister once sent me a series of photos from shows in which J and I were staring at each other like two smitten lovebirds onstage with the text,

"Subtle. No one can tell, for sure."

I no longer had to worry about (however terribly) hiding any of it. From anyone. Ever again.

I felt like Atlas on the best day of his life: as if someone had just walked up and told him that the world would be totally fine if he just set it down and walked away. He no longer had to feel responsible for any of it, and earth would just keep doing its own thing. He was free to do the same.

I was free to do the same.

Everyone who meant the most to me now knew.

I no longer had to grieve in private.

I had permission from J to tell our story on as big or as small of a scale as I needed or wanted.

Authenticity was not only allowed, it was being encouraged.

A new chapter had begun.

Healing could finally truly begin.

The wound could get some air without me constantly trying to cover it up with a blanket to hide it from the world.

I was free.

Free in J and free in Spirit.

The cage doors had been flung wide open, and the keys tossed into the river.

I flew away joyfully to join my love on a new adventure.

Free to go wherever the winds might take us.

Free to stop and drink the sweet nectar from the flowers.

Free to fly in whatever direction we pleased.

Two tiny, happy hummingbirds.

Frequently throughout my life, even before my spiritual gifts began to open up the way they are now, I have had dreams that have been unusually profound. They only happen periodically, and I never know when they are coming, but I have learned over time that when they appear they are a special gift. They are a message to me from the spirit realm. They are typically extra vivid, and I am able to recall every single detail. I have recounted a few of these dreams in this book. A few nights after I told my parents I had just such a dream; and it was by far the most vivid and potent dream that I have ever had in my life.

In the dream, I was in a long flowing red dress, and I was standing in front of a wall of fire that rose far above my head. Two wrought iron gates flanked me on either side, and they were slightly behind me. J was holding my hand and we were facing outward, away from the fire and the gates, but flames and smoke still flickered in between and around us. We were dancing, but suddenly there were demons running toward me, heading into the gated area and I immediately understood that we were at the gates of my heart.

J stepped behind me and wrapped me in his strong arms, and I begin to fight the demons with all of my power. I was keeping them from entering into my sacred heart space. I was protecting my fire, my love, from these vicious intruders. As I fought and fought, my powers got stronger and stronger, and I grew bigger with each passing battle. A few times, a demon would sneak to the side and try to attack me that way, but J would kick and punch them, always putting himself between them and me. Anytime I didn't see the blow coming, he jumped to my aid and took the hit, but for the most part, I defeated them on my own.

I didn't see the attack that did it, but one of the demons must have landed contact because suddenly I was badly wounded, and I couldn't stand. It felt like I was dying. J held me in his arms, carrying me like a child. I didn't even appear conscious. While he held me, he continued to fight the demons, never so much as letting a hair on my head touch the ground. Protecting both my body in his arms, and my heart space behind him at all costs.

I saw myself begin to heal.

The wounds began to smooth over beneath his kisses. He slowly sat me on my feet in front of him, a little at a time, until I was able to stand on my own again. He then turned me forward to face the battle yet again, and took his place behind me, assisting me once again when needed. He never let go of me. Always he had at least one arm around my waist as I fought harder and harder. At times my red hair blended in with the flames, and I felt like part of the fire. The fire was part of my power, and so was J. We were a force of love together.

I saw my face begin to age as I fought.

The lines got deeper, and my red hair begin to turn silver, just a hint of the fiery color that it had once been.

My fight began to slow.

The scene got quiet, and I saw myself lying in a bed with my family surrounding me. My niece, and my own daughter were there, both of them looking like their mothers look now.

J was pacing in the room, delighted. He was obviously excitedly anticipating something, and he would periodically come over and check my vitals and kiss my forehead.

I realized that I was dying.

All of a sudden, I saw myself go translucent and wavy, and my spirit began to rise up out of my body. It had risen no more than a centimeter when J stepped over and took my hands in his and pulled my spirit tight to him in a deeply loving embrace.

We kissed as we rose up into the heavens.

I began to see us all tangled up…a rolling together of spirit bodies where I could only get flashes of feet or hands or my own red hair, and we were laughing with glee.

We would dance together for a bit, and I could distinguish the forms of our former earthly bodies - separate entities, but glowing. And then we would tangle and roll again, and I couldn't tell us apart. I could hear laughter, but erotic murmurs and moans of pleasure as well.

We were reveling in each other in some form of spirit sex that delighted me to witness.

We couldn't leave each other alone.

It reminded me of how we were when he was alive. It had felt just like that energetically. No time, and absolutely no separation between us. So entangled that there was no end or no beginning of either of us as individuals.

I then saw us, just like that…in every conceivable place on earth together.

We were watching the Northern lights, with my head against his shoulder, and then suddenly, we were making love in this new spirit fashion…rolling in and out of the lights as they flashed. Amazed and dazzled by each other as much as we were the lights that accompanied us

I saw us at the pyramids, and J was laughing at me as I played with the desert creatures, but he wouldn't join me in trying to chase or ride them. Then suddenly there was sand flying in whirlwinds as we tangled back up together playfully in our sex.

We were on a pink sand beach, blowing it like fairy dust from our fingers and laughing together as we watched it fall like glitter.

Then I saw us in Hawaii and J was braiding flowers in my long red hair before he laid me down at the bed of a volcano and our lovemaking shook the earth harder than the rumbles from the belly of it. We made it a game to see if we could outdo her fiery groans.

We were in the jungle, then on grasslands, and back to beaches. I saw us occasionally pop onto animals' bodies, only to use them to make love to each other so that we could physically feel the sensation again. Rough, quick, and wild.

We would inhibit their bodies, like a game; animalistically ravishing each other, only to roll out of the animal bodies howling with laughter and delight. We would double over laughing and pleading with each other to do it again.

When night would fall, we danced and sang to each other sweetly. We stargazed on our backs and then arose high into the heavens until the starlight surrounded us with its brilliance. We ran between the stars themselves in a game of lover's chase, only to allow one another to be caught and wrapped back up into an embrace once more.

We explored, and laughed, and loved.

It was eternity, and I knew it.

But I still never wanted it to end.

The newness of each other never went away.

I would catch him watching me with adoration as I picked dandelions in a field or twirled by the sea. I would turn suddenly and find him staring at me with love pouring from his being, and immediately we would be in each other's arms again.

I couldn't get enough of him. He picked me flowers and sang to me…. still wooing and romancing me even though he no longer had to. He still made me weak with every interaction. I still wanted him fiercely though we were never separate. I submitted to him with glee at every turn.

When I was younger, I never gave that much thought to heaven. The religious teachers whose words I grew up memorizing were far more concerned with spreading the news about hell. When it came to heaven I just remember hearing that there would be "streets of gold, and mansions."

I never really cared about those things, so it really didn't seem that enticing. (Honestly, I always thought it felt super materialistic. We were going to care about what our houses looked like when we died?)

No one ever told me that heaven was being surrounded, encompassed by, and embodied in the greatest love that ever existed.

It was an eternity of worshipping and adoring; and being worshipped and adored. It was the sheer delight of love. It was making love, as in the very creation of love itself.

It was like the night J told me, "We just made love. We created it between the two of us. Made it and then released it out into the world. We uplifted the universe through our lovemaking."

Love *is*.

It has no beginning and no end.

It comes from us, but it also comes through us.

We create it, but it also creates us.

It is a cosmic dance that we can no more extract ourselves from than we can force our way into.

It just IS.

Heaven is a place where love is allowed to exist, undiluted.

It is love reveling in itself.

It is the DELIGHT in the neverending-ness.

It is the repetition of the waves crashing over and over and over again on the shore, only to wash back out to the deep and do it again.

Each time a little bit different, but also…the same.

The seed and the fruition.

Back to the seed.

The blossoming forth from the newness, only to disintegrate in order to experience the newness again.

Heaven isn't mansions and gold.

Heaven is made of the stuff that ignites our very soul.

It's the journey of the tiny ember… to the wildfire… and back again.

It is the melody of fire sung out into the universe while all of consciousness sings it back to you in a never-ending love song.

Six Months Later

I WAS SITTING on my bed, curled up with my dog, and lost completely in a book that had every bit of my attention. Suddenly, there was a flurry of energy at the foot of the bed and J appeared seated beside me looking a bit wild-eyed and excited.

"JEN! I have to tell you what just happened!" he exclaimed. "Stop reading for a second." He waved towards the book that I had already begun to fold the corner of to mark my spot.

Interactions with J were the norm these days, though I had certainly never seen him in this kind of state. I felt, heard, and saw him most of the time now. Our relationship had taken on a whole new quality and though I still found it unsettling at times, I was beginning to learn to trust this connection with all of my heart. My gifts had been steadily opening more and more over the last few months. I now received information from the spirit realm regularly and was learning to navigate and integrate it with my daily life. It felt like someone had been slowly lifting a blindfold from my eyes, leaving me with a clearer and clearer picture of what was happening beyond it. J was as visually solid and audibly clear to me now as if he were in the flesh. We spent most of our time with each other, and as of late, had been trying very, *very* hard to sexually connect.

I had bought books on sex magic and tantra (one of which I was wading through at this particular moment), and we had been dabbling with exercises in sexual energy alchemy together. We had been moderately successful with a few deeply connective experiences, but it was definitely still a work in progress. Not that the "practice" hadn't been exquisitely fun. It constantly reminded me of our sexual connection when he was in the physical and our general attitude of "let's just see what happens…". There were no "wrong roads" when you treated the whole experience like a playground of sorts.

I looked at him expectantly.

"You have my attention, babe. What's up?" I asked.

"Do you remember… when I was alive in the physical…there was a morning that I came to you in meditation and made love to you on your yoga mat?" he asked, earnestly.

"I do remember that. Though honestly, I had kind of forgotten about it…or just hadn't thought about it in a very long time. That was the strangest experience, J. I tried to talk to you about it right after and you had no idea what I was talking about. Remember?" I said. I thought back on the incident. I remembered how it had made me question my sanity at the time, and how I had been half convinced I had somehow made it up.

"I wasn't aware of it happening then…because it just happened NOW," he said. He watched my face carefully as he said it, obviously waiting for a reaction of some kind.

"Huh? I don't understand. It happened like…4 years ago. What do you mean?" I asked in confusion.

"I…me…this version of me that you are speaking to right now…just traveled back in time and made love to you in what would have been 4 years ago," he said, speaking the words slowly.

I felt my jaw fall open slightly as what he was saying began to register fully.

I thought back to the details of the encounter that morning.

I suddenly remembered that he had felt *so sad* to me, and I hadn't understood why.

"How is that even possible? How did you figure out how to do that?" I asked incredulously. I could barely wrap my mind around what he was telling me, even though the more that I thought about that moment in time, the more I knew that what he was saying must be true.

"I have a bit of a confession to make. I have known that I could go to any point in time for a while now. Time isn't like what you think it is, Jen. I promise to tell you more about that soon…but for now, just know that any point in time is accessible from the spirit realm. I had been going back frequently to the moments that we were together and watching them. Sometimes I would watch them from the outside… like a movie almost. I would be in the same space as you and I and just relive the sweetness of our time together by witnessing it again. Other times I would merge back into my own physical body just to feel what it was like to make love to you again with a body. Those were my happiest times, Jen. I go back there any chance I get just to hold you again. But it never occurred to me that I might be able to interact with you as I am right now. I never thought about trying to talk to you or touch you in my spirit form. Until today," he said. He paused, obviously emotional and trying to collect himself. I simply stared at him wide-eyed.

"I was more than a little surprised when you felt me sit down in front of you," he laughed softly, though he wiped a tear from his cheek as he said it. "How tapped in were you, love, that you felt that? I was so proud of you. *And you were so brave.* You let me kiss you and fuck you and merge my heart with yours…just… complete surrender to a *spirit*. I don't know how you weren't scared to death."

"I wasn't scared because I felt that it was really you. Of course, I had no understanding of what was actually happening, but knowing that it was you was enough. I would recognize you in any form, I feel certain," I replied.

"And by the way, you are giving me entirely too much credit. I don't think I

425

was very tapped in at all at that point, actually. You are such a STRONG spirit, J. I think anyone would have felt that," I said with a laugh.

"I'm not the only one who is strong. Do you remember me telling you that morning that I learned how to make love to you like that from a very powerful teacher? Look at what we've been doing across the realms the last few months, my dear. I've learned that from, and with, *you*," he said.

At this, I laughed out loud.

"I remember being so jealous when you said that to me then. I was so hurt at the thought of you sharing something like that with someone else," I said.

He touched my cheek tenderly. "You should have known better," he said softly.

The way he said it reminded me of the melancholy in his voice and energy that morning four years ago. I recalled how it had caused an emotional reaction in me at the time, though I hadn't understood why.

"You were so sad that morning because you knew all that was about to unfold. It makes so much sense now…" I let my words trail off.

"More than that, Jen," he looked at me with agony in his eyes, waiting patiently for the rest of it to click together like a puzzle piece.

It suddenly hit me in its fullness.

He was already dead when he came to me that morning.

What should have been obvious from the get-go suddenly hit me so hard that it knocked the breath out of me.

I had always looked back on that morning as a moment that I had somehow connected to J's higher self. I had landed on that "story" of what occurred that morning in order to find a meaning that I could accept and move on from. I had told myself that somehow, I had tapped into the spirit plane and been allowed to feel the nature of what we were so that I could feel validated about it when times were tough.

Now I understood that wasn't what had happened at all.

He had already been dead in that moment, and he had tried to prepare me for what was to come.

Our eyes met and he nodded solemnly.

"I knew I couldn't say or do anything that would change the course. And I knew if I let you know what was happening it would have terrified you and broken your heart, and you wouldn't have been able to stop it either. The best thing I could do was to give you something to hold on to. I just tried to pour every bit of my love into you so that you could feel it entirely. So that when you did lose me… you would remember that we once connected in the spirit plane so solidly that you experienced our love in its fullness. I wanted you to know that it was possible to reach each other there," he said earnestly.

"J…that is so beautiful," I whispered as I wiped tears from my eyes. I hadn't known enough to be grateful to him then, but now I knew it was the best gift that he had ever given me. In the back of my mind, that particular moment shared between us had been the thing that had kept me going. Part of me had been terrified that I had made it up somehow, but the other part of me had clung to it after he passed as the single shred of evidence that perhaps we hadn't been done after all.

In the moments that I nearly took my own life, that memory had always jumped up and waved to me. An experience that had been a testament to the impossible and the miraculous.

In one instant in time, I had seen, heard, felt, and tasted the infinite nature of our love. When all had felt lost, I had remembered that.

"Thank you," I whispered, tearfully. "I don't even know if *you* fully understand the gift that you gave me. It was the biggest reason why I never gave up. I almost checked out completely so many times….it was the memory of that moment that kept me here."

I thought about how well he had done. How he had equipped me to survive the most brutal of times in that single interaction. How once again, he was loving me beyond my capacity to comprehend.

I thought about the logistics of what had just happened, and the implications of what it all meant. I was more than a little mind blown. If J could go to any point in time from where he was at… didn't that mean he could go into the future as well? And if he could go into our past in this lifetime, could he go further back in time too? Could he visit our past lives?

"How much can you see, J? How much access do you have? Do you know how all of this is going to play out, love?" I asked him earnestly.

He sighed.

"When it comes to the future, I can see all the directions that are possible. I also can see the most probable path – the most likely direction is illuminated the most. But it's not set in stone, Jen. You still have free will. You can go in any direction you choose, and if you happen to not take the most probable path… everything that I see will shift," he said.

"Good to know. I think part of me just always assumed things were kind of set up or predestined for us in a lot of ways. What about the past? How much of that can you see? Just this lifetime, or more?" I asked.

"All of it. All of the lifetimes," he replied solemnly.

I stared at him in disbelief.

"Where was the first one?"

"A place that is mostly underwater now. It was called Lemuria," he said.

I paused. I had heard that word before. The very first time that we made love, I remembered that the two of us had both heard that word for the first time, though we hadn't known what it meant at the time. So "Lemuria" was a place?

"I can't believe you've been holding out on me like this," I said with a laugh. "What happened in Lemuria? Are you going to tell me about it or not?" I demanded.

He smiled at my impatience, and then put his hands on either side of my face and looked deeply into my eyes. "I'll tell you what, Jen. I'll do even better than that. I'll show it to you," he said.

And so began the next chapter in the most ancient of love stories….

For a sneak preview of the next volume of this story,
you may join my mailing list on my website:
http://www.themelodyofmissjen.com

If this book meant something to you, I would love to hear about it!
Please consider leaving a review on Amazon. (Unless you hated it,
then maybe just use the book for fire kindling or something
and pretend like it was just a fever dream.)

Opening quote sourced from:

Miller, Madeline, author. *The Song of Achilles*. N New York : Ecco, 2012

Made in the USA
Columbia, SC
25 September 2023

dc6f17c6-a174-44d4-b244-5d9b03823899R01